THE GENRE OF ARGUMENT

1430 W. Susquehanna Ave
Philadelphia, PA 19121
215-236-1760 I treehousebooks.org

THE GENRE OF ARGUMENT

Irene L. Clark
University of Southern California

Harcourt Brace College Publishers

Fort Worth   Philadelphia   San Diego   New York   Orlando   Austin   San Antonio
Toronto   Montreal   London   Sydney   Tokyo

Publisher:	Christopher P. Klein
Executive Editor:	Michael A. Rosenberg
Acquisitions Editor:	John Meyers
Product Manager:	Ilse Wolfe West
Developmental Editor:	Cindy Hoag
Project Editor:	Denise Netardus
Art Director:	Garry Harman
Production Manager:	Serena Manning
Cover Image:	© Keizo Nakajima/Tony Stone Images

ISBN: 0-15-502184-2
Library of Congress Catalog Card Number: 97-71706

Address for orders:
Harcourt Brace & Company
6277 Sea Harbor Drive
Orlando, FL 32887-6777
1-800-782-4479

Address for editorial correspondence:
Harcourt Brace College Publishers
301 Commerce Street, Suite 3700
Fort Worth, TX 76102

Web site address:
http://www.hbcollege.com

Harcourt Brace & Company will provide complimentary supplements or supplement packages to those adopters qualified under our adoption policy. Please contact your sales representative to learn how you qualify. If as an adopter or potential user you receive supplements you do not need, please return them to your sales representative or send them to: Attn: Returns Department, Troy Warehouse, 465 South Lincoln Drive, Troy, MO 63379.

Printed in the United States of America

7 8 9 0 1 2 3 4 5 6   066   9 8 7 6 5 4 3 2 1

To my husband, Bill,
and my children,
Elisa, Louisa, Clifton, and Justin

PREFACE

I first became interested in applying genre analysis to argumentation when I was teaching at the University of Utrecht in The Netherlands, working with PhD candidates in geography who wished to write publishable articles in English. These students were all high achievers in their field; yet, most of them were unsuccessful at writing articles in English, not because of poor language skills, but because they were unfamiliar with the conventions, that is, the "genre" of scholarly articles in the social sciences. Like many native-English-speaking students, the Dutch students had not analyzed the role of purpose and audience in constructing an effective argument, nor did they understand what constituted convincing evidence. Most importantly, they were not aware of the necessity of approaching a topic in terms of a problem to be addressed. I taught in Utrecht on two occasions, in 1989 and 1993, and during the more recent period, I developed several class lessons based on John M. Swales' concept of genre analysis, as described in his book, *Genre Analysis: English in Academic and Research Settings* (Cambridge University Press, 1990). Once the Dutch students understood that social science writing is a genre with an argumentative purpose achieved through particular features, their writing improved impressively, and it was at this point that I began to think about using this approach with composition students in the United States.

The Goal of This Book

The goal of this book is to help students understand the purpose and generic features of college argumentation. Chapter 1 focuses on the relationship of purpose to genre, emphasizing the relationship between purpose and other conceptual features. Chapter 2 discusses several strategies for exploring a topic and finding a thesis suitable for the genre of argument. Chapter 3 examines the crucial role of reason. Chapter 4 presents a three-pass approach to critical reading, emphasizing the importance of discerning a writer's credentials and agenda before accepting the premise of a text. Chapter 5 discusses the role of audience in argumentation and strategies for establishing credibility.

Chapter 6 presents various strategies of supporting a thesis characteristic of the genre of argument. Chapter 7 discusses methods of organizing and incorporating outside information in order to maximize the writer's credibility and avoid plagiarism. Chapter 8 examines the function of form and the role that narration and description play in advancing an argumentative claim. Chapter 9 discusses two critical strategies in argumentation, establishing causality and defining terms. Chapter 10 demonstrates suggestions for revision. The appendix presents both MLA and APA documentation systems and discusses possibilities for conducting research through the World Wide Web. The concepts discussed in each chapter are reinforced through exercises, writing assignments, group work, and readings. The book also includes several examples of actual student papers annotated to focus attention on their generic features.

The Features of Academic Argument

In *The Genre of Argument* academic argument is viewed as a *genre* with particular conceptual and stylistic features. The book's overall premise is that when students understand how genre is determined by purpose, they will gain insight into how purpose influences many other features of a successful argumentative text. These features include the representation of the writer within the text, the concept of audience, the choice of topic and issue, the approach taken to the topic, and the type of support and evidence presented, as well as formal conventions associated with academic argument. Deriving from recent discussions of genre theory, the book is based on the following concepts:

1. Academic argument is a definable genre with distinguishing characteristics that students can understand easily once they become aware of its context and purpose. Although each academic discipline may be defined in terms of particular approaches, devices, and patterns, "academic argument is more unified than the fragmentation of academic fields might imply" (Nelson, Megill, and McClosky 4).
2. The genre of academic argument can be defined not primarily in terms of form but rather in terms of rhetorical and social situations that invite written response. These situations construct the role of the writer and determine the writer's conception of audience.
3. An important characteristic of academic argument is the "problematizing" of a topic—that is, in developing a position or thesis for an argumentative writing assignment, the writer identifies a specific problem, assumption, idea, view, or situation that requires some form of reevaluation or reexamination that can be addressed in writing. Problematization thus constitutes an important heuristic for academic argument. (Barton)
4. Academic argument moves readers to consider what is being said, to think about the reasons and evidence presented, to acknowledge that the argument is compelling, and then to reevaluate and modify their point of view.
5. Writing a compelling argument supported by convincing evidence requires and develops the ability to critically evaluate published material and incorporate outside information into a text.

The Reconceptualization of Genre: Background

Traditionally, the word "genre" has been associated with notions of form and classifications of text, in particular with describing the formal features of a literary work. In a pedagogical context, this way of looking at genre has frequently suggested an emphasis on form, and to a certain extent, on form for form's sake. The most problematic application of this view completely separates form from context: students have been encouraged to insert content into formulaic slots within a text without questioning the rationale for doing so. A notorious example of this approach is the paradigm of the five paragraph essay, which many students apply indiscriminately to any writing task, without questioning why there should be five rather than four or six paragraphs or examining the relationship of one paragraph to another.

During the past ten years or so, however, genre has been reconceptualized in terms of **function.** While recognizing that genres can be characterized by regularities in textual form and substance, current thinking about genre looks at these regularities as surface manifestations of a more fundamental kind of regularity. The work of Freedman and Swales, among others, recognizes that although genres can be characterized by regularities in textual form, such regularity represents "typical ways of engaging rhetorically with recurring situations" (Freedman and Medway 2), and that similarities in textual form and feature derive from an effective response to situations that "writers encounter repeatedly" (Devitt 576). Because genres arise when writers respond appropriately to recurring rhetorical situations, the new concept of genre perceives generic conventions as deriving from suitability and effectiveness, rather than from arbitrary conventions.

To a great extent, this reconceptualized idea of genre builds on other theories of writing that have had an impact on the teaching of writing, particularly those that emphasize the functionality of text and the role of context in determining text effectiveness. Genre theory is consistent with rhetorical approaches, which focus attention on context, audience, and occasion and view writing as a way of responding to a specific reader (or readers) within a specific context on a specific occasion (Freeman and Medway 5). Genre theory is also compatible with social constructionist theory, which recognizes that the act of composing draws on previous interactions with others, and with speech act theory, which emphasizes the function of language as a way of acting in the world and the importance of context in creating meaning.

In accord with this emphasis on context, John M. Swales defines the concept of genre primarily by its common communicative purposes. Swales maintains that these purposes and the role of the genre within its environment have generated specific textual features, and he advocates a genre-centered approach to teaching as a means of enabling students to understand why a particular genre has acquired characteristic features.

Pedagogical Implications of Genre

The pedagogical implications of this reconceptualization of genre have raised considerable controversy among those who believe that genre **cannot** be taught but rather must be absorbed through the discourse community, those who feel that genre **should not** be taught explicitly because it will result in the blind adherence to form that characterized the original concept of genre, and those, such as myself, who argue that helping students acquire genre knowledge does not mean teaching form and formula as ends in themselves, but rather that it helps students understand what motivates the production of discourse so that they can develop appropriate response strategies. This position maintains that being able to produce an example of a genre is a matter not just of generating a text that adheres to certain formal characteristics; rather, the overt considera-tion of genre is a means of enhancing understanding so that students can apply generic conventions in a multiplicity of contexts.

A genre approach to argumentation can have significant impact on stu-dents throughout their university careers because a great deal of the writing students are required to do at the university, the sort of writing that is fre-quently referred to as "academic discourse," is really a form of argumentation, whether or not it is specifically labeled as such. Most college writing assign-ments, from the first-year essay to the content-area research paper, are actually *arguments* in the sense that they require students to establish and support a clearly stated thesis or position relative to a substantive and often controversial topic, to problematize that topic in order to establish an argumentative context for that thesis, and to establish a credentialed persona through the use of cita-tion and acknowledgment of a counter argument. However, this is the type of writing with which students often have the most difficulty, not only because they are unfamiliar with it as a genre, but also because the requirements of the assignment are often presented solely in terms of form rather than purpose. As a result, students confuse argumentation with exposition, and the papers they write then consist of a linear sequence of unprocessed material in the body of the essay, with evaluative comment (if it exists at all) postponed to the con-cluding paragraph.

In contrast to a number of argumentation textbooks currently on the mar-ket, which include large sets of topic-oriented readings, I wanted *The Genre of Argument* to be relatively short, enabling students to use it as a guide. Although the concept of the book is supported by a body of literature on the subject of genre, the premise of the book is actually quite simple. It explains the purpose behind college argumentation, shows students what an argumen-tative essay looks like and aims to accomplish, and then suggests strategies for helping students complete argument-based writing assignments. Once stu-dents understand these ideas, they will not only write more effectively in their composition classes but will also be able to apply this approach to academic argument to other writing tasks both within and beyond their university careers.

Acknowledgments

There are a number of people whose insights and suggestions have affected this book and whom I would like to thank. John Meyers, acquisitions editor at Harcourt Brace, who recognized the underlying purpose of this book and helped me focus each chapter accordingly; Cindy Hoag, my developmental editor, who painstakingly synthesized reviewers' comments so that I could apply them more effectively; Teeana Rizkallah, who provided not only assistance but also creative insights; Denise Netardus at Harcourt Brace, who worked with the book to completion; and the following reviewers: Micael Clarke, Loyola University of Chicago; Gay Lynn Crossley, Kansas State University; George Estreich, Duke University; James Farrelly, University of Dayton; Michael Flanigan, University of Oklahoma at Norman; Patricia Graves, Georgia State University; Sandy Jensen, Lane Community College; Joe Law, Texas Christian University; Richard Leahy, Boise State University; Alan Merickel, Tallahassee Community College; Gary Olson, University of South Florida; Jeanne Pattow, SUNY-Brockport; and Donald Pattow, University of Wisconsin at Stevens Point. Then, of course, there are my husband Bill, and my children Elisa, Louisa, Clifton, and Justin, who have always encouraged and supported me in everything I have written.

Irene Clark
University of Southern California
(IClark@Mizar.usc.edu)

Works Cited

Barton, Ellen. " Evidentials, Argumentation an Epistemological Stance." *College English* 55 (1993): 745-769.

Devitt, Amy J. "Generalizing About Genre: New Conceptions of an Old Concept." *College Composition and Communication* 44 (1993): 573-86.

Freedman, Aviva, and Peter Medway, eds. *Learning and Teaching Genre*. Portsmouth: Boynton/Cook, 1994.

Nelson, John, Allan Megill, and Donald McClosky. "Rhetoric of Inquiry." *The Rhetoric of the Human Sciences: Language and Argument in Scholarship and Public Affairs.* Ed. John Nelson, Allan Megill, and Donald McLoskey. Madison: U of Wisconsin P, 1987. 3-18.

Swales, John. *Genre Analysis.* Cambridge: Cambridge UP, 1990.

BRIEF CONTENTS

CONTENTS

Chapter 2
EXPLORING A TOPIC; FINDING A THESIS   34

nurturing roles, giving children the impression that they play a secondary role in the home.

The absence of and rivalry between women in many traditional fairy tales may be traced to actual conditions in which women died in childbirth or became dependent on male family members. Moreover, because these tales were often told by older women to their children or grandchildren, the stories reflect many elements of actual lived experience.

Chapter 3
THE NATURE OF PROOF   71

Chapter 4
EXPLORING THROUGH OUTSIDE READING   107

Chapter 5
CONSIDERING YOUR AUDIENCE: ESTABLISHING CREDIBILITY   149

Chapter 8
THE FUNCTION OF FORM   236

Chapter 9
TWO IMPORTANT STRATEGIES IN ARGUMENTATION: ESTABLISHING CAUSALITY AND DEFINING TERMS   280

APPENDIX   349

THE GENRE OF ARGUMENT

Used with permission of the Duke Unlimited Agency and Southwest Airlines.

Chapter 1

ARGUMENTATIVE WRITING IN COLLEGE: THE IMPORTANCE OF PURPOSE

Imagine yourself leafing through a magazine and coming upon a picture of an elegant but casually dressed gray-haired gentleman, smiling appreciatively as he eats a steak in what appears to be a "good" restaurant. Above the picture is the following quotation:

> "A Ruth's Chris Steak
> Is a Lot Like
> My Favorite Airline . . .
> . . . High In Customer Satisfaction,
> Sizzling And Right On Time."

Beneath the quotation is the signature of Herb Kelleher,

> Chairman/President/CEO
> Southwest Airlines

Farther down the page is the question:

> Where does he go to enjoy U.S. Prime steak?
> Ruth's Chris Steak House. Of course!

You probably have no difficulty understanding the meaning either of the picture or the statements because you recognize them as components of an **advertisement.** Most students are quite familiar with the **genre** of advertising—they understand the **purpose** of an ad and are aware of how its various **components** create its **form** and make it different from other types of writing.

Because familiarity with a genre is essential for anyone who wishes to reproduce it, this book aims to familiarize you with the **genre of argument** as it is used in the college classroom. Argumentative writing is an important component of most college classes, in courses throughout the disciplines, as well as in composition courses. When professors assign writing, they usually expect you to produce a particular genre of writing, in particular, a type of essay that establishes or *argues* a central point about a complex or problematic topic. Moreover, this expectation usually exists even if the professor does not specifically use the word *argument* or *argumentation,* and it is often the quality of the argument that most significantly influences the grade a paper will receive.

Argumentation, however, is a type of writing that students sometimes find anxiety-provoking because they have had little experience with it and tend to misunderstand its purpose. They think of it as more difficult than other types of writing, such as narrative writing, which tells a story, or expository writing, which presents information. But after students become aware of what argumentation is, they find it much more manageable and can write their essays more easily.

By approaching argument as a *genre, The Genre of College Argument* aims to take the mystery out of argumentation by showing how the purpose of an argumentative essay influences its other features such as:

- the *writer* as he or she appears in the essay
- the *audience* for whom the essay is intended
- the *topic* selected
- the *approach* to the topic
- the type of *support* and evidence used to develop the main point (also called the claim or thesis
- the *assumptions* underlying the main claim or thesis

Purpose affects not only the conceptual features of a text, it also affects its structure and style. In this chapter, I will show what a typical argumentative essay looks like in terms of its *structure* or *form;* and in subsequent chapters I will discuss stylistic choices and *documentation conventions* that are associated with the genre of argument. The premise of this book is that the better you understand how various features of argumentative writing help achieve its purpose, the more successfully you will be able to write essays in your college classes.

THE PURPOSE OF ARGUMENTATIVE WRITING

People sometimes think of an argument as a heated verbal interchange or quarrel, characterized by intense emotions and angry words; usually the person who "wins" an argument is the one with the greatest stamina and the loudest voice. Academic argument as a genre of writing, however, is characterized by reason, logic, and analytical thinking rather than by emotional excess, and its purpose is to convince its audience or readers of the truth of an idea, not to bulldoze them into surrender. If the essay is concerned with an emotionally charged or complex topic, it will probably not cause its readers to change their minds completely. But a well-developed essay can move them to at least *consider* the thesis or claim, *think* about the reasons and evidence, *acknowledge* that the thesis has merit, and then perhaps to reevaluate and modify their point of view somewhat.

FEATURES OF ARGUMENTATION AFFECTED BY PURPOSE

The Writer

How Is the Writer Influenced by the Purpose of Argumentative Writing?

All of us are more likely to accept another person's ideas if we think of that person as knowledgeable, trustworthy, logical, and fair, as opposed to ignorant, untrustworthy, illogical, and biased. In order to convince an audience that their ideas are worth considering, writers of academic argument thus aim to present themselves as people of intelligence, moral integrity, and good intentions. *Ethos,* or credibility, is created when an audience thinks of a writer in the following ways:

1. The writer must convince the audience that he or she is knowledgeable about the subject.

To become knowledgeable about the subject of the argumentative essay, the writer needs to research the topic and learn as much about it as possible within the time limits of the assignment. For example, if you are writing an essay arguing that children in public schools should be required to wear school uniforms, you should indicate to your reader that you know a lot about the controversy concerned with school uniforms. Otherwise, your reader is unlikely to accept your ideas.

2. The writer must indicate awareness and understanding of the ideas of others by presenting a balanced perspective on the topic.

The writer of an effective argumentative essay has examined multiple sides of an issue and indicates to the reader that he or she has done so. If you are writing about the controversy concerning school uniforms, you should indicate that you are familiar with both sides—that some people feel that uniforms stifle self-expression and individual freedom, but that others feel that uniforms actually promote self-expression and freedom because children can focus on learning rather than on clothing.

3. The writer should base his or her claims on logic and credible evidence.

Argumentative essays are written for readers who value logic and reason, readers who expect convincing evidence rather than empty assertions. If you are writing about the controversy concerning school uniforms, you should be able to cite authorities who have had experience with the effect of uniforms on children's behavior and performance in school. You should also be familiar with statistics about crimes committed in schools when children fight over brand-name clothing, or reports of gang-related incidents when children are mistaken for gang members as a result of their clothing. Simply making an assertion that uniforms are better (or worse) is insufficient within the genre of argument. You must be prepared to say *why* uniforms are better or worse and provide sound evidence for your ideas.

4. The writer must use language in such a way as to appear truthful and fair.

The genre of argument is written for a community that values truth and rational thinking. Such a community will not accept the ideas of a writer who appears biased or hysterical or who uses language to inflame rather than convince. Although you may feel strongly about your subject (and it's good to have strong feelings about topics you write about) you should aim for a measured tone that suggests that you are a careful person who thinks seriously about the statements you write. Overblown statements such as "school uniforms are a form of fascism" or "if students do not wear uniforms, they will never learn anything in school" are unlikely to convince an audience.

The Audience

For Whom Is Academic Argument Written?

When you write a paper for a college class, you may be under the impression that you are writing exclusively for your teacher. This is not an unreasonable assumption, because certainly your teacher is likely to be one of your readers. However, an argumentative essay is not usually intended for only one person. Rather, it is oriented toward a broader audience or readership consisting of educated people who tend to be convinced by reason and supported claims rather than by empty rhetoric and inflammatory assertions. Although this audience may not be completely knowledgeable about the topic being discussed, writers of academic argument presume an audience that is familiar with the purpose and conventions of academic argument and that will be able to understand what is being written if adequate context, background, and explanation are provided.

In considering the audience or readership for your college writing assignments, imagine that you have left a copy of your essay on a table in the college library. If you have explained and supported your position adequately and included sufficient background and context for the topic, an educated person who finds your essay should be able to understand its central point, even if he or she is not thoroughly familiar with the topic or the assigned writing task.

The Topic

What Sorts of Topics Are Suitable for Academic Argument?

How Much Background Should the Writer Provide?

The genre of argument is concerned with topics that generate controversy because they are problematic, unresolved, and complex. Suitable topics do not address questions of fact or taste but rather focus on questions on which more than one view is possible. An important characteristic of academic argument is that it deals with a problem or difficulty within the topic—that is, the writer identifies a specific problem, assumption, idea, view, or situation that requires some form of reevaluation, additional understanding, or reexamination that can be addressed in writing. Problems associated with the topic of school uniforms include the controversy over what effect uniforms have on individual creativity and the question of whether schools have the right to dictate what students wear. In establishing a context for an argumentative essay, the writer must present sufficient background information so that the reader understands the situation but not so much information that the reader becomes overwhelmed or confused.

Moreover, in deciding what information to include, it is also important to consider what may be considered "new" as opposed to "common" knowledge. *New* knowledge, such as a discussion of a little-known scientific term or, in the case of school uniforms, a study showing the impact of uniforms on students' performance in school, must be explained and the source of new knowledge must be acknowledged by a citation. *Common* knowledge, such as the fact that George Washington was the first president of the United States, is presumed familiar and requires no special acknowledgement or citation.

Approach to the Topic

What Kind of Approach Is Appropriate in Academic Argument?

Because argumentative writing is concerned with complex, unresolved, or problematic topics, thoughtful writers of academic argument understand that the thesis or claim that expresses their ideas is rarely true 100 percent of the time. Therefore, a great deal of academic writing is characterized by a *qualified* approach to a topic, and an effective thesis statement reflects that qualified approach. Writers may predict consequences or present an analysis of particular conditions or events, but they may also acknowledge that their statements are true only under certain conditions, discuss alternative points of view, or indicate the tentativeness of their observations by using qualifying words such as *seems, suggests, indicates, to some degree,* or *to a certain extent.* For the topic of school uniforms, an appropriate statement might be that school uniforms are *likely* to enhance academic performance or that they are *likely* to minimize gang-related incidents.

Support

What Kinds of Support and Evidence Are Used in Academic Argument?

A main point or thesis or claim in the genre of argument is supported by logic and reason, not by emotional rhetoric. The evidence cited should be from a reliable source and may take the form of appropriate examples, valid analogies, statements from credible authorities, and information from reputable published works. In using evidence obtained from statistics, you should consider how, where, when, and why the data was collected and examine carefully how it pertains to the claim being established. For the topic of school uniforms, appropriate evidence might consist of statements from school authorities or educators who have studied the effect of uniforms on student performance.

Assumptions

What Is the Role of Underlying Assumptions in Academic Argument?

Although adequate support is necessary in order for a rational audience to accept a claim, no thesis or claim will be convincing unless the writer and the audience share assumptions, beliefs, or principles that can serve as a common ground between them. For example, a mother might say to a teenager, "You should take a summer math class because it will help you become a better student." But because this claim is based on the assumption that being a good student is desirable, it will be convincing only if both the teenager and the mother share this belief. The teenager would then say, "Good idea, Mom. It's important for me to become a better student. Let me at that math class." Other assumptions are also implicit in this claim—the ideas that extra work in the present will have benefit in the future and that summers should be used for educational enrichment, to name two.

The teenager, however, might not share his mother's assumptions (teenagers often don't), and therefore he might say, "I don't care about being a good student. I want to spend time at the beach so I can have a toned, tanned body. My body is what is important to me." For a teenager, the future may seem far in the distance, too far to worry about when the sun is shining and the waves are splashing onto the shore. The teenager may conceive of summer as a time for relaxing or working on a tan, not for improving math skills. Therefore, the mother's argument about the importance of taking the math class would not be convincing to the teenager.

THE ROLE OF STRUCTURE

The features just discussed are characteristic of the genre of argument. However, if you are unfamiliar with college argumentation, you will also want to know how these features are incorporated into the text—that is, you will want to know what an argumentative essay actually looks like. The final section of this chapter will discuss the structure that an argumentative essay usually takes and will include some illustrative examples.

What Does an Argumentative Essay Look Like?

A Qualification about Structure

Academic argument usually conforms to a particular structure that has been in existence since the time of the ancient Greeks. This structure reflects the purposes and goals of argumentation, although this structure, like any other, is also a matter of convention, and all conventions are arbitrary, at least to some extent. This means that the goals of argumentation might be realized through a number of different essay forms, and indeed, writers wishing to exercise their creativity might attempt to devise such a form. Nevertheless, because this structure continues to dominate most academic writing and because most college professors expect assigned essays to appear in this form, you will want to become familiar with it, understand how it functions within the genre of argument, and incorporate that understanding into your writing.

Before I examine the components of this structure, discuss its purpose, or suggest strategies for using it or varying it, though, I would like to emphasize the importance of **questioning** how the formal features of any text help writers accomplish their purpose; mechanical adherence to any form stifles creative thought and results in a boring, ineffective essay. The structure of the essays you write should reflect careful thinking about the relationship of form to function.

For example, many students in high school are taught the form known as "the five-paragraph essay," which consists of an introduction, three body paragraphs, and a conclusion. The problem with the five-paragraph essay is that after students have been using it for several years, some of them then believe that *all* essays are required to have five paragraphs, no matter what subject is being discussed. Unaware that the value of any pattern is determined solely by whether or not it fulfills the writer's purpose, these students maintain a mechanical, uncritical perspective on their writing assignments, producing essays that are usually simplistic and boring. Form must follow content, not the other way around. So, whatever essay form you use, it is important to think about how form contributes to the purpose of argumentation—that is, to establish an adequately supported thesis or claim that will have an impact upon a reader.

Having made this qualification, I will now talk about the central components of an argumentative essay.

THE CLASSICAL FORM OF ARGUMENTATION

The classical argumentative structure consists of an introduction, which states the thesis or claim, a body, which supports that claim and addresses the opposing viewpoint, and a conclusion, which sums up the main ideas and perhaps restates the thesis. The components of this form, which are probably familiar to you, may be summarized as follows:

1. Introduction

In this component, which may consist of only one or two paragraphs, the writer indicates the topic, establishes briefly why it is controversial and significant, and presents the thesis or claim. The introduction may also include relevant background material. In some instances, it might summarize a viewpoint that the body of the essay will refute.

2. Body

The body of the essay consists of the following components:

The Nature of the Controversy

This explains the conflict or problem and summarizes various viewpoints as a way of indicating that the writer understands the ideas of others and has researched the topic thoroughly. This component might also define important key terms and include personal experience that is relevant to the topic.

Support for the Thesis

This is usually the longest and most substantive section of the essay. It supports the thesis with compelling reasons and evidence, which might include facts, statistics, data, statements by authorities, and illustrative examples. It may also establish common ground between the author and the intended readers of the essay.

Anticipation and Refutation of Opposing Viewpoints

In this section, the writer indicates areas where an opponent will probably disagree with the thesis. Discussing an opposing viewpoint adds strength to an essay because by indicating awareness of an opponent's point of view, the writer can then argue against it, showing how the ideas in the essay are superior.

3. Conclusion

This section provides a sense of closure by summarizing the writer's main argument. It may also suggest what action, if any, the readers ought to take, or it may postulate potential implications or consequences.

These are the various "parts" of an argumentative essay in terms of the classical structure. In subsequent chapters, I will discuss each of these parts in more detail and also suggest alternative ways you may wish to structure your essay.

Use of Outside Sources in an Argumentative Essay

Although some essay assignments may ask you to write from personal experience, most college writing assignments will require you to support your thesis with information from books and articles from the library or computerized data sources such as the Internet and the World Wide Web. When you include outside information in your essay, it is important to indicate to your reader the source from which you obtained it. To do so, conventions associated with argumentation require you to cite your source within the body of your essay and then compile a "Works Cited" or "References" page at the end of the essay that provides complete bibliographic information. Chapter 4 will discuss strategies for working with information from published works. The Appendix will discuss citation conventions.

ANALYZING AN ARGUMENTATIVE ESSAY

The following essay exemplifies the conceptual features, structure, and citation conventions associated with the genre of argument. It was written in response to an assignment concerned with the controversial topic of political correctness, which asked students to examine the extent to which policies mandating what can and cannot be said on college campuses are likely to cause benefit or harm to the university community. Examining this essay and its annotations can help you understand more fully how the conceptual features of argumentation discussed so far help fulfill its purpose. It will also give you a more complete picture of what an argumentative essay usually looks like in terms of form and structure.

Cyrus Chan

Political Repression: What PC Really Does

(The title provides insight into the main idea in the essay.)

(The introduction explains the controversy and discusses its background. It also presents the thesis.)

Although the United States prides itself on its tolerance of people of all races and ethnic origins, racial hatred and racially motivated crimes seem to be on the rise. Nineteen ninety-two saw race riots shake Los Angeles; that same year, David Duke, an ex-Klansman, ran with moderate

(The writer identifies his reference. He does not presume that the reader will automatically know who David Duke is.)

support for the office of president. Fear of racism and the violence associated with it has moved officials at colleges to mandate what can and cannot be said on campus. This movement has come to be known as political correctness or PC. However, although the political correctness movement is intended to benefit society by preventing hurtful speech against minorities and women, in actuality it serves to undercut one of the most important precepts of our educational system—the free exchange of ideas. Instead of fostering an environment conducive to understanding and learning, as its proponents maintain, PC suppresses discussion and meaningful interchange between students. Such suppres-

(The underlined sentence is the thesis statement using the word *although*.)

sion allows misconceptions of other races and sexes to fester in secret.

(This sentence expands on the thesis and indicates why it is important.)

(The body of this essay begins with the opposing viewpoint, a useful strategy for beginning an argumentative essay. The

writer indicates that he understands the opposing viewpoint,
but then he shows why he disagrees with it.)

Supporters of the PC movement maintain that their goal is to assist
the underprivileged (such as minorities and women) by creating an environment that "affirms the uniqueness and worth of each person" (Siegel
34). Although there is nothing wrong with this statement—indeed, it is
an admirable one—the way in which PC groups assert themselves to
maintain this goal is where the danger lies. In order to succeed in creating such an environment, proponents of PC have established or attempted
to establish "speech codes" that repress racist or sexist taunts by imposing penalties or other consequences for their use (Emerson 18).

Unfortunately, attempting to restrict what one may or may not say
frequently becomes a slippery slope. After one begins to forbid certain

(This is a main point.)

words to be said, other words also become forbidden, ultimately
destroying any hope for an environment dedicated to the pursuit of
knowledge and free inquiry. Even without speech codes, the necessity of
being PC has been so drilled in to students that some avoid even talking
about controversial topics: topics such as affirmative action or abortion
(Hentoff 372) for fear of saying something that might be misinterpreted. Moreover, schools with speech codes face another problem: the
fine line between freedom of thought and thought control. In the words
of Stanford president Donald Kennedy, after you start telling people
what they can't say, you will end up telling them what they can't think
(Hentoff 371).

(The writer cites an authority to lend credibility to his supporting point.)

At the University of Connecticut, speech codes have gone to the
extreme. One Asian-American student was actually thrown out of school

(The writer cites an example to support his thesis.)

for displaying her homemade poster that read, "bimbos should be shot on sight" before her expulsion was overturned in a federal district court (Emerson 18). It is troubling when students or teachers cannot voice their beliefs or views without being subject to abuse or harassment. But it is especially troubling when such speech codes do nothing to change the misunderstandings that perpetuate racism and sexism.

Advocates of speech codes argue that racist or sexist slurs create a climate of fear on campus, damaging students' feelings of self-worth and interfering with their ability to learn. However, it can also be argued that

(The writer cites an opposing viewpoint and then argues against it.)

students must learn to face these so-called nonpolitically correct words so that they can deal more effectively with them at a later time, when they are out in the world. During a debate about speech codes at Harvard Law School, a white student got up and said "that the codes are necessary because without them, black students would be driven away from colleges and thereby deprived of the equal opportunity to get an education" (Hentoff 372). However, a black student then countered this remark by saying that the white student had "a hell of a nerve to assume that he—in the face of racist speech—would pack up his books and go home. He'd been familiar with that kind of speech all his life and he had never felt the need to run away from it" (Hentoff 372).

(This example further supports the thesis and lends authority to the writer's point of view.)

Moreover, speech codes do little to create a better environment for minorities because they have no impact on people's ideas, and in that sense, they are actually dangerous. People are not going to stop thinking,

(This is another supporting point.)

even if they are restricted from expressing their ideas, and thoughts of racism and sexism aren't going to disappear simply because an adminis-tration establishes speech codes that hide what people think. Instead, by preventing the free exchange of ideas, such codes may prejudice people more, leaving a facade of tolerance that hides the anger and suspicion that lie beneath the surface. As the National Association of Scholars points out, "Tolerance is a core value of academic life, as is civility. College authorities should ensure that these values prevail. But tolerance involves a willingness not to suppress, but to allow divergent opinions" (401).

(This is another statement from an authority that adds credibility to the writer's main point.)

(The conclusion summarizes the writer's main point and indicates that the topic is important to think about because it has widespread societal impact.)

Freedom of expression is the essence of a democratic society, and by stifling free speech, the political correctness movement, with its speech codes and other forms of harassment, will ultimately harm our society. Campuses are no longer centers of intellectual discussion, but rather schools of indoctrination, hiding potentially serious problems festering under an externally imposed facade. Racism and sexism can be eliminated in our culture only by the understanding and mutual acceptance that come from the free exchange of ideas, not by externally imposed mandates and codes.

(The "Works Cited" section lists the sources referred to in the text. This essay cites sources using MLA citation form.)

Works Cited

D'Souza, Dinesh. "The Visogoths in Tweed." Writing about Diversity: An Argument Reader and Guide. Ed. Irene L. Clark. Fort Worth: Harcourt Brace, 361–369.

Emerson, Ken. "Only Correct." The New Republic 18 Feb. 1991: 18–19.

Hentoff, Nat. "Speech Codes and Free Speech." Writing about Diversity: An Argument Reader and Guide. Ed. Irene L. Clark. Fort Worth: Harcourt Brace, 370–375.

Siegel, Fred. "The Cult of Multiculturalism." The New Republic 18 Feb. 1991: 34–36.

Student Essay

In Joni's essay reproduced next, which is also concerned with the topic of political correctness, I have marked instances that indicate that she did not fully understand the requirements of the genre of argument. Read Joni's essay and the comments I have inserted. Then examine the analysis that follows.

PC Is Ridiculous!

(This title does not indicate the seriousness of the topic.)

(This introduction introduces the topic through
a definition. However, it does not lead smoothly
into a thesis statement, as did Cyrus's essay.)

A debate has scourged the United States for several decades regarding

(Actually, the debate has been going
on only during the past few years.)

the issue of "PC." The abbreviation is often confused with several different meanings, such as "personal computer" and "president's choice," but
instead I am addressing the coined term "political correctness." Every

(The abbreviation and mistakes one might
make in understanding it are not really
relevant to the main point of the essay.)

day the debate about PC becomes more prominent in the classroom, the
newspapers, and casual conversation, and people are getting sick of it.

(This last sentence uses an overly conversational expression
that is inappropriate to the genre of argument. Moreover, it
does not contribute to the advancement of the argument.)

(The body of this essay lacks cogent arguments with supporting points. It also does not indicate awareness of audience.)

The truth of the matter is actually simple. No matter what Stanley

(Actually, the matter is complex. If it were simple, it
wouldn't be a suitable topic for the genre of argument.)

Fish might claim, political correctness stifles free speech and will ulti-

(The writer does not identify Stanley Fish.)

mately lead to a completely repressive society. Even now, students are afraid to open their mouths and say what they really think because they

**(This is a slang expression that is inappropriate
to the genre of argument.)**

are afraid of being labeled "racist" or "sexist." Is this what education is about? Isn't it time we stopped being afraid of telling the truth?

**(This is an exaggerated statement that is
inappropriate to the genre of argument.)**

Political correctness has been taken to an extreme. People can't say that someone is "short" anymore. They have to say someone is "vertically challenged." It is now considered insulting to refer to a female person as a "girl" because we now have to say "woman." This is just

**(This is a trivial example that does not address the more
important issues associated with the topic.)**

ridiculous! Anyone who gets insulted from such trivial statements can't

**(Simply saying that something is ridiculous
is an inflammatory assertion.)**

be intelligent.

**(This is an exaggerated statement that is more likely to insult
the audience than to serve as a convincing argument.)**

**(The hysterical tone and extreme statements in this
conclusion detract from the writer's credibility.)**

Our country was founded on the Bill of Rights, and the First Amendment to that document guarantees freedom of speech. If the PC people continue to make policy in our colleges and universities, free speech will no longer be a guaranteed right for students. Are students supposed to be considered second-class citizens? Isn't the university a place where people can speak freely? The PC movement has gotten completely out of hand, and all policies concerned with it on campus ought to be eliminated.

Analysis of Joni's Essay

Following is an analysis of Joni's essay in terms of the conceptual features of academic argument discussed in this chapter.

The Writer

As a writer, Joni does not appear to be trustworthy, objective, logical, or fair. She presents only a limited perspective on the topic and uses a strident tone; moreover, she does not seem to have done much reading or research, nor does she indicate awareness and understanding of the ideas of others. Joni simply states her opinion without acknowledging that some people might disagree with her ideas. Phrases such as "This is just ridiculous! Anyone who gets insulted from such trivial statements can't be very intelligent" characterize a personal shouting match, not a thoughtful examination of a complex issue. Moreover, several statements in Joni's conclusion are exaggerated and not supported by careful evidence. Joni does not therefore present herself as a writer who is familiar with the purpose and conventions of the genre of argument.

The Audience

Joni does not seem to have considered her audience very much at all. She does not define "PC," assuming that her audience already knows what she is referring to, nor does she explain her reference to Stanley Fish. A reader who is not familiar with Joni's topic might well ask, "Who is Stanley Fish, and why is Joni arguing with him?" Moreover, Joni's tone indicates that she has not thought about how stridency and exaggerated claims will affect a reader. Few of us are likely to be convinced by a statement such as "Anyone who gets insulted from such trivial statements can't be very intelligent." In fact, most people would find a statement such as this quite insulting.

The Topic and the Context

Joni has chosen a topic that is appropriate for academic argument, but she has not indicated that she is aware of the controversy associated with it, nor did she provide sufficient background information. By not acknowledging an opposing position, Joni's stance in this essay appears one-sided.

Approach to the Topic

Joni approaches this topic as if she is having an emotionally heated interchange with an opponent. Her language is inappropriate to the genre of argument because she relies on unsupported assertions and unanswered questions.

Support

Joni does not provide compelling support for her statements. Her essay consists of unsupported claims and rhetorical questions.

Assumptions

Joni does not establish that she shares assumptions with her intended audience. She seems inclined to attack her opposition rather than to establish a basis for understanding.

You will also note that Joni does not incorporate information from outside sources, and so, of course, she cannot include a "Works Cited" section.

EXERCISE

A critical feature of the genre of argument is that it deals with a problem—that is, a facet of the topic that people may disagree with in some way, or an aspect of the topic that might be improved through reexamination, reevaluation, or change. For example, a problem associated with the topic of legalizing marijuana, at least according to some people, is that restrictions imposed on marijuana make it difficult to use it for medical purposes. These people also claim that enforcing the law against marijuana costs a great deal of money. Opponents of this position claim that marijuana is a dangerous drug and that a dangerous drug should not be made easily available.

To gain practice in finding problems within a topic, try to locate a problem that might lend itself to argumentative writing for each of the following topics. This exercise can be done either on your own or in small groups in class.

1. required courses in undergraduate education
2. athletics on campus
3. living in the dorms
4. short answer exams
5. animal rights
6. quotas in employment or educational settings
7. child-care centers in the workplace
8. part-time jobs for students
9. school uniforms

After locating a problem within these topics, choose one and see if you can formulate a position on it.

Working with the Readings
at the End of this Chapter

The readings at the end of this chapter were taken from academic and popular journals. Their purpose is to help you think about the the genre of argument and how it appears in different contexts. Before working with these readings, work in small groups to review the features of the genre of argument discussed in this chapter. Then, continuing to work in a group, select one of these essays and answer the following questions:

1. What is the purpose of the essay?
2. Does the essay address a controversial or complex topic?
3. What is the thesis or claim made in the essay? Can you locate it?
4. Does the writer of the essay indicate awareness of both sides of the controversy? Can you list at least two viewpoints on this topic?
5. Does the writer qualify any of the statements made in the essay?
6. Does the writer indicate awareness of audience? How and where?
7. What sort of tone characterizes the essay? Does the tone contribute to or detract from the credibility of the writer?
8. Examine the structure of the essay. How is it similar to and different from the classical argumentative structure discussed in this chapter?
9. Is the essay an example of the genre of argument? Why or why not?

EXERCISE

Select an ad from a magazine. In small groups discuss the following questions:

1. What is the purpose of this ad?
2. What features of this ad are similar to those associated with the genre of argument?
3. What features of this ad are different from those associated with the genre of argument?
4. What is the thesis of this ad? Could this ad be written as an essay? Why or why not?

Should Violence Go Unpunished?
Rushworth M. Kidder

Rushworth Kidder is a writer and journalist who writes about ethical issues. His books include *How Good People Make Tough Choices* (1995) and *Shared Values for a Troubled World.* This editorial is from the journal *Insights on Global Ethics* (December 1994/January 1995).

Some years ago in a conversation with Mexican novelist and diplomat Carlos   1
Fuentes, I asked him to define the central challenge facing Latin America. In words that echoed far beyond the Western Hemisphere, he spoke of "a history of unpunished violence."

I've thought of that phrase many times in recent weeks. No wonder: 2

- Haitian strongman Raoul Cedras, whose forces killed thousands of his fellow citizens, has been airlifted to a safe haven in Panama with his assets intact. He's now at work on his memoirs.
- South Africa's newly proposed Truth Commission is designed to investigate 33 years of apartheid-era jailings, tortures, and murders. But the perpetrators, once they've confessed, would be granted amnesty and could never be prosecuted or sued for their actions.
- Palestinian leader Yasir Arafat, after years of terrorism directed at Israeli civilians, won the Nobel Peace Prize. One member of the Nobel Committee, resigning in protest, noted that Arafat's past was "too tainted with violence, terrorism, and bloodshed" to deserve the award.

How *should* we punish violence?   3

That's one of the central moral questions of our time. Of the great ethical   4
dilemmas in human experience, none is so challenging as one that pits justice against mercy. On one hand, laws must be obeyed and the disobedient punished. That's what "justice" means. On the other hand, extenuating circumstances often impel us to temper the law with forbearance or compassion. When our judicial systems blend justice and mercy, giving miscreants no more (and no less) than they deserve, we say, "Good. That was fair."

But the problem with Cedras, Arafat, & Co. is of a different order. What off-   5
sets *justice,* here, is not *mercy* but *pragmatism.* The calculation is not, "Do these people deserve our compassion?," but "Will the world be more secure if they go unpunished?" These are, morally, two very different questions.

The answer to the first is quite simple: People who deliberately commit   6
deadly acts of political terrorism have not earned our compassion. One can also argue that true morality lies in following rules that can be applied universally. If that's so, what are we to make of a rule saying, "Everyone should be free to murder the innocent for political ends"? Universalize that rule, and violence erupts. Refuse to do so, and a measure of moral consistency is restored.

7   In fact, issues of amnesty are rarely argued this way. Instead, the utilitarian calculus is usually invoked. Will the security of the many be ensured by overlooking the crimes of a few? To answer "Yes," one has to assess two things: the numbers involved, and the probable course of the future. Numbers are no problem: Millions of Haitians are more important than a few thugs. But what of the future? Will Cedras fade, Haiti heal, and democracy bloom? Or will he prove to other would-be dictators that, if you're big enough and violent enough, you'll make a pile and ultimately walk free?

8   On these last questions, the jury's still out. Nor will it return any time soon—since we can never wait long enough to be able to say, "There, the future is at last complete, and now we know." This fall's crop of amnesty, sown widely and well tended, could lead to far more powerful democracies in Haiti, South Africa, and the Middle East. Or it could lead to a deeper history of unpunished violence. Is amnesty wise, or just expedient?

QUESTIONS

1. What point is Kidder making with this article? How does this point invite us to view the issue of amnesty for terrorists?
2. What assumptions does Kidder make about the personalities he discusses? What do you already know about Cedras, Arafat, and the Truth Commission? What don't you know?
3. Does this essay offer a reasoned argument, or would you say that it merely poses a problem? What is its purpose? Could you write an essay on it using the academic argument genre?
4. Who do you think is the audience Kidder addresses? Would your audience differ from his if you wrote an essay on this article? How? (Be specific!)
5. How do we perceive Kidder as the writer? Is he convincing? Does he sound authoritative? Why?
6. What kind of evidence would you need to find to write a well-supported essay on this issue?

Hazardous Waste and Gender Equity: Who Decides?

Rushworth M. Kidder

This article is from Rushworth M. Kidder's book *How Good People Make Tough Choices* (1995).

As an environmental chemist heading a hazardous waste laboratory, Peter employed both female and male professionals. Chemistry, to him, was perfectly gender-neutral.

But in the mid-1980s his company asked him to set up a lab to deal with one of the most toxic substances known: dioxin. He put in place all the standard safety precautions. But he deliberately hired chemists who were males or were females beyond child-bearing age. The reason: The best literature of the day suggested that children born to mothers exposed to dioxin experienced a higher-than-usual incidence of birth defects and neurological disorders.

Given the extensive publicity about the dioxin contamination of Times Beach, Missouri, in 1982, the lab was very successful. Then one day a bright company scientist—Camille, a married woman in her late twenties—requested a transfer into his lab. Though she was scheduled to leave the company in six months, she wanted a stint in the dioxin lab for the sake of her résumé, since few women had such backgrounds.

In interviewing her, Peter learned that she intended to have children in the future. She also made it clear that, were she not hired, she would sue for discrimination. Yet if he did hire her, and if her children subsequently suffered deformities, he knew the company could be legally liable for failing to protect her.

Peter's dilemma arose out of a conflict between two of his core beliefs. One was his sense of gender equity. The other was his profound concern for the care of infants and small children. He knew he should give Camille the job to further erode the gender barrier. Yet his own sense of personal responsibility caused him to worry deeply about possible harm to her children.

Peter later learned, as did the nation, that dioxin is not nearly as toxic as once thought, and that the disincorporation of Times Beach was probably unnecessary. At the time, however, based on the existing information, he faced an ethical dilemma of the justice-versus-mercy sort. Fairness dictated that he hire her. But compassion argued that—despite the fact that such a decision would be surely unpopular, probably illegal, and professionally difficult—he should not.

What to do? From an ends-based perspective, considering the greatest good for the greatest number, he might decide to hire her. He could argue that the need to defend gender equity for women chemists in general was worth the risk to a single baby—and that the risk of a law-suit that could shut down the operation and cost dozens of jobs was greater than the risk of a single dioxin exposure in a carefully run lab.

8   From a rule-based perspective, however, he might argue that, if such an action were made into a universal rule, every manager in every hazardous waste operation would have to act as though there were no differences between men and women—even though science suggested otherwise. The most important rule to live by, he might say, would be "Always protect the lives of children," rather than "Always promote the careers of women."

9   From a care-based perspective, he might argue that, if he were in Camille's position, he would want to be hired—although he might also want friends to warn him of consequences he perhaps hadn't fully considered.

QUESTIONS

1. The controversy in this issue arises from concern for the individual, as well as the best interest of the company. How would you state the specific issues involved in the example posed by Kidder? How would you state the larger implications of this problem, using the academic argument genre?

2. If you were to take a side on this issue, which side would you take? Would your opinion be an appropriate approach to the subject? What would be the purpose of your argument?

3. What kind of assumptions about this topic does Kidder make? What kind of assumptions would you need to make to write a persuasive argument on this issue?

4. Think about the elements involved in structuring an essay. Reflecting on the structure of the earlier readings, come up with three different structures for this argument. Which do you think is best? Why?

5. What kind of evidence would you need to support an academic argument on this topic?

AIDS Babies Deserve Testing
New York Times

This selection is from the *New York Times,* June 27, 1994.

All those concerned about babies infected with the virus that causes AIDS can 1
be grateful to Michael Dowling, New York's Commissioner of Social Services.
He, at least, has had the decency and common sense to guarantee that all AIDS-
infected babies in the foster-care system will be identified and cared for.

But what about the larger number of AIDS-infected babies who are not in 2
foster care? Their fate now hinges on the outcome of a legislative battle that pits
the health needs of the babies against the privacy rights of the mothers.

The core issue is whether there should be mandatory testing and identifi- 3
cation of all newborns so that those infected with the AIDS virus can be
treated—or simply mandatory counseling of all mothers to try to persuade
them to allow testing of themselves and their babies.

Each side in this clash claims its approach will be best for the children. But 4
from the evidence available, the likelihood that counseling alone will do the job
seems slight. The only sure way to identify these infants is through testing. The
state already tests all newborns, anonymously, to track the epidemic; it could
use or enhance that program to identify the infected infants who need medical
monitoring and treatment.

The dispute arises because there is no way to identify an infected newborn 5
without identifying the mother as infected; the babies contract the virus from
their mothers in the womb or at birth. Thus a mandatory test of any newborn
amounts to a mandatory test of the mother as well, subjecting her to possible
discrimination if her disease status becomes known. Under current state law,
neither the mother nor her child can be tested without written, informed consent.

Commissioner Dowling avoided this dilemma because his agency has legal 6
responsibility for the babies in its care; in effect, he is their surrogate parent.
Thus he provoked no opposition when he pledged recently to require routine
testing of all children who enter foster care and appear likely to have been
exposed to the virus.

But foster children account for only a minority of the several hundred AIDS- 7
infected babies born in New York State each year. Most of these babies leave the
hospital without being tested. They are thus robbed of any chance at early treatment. Nothing is done for them until they come down with symptoms of the
fatal illness.

Assemblywoman Nettie Mayersohn, of Queens, and State Senator Guy 8
Velella, of the Bronx, would rectify this neglect by disclosing the state's anonymous test results to the mothers. That may not go far enough. When individual

lives are at stake, the tests must be conducted more rigorously than those now performed for statistical purposes. Still, done properly, such testing could identify virtually every infected baby, and the mothers could then be counseled on the importance of medical follow-up.

9   But leaders of the key health committees in the Legislature are pushing bills, already approved in the Senate, that only call for mandatory counseling of new and expectant mothers. They argue that this would capture the great majority of infected children—and that babies would get better care if their mothers cooperated in treatment than if they were frightened away from the medical system because of mandatory testing.

10   Unfortunately, there is scant evidence that the counseling approach would work. The state already sponsors voluntary counseling programs for pregnant women and new mothers in 24 hospitals in AIDS-impacted areas; they typically fail to identify most of the infected babies. Counseling enthusiasts cite the success of Harlem Hospital; some 90 percent of all infected babies born there in 1993 were identified through counseling and voluntary testing. But even the founder of that program doubts its success could be replicated widely. And why neglect even 10 percent of the babies?

11   Mandatory counseling could be beneficial during prenatal care when doctors can actually save many babies from infection by treating the expectant mother with AZT. Since no one is seriously recommending that pregnant women be forced to take an AIDS test, counseling the mother-to-be on the benefits of testing is the only feasible approach.

12   But once a mother has delivered an infected baby, that infant deserves to be identified and given the best possible care. By all means, counsel the mother on the advantages of testing and treatment. But for the baby's sake, test the child whether the mother approves or not.

QUESTIONS

1. What is the specific problem addressed in this article?
2. What solution to the "AIDS babies" problem does the author offer?
3. Do you think this argument is convincing? Why? Why not?
4. Identify the author's sources. Do they seem reliable?
5. What does the author assume you already know about this topic?
6. Review the features of academic argument discussed in this chapter. Which of these features also characterize an editorial? How does an editorial differ from an academic essay?

Test-Tube Babies: Solution or Problem?
Ruth Hubbard

Ruth Hubbard (b. 1924), one of the first women in the sciences to be
tenured at Harvard University, first presented the ideas in this essay at
a meeting of the American Association for the Advancement of Science. Her other writings include *Looking at Women* (1979), edited
with Mary Sue Henifen and Barbara Fried; *Genes and Gender II; Pitfalls in Research on Sex and Gender* (1979), edited with Marian
Lowe; *Nature: Rationalizations of Inequality* (1983), and *Explod-
ing the Gene Myth* (written with her son, Elijah Wald). This essay was
published in *Technology Review* (1980).

In vitro fertilization of human eggs and the implantation of early embryos into
women's wombs are new biotechnologies that may enable some women to
bear children who have hitherto been unable to do so. In that sense, it may
solve their particular infertility problems. On the other hand, this technology
poses unpredictable hazards since it intervenes in the process of fertilization, in
the first cell divisions of the fertilized egg, and in the implantation of the
embryo into the uterus. At present we have no way to assess in what ways and
to what extent these interventions may affect the women or the babies they
acquire by this procedure. Since the use of the technology is only just beginning, the financial and technical investments it represents are still modest. It is
therefore important that we, as a society, seriously consider the wisdom of
implementing and developing it further.

According to present estimates, about 10 million Americans are infertile by
the definition that they have tried for at least a year to achieve pregnancy without conceiving or carrying a pregnancy to a live birth. In about a third of infertile couples, the incapacity rests with the woman only, and for about a third of
these women the problem is localized in the fallopian tubes (the organs that
normally propel an egg from the ovary to the uterus or womb). These short,
delicate tubes are easily blocked by infection or disease. Nowadays the most
common causes of blocked tubes are inflammations of the uterine lining
brought on by IUDs, pelvic inflammatory disease, or gonorrhea. Once blocked,
the tubes are difficult to reopen or replace, and doctors presently claim only a
one-in-three success rate in correcting the problem. Thus, of the 10 million
infertile people in the country, about 600 thousand (or 6 percent) could perhaps be helped to pregnancy by in vitro fertilization. (These numbers are from
Barbara Eck Menning's *Infertility: A Guide for the Childless Couple.* Prentice-
Hall, 1977. Ms. Menning is executive director of Resolve, a national, nonprofit
counseling service for infertile couples located in Belmont, Mass.)

Louise Brown, born in England, in July, 1978, is the first person claimed to
have been conceived in vitro. Since then, two other babies conceived outside

the mother are said to have been born—one in England, the other in India. In none of these cases have the procedures by which the eggs were obtained from the woman's ovary, fertilized, stored until implantation, and finally implanted in her uterus been described in any detail. However, we can deduce the procedures from animal experimentation and the brief published accounts about the three babies.

4   The woman who is a candidate for in vitro fertilization has her hormone levels monitored to determine when she is about to ovulate. She is then admitted to the hospital and the egg is collected in the following way: a small cut is made in her abdomen; a metal tube containing an optical arrangement that allows the surgeon to see the ovaries and a narrow-bore tube (called a micropipette) are inserted through the cut; and the egg is removed shortly before it would normally be shed from the ovary. The woman is ready to go home within a day, at most.

5   When the procedure was first developed, women were sometimes given hormones to make them "superovulate"—produce more than one egg (the usual number for most women). But we do not know whether this happened with the mothers of the three "test-tube" babies that have been born. Incidentally, this superovulation reportedly is no longer induced, partly because some people believe it is too risky.

6   After the egg has been isolated, it is put into a solution that keeps it alive and nourishes it, and is mixed with sperm. Once fertilized, it is allowed to go through a few cell divisions and so begin its embryonic development—the still-mysterious process by which a fertilized egg becomes a baby. The embryo is then picked up with another fine tube, inserted through the woman's cervix, and flushed into the uterus.

7   If the uterus is not at the proper stage to allow for implantation (approximately 17 to 23 days after the onset of each menstruation) when the embryo is ready to be implanted, the embryo must be frozen and stored until the time is right in a subsequent menstrual cycle. Again, we do not know whether the embryos were frozen and stored prior to implantation with the two British babies; we are told that the Indian one was.

8   In sum, then, there is a need, and there is a technology said to meet that need. But as a woman, a feminist, and a biologist, I am opposed to using it and developing it further.

Health Risks

9   As a society, we do not have a very good track record in anticipating the problems that can arise from technological interventions in complicated biological systems. Our physical models are too simpleminded and have led to many unforeseen problems in the areas of pest control, waste disposal, and other aspects of what is usually referred to as the ecological crisis.

10   In reproductive biology, the nature of the many interacting processes is poorly understood. We are in no position to enumerate or describe the many reactions that must occur at just the right times during the early stages of

embryonic development when the fertilized egg begins to divide into increasing numbers of cells, implants itself in the uterus, and establishes the pattern for the different organ systems that will allow it to develop into a normal fetus and baby.

The safety of this in vitro procedure cannot be established in animal exper- 11 iments because the details and requirements of normal embryonic development are different for different kinds of animals. Nor are the criteria of "normalcy" the same for animals and for people. The guinea pigs of the research and implementation of in vitro fertilization will be:

- the women who donate their eggs,
- the women who lend their wombs (who, of course, need not be the same as the egg-donors; rent-a-wombs clearly are an option), and
- the children who are produced.

The greatest ethical and practical questions arise with regard to the chil- 12 dren. They cannot consent to be produced, and we cannot know what hazards their production entails until enough have lived out their lives to allow for statistical analysis of their medical histories.

This example shows the inadequacy of our scientific models because it is 13 not obvious how to provide "controls," in the usual scientific sense of the term, for the first generation of "test-tube" individuals; they will be viewed as "special" at every critical juncture in their lives. When I ask myself whether I would want to be a "test-tube person," I know that I would not like to have to add *those* self-doubts to my more ordinary repertoire of insecurities.

A concrete example of a misjudgment with an unfortunate outcome that 14 could not be predicted was the administration of the chemical thalidomide, a "harmless tranquilizer" touted as a godsend and prescribed to pregnant women, which resulted in the births of thousands of armless and legless babies. Yet there the damage was visible at birth and the practice could be stopped, though not until after it had caused great misery. But take the case of the hormone DES (diethyl stilbesterol), which was prescribed for pregnant women in the mistaken (though at the time honest) belief that it could prevent miscarriages. Some 15 years passed before many of the daughters of these women developed an unusual form of vaginal cancer. Both these chemicals produced otherwise rare diseases, so the damage was easy to detect and its causes could be sought. Had the chemicals produced more common symptoms, it would have been much more difficult to detect the damage and to pinpoint which drugs were harmful.

The important point is that both thalidomide and DES changed the envi- 15 ronment in which these babies developed—in ways that could not have been foreseen and that we still do not understand. This happened because we know very little about how embryos develop. How then can we claim to know that the many chemical and mechanical manipulations of eggs, sperms, and embryos that take place during in vitro fertilization and implantation are harmless?

A Woman's Right?

16 The push toward this technology reinforces the view, all too prevalent in our society, that women's lives are unfulfilled, or indeed worthless, unless we bear children. I understand the wish to have children, though I also know many people—women and men—who lead happy and fulfilled lives without them. But even if one urgently wants a child, why must it be biologically one's own? It is not worth opening the hornet's nest of reproductive technology for the privilege of having one's child derive from one's own egg or sperm. Foster and adoptive parents are much needed for the world's homeless children. Why not try to change the American and international practices that make it difficult for people who want children to be brought together with children who need parents?

17   Advocates of this new technology argue that every woman has a right to bear a child and that the technology will extend this right to a group previously denied it. It is important to examine this argument and to ask in what sense women have a "right" to bear children. In our culture, many women are taught from childhood that we must do without lots of things we want—electric trains, baseball mitts, perhaps later an expensive education or a well-paying job. We are also taught to submit to all sorts of social restrictions and physical dangers—we cannot go out alone at night, we allow ourselves to be made self-conscious at the corner drugstore and to be molested by strangers or bosses or family members without punching them as our brothers might do. We are led to believe that we must put up with all this—and without grousing—because as women we have something beside which everything else pales, something that will make up for everything: we can have babies! To grow up paying all the way and then to be denied that child *is* a promise unfulfilled; that's cheating.

18   But I would argue that to promise children to women by means of an untested technology—that is tested only as it is used on them and their babies—is adding yet another wrong to the burdens of our socialization. Take the women whose fallopian tubes have been damaged by an infection provoked by faulty IUDs. They are now led to believe that problems caused by one risky, though medically approved and administered, technology can be relieved by another, much more invasive and hazardous technology.

19   I am also concerned about the extremely complicated nature of the technology. It involves many steps, is hard to demystify, and requires highly skilled professionals. There is no way to put control over this technology into the hands of the women who are going to be exposed to it. On the contrary, it will make women and their babies more dependent than ever upon a high-technology, super-professionalized medical system. The women and their babies must be monitored from before conception until birth, and the children will have to be observed all their lives. Furthermore, the pregnancy-monitoring technologies themselves involve hazard. From the start, women are locked into subservience to the medical establishment in a way that I find impossible to interpret as an increase in reproductive freedom, rights, or choices.

Health Priorities

The final issue—and a major one—is that this technology is expensive. It 20
requires prolonged experimentation, sophisticated professionals, and costly
equipment. It will distort our health priorities and funnel scarce resources into
a questionable effort. The case of the Indian baby is a stark illustration, for in
that country, where many children are dying from the effects of malnutrition
and poor people have been forcibly sterilized, expensive technologies are being
pioneered to enable a relatively small number of well-to-do people to have their
own babies.

In the United States, as well, many people have less-than-adequate access to 21
such essential health resources as decent jobs, food and housing, and medical
care when they need it. And here, too, poor women have been and are still
being forcibly sterilized and otherwise coerced into *not* having babies, while
women who can pay high prices will become guinea pigs in the risky technology of in vitro fertilization.

In vitro fertilization is expensive and unnecessary in comparison with 22
many pressing social needs, including those of children who need homes. We
must find better and less risky solutions for women who want to parent but
cannot bear children of their own.

QUESTIONS

1. What is the thesis of this essay?
2. What is the opposing viewpoint with which this essay is concerned?
3. What are the main arguments in favor of the author's thesis?
4. How is this essay from a professional journal similar to the genre of argument as it is explained in this chapter?
5. Do you agree with the thesis of this essay? Why or why not?

An Alternative View
of the Purpose of Psychosis

Harold H. Mosak and Samuel E. Goldman

Harold H. Mosak is a therapist who is particularly known for his writings on Adlerian psychology. Samuel E. Goldman writes about the influence of neurobiology on behavior. This essay originally appeared in *Individual Psychology: The Journal of Adlerian Theory, Research and Practice* (March 1995).

1   In a previous article Mosak and Fletcher (1973/1977) discussed the purposes of delusions and hallucinations. A retrospective glance makes transparent not only the purposes of these psychotic behaviors but affords glimpses of the nature and purposes of the psychotic process as well.

2   Adlerians tend to be content with the explanation that all psychopathologies are attempts to evade the life tasks. The psychotic refuses to think, feel, and behave consensually. Through the use of "schizophrenese" (Mosak & Maniacci, 1989) psychotics disturb communication, create social distance, and evade the consensual social task. From a superficial point of view these observations can be readily confirmed.

3   Given this view based upon evasion of the life tasks, Adler and other Adlerians of his generation were fond of labelling people who exhibited psychopathology with such pejorative terms as "cowards" and "misfits." These read more as accusations than diagnoses.

4   However, we can also observe psychotic behavior from another perspective. Dreikurs (personal communication) maintained that "psychotics are like normal people—only more so." This statement posed a puzzle, but the point Dreikurs was apparently making was that psychotics behaved according to the same "laws" that all people do although the forms these behaviors took might be highly idiosyncratic.

5   Like other people, psychotics are engaged in problem solving rather than merely avoiding behaviors. Instead of speaking of *evading* the life tasks, we may alternatively regard psychosis as an attempt to *solve* the life tasks. The psychotic solutions, unfortunately are, as Adler said, on the useless side of life—inferior, nonconstructive, nonconsensual, irrational, ineffective, and unsuccessful.

6   Ultimately, outside of the solutions to mundane life problems, psychotics are engaged in the same goal-seeking behavior as other people. Their self-ideal (Mosak, 1954) is based on "man's quest for significance" (Lombardi, 1975; Way, 1948)—to be somebody, to count, to belong, to possess an identity. Unable to find a place through the exercise of ability or of goodness—perhaps because their training or self-training in life has discouraged them—they seek signifi-

cance through the creation of psychotic thought, feeling, and behavior. How much more significant can someone be than if one is God? How much more significant can one be than if everyone is after him or her, threatening them, seeking to do them harm? If "they" are trying to steal his or her secrets, the psychotic is doubly significant, first because she or he possesses important secrets and second because others are persistently trying to steal them. In the manic episode one can be or do anything, and in the depressive episode one can proclaim, like the tragically heroic Prometheus, "Ye gods! How I suffer!" Not only do psychotics render themselves important in their own minds, their outward behavior invites the world to pay attention to them. People exhort them, reinforcing their feelings of importance and power. And to the extent they can actively or passively resist these efforts to change them, they gain even greater feelings of importance. The psychotics must resist (even when they passively comply) therapeutic interventions. Should therapy succeed and the psychotic behavior be eliminated, the psychotic will be robbed of his identity; the cure will transform the person into a "nobody," and that would be intolerable. If it were tolerable to be an insignificant nonentity, the person would not have chosen psychosis in the first place. Consequently, psychotics must tenaciously cling to their behavior, a resistance which has led to the fiction in some people's minds that the psychotic is incurable.

This conceptualization, in Adlerian terms, is dynamic in that it concerns itself 7 with the psychotic's line of movement. As such, the difficulties in psychotherapy can be explained in terms of how and why the individual attempts to achieve his or her self-ideal goals and maintain a place in the world rather than upon static psychology of possession explanations that the psychotic has a "narcissistic neurosis" rather than a "transference neurosis," and that only the latter have good prognosis. Those therapists with a biological orientation spare themselves the troubles inherent in the psychological understanding of the psychotic, as well as others, by embracing a psychology of possession, e.g., the psychotic has a biochemical disorder, and therefore interventions must be in terms of medication and somatic interventions. Much of the time these methods play into the hands of the psychotic in that the changing of medications and adjusting the dosages gives them the feeling that they count. To the extent that the medications are ineffective or require changing the dosages, the psychotic gets the feeling that she or he is more powerful than the medication or the doctor, and this feeling of power gives them a place. The medications themselves, while they may alleviate symptomatology, do nothing to give psychotics the feeling of place they so sorely need. When tranquilizers were introduced, a newsmagazine interviewed a psychotic woman who explained that after being administered tranquilizers, she still heard the devil talking to her but now she no longer answered back.

Does this mean that there is no place for biochemical explanations and 8 somatic interventions if we adopt the viewpoint stated here? Not necessarily. While Mosak (1994) does not rely upon medication in his treatment of schizophrenics, the principle of complementarity (Rychlak, 1993) leaves room for biological explanations. Rychlak posits four grounds for explanation which are "of equal stature"—"*Physikos, Bios, Socius, and Logos*" (p. 936). He writes further,

> Also, it will not matter if empirical findings supporting one grounding assumption fail to address explanations in another grounding assumption. The empirical findings in the *Bios* complement empirical findings in the *Logos:* they do not replace them. (p. 937)

Consequently, the debate between the proponents of these two views—psychological and biological—is largely irrelevant. The views are complementary rather then contradictory explanations of psychotic behavior. They are of equal stature; one explanation does not reduce the content of the other. Each explanation becomes the "spectacles" (Beecher, 1942; Beecher & Beecher, 1951; Bitter, 1985) through which human behavior is viewed, leading to certain forms of intervention. Rychlak (1993) summarizes it well.

> At a metatheoretical level we may debate the grounds to be used generally in psychology, and unabashedly commit to our favorite. But we should not hit each other over the head with such biases during the everyday efforts we put into building a scientific discipline. It seems to me that this tolerance of a colleague's ground would be a nice first step toward the unification of psychology that is being sought today by many psychologists. (p. 939)

References

Beecher, W. (1942). The meaning of theories. *Individual Psychology Bulletin, 2*(3), 46–49.

Beecher, W., & Beecher, M. (1951). What makes an Adlerian? *Individual Psychology Bulletin, 9,* 146–148.

Bitter, J. R. (1985). An interview with Harold Mosak. *Individual Psychology, 41*(3), 386–420.

Lombardi, D. (1975). *Search for significance.* Chicago: Nelson-Hall.

Mosak, H. H. (1954). The psychological attitude in rehabilitation. *American Archives of Rehabilitation Therapy, 2,* 9–10.

Mosak, H. H. (1994). Drugless psychotherapy with schizophrenics. *Individual Psychology, 51*(1), 61–66.

Mosak, H. H., & Fletcher, S. J. (1977). Purposes of delusions and hallucinations. In H. H. Mosak (Ed.), *On purpose* (pp. 239–245). Chicago: Alfred Adler Institute. (Original work published 1973)

Mosak, H. H., & Maniacci, M. (1989). An approach to the understanding of "schizophrenese." *Individual Psychology, 45*(4), 465–472.

Rychlak, J. F. (1993). A suggested principle of complementarity for psychology: In theory, not method. *American Psychologist, 48*(9), 933–942.

Way, L. (1948). *Man's quest for significance.* London: Allen & Unwin.

QUESTIONS

1. What is the controversy with which this essay is concerned?
2. What is the main thesis of this essay?

Calvin and Hobbes   by Bill Watterson

3. What idea do the authors use to begin their essay? How does that idea relate to the thesis of the essay?
4. What sort of evidence is used in this essay in support of the thesis?
5. What sort of audience does this essay address? How do you know?
6. How is this essay from a professional journal similar to the genre of argument as it is explained in this chapter?

Chapter 2

EXPLORING A TOPIC;
FINDING A THESIS

When you are assigned to write an argumentative essay in a college class, you may worry about how you will be able to find enough information about the topic to formulate a good thesis or claim. Should you sit around waiting for an inspiration? Should you head for the library immediately? Will you be able to discover good ideas just by thinking? This chapter focuses on several strategies for exploring a topic actively, beginning with your own experience and then moving beyond yourself to locate information elsewhere. The chapter also discusses several forms that a thesis can take within the genre of argument.

EXPLORING A TOPIC ACTIVELY

In some of your college classes, you may have the option of selecting your own topic; in others, your teacher may assign one. In either case, you should begin working on your paper by doing **something active**—it is not a good idea to just sit staring at a computer screen or chewing your fingernails, hoping that ideas will strike like a bolt of lightning. I suppose that some writers are inspired in this way—these are the writers depicted in film and story, who pace the floor and think until a brilliant notion emerges, springing like Athena from the head of Zeus. For most writers, though, ideas do not arrive in this way. Most writers discover ideas when they engage in preliminary writing activities that enable them to assess what they already know and believe about the topic.

Engaging in preliminary writing activities, of course, is no guarantee that you will discover wonderful, exciting ideas right away. In fact, you may find that you reject a lot of what you have written initially. Yet even if this happens, you will find that doing some form of preliminary writing will stimulate the discovery of at least something that is useful. If nothing else, it will highlight what additional information you might need.

BEGINNING WITH WHAT YOU KNOW: EXPLORATION QUESTIONS

A good place to begin the process of writing an argumentative essay is with what you know—that is, to reflect on experiences, facts, opinions, and values you already have about the topic. Understanding your own views on a topic will also help you figure out what you *don't* know about it, determine what you need to find out, and enable you to evaluate the material you find. One strategy for initiating work on any topic is to respond in writing to the following "**exploration questions**":

1. Is there a controversy associated with this topic?
2. Were you brought up to have an opinion on this controversy? What opinion did your family and community have on this topic?
3. How did your school experiences influence your conception of the topic? Did your teachers and classmates feel the same way about it as did your family? Were there any points of disagreement?
4. Can you think of at least two people who hold differing views about this topic? If so, describe these people and summarize what you believe are their points of view.
5. Has your opinion about this topic changed in any way? Why or why not?
6. Do you think that this topic is important for people to think about? Why or why not?

To illustrate how "exploration questions" can enable a writer to gain an understanding of a topic, let us imagine the following scenario:

A college student named Brian is currently in his first year at State College. State College is a large, well-known university that offers many opportunities, and Brian had entered State in the fall semester with the idea of majoring in business. However, after a semester at State, Brian is thinking about transferring to Northern College, a smaller school that is not as well known. Northern offers a major in environmental studies, which Brian would now prefer as his major.

Brian's problem is that his Uncle Stan is helping Brian with his college tuition, and Uncle Stan is, himself, a graduate of State. Brian's writing task is to convince Uncle Stan that Northern College would be a better choice.

To gain a better understanding of his "topic," Brian responded to the "exploration questions" just listed, an exercise that enabled him to become aware of other facets of the topic that he needed to clarify and investigate.

Brian's Responses

1. Is there a controversy associated with this topic?

The choice of which college to attend can be a controversial topic for some people. Some people, like my Uncle Stan, think that choosing the "right" college is an extremely important decision for being successful in life and that the "right" college means one that has a great business school where you can make lots of contacts. Other people think that the "right" college is one that has programs that are interesting to students. These people think that going to college to study business is not the only possibility and is not at all the right choice for someone who doesn't find business interesting.

2. Were you brought up to have an opinion on this controversy? What opinion did your family and community have on this topic?

I was brought up with the idea that being financially successful is important. Yet my mother always encouraged me to explore topics that interested me and that I felt were worthwhile. Actually, my mother is an elementary school teacher, and she didn't choose that field because she would be able to make a lot of money. On the other hand, a lot of my friends think that making money is everything and that studying business is a great way to do it.

3. How did your school experiences influence your conception of the topic? Did your teachers and classmates feel the same way about it as did your family? Were there any points of disagreement?

In school we were taught that doing something worthwhile is more important than just going for the money. My community service class in high school really opened my eyes to the possibilities of working to help the environment. My geography teacher last semester showed me that there is important work to be done in environmental policy. That class really sparked my interest and showed me that I could study something interesting and worthwhile and still make a decent living.

4. Can you think of at least two people who hold differing views about this topic? If so, describe these people and summarize what you believe are their points of view.

Uncle Stan thinks that going to a big, well-known school and majoring in business are the only way to go. He thinks that making a lot of money is the most important thing in life.

My geography teacher thinks I should go to a school that has a program that interests me. He thinks that making enough money is important but that doing something interesting and worthwhile is just as important.

5. Has your opinion about this topic changed in any way? Why or why not?

I used to agree with Uncle Stan. When I first began high school and saw the other kids with fancy cars and terrific clothes, I used to think that all I wanted to do was make a bundle of money so I could buy all that neat stuff. Now I think that doing something interesting and worthwhile is more important for me. I don't want to be poor, but I think I can make a living doing environmental studies because there are lots of jobs in that area.

6. Do you think that this topic is important for people to think about? Why or why not?

I think that choosing a school sometimes means choosing a profession, which is one of the most important decisions a person can make. I don't think that a person should choose a profession just for the money. On the other hand, you have to make enough to live. I think my idea to study environmental policy is a good compromise between the two.

Exploring Your Exploration

After you have written responses to the exploration questions, you should reread them, looking for ideas and directions that you can use in your essay or that you will need to explore further. In looking over his responses, Brian noted several ideas to use, as well as a few about which it would be good to find out more:

Question 1: Is there a controversy associated with this topic?

In his response, Brian had written that "other people" think that "business is not the only possibility" for having a successful professional life. In rereading this statement, he realized that aside from his geography teacher, he didn't really know any other people who felt this way. He decided that it might help convince Uncle Stan if he could find some specific people.

Question 2: Were you brought up to have an opinion on this controversy? What opinion did your family and community have on this topic?

In answering this question, Brian noted that he had referred to his mother's profession as an elementary school teacher, one that doesn't earn an extremely high salary. He then thought that maybe he should ask his mother about why she had chosen her career and find out if she was satisfied with her choice.

Question 3: How did your school experiences influence your conception of the topic? Did your teachers and classmates feel the same way about it as did your family? Were there any points of disagreement?

In answering this question, Brian had written that "there is important work to be done in environmental policy." Yet, he really didn't have specific information to support that statement. He decided that he would talk with his geography teacher about this and maybe do some research in the library to find out more specific information.

Question 4: Can you think of at least two people who hold differing views about this topic? If so, describe these people and summarize what you believe are their points of view.

In answering this question, Brian had written that Uncle Stan "thinks that making a lot of money is the most important thing in life" and that majoring in business is the only way to do this. As he thought about this, he realized that maybe some of the courses needed for the environmental studies major would be just as likely to earn him a good job after graduation. More information about this would be useful, Brian decided.

Question 5: Has your opinion about this topic changed in any way? Why or why not?

Because Brian's opinion had changed on this topic, he can use his previous opinion as a point of contact with Uncle Stan. Shared ideas, even when those ideas have changed, can be used as a bridge between you and your reader. Also, as in his response to question 4, Brian referred to "lots of jobs" in the area of environmental studies, a subject about which he will need additional information.

Question 6: Do you think this topic is important for people to think about? Why or why not?

Brian's answer to this question contained two possible points he could use: his awareness that he needed at least a reasonable salary to live and the reference to environmental studies as a compromise. These points might be included in his letter.

WRITING ASSIGNMENT

The director of the local preschool has decided to include a unit on fairy tales for all the children. Based on the readings in this chapter and on the fairy tales you are familiar with from your own culture, write an essay in which you address the following question:

Is it valuable for children to hear fairy tales? Why or why not?

In responding to this assignment, you should complete the following activities:

1. In small groups, discuss the fairy tales you liked best when you were a child. Why do you think you liked them? Would you tell these tales to your own children? Can you perceive anything harmful about these tales?
2. Write responses to the exploration questions.
3. Write a short, informal essay discussing the good and bad points of the fairy tales you liked best when you were a child.
4. Read Teeanna's responses and compare them with your own.
5. Read the following essays (at the end of this chapter):
    Bruno Bettelheim, excerpt from *The Uses of Enchantment*
    Armin A. Brott, "Not All Men Are Sly Foxes"
    Marina Warner, "The Absent Mother: Women against Women in Old Wives' Tales"
6. Revise your essay to respond to the question:

Is it valuable for children to hear fairy tales? Why or why not?

Your essay should have the characteristics of the genre of argument and should include at least some information from the readings.

Exploration Questions on the Topic of Fairy Tales

1. Is there a controversy associated with the topic of fairy tales?
2. Were you brought up to have an opinion on the topic of fairy tales? What opinion do you think your family and community have on this topic?
3. How did your school experiences influence your conception of the topic? Do you think your teachers and classmates feel the same way about this topic as does your family?
4. Can you think of at least two people who hold differing views about this topic? If so, describe these people and summarize what you believe are their points of view.
5. Has your opinion about the topic of fairy tales changed in any way? If it has, how has it changed?
6. Do you think that the topic of fairy tales is important for people to think about? Why or why not?

Teeanna's Responses

1. Is there a controversy associated with the topic of fairy tales?

The question of fairy tales is hotly debated. Some, like Bruno Bettelheim, feel that fairy tales teach young children how to deal with frightening emotions. Others, like Armin Brott and Marina Warner, are afraid that fairy tales teach children harmful attitudes about male and female roles in society. The question that arises from these arguments is: Do fairy tales help or harm children?

2. Were you brought up to have an opinion on the topic of fairy tales? What opinion do you think your family and community have on this topic?

I was encouraged to read everything I could get my hands on, and my parents never disapproved of anything I chose to read. As far as fairy tales were concerned, my mother gave me copies of the original Brothers Grimm and Hans Christian Andersen stories when I was very young. She felt that they would be good for my imagination and would teach me moral principles. My father's family comes from a different culture, a culture that does not value imagination like Americans do. Although he encouraged me to read as much as I could, he also thought that anything fictional was useless and that I would be better prepared for life if I chose more "sensible" topics: science, math, or history, for example.

3. How did your school experiences influence your conception of the topic? Do you think your teachers and classmates feel the same way about this topic as does your family?

When I started school, I hadn't yet read any Mother Goose stories. My mother thought they were silly, unlike the moral messages in the Brothers

Grimm and Andersen. My teachers and classmates were surprised that I didn't know stories like "Jack Sprat" and "Little Miss Muffet," and the children teased me. I got the feeling that I had missed out on something important, so I read all the Mother Goose tales. I thought they were silly. I've never understood why my teachers thought they were important for me to know.

4. Can you think of at least two people who hold differing views about this topic? If so, describe these people and summarize what you believe are their points of view.

Ms. X is a college graduate working in a feminist bookstore and is pregnant with her first child. She is concerned about what she should allow her child to read because she wants to avoid dangerous sexual stereotypes. She wants her child to respect him/herself, no matter what sex he/she turns out to be. Ms. X is afraid that fairy tales give children harmful ideas about male and female roles.

Ms. Q went to college with Ms. X and works for a counseling service. She is excited about Ms. X's baby because Ms. Q is going to be its godmother. She is not as concerned about sexual stereotypes in fairy tales. In fact, she thinks Ms. X should allow her child to read fairy tales because they teach children about how to feel good about themselves, even when they have "bad" thoughts.

5. Has your opinion about the topic of fairy tales changed in any way? If it has, how has it changed?

My opinion about fairy tales is different from my parents' view. I feel that fairy tales expand a child's mind by giving him or her new and unusual things to think about, and that they provide insight into how our culture has developed its value system. Bettelheim's essay shows how fairy tales allow children to think about things that are frightening to them, and Brott and Warner show how our society is reflected in fairy tales. I am not sure, however, that I feel that fairy tales are as potentially damaging as Brott and Warner say they are.

6. Do you think that the topic of fairy tales is important for people to think about? Why or why not?

I think that fairy tales are very important for people to think about. Fairy tales show us where we came from as a society and how our culture has changed. They expose us to impossible things that stimulate our imaginations and allow us to dream about making the impossible possible. These kinds of dreams teach inventors how to design new technologies, doctors how to develop new methods to treat disease, and politicians to imagine new forms of government.

Teeanna's Essay

The Role of Fairy Tales

Children have been reading fairy tales for generations, and until about 25 years ago, people tended to accept that fairy tales are an important part of a child's education. Today, however, some people are concerned about how fairy tales affect children. They say that they are too violent and instill harmful sexual stereotypes. However, although there may be violent elements in fairy tales, and although many of them do present stereotypical concepts of both men and women, fairy tales should still be part of a child's upbringing because they can teach children how to deal with complicated and difficult emotional stereotypes.

One of the most compelling arguments against fairy tales is that they expose children to gender-based stereotypes that perpetuate an old-fashioned and unflattering view of women. Many fairy tales such as "Cinderella" or "Sleeping Beauty" depict women as passive, waiting for a Prince Charming to show up on a white horse and rescue them. Those people who are concerned with the impact of fairy tales on children point out that this view of women presents an outmoded model of male-female relationships that is inappropriate to today's society.

In addition to depicting women as passive, many fairy tales characterize women as evil, witchlike beings who are consumed with jealousy and anger. Marina Warner points out that in many tales, women are extremely nasty to one another or to other women's children and that "fairy tales told by women contain vivid examples of female evil: wicked step-mothers, ogresses, bad fairies abound, while virtuous figures like Cinderella's mother, are dead from the start" (25). Warner traces these evil figures to the necessity in the past for women to guard their children's and their own positions in a male-dominated society, claiming that "if you accept Mother Goose tales as the testimony of women, as old wives' tales, you can hear vibrating in them the tensions, the insecurity, jealousy and rage of both mother-in-law and vice versa, as well as the vulnerability of children from different marriages" (28). Moreover, as Armin Brott points out, fairy tales are frequently unflattering to fathers as well, often depicting them as uninvolved or even absent from their families. Brott states that children's literature often ignores "men who share equally in raising their children" and contributes to "yet another generation of men who have been told . . . that mothers are the truer parent" (14).

In addition to their perpetuation of harmful gender stereotypes, fairy tales also contain considerable violence. In "Hansel and Gretel" the children face a witch who wants to eat them and finally defeat her by pushing her into her own oven. In the Brothers Grimm version of Cinderella, the evil stepsisters try to fool the Prince by cutting off parts of their feet so they will fit into Cinderella's tiny shoe. Later at Cinderella's wedding, birds peck out their eyes. Certainly it would seem as if these would be alarming things for a child to read.

Nevertheless, although one must acknowledge both the gender stereotypes and the violence, fairy tales should be retained in early childhood education because, as the psychologist Bruno Bettelheim asserts, they "teach children about the inner problems of human beings." Bettelheim points out that many of the elements present in fairy tales are those that children already think about. According to Bettelheim, children do not always think only good thoughts and sometimes have trouble feeling good about themselves because of this tendency. He tells us:

> . . . children know that they are not always good; and often, even when they are, they would prefer not to be. This contradicts what they are told by their parents, and therefore makes the child a monster in his own eyes. (7)

A new brother or sister may anger a child because he/she is not getting enough attention from the parent, and the child may then think that pushing the baby into an oven might be a good idea. The child understands that this is a horrible thing to do or even to think of doing, and therefore thinks that he/she is a horrible person as well. But if children can read about deeds such as this in a fairy tale, they can then pretend they are doing something awful, such as pushing the witch into an oven, and they will therefore feel less guilty about their own thoughts without acting on them.

Moreover, in many fairy tales, the hero or heroine must struggle against great difficulties—a hostile stepmother, as in "Cinderella," fierce jealousy, as in "Snow White," or threats from fearsome beings such as wolves, giants, or ogres, as in "Jack and the Beanstalk." Identifying with the protagonist, children learn "that a struggle against severe difficulties in life is unavoidable, is an intrinsic part of human existence—but that if one does not shy away, but steadfastly meets unexpected and often unjust hardships, one masters all obstacles and at the end emerges victorious" (Bettelheim 8). This is an important message for children to learn.

Finally, fairy tales are an important transmitter of culture, providing children with links to previous generations. Whatever gender stereotypes fairy tales might embody, other influences within the culture can counteract their potentially harmful effect. But the magic and imagination found in fairy tales cannot be replaced by the perhaps more politically correct but certainly less vital modern tales that do not force children to confront the dark side of human existence. Fairy tales should continue to be part of children's early years because they are psychologically and culturally beneficial, enabling children to grapple with the "inner problems of human beings" (Bettelheim 6).

Works Cited

Bettelheim, Bruno. "Introduction." The Uses of Enchantment. New York: Alfred A. Knopf, 1976. 3–11.

Brott, Armin. "Not All Men Are Sly Foxes." Newsweek 1 June 1992: 14.

Warner, Marina. "The Absent Mother: Women against Women in Old Wives' Tales." History Today 41 (April 1991): 22–28.

OTHER STRATEGIES FOR ASSESSING WHAT YOU KNOW ABOUT A TOPIC

Freewriting and Brainstorming

Exploration questions structure the direction of your thinking. But some writers prefer a less structured way to become conscious of personal knowledge, either by writing freely about a topic or by simply jotting down ideas. When you use these methods, the images and possibilities that come to mind often suggest others, leading you in new directions and enabling you to discover information that you didn't know you had.

Clustering

Clustering, like freewriting and brainstorming, can also be a useful means of beginning to explore a topic. It enables you to group ideas graphically and to

CLUSTERING

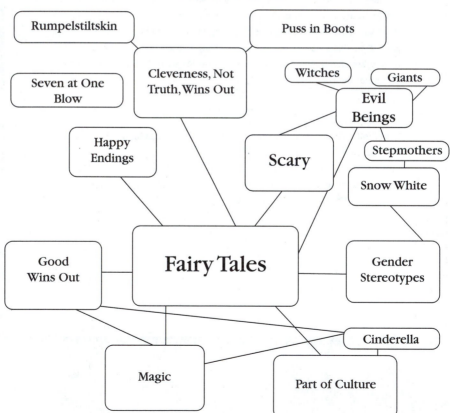

perceive possible connections between them. To cluster on a topic, write the central idea or topic in the center of a piece of paper and draw a circle around it. Around this centered word, write other words that are connected with it in some way, and draw circles around them, too. Connect these circles to your main circle. Now, around each of the words surrounding your main topic, write other ideas that come to mind and use lines to connect these ideas to others on the page. An example of a cluster on the topic of fairy tales appears on page 44.

MOVING BEYOND YOURSELF IN DISCOVERING INFORMATION

Becoming conscious of your own ideas and beliefs is an important first step in exploring a topic. But the genre of argument is not usually confined to personal topics, so it is important to move beyond your own immediate background and discover additional information. That information may include the following:

- relevant background material
- key terms associated with the topic
- the main viewpoints on the topic
- the main reasons usually cited in support of these viewpoints

Locating Relevant Background Material

Most, if not all, of the controversies you will be writing about for your college courses have their roots in the past, and in order for you to formulate an opinion about a controversy in the present, you will find it useful to understand what happened in the past. Even in the most everyday occurrences, such as deciding on where to live, the past can play an important role. Suppose you were hunting for an apartment and discovered that one was available in a building in a section of town that was close to a large river. Before you formed an opinion on whether or not this was a good place to live, you would surely want to know whether or not the river ever overflowed its banks in the past, if any sort of damage had been done, and what sort of compensation was available were it to happen again.

Controversies concerned with social issues usually have their roots in past conditions. For example, in a political science or sociology class, you may be discussing the question of whether special priority should be given to admitting minorities and women to colleges in order to attract these people into the workforce and to compensate for past discrimination. Such priorities are often implemented in affirmative action programs, and the issue of whether such programs are "fair" and the effect they have on society continue to generate controversy. However, in order to decide whether affirmative action programs are "fair" or whether they are necessary for promoting equal opportunity to formerly oppressed groups, one must look to the past to find out why such programs were recommended in the first place and the extent to which they have been deemed effective. To explore this issue, you might wish to investigate the civil rights movement of the sixties and become familiar with the conditions during that time. Thus, an important question to ask about most topics for argumentative writing is the following:

> **What do I need to know about the past in order to develop an informed opinion on this topic?**

Locating Key Terms Associated with the Topic

In addition to finding out about the past, exploring the background of a topic also involves locating key terms that are associated with it, terms that are likely to arouse strong feelings in a prospective audience. If you were researching the topic of affirmative action, it would be important for you to be aware of such key terms as "equal opportunity," "quotas," "reverse discrimination," or the Fourteenth Amendment. For every topic, there are key terms that appear most frequently; usually these are terms that are likely to elicit strong reactions. These terms are also useful for conducting searches in the library.

Locating the Main Viewpoints on the Topic and the Reasons Usually Cited in Support of These Viewpoints

When you begin to read about your topic, it is helpful to become aware of the major opposing viewpoints that people hold about it and to become familiar with the reasons usually cited in support of these viewpoints. Understanding the extreme views on a topic does not mean that you must choose one or the other or that the genre of argumentation involves a "winner" and a "loser" in a debate. On the contrary, writers of academic argument usually situate themselves somewhere in between extreme viewpoints, acknowledging that there is merit on both sides and adopting a thesis or claim that represents a compromise. However, in exploring a topic, it is a good idea to understand the extremes so that you can address them in your writing when appropriate.

EXERCISE

The following situations have generated controversy:

1. A community wishes to pass a law forbidding anyone between the ages of 16 and 18 from driving after 11 p.m.
2. A community wishes to organize a neighborhood watch to notify the police when a suspicious-looking person is seen.
3. California passed Proposition 187, which would make it illegal to provide social services to illegal immigrants.
4. An urban school wishes to require its students to wear school uniforms.

In small groups, explore each of these situations by answering the following questions:

1. What information about the past must be known in order to develop an informed opinion on this topic?
2. What key terms are usually associated with this situation?
3. What are the extreme viewpoints on this topic and the main reasons usually cited in support of these viewpoints?

THE ROLE OF THE THESIS

Exploring a topic both by examining your own experience and by finding additional information about the background, key terms, and opposing viewpoints will enable you to discover a main idea for your essay. This main idea, which is developed and supported throughout the essay, is called the *thesis*, although sometimes it is also called a *position* or *claim*, and I will use these terms interchangeably in this book. A thesis in the genre of argument usually appears in the form of a statement about a problematic situation or controversial issue, and it exerts control over other features of the essay, serving as a sort of glue that holds the essay together. In fact, readers who wish to gain an overview of the major focus of an essay will often skim for the thesis statement before reading the essay.

Three Ways of Phrasing a Thesis Statement

Three useful ways to phrase a thesis are as a *simple thesis* statement, as an *expanded thesis statement,* and as an *expanded thesis statement using the word "although."*

A Simple Thesis Statement

A simple thesis statement, as its name suggests, is a presentation of a position or main idea stated as a simple sentence. Brian, who is writing an essay about why he wants to transfer from one university to another, may state his thesis this way:

Northern College is a better choice for me than is State University.

For other topics, examples of simple thesis statements are as follows:

1. Speech codes are an acceptable feature of campus life.
2. Marijuana ought to be legalized.
3. Immigration laws in California should be more restrictive.

A simple thesis statement presents a main idea or position, but it gives no hint of a writer's reasons, nor does it give readers a sense of what the structure of the essay is going to be.

The Expanded Thesis Statement

A more elaborate type of thesis statement is the expanded thesis, which uses the word *because*. Writing an expanded thesis can be a useful way of clarifying an argument for yourself because it forecasts what you plan to say. Here are examples of how a simple thesis may be stated as an expanded thesis. Brian's expanded thesis:

Northern College is a better choice for me than is State because it offers programs in environmental studies, which is the field I wish to enter.

Expanded theses concerned with other topics:

1. Speech codes are an acceptable feature of campus life because creating a harmonious climate is more important than free speech.
2. Marijuana ought to be legalized because it has many medical benefits and because enforcement of restrictive laws is too expensive.
3. Immigration laws in California should be more restrictive because the local economy cannot afford to support illegal immigrants.

In an expanded thesis statement, the use of the word *because* indicates a *relationship* between the two parts of the thesis—the main idea and the reasons that will be used to support it. This relationship can also be suggested in other ways. For example, Brian could have written an expanded thesis as follows:

Northern College offers programs in environmental studies, has smaller class size, and fosters close interaction between professors and students. Therefore, it is a better college for me.

or

Northern College offers programs in environmental studies, has smaller class size, and fosters close interaction between professors and students, so it is a better college for me.

The use of the word *because* (either actually or implied) is a useful strategy for clarifying your thinking and for helping you to develop supporting points, so I suggest that you write an expanded thesis for all of your assignments, even if you decide you don't want to state it that way in your actual essay.

Thesis Statements Using "Although"

Another useful word that helps you clarify the goals of your thesis is *although. Although* often appears in a thesis statement to indicate how the thesis will differ from what is generally believed about the subject or how the thesis will differ from the *opposing viewpoint.* A reference to what is generally believed or to what an opponent may believe is characteristic of the genre of argument because it focuses attention on the viewpoint being refuted. Here are some examples of how the word *although* can help to focus a thesis statement:

Brian's Expanded Thesis Using "Although"

Although State College has an excellent reputation, Northern College is a better choice for me because it offers programs in environmental studies, has smaller class size, and fosters close interaction between professors and students.

Expanded Theses for Argumentative Essays Using "Although"

1. Although speech codes may sometimes interfere with the First Amendment right to free speech, they are an acceptable feature of campus life because creating a harmonious climate is more important.
2. Although marijuana has been considered a dangerous drug, it ought to be legalized because it has many medical benefits and because enforcement of restrictive laws is too expensive.
3. Although the United States has always offered a haven to immigrants, immigration laws in California should be more restrictive because the local economy cannot afford to support illegal immigrants.

Like *because,* the word *although* can be implied in other ways. Here is an example of Brian's thesis that implies the word *although* without actually using the word:

Despite the fact that State College has an excellent reputation, Northern College is a better choice for me because it offers programs in environmental studies, has smaller class size, and fosters close interaction between professors and students.

The use of the word *although* indicates to the reader that the writer is aware of the complexity of the topic and understands that others may have different points of view. *Although* therefore renders the thesis statement more "polite" or more "judicious." When writing an argumentative essay, you are more likely to have an impact on your readers by acknowledging their viewpoint and indicating that you understand and respect it, not by telling them that they are completely wrong. Argumentative essays are usually concerned with complex and controversial subjects about which the "truth" is difficult to "know" with absolute certainty. Thus, a thesis for an argumentative essay is one with which at least some people are likely to disagree, and often a position that one person may view as absolutely right may be viewed by another person as absolutely wrong (after all, that is why such positions are considered controversial). Therefore, you will be more successful if you approach your subject politely and judiciously, indicate that you understand the complexity of the subject, and acknowledge that you are aware of other points of view. The word *although* helps you to frame thesis statements that accomplish this purpose.

EXERCISE

Working in small groups, find the thesis or claim for each of the three essays at the end of this chapter. State each in three ways—as a simple thesis statement, as an expanded thesis statement, and as an expanded thesis statement using the word *although*.

Introduction to *The Uses of Enchantment*
Bruno Bettelheim

Bruno Bettelheim (1903–1990) was a widely respected child psychologist who emigrated to the United States after surviving the Nazi Holocaust. He wrote extensively about parent-child relationships, the psychological significance of fairy tales, and the Holocaust. His most famous works are *Individual and Mass Behavior in Extreme Situations* (1943), *Love Is Not Enough* (1950), and *The Uses of Enchantment: The Meaning and Importance of Fairy Tales* (1976), from which this excerpt was taken.

If we hope to live not just from moment to moment, but in true consciousness   1
of our existence, then our greatest need and most difficult achievement is to find meaning in our lives. It is well known how many have lost the will to live, and have stopped trying, because such meaning has evaded them. An understanding of the meaning of one's life is not suddenly acquired at a particular age, not even when one has reached chronological maturity. On the contrary, gaining a secure understanding of what the meaning of one's life may or ought to be—this is what constitutes having attained psychological maturity. And this achievement is the end result of a long development: at each age we seek, and must be able to find, some modicum of meaning congruent with how our minds and understanding have already developed.

Contrary to the ancient myth, wisdom does not burst forth fully developed   2
like Athena out of Zeus's head; it is built up, small step by small step, from most irrational beginnings. Only in adulthood can an intelligent understanding of the meaning of one's existence in this world be gained from one's experiences in it. Unfortunately, too many parents want their children's minds to function as their own do—as if mature understanding of ourselves and the world, and our ideas about the meaning of life, did not have to develop as slowly as our bodies and minds.

Today, as in times past, the most important and also the most difficult task   3
in raising a child is helping him to find meaning in life. Many growth experiences are needed to achieve this. The child, as he develops, must learn step by step to understand himself better; with this he becomes more able to understand others, and eventually can relate to them in ways which are mutually satisfying and meaningful.

To find deeper meaning, one must become able to transcend the narrow   4
confines of a self-centered existence and believe that one will make a significant contribution to life—if not right now, then at some future time. This feeling is necessary if a person is to be satisfied with himself and with what he is doing. In order not to be at the mercy of the vagaries of life, one must develop one's

inner resources, so that one's emotions, imagination, and intellect mutually support and enrich one another. Our positive feelings give us the strength to develop our rationality; only hope for the future can sustain us in the adversities we unavoidably encounter.

5   As an educator and therapist of severely disturbed children, my main task was to restore meaning to their lives. This work made it obvious to me that if children were reared so that life was meaningful to them, they would not need special help. I was confronted with the problem of deducing what experiences in a child's life are most suited to promote his ability to find meaning in his life; to endow life in general with more meaning. Regarding this task, nothing is more important than the impact of parents and others who take care of the child; second in importance is our cultural heritage, when transmitted to the child in the right manner. When children are young, it is literature that carries such information best.

6   Given this fact, I became deeply dissatisfied with much of the literature intended to develop the child's mind and personality, because it fails to stimulate and nurture those resources he needs most in order to cope with his difficult inner problems. The preprimers and primers from which he is taught to read in school are designed to teach the necessary skills, irrespective of meaning. The overwhelming bulk of the rest of so-called "children's literature" attempts to entertain or to inform, or both. But most of these books are so shallow in substance that little of significance can be gained from them. The acquisition of skills, including the ability to read, becomes devalued when what one has learned to read adds nothing of importance to one's life.

7   We all tend to assess the future merits of an activity on the basis of what it offers now. But this is especially true for the child, who, much more than the adult, lives in the present and, although he has anxieties about his future, has only the vaguest notions of what it may require or be like. The idea that learning to read may enable one later to enrich one's life is experienced as an empty promise when the stories the child listens to, or is reading at the moment, are vacuous. The worst feature of these children's books is that they cheat the child of what he ought to gain from the experience of literature: access to deeper meaning, and that which is meaningful to him at his stage of development.

8   For a story truly to hold the child's attention, it must entertain him and arouse his curiosity. But to enrich his life, it must stimulate his imagination; help him to develop his intellect and to clarify his emotions; be attuned to his anxieties and aspirations; give full recognition to his difficulties, while at the same time suggesting solutions to the problems which perturb him. In short, it must at one and the same time relate to all aspects of his personality—and this without ever belittling but, on the contrary, giving full credence to the seriousness of the child's predicaments, while simultaneously promoting confidence in himself and in his future.

9   In all these and many other respects, of the entire "children's literature"— with rare exceptions—nothing can be as enriching and satisfying to child and adult alike as the folk fairy tale. True, on an overt level fairy tales teach little

about the specific conditions of life in modern mass society; these tales were created long before it came into being. But more can be learned from them about the inner problems of human beings, and of the right solutions to their predicaments in any society, than from any other type of story within a child's comprehension. Since the child at every moment of his life is exposed to the society in which he lives, he will certainly learn to cope with its conditions, provided his inner resources permit him to do so.

Just because his life is often bewildering to him, the child needs even more 10 to be given the chance to understand himself in this complex world with which he must learn to cope. To be able to do so, the child must be helped to make some coherent sense out of the turmoil of his feelings. He needs ideas on how to bring his inner house into order, and on that basis be able to create order in his life. He needs—and this hardly requires emphasis at this moment in our history—a moral education which subtly, and by implication only, conveys to him the advantages of moral behavior, not through abstract ethical concepts but through that which seems tangibly right and therefore meaningful to him.

The child finds this kind of meaning through fairy tales. Like many other 11 modern psychological insights, this was anticipated long ago by poets. The German poet Schiller wrote: "Deeper meaning resides in the fairy tales told to me in my childhood than in the truth that is taught by life." (*The Piccolomini*, III, 4.)

Through the centuries (if not millennia) during which, in their retelling, 12 fairy tales became ever more refined, they came to convey at the same time overt and covert meanings—came to speak simultaneously to all levels of the human personality, communicating in a manner which reaches the uneducated mind of the child as well as that of the sophisticated adult. Applying the psychoanalytic model of the human personality, fairy tales carry important messages to the conscious, the preconscious, and the unconscious mind, on whatever level each is functioning at the time. By dealing with universal human problems, particularly those which preoccupy the child's mind, these stories speak to his budding ego and encourage its development, while at the same time relieving preconscious and unconscious pressures. As the stories unfold, they give conscious credence and body to id pressures and show ways to satisfy these that are in line with ego and superego requirements.

But my interest in fairy tales is not the result of such a technical analysis of 13 their merits. It is, on the contrary, the consequence of asking myself why, in my experience, children—normal and abnormal alike, and at all levels of intelligence—find folk fairy tales more satisfying than all other children's stories.

The more I tried to understand why these stories are so successful at 14 enriching the inner life of the child, the more I realized that these tales, in a much deeper sense than any other reading material, start where the child really is in his psychological and emotional being. They speak about his severe inner pressures in a way that the child unconsciously understands, and—without belittling the most serious inner struggles which growing up entails—offer examples of both temporary and permanent solutions to pressing difficulties.

15   When a grant from the Spencer Foundation provided the leisure to study what contributions psychoanalysis can make to the education of children—and since reading and being read to are essential means of education—it seemed appropriate to use this opportunity to explore in greater detail and depth why folk fairy tales are so valuable in the upbringing of children. My hope is that a proper understanding of the unique merits of fairy tales will induce parents and teachers to assign them once again to that central role in the life of the child they held for centuries.

Fairy Tales and the Existential Predicament

16 In order to master the psychological problems of growing up—overcoming narcissistic disappointments, oedipal dilemmas, sibling rivalries; becoming able to relinquish childhood dependencies; gaining a feeling of selfhood and of self-worth, and a sense of moral obligation—a child needs to understand what is going on within his conscious self so that he can also cope with that which goes on in his unconscious. He can achieve this understanding, and with it the ability to cope, not through rational comprehension of the nature and content of his unconscious, but by becoming familiar with it through spinning out day-dreams—ruminating, rearranging, and fantasizing about suitable story elements in response to unconscious pressures. By doing this, the child fits unconscious content into conscious fantasies, which then enable him to deal with that content. It is here that fairy tales have unequaled value, because they offer new dimensions to the child's imagination which would be impossible for him to discover as truly on his own. Even more important, the form and structure of fairy tales suggest images to the child by which he can structure his daydreams and with them give better direction to his life.

17   In child or adult, the unconscious is a powerful determinant of behavior. When the unconscious is repressed and its content denied entrance into awareness, then eventually the person's conscious mind will be partially overwhelmed by derivatives of these unconscious elements, or else he is forced to keep such rigid, compulsive control over them that his personality may become severely crippled. But when unconscious material *is* to some degree permitted to come to awareness and worked through in imagination, its potential for causing harm—to ourselves or others—is much reduced; some of its forces can then be made to serve positive purposes. However, the prevalent parental belief is that a child must be diverted from what troubles him most: his formless, nameless anxieties, and his chaotic, angry, and even violent fantasies. Many parents believe that only conscious reality or pleasant and wish-fulfilling images should be presented to the child—that he should be exposed only to the sunny side of things. But such one-sided fare nourishes the mind only in a one-sided way, and real life is not all sunny.

18   There is a widespread refusal to let children know that the source of much that goes wrong in life is due to our very own natures—the propensity of all men for acting aggressively, asocially, selfishly, out of anger and anxiety. Instead, we want our children to believe that, inherently, all men are good. But

children know that *they* are not always good; and often, even when they are, they would prefer not to be. This contradicts what they are told by their parents, and therefore makes the child a monster in his own eyes.

The dominant culture wishes to pretend, particularly where children are 19 concerned, that the dark side of man does not exist, and professes a belief in an optimistic meliorism. Psychoanalysis itself is viewed as having the purpose of making life easy—but this is not what its founder intended. Psychoanalysis was created to enable man to accept the problematic nature of life without being defeated by it, or giving in to escapism. Freud's prescription is that only by struggling courageously against what seem like overwhelming odds can man succeed in wringing meaning out of his existence.

This is exactly the message that fairy tales get across to the child in mani- 20 fold form: that a struggle against severe difficulties in life is unavoidable, is an intrinsic part of human existence—but that if one does not shy away, but steadfastly meets unexpected and often unjust hardships, one masters all obstacles and at the end emerges victorious.

Modern stories written for young children mainly avoid these existential 21 problems, although they are crucial issues for all of us. The child needs most particularly to be given suggestions in symbolic form about how he may deal with these issues and grow safely into maturity. "Safe" stories mention neither death nor aging, the limits to our existence, nor the wish for eternal life. The fairy tale, by contrast, confronts the child squarely with the basic human predicaments.

For example, many fairy stories begin with the death of a mother or father; 22 in these tales the death of the parent creates the most agonizing problems, as it (or the fear of it) does in real life. Other stories tell about an aging parent who decides that the time has come to let the new generation take over. But before this can happen, the successor has to prove himself capable and worthy. The Brothers Grimm's story "The Three Feathers" begins: "There was once upon a time a king who had three sons. . . . When the king had become old and weak, and was thinking of his end, he did not know which of his sons should inherit the kingdom after him." In order to decide, the king sets all his sons a difficult task; the son who meets it best "shall be king after my death."

It is characteristic of fairy tales to state an existential dilemma briefly and 23 pointedly. This permits the child to come to grips with the problem in its most essential form, where a more complex plot would confuse matters for him. The fairy tale simplifies all situations. Its figures are clearly drawn; and details, unless very important, are eliminated. All characters are typical rather than unique.

Contrary to what takes place in many modern children's stories, in fairy 24 tales evil is as omnipresent as virtue. In practically every fairy tale good and evil are given body in the form of some figures and their actions, as good and evil are omnipresent in life and the propensities for both are present in every man. It is this duality which poses the moral problem, and requires the struggle to solve it.

Evil is not without its attractions—symbolized by the mighty giant or 25 dragon, the power of the witch, the cunning queen in "Snow White"—and often it is temporarily in the ascendancy. In many fairy tales a usurper succeeds for a time in seizing the place which rightfully belongs to the hero—as the wicked sisters do in "Cinderella." It is not that the evildoer is punished at the story's end which makes immersing oneself in fairy stories an experience in moral education, although this is part of it. In fairy tales, as in life, punishment or fear of it is only a limited deterrent to crime. The conviction that crime does not pay is a much more effective deterrent, and that is why in fairy tales the bad person always loses out. It is not the fact that virtue wins out at the end which promotes morality, but that the hero is most attractive to the child, who identifies with the hero in all his struggles. Because of this identification the child imagines that he suffers with the hero his trials and tribulations, and triumphs with him as virtue is victorious. The child makes such identifications all on his own, and the inner and outer struggles of the hero imprint morality on him.

26   The figures in fairy tales are not ambivalent—not good and bad at the same time, as we all are in reality. But since polarization dominates the child's mind, it also dominates fairy tales. A person is either good or bad, nothing in between. One brother is stupid, the other is clever. One sister is virtuous and industrious, the others are vile and lazy. One is beautiful, the others are ugly. One parent is all good, the other evil. The juxtaposition of opposite characters is not for the purpose of stressing right behavior, as would be true for cautionary tales. (There are some amoral fairy tales where goodness or badness, beauty or ugliness play no role at all.) Presenting the polarities of character permits the child to comprehend easily the difference between the two, which he could not do as readily were the figures drawn more true to life, with all the complexities that characterize real people. Ambiguities must wait until a relatively firm personality has been established on the basis of positive identifications. Then the child has a basis for understanding that there are great differences between people, and that therefore one has to make choices about who one wants to be. This basic decision, on which all later personality development will build, is facilitated by the polarizations of the fairy tale.

27   Furthermore, a child's choices are based, not so much on right versus wrong, as on who arouses his sympathy and who his antipathy. The more simple and straightforward a good character, the easier it is for a child to identify with it and to reject the bad other. The child identifies with the good hero not because of his goodness, but because the hero's condition makes a deep positive appeal to him. The question for the child is not "Do I want to be good?" but "Who do I want to be like?" The child decides this on the basis of projecting himself wholeheartedly into one character. If this fairy-tale figure is a very good person, then the child decides that he wants to be good, too.

28   Amoral fairy tales show no polarization or juxtaposition of good and bad persons; that is because these amoral stories serve an entirely different purpose. Such tales or type figures as "Puss in Boots," who arranges for the hero's success through trickery, and Jack, who steals the giant's treasure, build character not by promoting choices between good and bad, but by giving the child the hope that even the meekest can succeed in life. After all, what's the use of choosing to

become a good person when one feels so insignificant that he fears he will never amount to anything? Morality is not the issue in these tales, but rather, assurance that one can succeed. Whether one meets life with a belief in the possibility of mastering its difficulties or with the expectation of defeat is also a very important existential problem.

The deep inner conflicts originating in our primitive drives and our violent 29 emotions are all denied in much of modern children's literature, and so the child is not helped in coping with them. But the child is subject to desperate feelings of loneliness and isolation, and he often experiences mortal anxiety. More often than not, he is unable to express these feelings in words, or he can do so only by indirection: fear of the dark, of some animal, anxiety about his body. Since it creates discomfort in a parent to recognize these emotions in his child, the parent tends to overlook them, or he belittles these spoken fears out of his own anxiety, believing this will cover over the child's fears.

The fairy tale, by contrast, takes these existential anxieties and dilemmas 30 very seriously and addresses itself directly to them: the need to be loved and the fear that one is thought worthless; the love of life, and the fear of death. Further, the fairy tale offers solutions in ways that the child can grasp on his level of understanding. For example, fairy tales pose the dilemma of wishing to live eternally by occasionally concluding: "If they have not died, they are still alive." The other ending—"And they lived happily ever after"—does not for a moment fool the child that eternal life is possible. But it does indicate that which alone can take the sting out of the narrow limits of our time on this earth: forming a truly satisfying bond to another. The tales teach that when one has done this, one has reached the ultimate in emotional security of existence and permanence of relation available to man; and this alone can dissipate the fear of death. If one has found true adult love, the fairy story also tells, one doesn't need to wish for eternal life. This is suggested by another ending found in fairy tales: "They lived for a long time afterward, happy and in pleasure."

An uninformed view of the fairy tale sees in this type of ending an unrealis- 31 tic wish-fulfillment, missing completely the important message it conveys to the child. These tales tell him that by forming a true interpersonal relation, one escapes the separation anxiety which haunts him (and which sets the stage for many fairy tales, but is always resolved at the story's ending). Furthermore, the story tells, this ending is not made possible, as the child wishes and believes, by holding on to his mother eternally. If we try to escape separation anxiety and death anxiety by desperately keeping our grasp on our parents, we will only be cruelly forced out, like Hansel and Gretel.

Only by going out into the world can the fairy-tale hero (child) find himself 32 there; and as he does, he will also find the other with whom he will be able to live happily ever after; that is, without ever again having to experience separation anxiety. The fairy tale is future-oriented and guides the child—in terms he can understand in both his conscious and his unconscious mind—to relinquish his infantile dependency wishes and achieve a more satisfying independent existence.

33   Today children no longer grow up within the security of an extended family, or of a well-integrated community. Therefore, even more than at the times fairy tales were invented, it is important to provide the modern child with images of heroes who have to go out into the world all by themselves and who, although originally ignorant of the ultimate things, find secure places in the world by following their right way with deep inner confidence.

34   The fairy-tale hero proceeds for a time in isolation, as the modern child often feels isolated. The hero is helped by being in touch with primitive things—a tree, an animal, nature—as the child feels more in touch with those things than most adults do. The fate of these heroes convinces the child that, like them, he may feel outcast and abandoned in the world, groping in the dark, but, like them, in the course of his life he will be guided step by step, and given help when it is needed. Today, even more than in past times, the child needs the reassurance offered by the image of the isolated man who nevertheless is capable of achieving meaningful and rewarding relations with the world around him.

QUESTIONS

1. What is Bettelheim's purpose in writing this essay? Identify the thesis and key concepts that Bettelheim uses to explain his position.
2. What kind of literature did you read as a child (or to your child)? What kind of message do you think you got from it? Did it add to your insight into life? How?
3. Bettelheim is referring to the original form of fairy tales, like those from the Brothers Grimm and Hans Christian Andersen. These versions are quite different from many of today's popular versions, like Disney's *Little Mermaid* or *Aladdin*. Compare these different versions. What do you think Bettelheim would say about these differences? What would you say yourself?
4. How does Bettelheim use personal experience to explain his theories? Try writing a similar explanation based on your own experiences with children's literature.
5. Do you agree with Bettelheim's attitude toward "safe" stories for children? Can you offer examples of "safe" stories? How about children's programming on TV, movies, the Internet?
6. Can you identify the genre of fairy tales based on Bettelheim's description? What are the essential elements of the fairy tale?

Not All Men Are Sly Foxes
Armin A. Brott

Armin Brott is a freelance writer living in Berkeley, California. He has written for a number of magazines, including *Family Circle, Nation's Business,* and *The Saturday Evening Post.* (This article is from *Newsweek,* June 1, 1992.)

If you thought your child's bookshelves were finally free of openly (and not so-openly) discriminatory materials, you'd better check again. In recent years groups of concerned parents have persuaded textbook publishers to portray more accurately the roles that women and minorities play in shaping our country's history and culture. "Little Black Sambo" has all but disappeared from library and bookstore shelves; feminist fairy tales by such authors as Jack Zipes have, in many homes, replaced the more traditional (and obviously sexist) fairy tales. Richard Scarry, one of the most popular children's writers, has reissued new versions of some of his classics; now female animals are pictured doing the same jobs as male animals. Even the terminology has changed: males and females are referred to as mail "carriers" or "firefighters." 1

There is, however, one very large group whose portrayal continues to follow the same stereotypical lines as always: fathers. The evolution of children's literature didn't end with "Goodnight Moon" and "Charlotte's Web." My local public library, for example, previews 203 new children's picture books (for the under-5 set) each *month*. Many of these books make a very conscious effort to take women characters out of the kitchen and the nursery and give them professional jobs and responsibilities. 2

Despite this shift, mothers are by and large still shown as the primary caregivers and, more important, as the primary nurturers of their children. Men in these books—if they're shown at all—still come home late after work and participate in the child rearing by bouncing baby around for five minutes before putting the child to bed. 3

In one of my 2-year-old daughter's favorite books, "Mother Goose and the Sly Fox," "retold" by Chris Conover, a single mother (Mother Goose) of seven tiny goslings is pitted against (and naturally outwits) the sly Fox. Fox, a neglectful and presumably unemployed single father, lives with his filthy, hungry pups in a grimy hovel littered with the bones of their previous meals. Mother Goose, a successful entrepreneur with a thriving lace business, still finds time to serve her goslings homemade soup in pretty porcelain cups. The story is funny and the illustrations marvelous, but the unwritten message is that women take better care of their kids and men have nothing else to do but hunt down and kill innocent, law-abiding geese. 4

The majority of other children's classics perpetuate the same negative stereotypes of fathers. Once in a great while, people complain about "Babar's" 5 colonialist slant (little jungle-dweller finds happiness in the big city and brings civilization—and fine clothes—to his backward village). But I've never heard anyone ask why, after his mother is killed by the evil hunter, Babar is automatically an "orphan." Why can he find comfort only in the arms of another female? Why do Arthur's and Celeste's mothers come alone to the city to fetch their children? Don't the fathers care? Do they even have fathers? I need my answers ready for when my daughter asks.

6   I recently spent an entire day on the children's floor of the local library trying to find out whether these same negative stereotypes are found in the more recent classics-to-be. The librarian gave me a list of the 20 most popular contemporary picture books and I read every one of them. Of the 20, seven don't mention a parent at all. Of the remaining 13, four portray fathers as much less loving and caring than mothers. In "Little Gorilla," we are told that the little gorilla's "mother loves him" and we see Mama gorilla giving her little one a warm hug. On the next page we're also told that his "father loves him," but in the illustration, father and son aren't even touching. Six of the remaining nine books mention or portray mothers as the only parent, and only three of the 20 have what could be considered "equal" treatment of mothers and fathers.

7   The same negative stereotypes also show up in literature aimed at the *parents* of small children. In "What to Expect the First Year," the authors answer almost every question the parents of a newborn or toddler could have in the first year of their child's life. They are meticulous in alternating between references to boys and girls. At the same time, they refer almost exclusively to "mother" or "mommy." Men, and their feelings about parenting, are relegated to a nine-page chapter just before the recipe section.

8   Unfortunately, it's still true that, in our society, women do the bulk of the child care, and that thanks to men abandoning their families, there are too many single mothers out there. Nevertheless, to say that portraying fathers as unnurturing or completely absent is simply "a reflection of reality" is unacceptable. If children's literature only reflected reality, it would be like prime-time TV and we'd have books filled with child abusers, wife beaters and criminals.

9   Young children believe what they hear—especially from a parent figure. And since, for the first few years of a child's life, adults select the reading material, children's literature should be held to a high standard. Ignoring men who share equally in raising their children, and continuing to show nothing but part-time or no-time fathers is only going to create yet another generation of men who have been told since boyhood—albeit subtly—that mothers are the truer parents and that fathers play, at best, a secondary role in the home. We've taken major steps to root out discrimination in what our children read. Let's finish the job.

QUESTIONS

1. This book gives you a series of exploration questions to help you examine controversial issues when writing in the college argument genre.

Brott asks similar questions in his own exploration of children's literature. What are these questions? How do they support his argument?

2. Brott admits that fathers in today's families are often not involved in
child-rearing. With this in mind, how important is it that children's literature represent a present, loving father? What do you think Bettelheim
would say about this portrayal of the family? What do you say?

3. Why should we consider Brott an authority on this subject? How did he
conduct his research? If you were to refute his argument, how would
you conduct your research?

4. Assuming that Brott is correct and that children's literature fails to represent the father in a positive light, what kind of impact would this have
on a child? What kind of behavior would you expect from an adult who
read this material as a child? How did it affect your parents, for example?

5. What does Brott mean when he says that "children's literature should be
held to a high standard"? Can you provide examples of this type of
book? Would he suggest fairy tales, as Bettelheim does?

The Absent Mother: Women against Women in Old Wives' Tales

Marina Warner

Marina Warner is Tinbergen Professor of Cultural Studies at Erasmus University, Rotterdam. This essay was adapted from her inaugural lecture in January 1990.

1   Plato defined fairytales, in the oldest theory about them, as tales told by nurses. Possibly the earliest story extant that recognisably anticipates the classic fairytales—*Cinderella* and *Beauty and the Beast*—is Apuleius' *Cupid and Psyche,* interpolated in his metaphysical comedy, *The Golden Ass,* written in the second century AD. In the novel, a young bride is captured by bandits and separated from her husband and thrown into a cave; there, a disreputable old woman chooses to tell her the story of Psyche's troubles before she reaches happiness and marriage with Cupid. It is "an old wives' tale." she says, (*anilis fabula*) and it will distract her from her troubles.

2   Charles Perrault, in his preface to the fourth edition of his classic collection of fairytales, first published in 1695, under the title *Contes du Temps Passé* or *Contes de ma Mère l'Oye,* issued an apologia on their behalf, linking them explicitly to the comic tradition of Milesian tales to which Apuleius belongs, and comparing his own, directly with *Cupid and Psyche:* It is "*une fiction toute pure et un conte de vieille comme celuy de Peau-d'Ane* (Donkey skin)," which was also told, he went on, by old women, grandmothers and governesses to the children in their charge. However, the moral of *Cupid and Psyche* is impenetrable, he wrote, while his own is patently clear.

3   The femaleness of fairytale as a genre manifests itself historically, through attested storytellers, literary interpreters, and their audiences. The *veillées,* as storytelling gatherings were called in France, offered women an opportunity to talk—to preach—which was forbidden them in other situations, the pulpit, the forum, and frowned upon and feared in the spinning rooms and by the wellside. Though male collectors have dominated the publication of popular wondertales, from the Venetian, Giovan Francesco Straparola, who published the rumbunctious *Le piacevoli notti* in 1550, to indefatigable nineteenth-century folklorists like the Scotsman, Andrew Lang, who created the Blue, Green, Red et al. Fairy Books, at the turn of the century and after, women have not been laggards in the related fields of folklore and children's literature. Female talespinners outnumber males by ten to one in the forty-one volume *Cabinet des fées,* an anthology of seventeenth- and eighteenth-century fairy stories.

4   It reveals the durable affinity of the female sex with fairytale that Straparola's talespinners (like Boccaccio's before him) figure as so many Schehezerades, using narrative to bring about a resolution of mercy and justice. Andrew

Lang relied on his wife Leonora Alleyne, as well as a team of women editors, transcribers, and paraphrasers to produce the many volumes of fairystories and folktales from around the world. Oscar Wilde's father, a doctor in Merrion Square, Dublin in the mid-nineteenth century, used to ask for stories as his fee from his poorer patients: he then wrote them down. Many of these were told to him by women. The sources used by Calvino for his classic anthology of Italian folktales were chiefly women and mostly illiterate.

The matter of fairytales reflects lived experience, with a slant towards the tribulations of women, and especially young women of marriageable age; the telling of the stories, (assuming the presence of a Mother Goose either as an historical source, or a fantasy of origin), gains credibility as a fatalistic record of lives lived, of characters known, and shapes the expectations of the young in a certain direction.

The orality of the genre remains central even in the most artificial and elaborate literary versions or inventions of the Victorians. It is often carried in the texts through an imagined narrator, (a grandmotherly or nanny type, called Gammer Gurton or Mother Hubbard, as well as Mother Goose or some such cosy name); the consequent style imitates speech, with chatty asides, plentiful exclamations, direct appeals to the imaginary circle round the hearth, rambling descriptions, gossipy parentheses, and other bedside or lap-like mannerisms create an illusion of collusive intimacies, of home, of the bedtime story, the winter's tale.

Yet, while fairytales tend to shore up traditional views, and circulate the lessons of the *status quo,* they can also act as fifth columnists, burrowing from within; utopian yearnings beat strongly in the heart of fairytale. Many writers, Salman Rushdie included, hide under its guileless and apparently childish façade, wrap its cloak of unreality around them, and adopting its traditional formal simplicities, attempt to challenge received ideas, many of them to do with the expectations of the sexes. Feminism and the fairytale have been strongly associated, in the saints' lives which are entangled in many stories, in the writings of the French *precieuses* and their disciples, like Marie-Jeanne Lheritier, Marie-Catherine d'Aulnoy, Gabrielle-Suzanne de Villeneuve, and Jeanne-Marie Leprince de Beaumont, who all campaigned through their fairytales for women's greater independence, and against arranged marriages.

Nineteenth- and early twentieth-century writers of both sexes also struggled to shape an egalitarian, communal, anti-materialist ethic, like John Ruskin with *The King of the Golden Mountain,* and Frank L. Baum, in *The Wizard of Oz* books, where he fantasised a feminine realm of justice and kindness. The contrary directions of the genre, towards acquiescence on the one hand, and rebellion on the other, are linked to its fabulism, intrinsic to its role of moral arbitration and soothsaying: the teller matters less than the audience whom he or she addresses, and so the teller struggles to locate and find that audience who will receive the stories' message with favour.

Children emerge as hearers because they are less likely to be committed already to a certain way of thought, and can be moulded; when adults want to mark their difference from their peers they take refuge in make-believe that

they have become childlike again, fantastical, receptive, irrational, uncon-
strained by convention.

10   The extraordinary fad for fairytale that the court and the salons fostered in
the years 1694–99 in France coincided with the growing aristocratic enthusiasm for the Child Jesus and for Christ's demonstrative affection for children
("Suffer the little children to come unto me"; "Be ye as little children"). At the
same time, Louis XIV's capricious policies, his wars and depredations, were
plunging the country—and even the nobles—into ruin.

11   The fairytale offered a coded way to dissent at a time of tough censorship
and monarchical control, it created a picture of a possible escape from tyranny,
and it used the naive setting of childish beliefs in magic, the simple structure of
the marvellous tale with its binary oppositions and neat resolutions. They could
adduce the unimpeachable claim of the genre to time-honoured, authentic,
native tradition in order to mount a critique of the times. When writers want to
speak their minds, they can step up onto a rostrum and put the matter openly,
and risk that rostrum changing to a scaffold. Or they can pretend to be little old
grannies telling wellworn homespun stories filled with the nonsense of dyed-in-
the-wool wisdom.

12   Fairytale offers a case where the very contempt for women opened an
opportunity for them to exercise their wit and communicate their ideas:
women's care for children, the prevailing disregard for both groups, and their
presumed identity with the simple folk, the common people, handed them
fairytales as a nursery indeed, where they might seed their own gardens and
foster their own flowers.

13 Fairytales told by women contain vivid examples of female evil: wicked step-
mothers, ogresses, bad fairies abound, while virtuous figures like Cinderella's
mother, are dead from the start.

14   In many famous stories, like *Beauty and the Beast,* the absence of the
mother from the tale is often declared at the start, without explanation, as if
none were required. Thus Beauty appears before us, in the opening paragraph
of the first, elaborate version by Madame de Villeneuve in 1740, as a daughter to
her father, and a sister to her six elders, a Biblical seventh child, the *cadette,* the
favourite: nothing is spoken about her father's wife.

15   One reason for this is historical, for the wondertale, however far-fetched
the incidents it includes, or fantastic the enchantments it relates, takes on the
colour of the actual circumstances in which it was told: while the elements
remain familiar and the tales' structure dependably dialectical, the variant versions of the same story often reveal the particular conditions of the society
which told it and retold it in this form: the absent mother can be read literally
as exactly that: a feature of the family before our modern era, when death in
childbirth was the most common cause of female mortality.

16   Children whose fathers had died, often stayed in the paternal house to be
raised by their grandparents or uncles and their wives, while their mothers
were made to return to the homes of their youth and forge another, advanta-

geous alliance for her native family. However widows remarried less frequently than widowers, who, in almost all cases under the age of sixty in Tuscany in the fifteenth century, for instance, took another wife and started another family. In France, in the seventeenth and eighteenth centuries, 80 per cent of widowers remarried within the year.

The antipathy of stepmothers to children of earlier unions marks stories 17 from all over the world, from the ancient world to the present day, and exhibits the strains and knots in different types of households, from patrilineage in conflict with dotal rights, to the tensions of polygamy. One tale from Dahomey, written down in 1958, tells how a dead mother manages to kill a wicked stepmother from beyond the grave with a handful of palm nuts.

Both the psychoanalytical and the historical interpreters of fairytale enter 18 stories like *Cinderella, Snow White,* or *Beauty and the Beast* from the point of view of the protagonist, the orphaned daughter who has lost her real mother and is tormented by her stepmother, or her sisters, sometimes her stepsisters; the interpreters assume that the reader or listener naturally identifies with the heroine—which is of course commonly the case. But that perception sometimes also assumes that because the narrator makes common cause with the protagonist, she identifies with her too. This may be an error. Fairytales are not told in the first person of the protagonist, and though she engages our first attention as well as the narrator's, the voice of the latter is located elsewhere.

If we imagine the characteristic scene, the child listening to an older person 19 telling this story, we may find the absent mother present in the narrator herself. When the mother disappears, she has been conjured away by the storyteller, who dispatches the child listeners' natural parent, replaces her with a monster, and then often produces herself within the pages of the story, as a good old fairy, working wonders on their behalf. Thus the older generation speaks to the younger in the fairytale; pruning out the middle branch on the family tree as rotten or irrelevant, and thereby lays claim to the devotion, loyalty and obedience of the young over their mothers' heads: this is the classic Cinderella story.

Such an old woman storyteller may be a grandmother, or a mother-in-law. A 20 woman in this situation had good reason to feel intense rivalry with her son's wife, when she often had to strive to maintain her position and assert her continuing rights to a livelihood in the household. If she was widowed, her vulnerability became more acute. Christiane Klapisch-Zuber uses the chilly phrase "passing guests" when she describes the condition of wives in the house, both symbolic and geographic, into which they have married, in fifteenth-century Florence.

The conflicting claims on women of their paternal and marital homes con- 21 tinued throughout their lives and exacerbated their insecurity and stirred up much misery and misogyny in consequence, and Italian fairytales reflect this turbulence, filled as they are with wicked stepmothers and other female tyrants. English wills of the seventeenth century show that widowed parents were customarily cared for in the household of their eldest child: the right to shelter, the family hearth, bed and board, was granted and observed. However, as *King Lear*

reveals, in the case of a widower, the exercise of such a right could meet fero-
cious resistance and reprisals. Just as Cordelia is a fairytale heroine, a wronged
youngest child, a forerunner of Cinderella, so Goneril and Regan are the wicked
witches, ugly sisters: the unnatural daughters whom fairytales indict. In Florence, some widows who wished to return to the family of their birth, as they
had a right to do, were forced to bring suits against their children in the marital
household in order to wrest back the dowry which was also theirs by right and
necessary to their survival outside.

22   Women lived longer than men, then as now, and there were more old
female dependents, (like the old nurse, Anfisa, in *The Three Sisters*), than King
Lears. Olga, who takes in the old woman when her brother's wife Natasha has
brutally assaulted her as a good-for-nothing parasite, and thrown her out of the
house where she has worked her whole life, shows a Cordelia-like spirit of gen-
tleness and courage.

23   In France, after the revolution, a widow did not retain her keys to the
household or to the family's business. Thus dispossessed by her husband's
death, she was often only grudgingly provided for by his legatees; destitute and
homeless old women were a feature of nineteenth-century society. Yet at the
same time, the rights of grandparents began to be considered: in 1867, for
instance, an important law was passed allowing the mother's parents to visit
children who had remained in their father's custody after a divorce. This sign
that grandparents' role in a child's upbringing was being recognised and valued
coincides exactly with the publication of many editions of *Contes* in which an
old woman is telling children tales by a fireside, both in France and England.

24   But the woman who threatens society by her singleness and her dependency was not always a widow; she could be a spinster, an unmarried mother,
an old nurse or servant in a household. In the centuries when the image of
Mother Goose was being disseminated through numerous editions of fairytale
collections, "there was," writes Michelle Perrot, "in a radical sense, no place for
female solitude in the conceptual framework of the time." She quotes Michelet:
"The woman who has neither home nor protection dies." Yet there were many
such and they had to survive, however precariously. The census of 1851 in
France showed that 12 percent of women over fifty had never married, and 34
per cent were single; this ratio remained the same nearly fifty years later.

25   The old wives who spin their tales are almost always represented unat-
tached: spinsters, or widows. Mother Goose is the anomalous crone, the
unhusbanded female cut loose from the moorings of the patriarchal hearth; kin
to the witch and the bawd. It is not difficult to see that the storyteller may be
speaking from a position of acute vulnerability, the kind that makes enemies in
the heart of the family.

26   The storyteller's mirror image is the ragged old woman whom the heroine
meets by chance, who turns out to be a powerful fairy in disguise; she rewards
virtuous sweet-talking girls who perform acts of kindness to her, like giving her
food and drink, while their wicked mother, and the unkind daughter who
resembles her, scorn the old woman as useless and will not provide for her.

Again, paying attention to the structure of the story, one can assemble a picture of strain across three generations, in which the old struggle to survive and plead for the mercy of the young.

The wicked stepmother who has become the stock figure of fairytale first appears as a mother-in-law, in Apuleius's *Cupid and Psyche*. In *The Golden Ass* fairytale, Cupid's mother, the goddess Venus, orders her son to destroy Psyche, her rival in beauty, but instead Cupid falls in love with her; he then visits her only at night, making love to her invisibly in an enchanted place. Eventually, her spiteful and jealous sisters goad her into spying on him while he sleeps, telling Psyche that he must be "a savage wild beast." Her fatal female curiosity— the familiar lesson—overcomes her and a drop of oil from the lamp spurts up with the flame on to the sleeping god's shoulder; he wakes, reproaches her furiously, and then everything—her fairy surroundings, as well as her divine groom—disappears. 27

In the fifteenth century, before the first extant variations on the tale were written down as fairy stories, *Cupid and Psyche* was chosen by *cassone* painters as a fitting theme for the trousseau chests brides took to their new home; alongside other tales of wronged daughters and aberrant marriages, like Patient Griselda, Potiphar's wife, and Helen of Troy, Psyche's troubles and eventual triumph could suitably furnish the room of a bride and help her keep in mind the pitfalls and the vindication of her predecessors in wedlock. Francesco di Giorgio, (on a *cassone* panel in the Berenson Collection at I Tatti), chose the scene where Venus's vicious sidekick is dragging Psyche by her hair into the goddess's presence. 28

The stories of *Cinderella, Beauty and the Beast, Snow White* have directly inherited features from the plot of Apuleius's romance, like Psyche's wicked sisters, the enchanted bounty in her mysterious husband's palace, and the prohibitions that hedge about her knowledge of his true nature. At a deeper level, they have also inherited the stories' function, to tell the bride the worst, and shore her up in her marriage. The more one knows fairytales the less fantastical they appear; they are vehicles of the most grim realism, expressing hope against all the odds with gritted teeth. As Angela Carter has written, they are marked by a mood of "heroic optimism." 29

The Wicked Stepmother makes another savage appearance as a mother-in-law in the *Vita* of Saint Godelive, patron saint of Bruges, an historical figure who was born around 1050 and married to Berthulphe de Ghistelles. According to the contemporary account of the priest, Drogo, she gave away food and goods to the poor behind his back, but was saved from detection by angels who replaced what she had taken. Hagiography and fairytale are often intertwined, and Godelive's story then takes a familiar turn and relates how Berthulphe's mother was furious at the match, how Berthulphe himself neglected his wife by his frequent absences and maltreated her when they were together, until finally, mother and son conspired to murder her. She was held head down in a pond and throttled by their servants. She was then put back to bed to make out she 30 had died in her sleep. Berthulphe remarried, but he later repented, made the pilgrimage to Jerusalem, and returned to become a monk. Godelive was canonised in 1084, very soon after her death, for miraculous cures had taken place: the blindness of one of her successor's children was suddenly lifted, and this was attributed to Godelive's intercession—a kind stepmother working wonders beyond the grave and making amends for the wickedness of the other mother in the story.

31   The proliferation of mother figures in the most conventional literary fairy-tale does not only reflect wishful thinking on the part of children, though I would not deny that fantasies of gratification and power over parents play their part; the aleatory mothers of Madame de Villeneuve's *Beauty and the Beast* reflect the conditions of aristocratic and less than aristocratic life in early modern France. Beauty, the heroine, was brought up in a foster home, discarded by her biological mother, like many other protagonists, when the fairies cast her out (the fairies figure as thinly disguised Versailles mignons and schemers) and compelled her to give up her child. For his part, the Beast has been cared for by his mother's closest friend. When he grows up she attempts to seduce him and then does him violence when he rejects her.

32   It is not hard to glimpse personal histories in these seemingly far-fetched schemata: Mme de Villeneuve herself lived with Crébillon *père* as her patron and protector, though not her lover. His son, the playwright, Crébillon *fils,* took up writing fairytales in the satirical, semi-licentious tone that became *à la mode* in the 1720s. Improvised families of this sort were not uncommon in the *ancien régime.*

33   In Mlle Lheritier's even more complicated and apparently far-fetched tale, *La Robe de Sincérité* of 1695, the relations of wet nurses, foster parents, guardians, court patrons and godparents can be glimpsed as family networks interpenetrating and combining with the natural, biological family. It is significant that in English, French, and Italian, for instance, the very word "mother" designated many women who were not natural mothers, nor women acting directly in lieu of her, like a foster parent, but occupied in some way with the care of other, often younger women—and sometimes men: Mère Arnault at the convent of Port Royal, *la mère maquerelle*—the notorious Madame of a brothel in colloquial speech, (like Hogarth's notorious Ma Needham in *The Progress of a Harlot*) or the *mères* of the *compagnons* who take part in the *Tour de France,* and still meet their chosen champions at different stations on the route.

34   In England, midwives and other female carers as well as wise women and witches were granted the status of Mother in common parlance; the *Oxford Dictionary* declares it was "a term of address for an elderly woman of the lower class." In usage, it also implies something subtly marginal, with a whiff of the comic, to do with taboo mysteries of the body and the associated matters of life and death. Mother Trot, for instance, as in *Tell-troth's New Year Gift* of 1593, would be related to Old Dame Trot, of nursery rhyme witchery, and both are popular descendants of Trotula, the author of the midwifery manual of the Mid-

dle Ages, who may or may not be an historical figure, but certainly gave her name to venereal and obstetric lore of all kinds.

In the borough where I live in London there were, until recently, two pubs 35 whose names recalled two such characters, *Mother Red Cap* and *Mother Shipton,* the last a byword in witchcraft and prophecy who was first mentioned in a pamphlet of 1641. Both have changed their names: one to *The World's End,* the other to *The Fiddler's Elbow.* The old names no longer held any meaning for their customers, and this is a symptom, in my view, of a larger alteration in consciousness: the meanings of the word "mother" are becoming more and more restricted to the biological mother in the nuclear family. The implications of the stock villain in fairytale, the wicked stepmother, have been dangerously attenuated as a result.

The experiences fairy stories recount are remembered, lived experiences 36 of women, not fairytale concoctions from the depths of the psyche; they are rooted in the social, legal and economic history of marriage and the family, and they have all the stark actuality of the real, and the power real-life has to bite into the psyche and etch its design: if you accept Mother Goose tales as the testimony of women, as old wives' tales, you can hear vibrating in them the tensions, the insecurity, jealousy and rage of both mothers-in-law against their daughters-in-law and vice versa, as well as the vulnerability of children from different marriages. Certainly, women strove against women because they wished to promote their own children's interests over those of another union's offspring; the economic dependence of wives and mothers on the male breadwinner exacerbated—and still does—the divisions that may first spring from preferences for a child of one's flesh, a child to whom the mother has been bonded physically. But another set of conditions set women against women, and the misogyny of fairytales reflects them from a woman's point of view: rivalry for the prince's love.

The effect of these stories is to flatter the male hero; the position of the man 37 as saviour and provider in these testimonies of female conflict is assumed, repeated and reinforced—which may be the reason why such "old wives' tales" found success with audiences of mixed men and women, boys and girls, and have continued to flourish in the most conservative media, like Disney cartoons.

QUESTIONS

1. What are the key concepts of Warner's essay? Is her purpose similar to that of Bettelheim? How about Brott? Is she talking about the same audience they spoke of?

2. Warner mentions several stories from classical, biblical, and medieval sources. Which stories were you familiar with before you read this essay? Do you think she has given enough information about these tales? What else do you think you need to know before venturing an opinion on her argument?

3. How does Warner establish an authoritative voice? Is she believable? Why?
4. Do you agree that the purpose of "old wives' tales" is to flatter men? Provide examples to support your position on this issue.
5. What is the function of the fairy tale, according to this essay? Who wrote fairy tales (according to Warner), and whom were they written for? Does she provide support for these positions? What is it?
6. If Warner had completed a list similar to the exploration questions you've been given, what would her answers have been?

Chapter 3

THE NATURE OF PROOF

Essays written within the genre of argument are intended for rational audiences who base their decisions on reliable information and well-constructed logic, rather than on whim or prejudice. Cogent proof is an essential feature of academic writing. Even if you have a fluent writing style and have developed effective strategies for organizing information, your argumentative essay will not achieve its purpose if you do not support your thesis or claim with good reasons. This chapter is concerned with several strategies used in the genre of argument to prove a claim, focusing on three types of appeal: appeal to logic and reason (*logos*), appeal to the character of the writer (*ethos*), and appeal to the feelings of the audience (pathos). It will emphasize the importance of appealing to people's understanding and common sense through logic and reason (*logos*) and discuss Aristotelian and Toulmin logic. This chapter also includes a section on logical fallacies.

THE IMPORTANCE OF REASON

Because academic argument is written for an audience that is presumed rational, reason is an important element in an argumentative essay. I would like to stress, however, that I used the phrase "presumed rational" in the last sentence because we all know that even rational people are not rational all the time and don't always make rational decisions. For instance, if, during a school election, someone makes the claim that Jennifer is a good candidate for school president but cites no reasons in support of that claim, the rational response would be for no one to vote for her. But some students, even those who are usually rational, might not base their choice of candidate completely on rationality and might decide to vote for Jennifer anyway—maybe because she has long hair or because she can whistle "Home on the Range" through a straw or just because they like her.

You may be asking, then, why you should appeal to your reader primarily on the basis of reason, rather than emotion, if people are not always rational. Wouldn't a well-crafted, emotionally charged appeal be more effective in convincing an audience? The answer is that the genre of argument, *by definition,* presumes a rational audience, and therefore your essay should be addressed to an audience that you perceive as rational. This means that you must use good reasons to support your thesis, even if you think you could write an equally convincing essay simply because of your own expertise on the topic or because the topic lends itself to some emotionally charged examples that are likely to appeal to your readers' feelings.

This requirement that a writer include well-developed reasons in support of a thesis is a primary characteristic of the genre of argument that distinguishes it from other genres, even those with the similar goal of having an impact on an audience. For example, a famous runner might write a letter to a school coach endorsing a particular brand of running shoes without citing any reasons for his choice, and the coach might decide to buy that brand for the school team, simply on the basis of the credibility or ethos of the writer. Or a concerned member of a community might address a letter to a charitable organization describing a lonely puppy, whimpering for its mother in an animal shelter, and the organization might decide to donate money to the shelter, simply on the basis of that emotional appeal (pathos). But even though both letters might achieve their desired goals of affecting an audience, neither the letter to the team nor the appeal to the charitable organization can be considered academic arguments if they don't include clearly stated reasons.

Here are some examples of how reasons are used to support a claim in the genre of argument:

Brian's claim: Brian is a college student who wishes to transfer from State College to Northern College.

Claim: Northern College is a better choice for me than is State.

> Reason 1: Northern College offers programs in environmental studies.
> Reason 2: Northern College offers small classes.
> Reason 3: Northern College fosters close interaction between professors and students.

Opposing claim: State College is a better choice for Brian than is Northern. (This is Brian's Uncle Stan's idea.)

> Reason 1: State College offers a good program in business.
> Reason 2: State College has a good reputation.
> Reason 3: Uncle Stan has a degree from State College and has had a successful professional life.

Claim: Colleges should have speech codes restricting sexist or racist speech.

> Reason 1: Unlimited free speech can be devastating to those injured by it.
> Reason 2: Speech codes are needed to prevent racist and sexist remarks.

Reason 3: It is the function of higher education to help students refrain from hurtful remarks about other groups.

Opposing claim: Colleges should not have speech codes restricting sexist or racist speech.

Reason 1: Speech codes are an infringement of First Amendment rights.
Reason 2: Speech codes cannot prevent racist or sexist thinking.
Reason 3: The university should be concerned with learning, not with dictating codes of behavior.

EXERCISE

1. Read "The Case for Torture" by Michael Levin at the end of this chapter. What is Levin's claim? What reasons does Levin cite in support of his claim?
2. Sometimes reasons are implied through a narrative rather than stated explicitly. Read "A Crime of Compassion" by Barbara Huttman. What is Huttman's claim? What reasons are suggested by her narrative?

THE TRADITION OF REASON

In his *Rhetoric,* the Greek philosopher Aristotle defined three approaches to argumentation: *ethos* (Greek for "character"), which refers to the trustworthiness or credibility of the writer or speaker, *pathos* (Greek for "emotion"), which refers to the emotional appeal of an argument so that it affects the reader's feelings, and *logos* (Greek for "word"), which refers to the internal consistency of the argument, in particular the logic of its reasons and the quality of the supporting evidence. Aristotle claimed that all three of these components are important, but he emphasized the role of reason.

The Relationship between Inductive and Deductive Argument

Inductive and deductive reasoning are both used in the genre of argument, and although they are usually distinguished from one another, they are also closely related. An inductive argument is based on a number of examples from which the writer has drawn a conclusion. For example, suppose you had made several trips to a tropical island and each time had gotten sick when you had eaten a yellow fruit with purple spots. Later on, you learn that other travelers have also gotten sick from this fruit, and you would probably then conclude that this fruit can make people sick. Induction thus moves from specific examples to a generalization based on examples. Therefore, if you say, "Yellow fruit with purple spots makes people sick," you have made a claim based on induction.

Having drawn this conclusion, let us now suppose that you travel once again to the same tropical island. But this time, when someone offers you a piece of yellow fruit with purple spots, you immediately turn it down, based on the conclusion that it will make you sick. In this case, you have applied a general principle (yellow fruits with purple spots make people sick) to a specific example (this particular piece of yellow fruit with purple spots will make me sick), thereby making a claim based on deduction. A deductive argument is based on a general principle that is applied to a specific case. But the general principle *originated* through inductive reasoning.

INDUCTIVE REASONING

Both inductive and deductive reasoning are used in the genre of argument. If your thesis or claim is based on a generalization from examples, you have used inductive reasoning. The following interchange is an example of inductive reasoning:

SANDRA: I am going to make a fruit salad for the Fourth of July party.
DAVID: Don't buy your fruit at Fruitful Farms Supermarket. They have a terrible selection, and every time I go in there, the fruit is dried out and wilted looking.

In this interchange, David indicated that he has had experience with fruit at Fruitful Farms Supermarket. His conclusion was reached inductively, in that it was based on several specific instances in which he had frequented the store. Actually, a lot of what we know about the world and most of what we have been told about the world have been obtained through induction—that is, by generalizing from a few examples. For example, I grew up in New York City, where there are no leopards roaming the streets (usually), and I have never encountered a live leopard except in a zoo. I have, however, seen leopards in pictures or films, and those that I have seen have spots and look like large cats. I therefore regard the few I have seen as typical leopards and believe that most leopards have spots and look like large cats. Similarly, although none of us has heard every dog bark or seen every fish swim, we would feel safe predicting that, in general, dogs bark and fish swim.

Inductive reasoning is often associated with a question to be answered, either a casual question, such as "How good is the fruit in Fruitful Farms Supermarket?" or, in scientific writing, "Does a particular decongestant clear stuffy sinuses?" In science or social science writing, the tentative answer to the initial question is called the *hypothesis*. After the writer has framed a question and postulated a hypothesis, then he or she gathers all the available evidence that pertains to the question and that may contribute to the answer. Finally, on the basis of this evidence, the writer draws a conclusion, sometimes called an inference, which provides an answer to the question. Here is an example:

Question: How did this glass on the kitchen floor get broken?

Evidence: We own a gray cat.
                   There is gray cat hair on the counter.
                   There are small paw prints on the counter.

Conclusion: The cat jumped onto the counter, knocking the glass onto the
                   floor.

This conclusion seems obvious because it takes all the evidence into account.
But if it turns out that we did not own a cat, the rest of the evidence would be
quite mysterious. Also, even if the conclusion seems believable, it is not necessarily true. Perhaps the cat did jump onto the counter, but it is also quite possible that someone else knocked the glass onto the floor.

Inductive arguments are usually more complex than this example, and
because conclusions in induction are not usually certain but only probable, writers
who use inductive reasoning must make an *inductive leap* to move from evidence
to a sound conclusion. Valid conclusions in inductive reasoning must be based on
samples that are **sufficient** and **typical** (this, of course, also pertains to statistics
or examples), or else you will be generalizing from too few examples or committing what Anthony Weston refers to as the "person who" fallacy (*A Rulebook for
Arguments,* 2nd ed. Hackett Publishing: Indianapolis, 1992). If you say, "The dangers of smoking are greatly exaggerated. I know *a person who* smoked three
packs a day and lived to be 100," you are basing a conclusion on only one person,
which constitutes an insufficient sample. If you use inductive reasoning to support
a thesis or claim, you must check that your sample has been adequate. Otherwise,
you will be drawing a hasty conclusion from an unrepresentative example.

Generalizing from an insufficient sample is often the cause of unfair stereotyping. If you say, "Don't hire this person. I once knew someone from his country, and that person was dishonest," you are assuming that all people from a
particular country have the same degree of honesty, a position that is unlikely
to be true and that a rational audience is unlikely to accept.

EXERCISE

In small groups choose a facility or situation associated with your college from
which you have drawn a conclusion based on induction. Some possibilities
include the food in the cafeteria, lines at registration, using the library, or the
computer center.

Induction and Probability:
The Necessity to Qualify

An inductive argument usually moves from a series of specific instances to a
generalization that represents a degree of probability. Before Dr. Jonas Salk

could claim that his vaccine prevented polio, he had to have tested it on a group that was both typical and of adequate size. He then concluded that it was probable that his vaccine could prevent polio in anyone. But for issues concerned with human behavior or opinion, it is not as easy to generalize from specific instances because there are bound to be many exceptions. It is therefore necessary to qualify your statements to indicate that you are aware of possible exceptions. If you survey a number of businesses and discover that female employees cite problems of inadequate child care as their most pressing concern, that does not mean that every female employee will necessarily feel the same way. However, you can qualify statements you make about this subject by using qualifying words such as *many, a number of,* or *most* so as to avoid simplistic and hasty conclusions. For instance, you can state that for *many* employees, inadequate child care represents a significant problem in the workplace.

In another example, suppose that your roommate, Sophia, throws her clothes onto the floor every day. You might assume that she will continue to do so throughout her college years, but this assumption is based only on probability. Even though Sophia has thrown her clothes onto the floor every day of the semester, it is possible that she may change her habits and start to put her clothes away neatly. Induction is involved with probability, not with certainty, so it is important to use expressions such as *it is likely that, to a certain extent,* or *for the most part* to qualify your statements.

DEDUCTIVE REASONING: THE SYLLOGISM AND THE ENTHYMEME

Although a rational audience will not accept a claim without support, no thesis or claim will be convincing unless the writer and the audience share assumptions, beliefs, or principles that can serve as a common ground between them. An assistant manager might say to his boss:

"We should have an office Christmas party because it will generate a sense of friendship among employees."

This statement is based on the assumption that it is desirable for employees to feel friendly toward one another. The boss, however, may not share this assumption and may be concerned only with how much money such a party is likely to cost. She would thus not be in favor of the Christmas party on the basis of this reason. However, if the assistant manager could convince his boss that employees who are friendly toward one another feel a sense of allegiance to a company and thus are likely to work harder, she might be convinced to hold the party.

The Syllogism

As a way of making explicit the connections between a statement, its support, and its underlying assumptions, Aristotle created a three-part structure called a *syllogism,* which consists of three statements: a major premise, a minor premise, and a conclusion. Here is an example of a famous syllogism:

Major premise: All persons are mortal.

Minor premise: James is a person.

Conclusion: James is mortal.

In this example, the major premise is an assumption or a belief about the world that every rational person shares, a truth that is self-evident and obviously true. The minor premise is a related but more specific statement, and the conclusion is a claim that is drawn from these premises. In the preceding example, the major premise "All persons are mortal" is self-evident, and because the minor premise follows from it, any person reading this three-part statement will have to accept the conclusion or claim. When an audience accepts the major premise as true, and if the minor premise and conclusion follow consistently from it, then the argument is said to be *valid* and the audience must accept the conclusion.

The syllogism is associated with deductive arguments, which proceed from a general premise or assumption to a specific conclusion, and it is deductive logic that people often mean when they use the term *logic.* In terms of form, deductive arguments imply that if a minor premise follows from the major premise and if all the statements in the syllogism are true, then the argument is valid and the conclusion is true. If the syllogism is not logical, however, then the argument is not valid and the conclusion will not be true. Here is an example of a syllogism that is not logical and therefore does not compel the acceptance of the conclusion as valid:

Major premise: All canaries are birds.

Minor premise: All parakeets are birds.

Conclusion: Therefore, all canaries are parakeets.

This conclusion is, of course, silly. But how did such a silly conclusion derive from two premises that are true? The explanation is that although both canaries and parakeets are birds, the term *parakeets* does not appear in the major premise. This error arose, then, because the form of the syllogism was incorrect, and the conclusion is therefore not valid.

Sometimes, the form of the syllogism is logically correct, but the conclusion will still not be true because the major premise is not true. Here is an example:

Major premise: All birds are red.

Minor premise: Carol's parrot is a bird.

Conclusion: Therefore, Carol's parrot, Finnegan, is red.

Of course, we know that not all birds are red. In fact, Finnegan happens to be green; not all birds, including parrots, are red. This conclusion is not true because the major premise is false. Although the form of the syllogism is correct, the conclusion is not true. For an argument to be convincing, a syllogism must be both logical and true.

The Enthymeme

A shortened version of a syllogism that leaves the major premise unstated is the *enthymeme,* which consists of a claim with a *because* clause. The expanded thesis I referred to in Chapter 2 was actually an enthymeme, which may be defined as an incomplete logical statement that presumes the acceptance of the unstated major premise and will not be valid without it. Here is how a syllogism may be stated as an enthymeme:

James is mortal because he is a person.

This claim is both valid and true because all logical people accept the major premise or underlying assumption that "All persons are mortal."

Aristotle's concept of the syllogism is based on the notion that there are well-established truisms and that for some topics, these truisms are still considered valid. However, there are also many assumptions that are not shared by all. For example, the following syllogism could be applied to Brian's decision to change his major to environmental studies:

Major premise: Students should choose a major based on interest.

Minor premise: Brian is interested in environmental studies.

Conclusion: Brian should major in environmental studies.

As an enthymeme, this argument can be stated as follows:

Brian should major in environmental studies because this major interests him.

However, although many of us would share the assumption that students should choose a major based on interest, not everyone does. Brian's Uncle Stan, for example, might not think that interest in a major is important at all, and therefore that basis for a claim would not convince him.

Because your audience must share the underlying assumptions behind your claim in order for your argument to be convincing, it is important to be aware of those assumptions as you develop your ideas and draft your argument. By focusing on the assumptions that both he and Uncle Stan might share, Brian might be able to make a more convincing case about his choice of environmental studies as a major. He might, for instance, focus on Uncle Stan's concern with making a living and emphasize that an environmental studies major could lead to a good job. Brian might then reframe his argument as follows:

Major premise: Students should choose a major that will lead to a good job.

Minor premise: Environmental studies is a major that leads to a good job.

Conclusion: Brian should major in environmental studies.

Or, stated as an enthymeme:

Brian should major in environmental studies because it is a major that leads to a good job.

EXERCISE

For the audience cited in each situation, work in small groups to decide which of the following reasons are most likely to be convincing. Support your decision by describing what you believe are the values of each particular audience.

1: Audience: your composition teacher

    A: I need an extension on my research paper because I need extra time for studying chemistry this week.

    B: I need an extension on my research paper because I want to locate some additional materials in the library.

2: Audience: an administrator at your school

    A: Students should sit in on university curricular committees because they need to know what sorts of changes are being planned.

    B: Students should sit in on university curricular committees because they can provide school officials with important insight into student needs.

3: Audience: parents of teenagers at a local high school

    A: The school should fund an end-of-year retreat for students because they worked hard and deserve a treat.

    B: The school should fund an end-of-year retreat for students because it will enable them to discuss important cultural and ethical issues and to plan for the following year.

Examining Syllogisms and Enthymemes

Because Aristotle's concept of formal logic pertains only to the structure of the argument, not necessarily to its truth, it is important to question whether or not the major premise in an enthymeme or syllogism is actually and unconditionally true or whether it simply expresses an idea that most people feel is true. The enthymeme *John is mortal because he is a person* contains the unstated assumption that *All persons are mortal,* which is a statement that all rational people believe is true. But in the enthymeme *Brian should major in environmental studies because it interests him,* the unstated assumption, *Students should choose a major based on interest,* is one that only some people might agree with. Some people might feel that college freshmen are too young to know what interests them because their interests might change as they become aware of new courses and fields. Others might feel that students should choose a school based on its reputation, not on whether it offers any particular major. Or, like Uncle Stan, they might feel that the choice of major should be determined by professional opportunity, not necessarily by interest.

EXERCISE: FOR GROUP DISCUSSION

For the following enthymemes, identify the unstated major premise. Rewrite each enthymeme as a syllogism. Then discuss whether or not you believe these assumptions are true.

1. Buy this beauty product because it will make your skin look younger.
2. Mrs. Smith is a wonderful teacher because she is patient.
3. *Jurassic Park* is a terrific movie because it has unusual special effects.
4. The political correctness movement is dangerous to society because it threatens freedom of speech.
5. The women's movement has threatened the stability of the family because it has taken women out of the home.
6. Studying a musical instrument is good for kids because it involves discipline.
7. Participating in sports is good for kids because it teaches coordination.
8. Ted is a bad manager because he always thinks he is right.

EXERCISE: THINKING ABOUT INDUCTION AND DEDUCTION

Examine the following statements and decide which are based on inductive reasoning and which on deductive. Then decide whether or not these statements are well reasoned. Discuss your observations in small groups:

1. John is one of our most punctual employees. In fact, he has never been late to work in the past five years since he joined the firm. Because he

didn't come in on time today, I assume that something serious must have happened to him.

2. People who collect snakes usually like other reptiles as well. Lisa has a large snake collection, so I think she will also like this iguana.
3. Mexican women are very warm and loving with babies, so I suggest that you hire Maria as a nanny because she comes from Mexico.
4. Students in the United States have not been given adequate preparation in geography. Seth was educated in the United States, so it is unlikely that he knows anything about geography.
5. Louisa is very athletic and works out at the gym every day, so she will probably be able to learn mountain-climbing techniques easily.
6. Justin is especially interested in electronics, so if you wish to interest him in your product, you should demonstrate its technical applications.
7. Clifton successfully negotiated a number of mergers in his previous job, so I suggest that you consult him about the upcoming acquisition.

EXERCISE

Read "Bottle Babies: Death and Business" by Leah Margulies. Identify all of the facts that Margulies cites to arrive at her conclusion. How does she establish causation? Does she account for other possible causes?

ERRORS IN REASONING

Statements based on poor logic and mistaken belief are called *fallacies,* and although numerous attempts have been made to categorize them, many of them overlap with one another. In writing an argumentative essay, it is not necessary that you study an exhaustive list of fallacies, but it is useful to become at least somewhat familiar with some of them so that you can avoid using them in your own writing and can detect them in the sources you use. The following is a list of the more common fallacies:

Slippery Slope Argument

This is an argument that assumes that one action will lead to another similar action that in turn will lead to another and to another, ultimately resulting in something quite undesirable. An example of a slippery slope argument is the following:

Doctor-assisted euthanasia will ultimately lead to mass suicide. In the beginning, only people with incurable, painful illnesses will request to die. Then others with less drastic conditions will request it. Before you know it, people with even minor illnesses will begin thinking of assisted death as a viable option.

Slippery slope arguments are used quite frequently in the context of a variety of social or policy situations. "Smoking marijuana will ultimately lead to heroin addiction" is a popular version. Another is "If you forbid people to smoke in restaurants, they soon will not be able to smoke at all." The essence of a slippery slope argument is that after a first step is taken, a descent all the way down is inevitable.

Black and White Thinking

This is a form of reasoning that presumes an "either-or" situation, such as the following:

Either we enroll in that painting course, or we will never learn to paint.

This statement does not consider that we might learn to paint through some other means.

Hasty Generalizations

Hasty generalizations are caused by drawing conclusions from insufficient evidence. Hasty generalizations are often used to condemn a whole group of people on the basis of an inadequate sample, such as in the following statement:

Let's invite Stewart to be a club member. He's Jewish, and all Jews are rich.

Hasty generalization leads to stereotyping.

False Cause

Related to the fallacy of hasty generalization is the false cause, which assumes causal connections where none may exist, as in the following statement:

As soon as mandatory busing was instituted in the town of Rockport, many families began moving out of town.

This statement presumes that it was mandatory busing that caused people to move, when, in actuality, the move also coincided with the closing of one of the town's major industries.

False Authority

Authorities from one field are sometimes cited as if they were authorities in another, a fallacy that is used commonly on television, when celebrities are used to endorse particular products that they may know little about. If a celebrity endorses a particular ideology, you should not immediately assume that it is then worthwhile.

Red Herring

The term *red herring* is derived from the idea that a pack of dogs would be distracted from a scent if a herring with a strong odor was dragged across the trail. In argumentation, a red herring means that the writer has brought in a point that has little or nothing to do with the issue being discussed. An example of a red herring would be as follows:

Brian should not enroll in State College because it doesn't offer a major in environmental studies.

Anyway, State College places too much emphasis on sports.

Attack on the Person Rather than on the Issue (Ad Hominem Arguments)

Arguments that attack the person rather than the issue are extremely common in controversies concerning social issues. An example of a statement using this form of fallacious reasoning is as follows:

Don't listen to what Angela has to say. She's just a typical dumb blond.

A Caution about Fallacies

Some textbooks provide a long and detailed list of fallacies, and by doing so they imply that all fallacies can be easily classified and that by identifying them you will be able to write convincing argument. My intention here, however, is simply to alert you to the possibility that reasoning can be false in a number of ways so that you scrutinize your own arguments more carefully and approach those of others with a critical perspective.

TOULMIN'S SYSTEM OF INFORMAL LOGIC

In *The Uses of Argument,* the British philosopher Stephen Toulmin has adapted formal logic to focus more directly on audience, anticipating the possible reactions of readers. Toulmin postulates an audience that might initially be in opposition to the claim, an audience that might question and weigh the argument, but that can be convinced of the claim's merit if the writer establishes common ground. Unlike formal logic, which is based entirely on the structure of the syllogism, Toulmin's system acknowledges that most major premises are not as easily accepted as the classic "All persons are mortal." He therefore includes another term, called the "backing," which provides a backup even for the major premise in an argument. His system thus focuses greater attention on the underlying assumptions behind all claims and acknowledges the importance of clarifying and qualifying an argument to suit particular situations. Toulmin's system thus is well suited for the genre of argument, which presumes a diverse readership in which not everyone will share underlying assumptions.

The Elements of Toulmin's System

Toulmin's system conceives of argument as consisting of six elements, the first three corresponding to the major premise, minor premise, and conclusion of a syllogism. In Toulmin's system, the major premise is called the *warrant,* the minor premise is called the *grounds,* and the conclusion is called the *claim.* Let us examine how Toulmin's system differs from the syllogism and how writers of academic argument can utilize this system in framing and evaluating ideas. In Toulmin's system, the claim is pretty much the same as the conclusion in a syllogism. To use one of the examples discussed earlier, a claim would be that *Brian should major in environmental studies.* The grounds in Toulmin's system are similar to the minor premise in a syllogism, except that they consist not of just one statement, but rather of all the evidence, facts, and information that can be used in support of the claim. Thus, for the claim that *Brian should major in environmental studies,* the grounds might consist of all of the information about what opportunities are actually available, statistics on job possibilities, projections of future trends, and so forth. The grounds thus include not only the reasons for a claim, but also all the evidence that can be used in support of those reasons.

The warrant in Toulmin's system is similar to the major premise of a syllogism—that is, it consists of a general statement from which the grounds and the claim follow logically. An example of a warrant is the statement, "Students should choose a major based on professional opportunity." However, Toulmin acknowledges that most warrants are not as easily accepted or as self-evident as the syllogism of formal logic presumes. He therefore provides a fourth element to the list of elements called a *backing,* which provides support for the warrant. For the warrant that "Students should choose a major based on professional opportunity," the writer might provide information from professional organizations substantiating that their employees majored in the subjects they are now working in professionally or statements from people working in the field indicating that their major was of major importance in establishing a career, and so forth.

The other additional elements in Toulmin's system are concerned with limiting the claim. These are called *qualifiers* and *conditions of rebuttal. Qualifiers* limit the absoluteness of a claim by indicating the extent to which it is true. By being aware of qualifiers, the writers of academic argument may modify their claims by using expressions such as *probably, possibly,* or *very likely.*

Or else they may indicate specific instances that limit the claim. Brian's claim might thus be modified as follows: "Brian should major in environmental studies, assuming that his academic goal is to choose a career" or "Brian should major in environmental studies at this point in his studies" (he might be exposed to other courses that give him new career opportunities).

Conditions of rebuttal point out instances in which the claim or warrant might not be true or other ways in which the audience might object to what the writer is arguing. In the example we have been working with, an audience might argue that professional opportunity is not the only basis on which to select a major. Therefore, the claim might be modified as follows:

Brian should major in environmental studies, as long as his interest in the subject continues.

This statement anticipates that some readers might say, "Professional opportunity is a good basis for choosing a major, assuming the student is interested in the field." These readers feel that professional opportunity alone is not enough of a rationale for making this kind of decision.

The strength of Toulmin's system is that it anticipates the reaction of the audience and acknowledges the importance of using qualifiers to modify assertions. The other strength is that it acknowledges that readers are likely to bring up exceptions to both the warrant and the claim and it recognizes that writers of argumentation must anticipate these exceptions.

The six elements of Toulmin's system are shown in the following model:

Enthymeme: Brian should major in environmental studies because it offers professional opportunities.

Claim: Brian should major in environmental studies.

Qualifier: at this point in his life

Grounds: information about the professional opportunities in the field

Warrant: Students should choose a major based on professional opportunities.

Backing: Successful professionals who were polled indicated that it was beneficial for them to have majored in a subject that was directly related to the field they entered.

Conditions of rebuttal: unless he is no longer interested in the field

Comparing the Syllogism and the Toulmin Model

The syllogism, developed over 2,000 years ago, and Toulmin's more recent model of argument are similar in many ways, and both are useful for understanding the reasoning that is involved in the genre of argument. In both the syllogism and the Toulmin model, the three main elements of an argument correspond to one another. The major premise, minor premise, and conclusion of the syllogism are similar to the warrant, grounds, and claim of Toulmin's model. However, there are notable differences between them as well. Whereas the *major premise* in a syllogism is usually an accepted assumption that does not need to be proved (all persons are mortal), the warrant in the Toulmin model (students should choose a major based on professional opportunities) is not nearly as well established. The Toulmin model recognizes that the validity of the warrant needs to be established in order to link the claim and the grounds. The *backing,* therefore, provides the necessary support for the warrant.

Toulmin's model also suggests the necessity for qualifying the claim. The *qualifier,* which is sometimes manifested in words such as *probably* or *at this time,* indicates that claims are not static, and the *conditions of rebuttal* further limit the absoluteness of the argument. Toulmin's model thus reflects the complexity and flexibility of the genre of argument intended for a modern audience.

EXERCISE

1. Restate and define the three major elements in Toulmin's system. In writing, explain why warrants are important in convincing an audience. For the following claims and grounds, find the implied warrants:

   A: You should send your child to summer camp. It will enable him to participate in sports.

   B: You should take Professor Johnson's political issues class. It will enable you to understand current controversies.

   C: You should not use Styrofoam cups. They pollute the environment.

   D: You should hang around at the Polo Lounge. You'll be able to meet rich people there.

2: Read an article in a newspaper or magazine and respond in writing to the following questions:

   A: What is the argument concerned with?

   B: What is the writer's thesis or claim?

   C: What grounds does the writer use?

   D: What is the warrant implied in the claim?

   E: What strategies does the writer use to convince his or her audience?

The Role of Ethos

Chapter 1 emphasized that it is important for the writer of an argumentative essay to demonstrate that he or she is knowledgeable, trustworthy, logical, and fair because audiences are most likely to accept the ideas of those with good character or *ethos*. Ethos is also important when you refer to authorities and experts in their fields within your own essay. Unless the person is extremely well known, or unless you are writing to a specialized audience that is familiar with the names of the experts in the field, it is a good idea to include information that testifies to the expertise of your reference. For example, in an essay concerned with fairy tales, you might wish to indicate to your reader that someone whose ideas you are using to support your position is a well-known child psychologist. You might therefore present this information as follows:

Dr. Richard Smith, director of the Stanford Institute of Child Development, asserts that fairy tales are very important in early childhood.

By including information about those people you quote, you are maximizing the likelihood that your audience will accept what they have to say.

The Role of Pathos

Pathos is used to arouse the emotions of the audience, primarily through emotional language that includes vivid descriptions and moving narratives and anecdotes. All of us are familiar with the use of emotional appeals in advertising; similarly, an essay discussing the need for an AIDS facility will be more effective if it includes moving examples depicting the misery of AIDS victims than if it simply cites statistics about the spread of AIDS. Remember, though, that when you appeal to your audience using emotional language, the references should be appropriate to the tone and purpose of the genre of argument. Overly sentimental or hysterical language will detract from the effectiveness of your essay, as will appeals to emotion that may tug at your audience's heartstrings but that are extraneous to your thesis.

EXERCISE: HOW ARE ADS SIMILAR TO AND DIFFERENT FROM THE GENRE OF ARGUMENT?

1. Working in small groups, examine one of the advertisements included on pages 89–91 and answer the following questions:

A: What is the purpose of the ad?

B: What is the claim made by the ad?

C: How does the ad appeal to reason (logos)?

D: How does the ad appeal to authority (ethos)?

E: How does the ad appeal to the emotions of its audience (pathos)?

F: Which features of the ad are similar to those in the genre of argument?

G: How is the ad different from an argumentative essay?

2. Choose one ad and rewrite it as an argumentative essay. Which features carry over easily? Which features do not? What sort of material did you have to add?

If Penny Scott had a ValuePoint™ with a three-year warranty, she could spend her time worrying about what's really important – like her annual review, the slides for the meeting and her two-year-old son's recent mastery of the word "no."

The IBM Performance Series.
Now available to Penny Scott.
And everyone else.

For more information, contact
your authorized dealer
or call our Personal Systems
HelpCenter at 1-800-772-2227.

IBM®

Used with permission of the IBM Corporation.

There are times
when you don't want caffeine.

CAFFEINE FREE
DIET COKE®

All the cola you need and none of the caffeine.

© 1996 The Coca-Cola Company. "diet Coke" and the Dynamic Ribbon device are registered trademarks of The Coca-Cola Company.

Used with permission of The Coca-Cola Company. The Coca-Cola Company is the owner of the trademarks "diet Coke," "Caffeine-free diet Coke," and the Dynamic Ribbon device.

One of those rare occasions when the sequel is even better than the original.

Technologically speaking it had no rivals. It had innovations designed to protect its passengers and the planet on which they live. And seventeen awards including Best Car in the World in its class for three years in a row.*

So what do you do next? At Mercedes-Benz you have a cup of coffee and get back to work.

Which brings us to the 1995 S-Class sedans. Even standing still the S320 easi- ly leaves other cars behind.

Even the low beams now perform 35% better.

The wheelbase has been lengthened and the body streamlined for a sleeker, more elegant look. But get

Introducing the New S-Class

a good look because its 3.2 liter in-line 6 can take it from 0−60 in 8.9 seconds, a mere four-fifths of a second behind its 8-cylinder counterpart.**

Though Mercedes-Benz invented the crumple zone and helped pioneer the air bag, it's the accident avoiding capabilities of the S-Class that are its most impressive safety features. Recirculating ball steering provides handling precision more typical of sports cars than luxury automobiles and, standard for 1995, every S-Class automobile will have a sophisticated traction control system. Even the telephone

For every new S-Class there's a standard traction control system.

is voice activated so you need not take your hands off the wheel.***

Finally, there's one last line that's been streamlined. The bottom one. Which is in itself a feat of engineering when you consider IntelliChoice's The Complete Car Cost Guide named the 1994 S320 and S420 sedans among the cars named "Best Overall Value" in their class.

Call 1-800-FOR-MERCEDES for more information on the 1995 Mercedes-Benz S-Class, a car with only one rival. Its predecessor.

The New S-Class

*auto motor und sport, Germany **Stated rates of acceleration are based upon manuf.'s track results & may vary depending upon model, environmental & road surface conditions, driving style, altitude above sea level & vehicle load. ***Standard equipment on S600 optional on all other S-Class models. For safety reasons, the driver should not use the cellular telephone while the vehicle is in motion. ©1994 Mercedes-Benz of North America, Inc., Montvale, N.J., Member of the Daimler-Benz Group.

Used with permission of Mercedes-Benz of North America.

The Case for Torture
Michael Levin

Michael Levin is a professor of philosophy at the City College of New York. This piece was first published in *Newsweek* (June 7, 1982).

1   It is generally assumed that torture is impermissible, a throwback to a more brutal age. Enlightened societies reject it outright, and regimes suspected of using it risk the wrath of the United States.

2   I believe this attitude is unwise. There are situations in which torture is not merely permissible but morally mandatory. Moreover, these situations are moving from the realm of imagination to fact.

3   **Death:** Suppose a terrorist has hidden an atomic bomb on Manhattan Island which will detonate at noon on July 4 unless . . . (here follow the usual demands for money and release of his friends from jail). Suppose, further, that he is caught at 10 A.M. of the fateful day, but—preferring death to failure—won't disclose where the bomb is. What do we do? If we follow due process—wait for his lawyer, arraign him— millions of people will die. If the only way to save those lives is to subject the terrorist to the most excruciating possible pain, what grounds can there be for not doing so? I suggest there are none. In any case, I ask you to face the question with an open mind.

4   Torturing the terrorist is unconstitutional? Probably. But millions of lives surely outweigh constitutionality. Torture is barbaric? Mass murder is far more barbaric. Indeed, letting millions of innocents die in deference to one who flaunts his guilt is moral cowardice, an unwillingness to dirty one's hands. If *you* caught the terrorist, could you sleep nights knowing that millions died because you couldn't bring yourself to apply the electrodes?

5   Once you concede that torture is justified in extreme cases, you have admitted that the decision to use torture is a matter of balancing innocent lives against the means needed to save them. You must now face more realistic cases involving more modest numbers. Someone plants a bomb on a jumbo jet. He alone can disarm it, and his demands cannot be met (or if they can, we refuse to set a precedent by yielding to his threats). Surely we can, we must, do anything to the extortionist to save the passengers. How can we tell 300, or 100, or 10 people who never asked to be put in danger, "I'm sorry, you'll have to die in agony, we just couldn't bring ourselves to . . ."

6   Here are the results of an informal poll about a third, hypothetical, case. Suppose a terrorist group kidnapped a newborn baby from a hospital. I asked four mothers if they would approve of torturing kidnappers if that were necessary to get their own newborns back. All said yes, the most "liberal" adding that she would like to administer it herself.

7   I am not advocating torture as punishment. Punishment is addressed to deeds irrevocably past. Rather, I am advocating torture as an acceptable mea-

sure for preventing future evils. So understood, it is far less objectionable than many extant punishments. Opponents of the death penalty, for example, are forever insisting that executing a murderer will not bring back his victim (as if the purpose of capital punishment were supposed to be resurrection, not deterrence or retribution). But torture, in the cases described, is intended not to bring anyone back but to keep innocents from being dispatched. The most powerful argument against using torture as a punishment or to secure confessions is that such practices disregard the rights of the individual. Well, if the individual is all that important—and he is—it is correspondingly important to protect the rights of individuals threatened by terrorists. If life is so valuable that it must never be taken, the lives of the innocents must be saved even at the price of hurting the one who endangers them.

Better precedents for torture are assassination and pre-emptive attack. No 8 Allied leader would have flinched at assassinating Hitler, had that been possible. (The Allies did assassinate Heydrich.) Americans would be angered to learn that Roosevelt could have had Hitler killed in 1943—thereby shortening the war and saving millions of lives—but refused on moral grounds. Similarly, if nation A learns that nation B is about to launch an unprovoked attack, A has a right to save itself by destroying B's military capability first. In the same way, if the police can by torture save those who would otherwise die at the hands of kidnappers or terrorists, they must.

Idealism: There is an important difference between terrorists and their vic- 9 tims that should mute talk of the terrorists' "rights." The terrorist's victims are at risk unintentionally, not having asked to be endangered. But the terrorist knowingly initiated his actions. Unlike his victims, he volunteered for the risks of his deed. By threatening to kill for profit or idealism, he renounces civilized standards, and he can have no complaint if civilization tries to thwart him by whatever means necessary.

Just as torture is justified only to save lives (not extort confessions or recan- 10 tations), it is justifiably administered only to those *known* to hold innocent lives in their hands. Ah, but how can the authorities ever be sure they have the right malefactor? Isn't there a danger of error and abuse? Won't We turn into Them?

Questions like these are disingenuous in a world in which terrorists pro- 11 claim themselves and perform for television. The name of their game is public recognition. After all, you can't very well intimidate a government into releasing your freedom fighters unless you announce that it is your group that has seized its embassy. "Clear guilt" is difficult to define, but when 40 million people see a group of masked gunmen seize an airplane on the evening news, there is not much question about who the perpetrators are. There will be hard cases where the situation is murkier. Nonetheless, a line demarcating the legitimate use of torture can be drawn. Torture only the obviously guilty, and only for the sake of saving innocents, and the line between Us and Them will remain clear.

There is little danger that the Western democracies will lose their way if 12 they choose to inflict pain as one way of preserving order. Paralysis in the face of evil is the greater danger. Some day soon a terrorist will threaten tens of thousands of lives, and torture will be the only way to save them. We had better start thinking about this.

QUESTIONS

1. What is the point of this essay? Rewrite the major premise in the form of the expanded thesis statement using the word *although*.
2. Does Levin use deductive reasoning, inductive reasoning, or both? Identify.
3. What are Levin's claims? Does he provide opposing claims? Are they appropriate for an essay written in the academic argument genre?
4. Can you find the six elements of the Toulmin system?
5. We have looked at two basic models of reasoning: the syllogism and the Toulmin system. Do you think this essay represents one of these models more than the other? How? Why?
6. Does Levin's use of reasoning affect how we read his argument?

A Crime of Compassion
Barbara Huttman

Barbara Huttman is a nurse and author of several articles and books, including *Code Blue: A Nurse's True-Life Story* (1982). This essay is from *Newsweek* (August 8, 1983).

"Murderer," a man shouted. "God help patients who get *you* for a nurse."   1

"What gives you the right to play God?" another one asked.   2

It was the Phil Donahue show where the guest is a fatted calf and the audi-   3
ence a 200-strong flock of vultures hungering to pick up the bones. I had told them about Mac, one of my favorite cancer patients. "We resuscitated him 52 times in just one month. I refused to resuscitate him again. I simply sat there and held his hand while he died."

There wasn't time to explain that Mac was a young, witty, macho cop who   4
walked into the hospital with 32 pounds of attack equipment, looking as if he could single-handedly protect the whole city, if not the entire state. "Can't get rid of this cough," he said. Otherwise, he felt great.

Before the day was over, tests confirmed that he had lung cancer. And   5
before the year was over, I loved him, his wife, Maura, and their three kids as if they were my own. All the nurses loved him. And we all battled his disease for six months without ever giving death a thought. Six months isn't such a long time in the whole scheme of things, but it was long enough to see him lose his youth, his wit, his macho, his hair, his bowel and bladder control, his sense of taste and smell, and his ability to do the slightest thing for himself. It was also long enough to watch Maura's transformation from a young woman into a haggard, beaten old lady.

When Mac had wasted away to a 60-pound skeleton kept alive by liquid   6
food we poured down a tube, IV solutions we dripped into his veins, and oxygen we piped to a mask on his face, he begged us: "Mercy . . . for God's sake, please just let me go."

The first time he stopped breathing, the nurse pushed the button that calls   7
a "code blue" throughout the hospital and sends a team rushing to resuscitate the patient. Each time he stopped breathing, sometimes two or three times in one day, the code team came again. The doctors and technicians worked their miracles and walked away. The nurses stayed to wipe the saliva that drooled from his mouth, irrigate the big craters of bedsores that covered his hips, suction the lung fluids that threatened to drown him, clean the feces that burned his skin like lye, pour the liquid food down the tube attached to his stomach, put pillows between his knees to ease the bone-on-bone pain, turn him every hour to keep the bedsores from getting worse, and change his gown and linen every two hours to keep him from being soaked in perspiration.

8   At night I went home and tried to scrub away the smell of decaying flesh that seemed woven into the fabric of my uniform. It was in my hair, the upholstery of my car—there was no washing it away. And every night I prayed that his agonized eyes would never again plead with me to let him die.

9   Every morning I asked the doctor for a "no code" order. Without that order, we had to resuscitate every patient who stopped breathing. His doctor was one of the several who believe we must extend life as long as we have the means and knowledge to do it. To not do it is to be liable for negligence, at least in the eyes of many people, including some nurses. I thought about what it would be like to stand before a judge, accused of murder, if Mac stopped breathing and I didn't call a code.

10   And after the 52nd code, when Mac was still lucid enough to beg for death again, and Maura was crumbled in my arms again, and when no amount of pain medication stilled his moaning and agony, I wondered about a spiritual judge. Was all this misery and suffering supposed to be building character or infusing us all with the sense of humility that comes from impotence?

11   Had we, the whole medical community, become so arrogant that we believed in the illusion of salvation through science? Had we become so self-righteous that we thought meddling in God's work was our duty, our moral imperative, and our legal obligation? Did we really believe that we had the right to force "life" on a suffering man who had begged for the right to die?

12   Such questions haunted me more than ever early one morning when Maura went home to change her clothes and I was bathing Mac. He had been still for so long, I thought he at last had the blessed relief of coma. Then he opened his eyes and moaned, "Pain . . . no more . . . Barbara . . . do something . . . God, let me go."

13   The desperation in the eyes and voice riddled me with guilt. "I'll stop," I told him as I injected the pain medication.

14   I sat on the bed and held Mac's hands in mine. He pressed his bony fingers against my hand and muttered, "Thanks." Then there was the one soft sigh and I felt his hands go cold in mine. "Mac?" I whispered, as I waited for his chest to rise and fall again.

15   A clutch of panic banded my chest, drew my finger to the code button, urged me to do something, anything . . . but sit there alone with death. I kept one finger on the button, without pressing it, as a waxen pallor slowly transformed his face from person to empty shell. Nothing I've ever done in my 47 years has taken so much effort as it took *not* to press that code button.

16   Eventually, when I was as sure as I could be that the code team would fail to bring him back, I entered the legal twilight zone and pushed the button. The team tried. And while they were trying, Maura walked in the room and shrieked, "No . . . don't let them do this to him . . . for God's sake . . . please, no more."

17   Cradling her in my arms was like cradling myself, Mac, and all those patients and nurses who had been in this place before who do the best they can in a death-denying society.

So a TV audience accused me of murder. Perhaps I am guilty. If a doctor had 18
written a no-code order, which is the only *legal* alternative, would he have felt
any less guilty? Until there is legislation making it a criminal act to code a
patient who has requested the right to die, we will all of us risk the same fate as
Mac. For whatever reason, we developed the means to prolong life, and now
we are forced to use it. We do not have the right to die.

QUESTIONS

1. How does Huttman's approach in this essay compare with Levin's essay?
   Is the reasoning different? How and why?
2. What assumptions about life and death do Huttman and Levin make? Are
   both positions reasonable? Can you construct an enthymeme that would
   cover both cases?
3. What is Huttman's purpose in telling Mac's story? Why is her description
   of her experience on the Donahue show important?
4. What is Huttman's warrant? Grounds? Claim? Does she provide backing,
   qualifiers, or conditions of rebuttal?
5. Are there any logical fallacies in the article? What are they? Would you be
   able to rewrite this story without using fallacies, using the academic
   argument form?
6. Is Mac's death a powerful story? Does its power come from its logic or
   from Huttman's stance on the issue of euthanasia? How does she support her position?

Bottle Babies: Death
and Business Get Their Market
Leah Margulies

Leah Margulies was a prominent protester against businesses promoting unsafe products in Third World countries. She served as director
of the Infant Formula Program of the Interfaith Center on Corporate
Responsibility, an ecumenical agency of the National Council of
Churches. This article originally appeared in *Newsweek* (August 8,
1983).

1   *Caracas, Venezuela, July 1977:* In the emergency room of the Hospital de
Niños, a large facility in the center of the city, lie 52 infants. All are suffering
from gastroenteritis, a serious inflammation of the stomach and intestines.
Many also suffer from pneumonia. According to the doctor in charge, 5,000
Venezuelan babies die each year from gastroenteritis, and an equal number die
from pneumonia. The doctor further explains that these babies, like many who
preceded them and those who would follow, have all been bottle-fed. He
remarks, "A totally breast-fed baby just does not get sick like this."

2   Poverty, inadequate medical care, and unsanitary conditions make bottle
feeding, to quote a government nurse in Peru, "poison" for babies in the developing countries. Yet bottle feeding is rapidly becoming the norm in Third World
countries. In 1951, almost 80 percent of all three-month-old babies in Singa-
pore were being breast-fed at the age of three months; twenty years later, only 5
percent of them were at the breast. In 1966, 40 percent fewer mothers in Mexico nursed their six-month-old babies than had done so six years earlier.

3   The end result of this significant change in human behavior is higher morbidity and mortality rates among bottle-fed babies. Many well-known studies
provide evidence of the relation between bottle feeding and infant malnutrition, disease, and death. Of course, it is impossible to know how many babies
are getting sick or dying because of bottle feeding, but the number is large and
growing throughout the developing world. Dr. Derrick Jelliffe, head of the
Department of Population, Health, and Family Planning at the UCLA School of
Public Health, conservatively estimates that about 10 million babies a year suffer
from malnutrition related to bottle feeding. The phenomenon is literally world-
wide. According to medical reports of malnutrition among Eskimo children in
the Baffin Zone of Canada, almost 5 percent of the infants born there in 1973–74
had to be flown to Montreal for emergency treatment, and doctors believe that
one of the major causes of this tragic development was bottle feeding.

4   At the center of the bottle-feeding controversy are the promotional practices of the corporations who sell bottles and powdered baby milks in the Third
World. Critics believe that promotion of these powders to mothers who do not

have the facilities to properly prepare the feeds is a deadly way to make a profit. However, despite the increased activity of critics and acknowledgments by industry that improper bottle feeding can be dangerous, sales of infant formulas in poor countries are still escalating.

The corporations that sell infant formula in the Third World run the gamut 5 from prestigious American, Swiss, British, and Japanese multinational corporations—like Abbott, American Home products, Bristol-Myers, Nestlés, and Cow and Gate—to local fly-by-night manufacturers trying to cash in. The concentrated campaign to attract Third World consumers began in the late 1950s. Soon a body of literature arose to help business conquer this almost virgin territory. For example, various articles advised foreign marketers that, in the absence of a middle class, they should consider the urban poor as an important potential market.

Business began to understand the market potential of a poor population 6 with many unfulfilled needs. Often the real needs of the poor could be obscured by a corporate sales strategy which promised the satisfaction of newly created needs. Mass media—TV, radio, and newspapers—could convey the promise that new products would meet these new needs. *Fortune* magazine heralded this new age with an article entitled, "Welcome to the Consumption Community." It was therefore not surprising that when the "Community" of infant formula consumers in the United States began to shrink as postwar birth rates declined and middle-class women in the developed countries decided they had been deprived of the experience of breast-feeding and began turning to the more natural way, the corporations turned to the ripe Third World market.

For the companies, baby formula sales strategies have paid off. Unfortu- 7 nately no reliable statistics on infant formula sales are publicly available, although sometimes companies have inadvertently revealed the extent of their commitment to the product. World-wide sales of formula are estimated to total around $1 billion, with Nestlé's figure at roughly $300–400 million. Nestlé reportedly controls approximately half of the formula market in developing countries.

Whatever the sales figures at present, they will undoubtedly increase in the 8 future. Bristol-Myers, for instance, has consistently reported sales gains for its Enfamil infant formula. Moreover, the upward trend, for the other companies as well as for Bristol-Myers, shows few signs of abating. Of course, sales figures do not tell the full story. Profit rates for infant formulas are also thought to be quite high. According to a 1977 supermarket sales printout from Brazil, commercial formula enjoyed a 72 percent profit margin, while all other supermarket products ranged between 15 percent and 25 percent.

What Is It?

What kind of product is infant formula? It is a highly processed food, based pri- 9 marily on cow's milk. While the fat content and sugar source are patterned after mothers' milk, the company's claim that it is "nearly identical to mother's milk" is ridiculous. Maternal milk is a living substance, unique in many ways. Besides supplying the proper quantities of protein, fats, and other nutrients, it protects the infant from disease by providing antibodies important to the development of the immunization system. Formula does not have the digestibility of mothers' milk. Sometimes the product is sold premixed, but in the Third World it is more often sold as a powder that requires measured amounts of pure water for the proper reconstitutions. Sterilized bottles and nipples are also necessary.

10   There are a number of reasons why infant formula sells so well in the Third World. A mother in a developing country often finds herself in situations totally unlike those her mother ever experienced. She may, for instance, work outside the home, listen to the radio, or watch TV. These situations can be disorienting, and new values and attitudes must be formed in order to deal with them. Newly acquired values such as social mobility, as well as a high regard for modern products and medical expertise, make her a particularly vulnerable target for sophisticated formula marketing campaigns. The smiling white babies pictured on the front of formula tins can lead her to think that rich, white mothers feed their baby this product and that therefore it must be better.

11   Going into a hospital to give birth can be an especially frightening situation for a young Third World woman. Since in many countries only a small proportion of women attend the prenatal clinic (if there is one), a mother's maternity stay may be one of the few times in her life that she will go into a hospital. Any products given to her in this environment will seem to carry medical endorsement.

12   Imagine the reaction of a Third World mother in her home, or a group of mothers in a clinic or hospital attending a class, to a woman in a crisp nurse's uniform. The woman may or may not be a nurse. She begins her speech, tactfully enough, by reassuring them that "breast is best," but she ends by extolling the virtues of her company's product over the natural method. Capitalizing on the respect given a nurse, the use of a "milk nurse" implies a connection between the health care profession and the commercial product.

13   In developed and developing countries alike, one of the hospital practices most damaging to breast-feeding efforts—and one implicitly supported by company promotional practices—is the separation of mothers and infants shortly after birth. During the twelve to forty-eight hours of separation, the infants are bottle fed in the nursery. Mothers are sometimes given antilactation shots during this period. Thus when a mother is finally reunited with her baby, switching from bottle to breast is made more difficult. Furthermore, if the hospital has no incentive to teach her, the woman is even less likely to breast-feed. Formula companies create a strong climate for their products with their constant offers to set up bottle sterilization and preparation facilities, to equip nurseries, and to provide free supplies of formula. Busy doctors and nurses are led to adopt the postnatal separation strategy by the willingness of formula companies to make this approach easier than breast-feeding.

14   Medical personnel are a prime target for promotion because they are the direct link to mothers. Although it is the patient who ultimately pays for the product, doctors tell her what to buy, and the difference in backgrounds of doctor and patient may well lead to an inappropriate choice. As Dr. John

Knowles, president of the Rockefeller Foundation, stated in a letter to the chairman of Bristol-Myers:

> The problem is not a "scientific" one. The problem is poverty and the inadequate home environment which makes the use of prepared formulae so lethal. This the physician is not uniquely qualified to understand. In fact, he may be precisely the most unqualified to understand, since he undoubtedly comes from a different socio-economic background and may have no idea of the home conditions of the poorest mothers of his own society.

Many dedicated physicians face a real dilemma when dealing with the promotion efforts of formula companies. Their hospitals and clinics are often woefully short of medical equipment and supplies. Under such circumstances, it may seem harmless, indeed charitable to agree to give away free samples of infant formula to mothers in exchange for the company's gift of medical stocks or a new nursery. One hospital administrator in Malaysia has explained. "It is a very corrupting influence. You are always aware that you could have virtually anything you ask for." 15

Marketing for Babies

These marketing strategies are consciously decided upon and implemented through instructions to sales personnel, milk nurses, and distributors. Note the following extract from American Home Products selling instructions for 1975: 16

> *Selected Doctors:* 40–50 doctors per territory including 5 or 6 VIP's. These doctors should all be selected on the basis of their known influence on the selection of formula by mothers and by hospital or clinic maternity services.
>
> *Sampling:* . . . Maternity services should be given primary allocation of free samples, geared to producing potential sales.

Companies believe, and with good reason, that the product a mother goes home with is the product she will be loyal to. A 1969 study of 120 mothers in Barbados showed that 82 percent of the mothers given free samples, whether in a hospital or at home, later purchased the same brand. Thirty-two percent of them admitted that they were influenced by the free sample.

This aggressive market penetration and consumer creation are particularly destructive because they affect the most important resource developing countries have—people. In Chile in 1973 three times as many deaths occurred among infants who were bottle fed before three months old than among wholly breast-fed infants. A research team inspecting feeding bottles there discovered a bacterial contamination rate of 80 percent. Poverty and underdevelopment lead to abuse of even legitimate baby milk substitutes. Poor mothers cannot afford them in the quantities needed. Water is often contaminated, and the necessary boiling is rarely possible. Illiteracy makes it difficult to follow proper directions. Early weaning of infants from the breast to bottled infant formula is accompanied by increasing cases of diarrhea and gastroenteritis. Improperly attended—as they are likely to be due to inadequate medical care—these disorders result in many deaths. 17

18   Malnutrition is another common result and has been described as "com-
merciogenic malnutrition." This is not meant to imply that the manufacturers
are solely responsible but simply that this type of malnutrition has nothing
directly to do with underdevelopment and lack of food resources. As Dr.
Michael Latham, a pediatrician and Cornell University professor of nutrition
stated, "Placing a baby on the bottle in the Third World might be tantamount to
signing that baby's death certificate."

19   A 1975 Pan American Health Organization study found that childhood
deaths from malnutrition peaked in the third and fourth months of life, because
of the early abandonment of breastfeeding. The study covered some 35,000
deaths in fifteen countries. Medical studies linking bottle feeding with infant
mortality and morbidity cover practically all areas of the Third World and some
developed countries as well. A 1977 study in Cooperstown, New York, compared
164 breastfed infants with 162 formula-fed infants; significant illnesses increased
as breast-feeding declined. In 1970 a study in Jamaica, West Indies, revealed a
higher incidence of gastroenteritis in the first four months of life among partly or
wholly bottle-fed babies than among breast-fed babies. Other studies have
reported similar results from Chile, Lebanon, Israel, Lagos, and others.

20   Hospital reports and personal testimony from doctors and nurses confirm
these findings. Doctors in Jamaica have reviewed the records of thirty-seven
seriously ill infants admitted in 1975 into their hospital, the Tropical Metabolism
Research Unit in 1975. Twenty-five of the thirty-seven patients had been fed a
brand-name infant formula. The average body weight of the babies was only 58
percent of the normal value. Their families were simply not equipped to safely
bottle feed. About one fifth of the mothers were illiterate. The remainder were
able to sign their names but were functionally illiterate. It was highly unlikely
that they would be able to read, no less understand written directions.

21   Nearly all the families lived in cramped, over-crowded, and unsanitary conditions, with an average weekly income of sixteen dollars. A tin of baby formula
costs approximately two dollars and a baby needs two cans a week if exclusively formula-fed. Despite optimal medical care, five of these babies died. The
case studies graphically show the inevitability of bottle contamination and dilu-
tion—the key culprits leading to illness and malnutrition.

22   Since 1970 when the Protein Advisory Group (recently dismantled) of the
United Nations first met with the baby formula industry, there has been a growing international campaign aimed at stopping unethical promotional practices.
In 1973, the Protein Advisory Group published guidelines for promoting infant
nutrition and included the need for restrictions in advertising. In 1974, the
World Health Assembly called for a critical review of company promotion, and
the issue has been discussed extensively at medical conferences, international
seminars, in U.N. papers, etc. Most recently, on January 31, 1978, the World
Health Organization announced, "The advertising of food for nursing infants or
older babies and young children is of particular importance and should be prohibited on radio and television . . . finally, the distribution of free samples and
other sales promotion practices for baby foods should be generally prohibited."

In 1975 the International Pediatrics Association issued a series of recom- 23 mendations to encourage breast-feeding. The section entitled "Curtailing Promotion of Artificial Feeding" reads:

1. Sales promotion activities of organizations marketing baby milks and feeding bottles, that run counter to the general intent expressed in this document, must be curtailed by every means available to the profession, including, where necessary and feasible, legislation to control unethical practice.
2. Dissemination of propaganda about artificial feeding and distribution of samples of artificial baby foods in maternity units should be banned immediately.

In the U.S. recently, considerable interest has centered around the stock- 24 holder lawsuit against Bristol-Myers (Mead Johnson Division). The Sisters of the Precious Blood have charged the company with making "false and misleading statements" about their overseas promotion and sales of infant formula. The statements appeared in a proxy report to stockholders, which is required by law to be accurate. In May 1977, a U.S. district court judge dismissed the case, stating that the Sisters had not shown that they, as shareholders, had been caused "irreparable harm" by the alleged misstatements. The judge declined to comment on the accuracy of the company's proxy report. The nuns appealed this decision.

Then in the first weeks of 1978, the Sisters signed an out-of-court settle- 25 ment with Bristol-Myers. The settlement stipulates that a report be sent to all shareholders of the company, outlining the legal action and the positions of both parties. The Sisters' statement in the report contains affidavits from five countries and an analysis of their current criticisms of company practices. The company's statement announces a more stringent interpretation of its Code of Policies and Practices and the fact that it has discontinued the use of milk nurses in Jamaica. Industry critics view the settlement as an important step toward convincing the companies that public opinion has changed the social climate in which marketing takes place: What was at one time an "acceptable" social cost no longer is the case, primarily because of increased public knowledge and protest.

The findings of the lawsuit have prompted local consumer advocacy 26 groups in the United States to join forces in a coalition called INFACT (Infant Formula Action). These groups believe it vital to keep pressuring Nestlé—the largest manufacturer of baby formula in the Third World—to desist from its promotion tactics. The Minnesota-based Third World Institute has initiated a consumer boycott which is quietly spreading throughout the U.S. In addition, church groups, acting in their capacity as stockholders in the American companies, are continuing their efforts to further restrict the promotion these companies engage in. This year two new shareholder resolutions were filed with American Home Products and Carnation, both of whom widely advertise their condensed milk in the Third World.

Because of this growing condemnation of industry practices, the companies have made some attempts to deal with their critics. In most cases however, the concessions do not significantly alter the outcome of formula promotion. There have been a number of changes:

- After blatant advertising, especially mass-media promotion had made some of the companies highly vulnerable to criticism, these companies switched the focus of their promotion efforts to the medical profession. This new marketing approach is more sophisticated, less risky, and far more effective. Via mass media, everyone heard the message, whether they were potential customers or not. Now marketing focuses more directly on the consumer through the use of health workers. For example, in a poverty hospital in the Philippines, name tags with a prominent brand-name logo are found on each crib in the nursery. Nestlé wrist labels have also been provided. There and elsewhere, while the most blatant ads have been curtailed, direct consumer promotion continues in the hospitals themselves and appears to be sanctioned by the medical authorities.

- In the past, critics charged that companies encouraged the abandonment of breast-feeding. Now the companies agree that bottle feeding to the exclusion of breast-feeding is not desirable. They talk about "supplementation." However, mixed feeding has also been shown to be quite dangerous. Consuming smaller amounts of contaminated and diluted formula is preferable, one assumes, but it is not the answer. Furthermore, the encouragement of supplementation in fact undermines breast-feeding. According to most medical experts, supplementation negatively affects the production of human milk.

- Critics have also complained about milk nurses and the ethics involved in employing nurses as a company sales force. Again, the companies have adapted. They often change the colors of the uniforms, add belts, call them "company representatives," and may even agree to alter somewhat milk-nurse sales techniques. But visits to hospitals and homes continue, and the nurses are still being lured away from government health services.

- A more significant adaptive technique is that of employing nutritionists and other highly trained professionals. In Venezuela, for example, Nestlé employs no milk nurses but several nutritionists. These nutritionists interact on a regular basis with Ministry of Health, nutrition, and hospital personnel. One Nestlé nutritionist in Caracas appears to have been totally integrated into the health care team at Maternidad Hospital as she made her rounds with the paid hospital staff. This type of interaction between government and business personnel raises serious ethical questions about the extent to which industry's point of view should be institutionalized within government health services.

- When critics argued that formula was being promoted to the poor, the companies responded that formula is priced above the income of poor people and is purchased almost exclusively by upper-income groups. But the companies have provided no evidence to confirm this argument. Indeed, there is more than adequate proof that the products are being promoted and sold indiscriminately to mothers who have neither the financial nor the sanitary facilities to use the products safely. Since July 1977 alone, documentation confirms the presence of promotional displays in markets, pharmacies, and grocery stores in the mountain villages of India, the barrios of Caracas, and the slums of Manila.

■ In response to these kinds of intense promotion efforts, the critics finally called for regulation of the formula industry. The industry, in turn, has responded with "self-regulation," which mainly consists of business codes. There are now several codes of ethics, some more stringent than others. All, however, share two inherent weaknesses.

First, the codes legitimize promotion to the medical profession and characterize the latter as "intermediaries" between the baby food industry and the mother. However, given the desperate shortages of medical personnel in developing countries and the constant pressure exerted on existing workers by the companies, it is very difficult for these intermediaries to be impartial. 28

Second, insuring that the companies will adhere to their self-imposed restrictions is virtually impossible in the absence of regular scrutiny by an independent body. In August 1977, a Bristol-Myers milk nurse was interviewed by this author on the ward of the largest public hospital in Jamaica. The milk nurse had in her hand a list of mothers she intended to visit in their homes. She had copied the names from ward lists. In an interview just two days before, the chief medical officer of Jamaica had explained that government policy prohibited milk nurses from entering public hospitals. The milk nurse's actions were therefore doubly in violation of Bristol-Myers's code of ethics which specifically requires cooperation with government health policies as well as the solicitation of references from medical professionals for all home visits. The publicity surrounding this incident most likely influenced Bristol-Myers's decision to discontinue milk nurses in Jamaica. 29

Stopping the promotion of infant formula products will not, in and of itself, eliminate malnutrition. Infant formula products could still be sold under carefully controlled and supervised conditions and still be misused because the existing social and economic conditions make proper usage virtually impossible. An end to malnutrition will ultimately require massive changes in the distribution of wealth, land, and power. But that is no reason not to take intermediate steps. The shifts in promotion thus far are adaptations to a new business climate and clearly prove that the formula industry is vulnerable to pressure. 30

If promotion could be eliminated entirely, health care institutions and governments would be freer to develop their own capacity to handle the monumental health problems that face Third World countries. To accomplish this, the public needs a strategy. It must include the continuous monitoring and disclosure of corporate activity; cooperation between concerned health professionals, 31 international agencies, and advocacy groups; and the development of an increasingly larger audience of people who share the belief that business must be held accountable for unethical practices, however costly and inconvenient. As Dr. Alan Jackson of the Tropical Metabolism Research Unit in Jamaica stated in a recent interview:

> When you spend your time working with children who are malnourished and you see children dying because they are either getting wrong food or food prepared improperly, it has a devastating effect upon you. It's very hard to think that people who are involved in selling, encouraging people to buy infant preparation, can carry on in this kind of a way, and at the same time pretend that they are not involved in the end results, which is malnutrition, malnourished children.

QUESTIONS

1. Identify the six elements of the Toulmin system. Can you locate the conditions of rebuttal? Are they convincing? Why?
2. Is this text written in the genre of academic argument? Could it be revised and rewritten in another genre?
3. Although Margulies is writing about baby formula, her argument also pertains to larger issues. What are those issues? Does her use of logic in the baby formula example connect it to these other issues? How?
4. Taking into account the literacy rate and the lack of pure water and sterile conditions, what is the logic behind the Third World mothers' use of commercial baby formula? Reconstruct the syllogism they use. Do you feel that they have enough information to make an informed choice?
5. Are there any fallacies in the counterargument offered by the large American corporations? Do fallacies make these companies seem dishonest, or is it possible that Margulies has "poisoned the well"?
6. If you were writing a rebuttal of Margulies's essay, which of her points would you attack? How would you attack them using logic to make your point?

Chapter 4

EXPLORING THROUGH
OUTSIDE READING

In addition to exploring a topic from the perspective of your own experience, the genre of academic argument requires that you incorporate what others have written about your topic in published works. This means getting acquainted with the library (discussed in the Appendix), finding useful material to work with, and evaluating its quality by reading critically. Of course, if you are writing about a topic that is relatively unfamiliar to you, you may be wondering how you can know whether or not to trust a particular source. Simply because a book or article has been published does not mean that it is valid or even true. So how can you figure out if a published work is reliable?

Given the quantity of available material, there is, of course, no simple answer to this question. However, if you develop the skill of *critical reading,* you will become aware of criteria you can use for making an informed decision about a published work. This chapter is concerned with the process of evaluating published material using a three-pass approach to critical reading.

CRITICAL READING AND THE
ONGOING CONVERSATION

To introduce the idea of critical reading, I would like you to imagine that you have arrived at a party at which a heated discussion is already going on. Wishing to join the conversation, you approach the group and listen for a while, trying to figure out whose point of view you found worthwhile. Suppose, though, that all of the speakers are strangers to you and that you know nothing about their backgrounds or interests. How, then, would you know whose opinion to take seriously? What criteria would you use to evaluate what is being said? On what basis would you be able to decide?

Reading a published work, whether in the form of a newspaper or magazine article or material from a book, is somewhat like entering an ongoing conversation—in fact, the rhetorician Kenneth Burke, among others, has made exactly that point—moreover, when you are not familiar with the topic, the process of research is uncomfortably similar to entering a room full of strangers. I make this comparison because as a student who is being asked to develop a thoughtful position on a complex topic, you have to be aware that most of the controversies you encounter in print have been going on for some time and that many of those who are writing about these controversies, like the guests at the party, have been involved in the discussion long before you arrived. The comparison also suggests that deciding which points of view are believable will be a real challenge for you.

Nevertheless, although it is difficult to assess the value of a published work, becoming aware of what you already know about the subject and using clues from the text will enable you to make an informed judgment. In first examining a published work, you should ask yourself the following questions:

1. What do I already know about this topic?
2. What do I know about the writer of the book or article? Does the text provide information about the writer?
3. Can I assess the quality of the argument based on tone, language, and evidence?

What Do I Already Know about This Topic?

In terms of the conversation at the party, one way you would be able to decide which speaker is credible would be to reflect on how much you already know about the topic being discussed and then to compare what you know with what you hear in the discussion. In fact, without some basic knowledge about the topic, you would not be able to assess anyone's opinion and would first have to acquire some basic information. If, for example, the speakers were debating the merits of various laptop computers, you would be unable to decide whose recommendation to believe if you knew nothing at all about laptop computers, had no idea what computers do, and had never used any sort of computer. The first requirement for participating in the conversation, then, would be that you know at least something about the subject matter. Exploration questions can help you understand what you already know and believe about the topic, and if you discover that you know nothing about it at all, I suggest that you consult sources that will provide you with at least an overview. An encyclopedia, an almanac, or an introductory book on the topic can usually provide you with at least some context and background.

In terms of the ongoing discussion at the party, the more similar a particular position is to a viewpoint you already hold, the more likely you would be to agree with it. So, if the topic under discussion was the merits of the Zoink laptop computer, and if you yourself had used a Zoink and liked it, knew others who felt the same way, and had read about the merits of the Zoink, you would be likely to agree that the Zoink is the best laptop computer on the market. Under these circumstances, you would be disinclined to change your mind unless you became aware of a new piece of information.

In addition to understanding the topic of the discussion and being aware of your own views on it, you would also be in a better position to evaluate what was being said if you knew something about the reason that the discussion was being held. Had someone requested the name of a reliable, reasonably priced laptop computer, or was the discussion concerned with deciding which computer is the most technologically advanced? Had something happened recently that had sparked the debate (the release of a new model, for example)? Had the topic been raised in the context of a presumed health hazard from laptop computers? Are there any particular groups or organizations associated with a particular perspective on this controversy?

What Do I Know about the Writer?

In terms of the party metaphor, you would also be more qualified to decide whose opinion to trust if you knew something about the participants, in particular about their qualifications for discoursing on this topic, and about what their motives or agendas might be in this discussion. For example, if you discovered that the gentleman in the red jacket happened to be the president of Zoink Computers, Inc., you would be somewhat suspicious of his endorsement of this particular model because he would obviously have a specific motive or agenda to promote. On the other hand, if the man in the blue T-shirt bearing the slogan "Computers Will Destroy Humanity" was yelling that Zoink computers are infected with all sorts of dangerous viruses, causing users to break out in unsightly rashes, yet he provided no specific evidence to support his claim (and, in fact, was a member of the Delete Computers Society), you would also distrust *his* position. And finally, if you realized that the gentleman with the large mustache was a notorious liar who enjoyed fueling discussions whether or not he had any real information to contribute, you would not pay too much attention to *his* viewpoint, either. However, if the woman in the gray suit introduced herself as a research consultant who evaluated laptop computers for a well-known corporation, and if she indicated (in measured tones) that, based on her extensive research and personal experience, the Zoink is undoubtedly the best model on the market, you would be most likely to trust her opinion, rather than those of the other participants in the debate. In fact, even if you already had an opinion on the topic, you might reevaluate your own point of view, if you were sufficiently impressed with what she had to say.

Can I Assess the Quality of the Argument Based on Tone, Language, and Evidence?

Generally, we tend to be convinced by arguments that are supported by clear reasons and that use evidence to support their major claims. We also tend to trust writers who appear calm and who speak in measured, rather than hysterical, tones. In terms of the party metaphor, we would probably be more likely to trust the woman in the gray suit who seemed balanced and restrained, rather than the man in the T-shirt who was yelling.

Now I must also point out that it is the *quality of the ideas,* not the style of presentation, that you should ultimately focus on in deciding which opinions to trust because style is something that can be easily distorted. Television commercials, in particular, tend to use people who seem calm and knowledgeable, and viewers find themselves trusting what such people have to say, even when the viewers know that the spokespersons are simply actors who are being paid to endorse a particular product. On the other hand, if someone is hysterical, it does not necessarily mean that his or her opinion is not worthwhile—perhaps the situation is sufficiently alarming so that hysteria is the appropriate response. Furthermore, an obvious self-interest is not always a reason to distrust an opinion. Perhaps the president of Zoink Computers has done a great deal of research, knows a lot about computers, and wants to produce the best computer on the market. In this case, despite the fact that he stands to profit from the sale of Zoinks, his ideas could be worth believing.

TAKING CHARGE OF YOUR READING THROUGH THE THREE-PASS APPROACH

When people are inexperienced in working with published works, whether in the form of articles or books, they often approach them passively—that is, they note that the title seems related to their topic, and then they simply begin reading, trying to understand the meaning of the text. The problem with this approach is that it adheres to a submissive, rather than to a "take charge" model of the reading process. Reading submissively implies that the work exists as a separate, valid, believable entity, worthy of serious consideration simply because it has been published. Moreover, the submissive approach does not include the reader-initiated activities of reflecting on the subject and context of the work, questioning the motives, agendas, and qualifications of its author, or evaluating the quality of the argument.

If you recall the party discussion scenario just outlined, the submissive approach to reading puts you, as the reader, at a great disadvantage because you will not be aware of all the factors necessary for evaluating the validity of what you are reading. Such an approach is as if you had entered the party, had been immediately cornered by the man in the blue T-shirt, who was screaming about the rash he had contracted from his Zoink laptop, and had listened only to his point of view, without reflecting on your own perspective, understanding the context of the discussion, or questioning the reliability of the speaker.

To avoid being a passive reader, you should keep the following principle in mind:

Very few, if any, articles or books are written simply to present information in a completely objective way.

Even what seems to be the most coldly and objectively written scientific piece of writing has at its foundation a complex set of beliefs about how the world is or ought to be, and if you are aware of what those might be, you will be in a better position to evaluate the text and decide whether or not to believe what it says. Competent readers engage actively in the reading process. They approach a published work by trying to learn as much information about it as possible before beginning to read it. Then, after they decide that the text is worth reading, they interact with it energetically, almost as if they were having a conversation with the author.

THE THREE-PASS APPROACH: AN OVERVIEW

The three-pass approach will enable you to evaluate the credibility of the articles and books you read, so that you will be able to decide whether or not to use them in your essays. At first, the method will seem to involve a lot of work, and maybe you will think initially that it is not worth your time. Keep in mind, though, that with practice the first two steps quickly become collapsed into one and that any new method may seem cumbersome at first but eventually becomes easy to use. Here, then, is an overview of the three-pass approach:

1. The First Pass—Reflection and Quick Overview

During the first pass, you reflect on the subject and context of the controversy, evaluate the qualifications and motives of the author, and examine the text for additional clues, such as the title, publication information, and easily discernible strategies of organization.

2. The Second Pass—Reading for Meaning and Structure

During the second pass, you read the text for meaning to determine what it is saying. To aid understanding, you use structural clues within the text and summarize main points.

3. The Third Pass—Interacting with the Text

During the third pass, you interact with the text, actively engaging in a critical dialogue with it, in order to determine how much of it to accept. In this pass, you distinguish between fact and opinion, evaluate the type of evidence cited, decide whether the writer is aware of the complexity of the topic, and pay close attention to how language is being used to shape the reader's perspective.

THE FIRST PASS: REFLECTION AND QUICK OVERVIEW

The first pass over a published work involves assessing what you already know about the subject matter, the context, and the author, and then examining the easily detectable surface clues that the work provides. Before you begin reading a published work, ask yourself the following questions:

1. What do I know about the subject matter of this work? Have I been brought up to have an opinion on this topic? Have I heard discussions on this topic or read anything about it? Is there a controversy associated with this topic?
2. What is the context of the controversy about this topic? Is there some action or policy associated with it? Was it written in response to another piece of writing? For whom is this work being written? Do I know anything about any groups associated with this controversy?
3. What do I know about the author? Does the author have a title or position that would indicate his or her qualifications or a particular agenda? Can I speculate on what the motive of the author might be?

Clues about the Text

After you have reflected on the subject and context of the controversy, and on the potential agenda of the author, you should then peruse the work for surface clues that can provide you with additional information. These clues include publication information, such as the title, the type of publication, and the copyright date, and organizational clues, such as section headings and boldfaced subtitles (for an article), or chapter headings and the table of contents (for a book). If you know something about the topic, you can get a sense of where the author is situated in the controversy by looking at the bibliography, if there is one, noting which sources the author has cited and whether or not you can recognize any names or publications. Then, in a brief glance, you should try to determine the type of evidence cited, such as the use of charts or graphs or the inclusion of statistics.

Begin by examining the title and thinking about what the title might suggest about the author's attitude toward the subject or purpose in writing. See if you can figure out what the article or book might be about simply on the basis of the title. Then, if the work is an article in a magazine or journal, try to grasp the overall approach or agenda of that publication. Some journals are known to endorse a particular political approach, so that you will be able to predict what the overall thrust of an article might be by thumbing through it to see what other articles appear along with the one you are thinking of reading. If biographical information about other authors appears, read through it and see what other authors are included and the kind of backgrounds they have. Finally, check the copyright date. For some topics, the fact that a particular article was written 15 or 20 years ago might not matter at all. For other topics, it might matter a great deal. Reflect on whether or not the date of publication will affect the believability or validity of the work.

Sometimes you can get a sense of an article by reading an abstract or by skimming over section subheadings or words that appear in boldface. Think about how these subheadings relate to the title, or, if the work you are about to read is a book or a chapter from a book, see if there is a chapter summary at the beginning or end of each chapter or group of chapters that will provide you with additional clues. Frequently, if you skim over the first few and last few paragraphs of an article or chapter, you can quickly understand its main point.

Of course, not every article or book you come upon will be easily accessible to immediate scrutiny. Nevertheless, even those that are not written by readily identifiable authors with easily predicted agendas, or those that do not state their main points explicitly, will usually yield at least *some* useful information during the first pass. Even if you find out very little information about the text, looking for clues in this way will at least help you begin looking at the work with a critical eye.

THE SECOND PASS: READING FOR MEANING AND STRUCTURE

During the second pass, you should read the material through reasonably quickly and write a summary of it so that you can easily refer back to it without having to reread it. Use the summary to encapsulate its overall point, as well as to record component supporting points, and make the summary sufficiently complete so that even a reader who has not read the article will be able to understand what it is about. Also be sure to write down all information you would need to be able to locate the article again if you wish to use it—that is, for an article, include the title, the author, the title of the journal, issue number, pages, and date; for a book, include the author, title, and publication information, such as publisher, place of publication, and date.

In reading a text for meaning, it is a good idea to focus attention on its purpose and structure—that is:

Is it a response to another point of view? Can you situate it in a conversation? Is there a controversy associated with it?

Does the article or book compare and contrast two or more ideas or recommendations?

Does it make a point about cause and effect?

Does it pose a question and then answer it?

Does it trace the history of something, structuring its information chronologically?

Is it developed through the use of many examples?

During the second pass, you will understand the text more easily if you think about how it has been organized, noting how different facets of the topic relate to the author's main point. Look also for signals in the text that indicate that a shift of some sort is about to occur, noting how new content is introduced—subheadings are good indicators of this, but sometimes the author uses transitional sentences.

One point to note about the second pass is that after a quick read, you may decide that the work is not worth reading after all. Remember that there has been a lot written that may not be worth your time. Understanding the meaning of a text through a relatively quick appraisal can thus prevent you from expending unnecessary effort.

THE THIRD PASS: INTERACTING WITH THE TEXT

After you understand the meaning and structure of the text, now is the time to take charge of your reading, which means reading critically with a questioning attitude toward your material and interacting with it as much as possible. Now is the time for you to enter the conversation, not accepting what you read unless the evidence is convincing. Keep in mind what you have learned about the author's agenda or qualifications for writing this particular article or book, and use that information to formulate critical questions as you read. Here is a detailed discussion of the third pass:

1. Is the Argument Consistent with What You Believe Is True or Possible about the World and about Human Behavior?

Your View of the World and Your Belief about Human Nature

In order for an argument to convince a reader, it must be consistent with what the reader believes is true and possible in the world and with his or her concept of human nature. Our view of the world and our beliefs and ideas about humanity serve as a kind of filter through which we can assess the quality of the information we receive, and the more we experience and read, the more we adjust our worldview to accommodate new information. We believe, for example, that it is possible to fly from California to New York in about five hours, so that if a friend left my home in L.A. at 2 p.m. and then called me at 8 p.m., claiming that he was in New York, I would probably believe him (unless I suspected that he was playing some sort of joke or had a reputation for lying, etc.). But if my friend left my home in L.A. at 2 p.m. and then called me at 2:30, claiming to be in New York, I would be unlikely to believe him even if he claimed that he had been whisked there in a new form of airplane.

Similarly, our concept of human nature—that is, what we believe human beings are likely to do or are capable of doing—is another source by which we evaluate what we read. To cite an obvious example of how your worldview and concept of human nature contribute to the credibility of an idea, imagine the difficulty you would have in convincing a local school board that a night watchman is needed to prevent aliens from landing on the school football field at night, because most people do not believe that aliens constitute much of a problem on a nightly basis (in fact, only some people think that aliens exist at all). On the other hand, it would probably not be at all difficult to convince the school board that a night watchman is necessary to prevent thieves from stealing expensive computer equipment from the science lab. Our worldview tells us that there are, indeed, such things as thieves, and our concept of human nature tells us that, unfortunately, some human beings will avail themselves of the opportunity to steal, unless reasonable precautions are taken.

On an issue such as whether or not to have a night watchman at the local high school, most people would probably have little difficulty reaching agreement (assuming that the funding was available). However, on controversial, complex topics, people will often disagree because they have differing concepts of human nature. Moreover, people sometimes make statements about human behavior on the basis of what they *wish* were true, rather than on what the evidence suggests is really the case. Because we often wish that everyone was motivated by only the most noble of impulses and that deep down everyone wants to do the "right" thing, we often have difficulty believing stories that suggest otherwise, particularly about those we have set up as heroes or role models. Thus, when a president of a country or a film star or sports celebrity behaves poorly or even illegally, many people refuse to believe even what seems evidently true. Many people seem to want to be deceived, easily believing reports that to others seem completely preposterous—belief in paranormal events or a chance at winning the lottery, for example.

In the third pass, then, you question the extent to which a particular argument is consistent with your worldview and concept of human nature. You ask yourself whether the main point makes sense to you according to your own experience and what you believe is likely to be true. If it is not, you would then attempt to view the issue from the author's point of view, trying to understand why the author espouses these beliefs.

2. Is the Argument Supported with Appropriate and Believable Subpoints, Examples, and Facts?

Distinguishing Fact from Opinion

One task of reading a text interactively is to be on the alert for statements that may appear to be facts but that are actually opinions that are presented as if they were facts. An effective way to detect the difference, though, is to notice whether or not the main points are supported with specific appropriate details and subpoints or instead consist simply of observations that the author *thinks* are true. Keep in mind that, unless a writer is an acknowledged authority, you really have no reason to accept his or her point of view and that even an expert is obliged to provide supporting evidence. For example, examine Jenny's paragraph that follows, which is concerned with the question of whether homework should be assigned to children in elementary school:

1) Although many teachers and parents believe that homework is an important part of a child's elementary school education, homework in the elementary grades does little or nothing to help children learn. 2) Moreover, it detracts from a child's physical development and family life. 3) Young children need time after school to play in the fresh air and get physical exercise, and homework requires them to stay indoors, working on their schoolwork. 4) Moreover, most homework assignments are nothing more than busywork, assigned by teachers because they have always done so. 5) Homework also contributes to children's anxiety about school because the responsibility of getting homework done weighs on their minds, interfering with their ability to enjoy learning. 6) Finally, the need to supervise a child's homework puts too much stress on parents, who are already too busy trying to work and maintain family life.

In this paragraph, Jenny has written a number of statements that are stated as if they are facts but that are actually Jenny's own opinion of what she believes to be facts. To determine the extent to which you should be convinced by Jenny's paragraph, read each statement carefully with a questioning attitude, reflecting on the nature of the support Jenny has provided.

1. Although many teachers and parents believe that homework is an important part of a child's elementary school education, homework in the elementary grades does little or nothing to help children learn.

This is Jenny's topic sentence. It expresses the idea that her paragraph is going to develop, and Jenny states it definitively. The implication of the statement is that homework should *never* be assigned in elementary school, and you might begin by reflecting on your own experience with homework, or that assigned to your own children, and the extent to which you agree with this idea.

2. Moreover, it detracts from a child's physical development and family life.

This is an extension of Jenny's thesis, and you might reflect on whether you think that this statement is a fact or only Jenny's opinion. You might ask, "How does homework detract from a child's physical development and family life?" Another point to consider is "How much homework would have this effect?" You also might ask, "How does Jenny know this?"

3. Young children need time after school to play in the fresh air and get physical exercise, and homework requires them to stay indoors, working on their schoolwork.

You will probably agree that children need fresh air and physical exercise. But you might feel that Jenny's statement is an exaggeration. Unless children are assigned hours and hours of homework, it is unlikely to interfere very much with their play and exercise time.

4. Moreover, most homework assignments are nothing more than busywork, assigned by teachers because they have always done so.

This is Jenny's opinion, presented as if it were a fact. You might ask, "How does Jenny know that most homework assignments are nothing more than busywork?" or "What is the difference between homework that is worthwhile and homework that is 'just busywork'?"

5. Homework also contributes to children's anxiety about school because the responsibility of getting homework done weighs on their minds, interfering with their ability to enjoy learning.

Once again, you might question how Jenny knows this. Can she cite the statements of people whose children have suffered anxiety due to homework? Additionally, Jenny does not refer to the possibility that assuming responsibility for homework might be beneficial for children in that it could help them develop a sense of responsibility. The role of homework in fostering responsibility and aiding learning is an issue that people are currently debating, so there is considerable discussion about this topic that Jenny could read and that might help her develop her ideas. However, in this paragraph, Jenny has not indicated that she has "joined the conversation." She is simply voicing her own opinion.

6. Finally, the need to supervise a child's homework puts too much stress on parents, who are already too busy trying to work and maintain family life.

This is once again an assertion, not a statement of fact, although it is presented as if it were. How does Jenny know that homework puts stress on family life? Is she simply basing her statements on what may have been the case in her own family?

Evaluating the Assumptions behind the Thesis

During the third pass, it is important to try to understand the assumptions that lie behind the author's position, that is, the underlying values or statements about the world that provide the foundation for the main idea. The assumptions behind the text provide the basis for the author's point and are used to justify what the author is saying. For example, Jenny's paragraph is based on a number of assumptions that derive from her view of homework. Some of these assumptions are as follows:

- that anything that detracts from free time is not good for children
- that giving a child responsibility for homework is harmful because it causes anxiety
- that learning takes place only in the classroom under the supervision of a teacher
- that parents should not be involved in schoolwork

After you are aware of the assumptions behind a work, you are in a better position to evaluate the quality of the argument and the extent to which you accept it. In the example of Jenny's paragraph, you may decide that you do, indeed, agree with it. But, on the other hand, you may also feel that homework can be beneficial.

3. Is the Evidence Reliable?

The Quality of the Reasoning

Some arguments appear to be well thought out, but are really based on fallacious reasoning that cannot withstand careful scrutiny. To evaluate the quality of the reasoning, question whether or not the author's reasons seem logical to you, and be on the alert for arguments based on fallacies, which are discussed in Chapter 3.

An active reader also looks closely at the kind of evidence used to support an argument before deciding to accept it. Evidence in an argumentative essay can take many forms, such as statements from authorities and statistics, and it is important for a careful reader to examine that evidence with a questioning attitude.

Appeals to Authority in a Published Work

Because no one is qualified to make judgments about every topic, writers often use the statements of experts to provide support. However, as an active reader, you should check that a statement from an authority does indeed substantiate what the author is saying and that the authority can really be trusted. Try to find out who these experts are before accepting what they say as absolute truth, and evaluate their statements carefully. Sometimes a statement by an authority is quoted out of context, or authorities in one field are quoted as experts in fields that they really know little about (the use of athletes or movie stars to endorse products is an example of this). Keep in mind that you do not have to accept everything that you read just because an alleged "expert" says that something is so. Maintain a skeptical attitude, and look for other perspectives on the topic before completely accepting a particular point of view, particularly if it does not seem sensible to you.

Statistics

Statistics constitute another means of supporting an argument, and they can be a very convincing means of support. In fact, many students are under the impression that when an article includes statistics, the article is then automatically more reliable. A critical reader is aware, however, that although statistics can often provide valid support, they can also be used to distort rather than to clarify an argument. As an active reader, then, be wary of statistics—they may not mean what they are initially suggested to mean and can be used to suit an author's purpose.

Moreover, statistics can be reported inconsistently. During the Persian Gulf War, *Time* magazine reported the number of Iraqi troops attacking Kuwait as 430,000 (November 12, 1990), 360,000 (October 1, 1990), 50,000 (September 1, 1990), and 100,000 (August 1, 1990). If you wanted an accurate reporting of how many troops Iraq sent to Kuwait during this period, you would need to consult additional sources.

4. Is the Text Stylistically Trustworthy?

Detecting Vagueness and Distortion in Language

Trying to figure out what a text is really saying is sometimes like trying to read through a rain-swept window. And particularly when writers attempt to manipulate, rather than convince, their readers, they sometimes use language to disguise meaning, so that readers have difficulty knowing whether to trust what they read. An important characteristic of a stylistically trustworthy text is that it uses language to communicate with readers, not to confuse them; therefore, you, as an astute reader, should be on the alert for the following stylistic techniques that can sometimes muffle the meaning of a text:

- interpretive words
- words used for emotional effect
- excessive use of abstract rather than concrete language
- ambiguity and distortion

Interpretive Words

Reading with a questioning, critical attitude involves becoming alert to words that *interpret* as opposed to words that simply state the facts. For example, examine the following two statements:

1. A beautiful woman was sitting in the cafe, her elegant hand lightly holding a coffee cup.
2. A woman in her mid-30s with long black hair was sitting in the cafe, her slender fingers lightly holding a coffee cup.

If you read the statements carefully, you will perceive that in the first statement, the reference to the woman as beautiful is only an opinion, the opinion of the author (the author thinks the woman is beautiful, and the author wants the reader to think that the woman is beautiful), whereas the second statement presents particular facts (the woman's age, the color and style of her hair, the slenderness of her fingers, which also suggests that the woman is probably slender because it is unlikely that the author would mention the slenderness of the woman's fingers if she was overweight). One method of distinguishing between facts and opinion, then, is to become sensitive to the many words that interpret, words such as *ugly, dangerous, elegant, bad, best,* and so forth.

Of course, it is not necessarily "bad" to use interpretive language, and indeed no text is entirely interpretation-free. However, in interacting with a text, it is a good idea to be sensitive to interpretive language and of the extent to which that interpretation either enhances or clouds the argument.

Words Used for Emotional Effect

Many words have positive and negative overtones and tend to trigger emotional responses in their readers or hearers. Because such words stimulate an immediate response, they are sometimes used by writers as a shortcut to providing adequate support. Saying that someone is a "bleeding heart," for example, suggests that such a person is inclined to spend money recklessly in a misguided impulse to help the human race. A writer may thus use this term without indicating what sort of spending or what type of misguided humanitarian impulse he or she may mean. Other examples of emotionally loaded language are *nerd, loser,* or *hippie.* Moreover, not all emotionally charged words are negative. *Democracy, freedom,* and *family* are examples of words that stimulate an immediate positive response among readers. Whether such words are positive or negative, be on the alert for extreme statements and exaggerated expressions—they can generate a disproportionately emotional response that can affect your judgment.

For example, reacting against the political correctness movement on college campuses, Dinesh D'Souza writes that the "college classroom" has been transformed from

> a place of learning to a laboratory of indoctrination for social change. Not long ago most colleges required that students learn the basics of the physical sciences and mathematics, the rudiments of economics and finance, and the fundamental principles of American history and government. Studies by the National Endowment for the Humanities show that this coherence has disappeared from the curriculum. As a result, most universities are now graduating students who are scientifically and culturally impoverished, if not illiterate.

"The Visogoths in Tweed," *Forbes* magazine, 1991

In this passage, D'Souza has used several terms that are likely to trigger a strong reaction in his reader, such as "laboratory of indoctrination," suggesting a dictatorial *1984*-like atmosphere, and the reference to students as "scientifically and culturally impoverished, if not illiterate." In essence, D'Souza is implying that the PC movement is responsible for lack of freedom, cultural impoverishment, and illiteracy on college campuses.

Excessive Use of Abstract Rather Than Concrete Language

In his famous and often-anthologized essay, "Politics and the English Language," George Orwell argues that politicians often use abstract language to desensitize the reader to what a politician may actually be writing:

> . . . political language has consisted largely of euphemism, question begging, and sheer cloudy vagueness. Defenseless villages are bombarded from the air, the inhabitants driven out into the countryside, the cattle machine gunned, the huts set on fire with incendiary bullets: This is called pacification. Millions of peasants are robbed of their farms and sent trudging along the roads with no more than they can carry. This is called transfer of population or rectification of frontiers . . .

Orwell's point pertains to a writing style that still exists today. Bureaucratic language, in particular, is often characterized by a high degree of abstraction, the idea being that the reader becomes numb or bored and hence more willing to accept what may be outrageous or preposterous statements.

Another form of ambiguity occurs when words are not adequately defined, a technique that is particularly common in advertising. A facial soap ad claims that the product will "enhance the beauty you were born with," but does not specify what "enhance" means in this context or define what "the beauty you were born with" means. In examining a text with a critical eye, be especially suspicious of words that are not adequately defined; words such as *family values* or *work ethic* are used frequently to put down a particular ethnic or racial group, yet the words are left undefined.

THE THREE-PASS APPROACH: USING THE METHOD

To illustrate how the three-pass approach can help you gain insight into a source, read the article "Educating Tomorrow's Workers: Are We Ignoring Today's Girls?" at the end of this chapter. Here is how the three-pass approach could work with this article:

The First Pass

On first encountering the article, you might begin by asking the following questions:

1. How can your own experience help you understand the article?

Have you had any experiences personally or witnessed or been told about any experiences that suggest that the educational system ignores women or discriminates against women in some way? Do you feel that discriminatory practices do not exist?

2. What do you already know or believe about the topic that is suggested by the *title* and the *subtitle*?

The title is "Educating Tomorrow's Workers," and the subtitle raises the question, "Are We Ignoring Today's Girls?" Although the main point of the article is not directly stated here, you might presume that the article's answer is probably "yes" and that the article is concerned with the harm allegedly done to tomorrow's workers because of this problem. On the basis of the title and the subtitle, then, you might assume that the article focuses on ways that the educational system is ignoring women.

3. Where was this article published? Will where it was published indicate something about the perspective being emphasized?

The note indicates that it was published in *National Business Woman* in the summer of 1992 and that it was written by Marcia Eldredge, who is identified as the "assistant editor of *National Business Woman*." On the basis of the journal and the identity of the author, then, you might presume that the article probably has a particular agenda to promote, most likely that of calling attention to educational inequities against women.

4. Who is the intended audience for this article—that is, who is likely to read *National Business Woman*?

Is the journal read mostly by women who are in business, as the journal's title suggests? Or do other people also read the journal, businessmen, for instance, or people who are not in business?

5. What can you learn from the first and final paragraphs of the article?

The first paragraph indicates that the article is concerned with a report published recently by the American Association of University Women and titled "How Schools Shortchange Girls," and states the thesis of the article quite explicitly, that is, that despite the passage of civil rights acts addressing women, "the rights won on Capitol Hill do not always translate into action for those they are designed to protect," thereby endangering America's competitive business edge. The final paragraph summarizes the main point of the AAUW report and makes the additional point that "what is good for America's school girls will be better for higher education and could ultimately be great for America's competitive business edge."

The Limits of the First Pass

Answering these questions during the first pass can be helpful. But unless you were very familiar with this journal, you would not necessarily know the answers to questions about its intended audience. Also, even if you can identify the writer's agenda, that does not mean that the article is not worth reading or that the author is not worthy of trust. In fact, someone who is an assistant editor of a business-oriented journal is probably well qualified to discuss the impact of education on business and is probably well educated. This person may have a background in journalism as well as business and may be especially concerned with the importance of presenting information fairly. However, awareness of a potential agenda can alert you to possible bias, which might be reflected in a one-sided or unintentionally distorted presentation of information or facts.

The Second Pass

During the second pass, you quickly appraise the article, reading it for meaning and trying to get a sense of how it develops its main point. A quick perusal of "Educating Tomorrow's Workers" indicates that the author uses subheadings to note various times and life stages that place women at an educational disadvantage. These subheadings are as follows: "Early Education," "The Later Years and Self-Esteem," "Teen Pregnancy," "Math and Science," "Special Education," "Public Boys School Rejected," and "Testing." These subheadings can be used to structure the summary, which might read something like this:

In "Educating Tomorrow's Workers: Are We Ignoring Today's Girls?" Marcia Eldredge discusses a report recently published by the American Association of University Women (AAUW) that points out that despite antidiscrimination legislation passed in the early seventies, women still suffer inequities in education. According to the report, these inequities can be traced to unconscious attitudes of teachers during the early years, social pressure and loss of self-esteem during late adolescence, to the perception that teen pregnancy is only a female problem, to gender-biased curriculums and tests, and to a continued stereotyping of students. The article expresses concern that an inequitable educational system is not good for American business, causing the nation to lose its competitive edge.

The Third Pass

During the third pass over "Educating Tomorrow's Workers: Are We Ignoring Today's Girls?" You could evaluate the text by responding to the following questions:

1. Is the argument consistent with what you believe is true or possible about the world and with your concept of human nature?

In asking yourself this question, you might reflect on your own view of the educational system and the extent to which you believe that most educators are sensitive to potential bias against women. Do you believe in the possibility that unconscious bias exists both in the treatment of women in schools and in the creation of a curriculum? If so, then you will be inclined to trust the observations of the author and the report she is discussing.

2. Is the argument supported with appropriate and believable subpoints, examples, and facts?

In evaluating the support provided in this article, you might note that the author cites specific points from the report. However, in some instances, the report itself makes assertions that may not necessarily be true, such as the statement that "school is only one place where they [girls] are reminded of their treatment as second-class citizens." This is a statement that might be open to question and that some might view as an exaggeration. Similarly, under the section "Special Education" the author attributes the presumed neglect that girls suffer to the fact that they are able to sit quietly and are less likely to misbehave, another questionable assumption. However, overall, the author's statements tend to be well supported.

3. Is the evidence reliable?

Although it is sometimes impossible to evaluate the reliability of statistics unless you are very familiar with the subject and the method of sampling, this article cites figures that seem consistent and realistic; moreover, the author uses them judiciously, not making outrageous claims. For example, in the third paragraph, the author cites figures showing that few women hold leadership positions, even in the field of education, where women usually succeed. The discussion of the gender bias in the Scholastic Aptitude Test also seems accurate.

4. Does the argument acknowledge the complexity of the topic?

In some instances, the author acknowledges that other causes beside inequities in the educational system may be responsible for women's lack of professional equality with men. In particular, the author admits that the "report allows that schools are not responsible for the inequality women face in society." For the most part, however, the author is discussing a report that makes a strong case in favor of one position, and the author herself seems strongly in favor of it.

5. Is the text stylistically credible?

The author uses a measured tone, devoid of language that is inflammatory or hysterical. Consequently, the article overall seems believable.

A FORM FOR CRITICAL READING

In this chapter, I have discussed a three-pass approach to reading an outside source, a method that will enable you to "join the ongoing conversation" about issues for your argumentative essays. Some of you may be thinking, though, that analyzing a text in this way will take more time than you are in the habit of devoting to your reading and that you prefer to complete your reading as quickly and efficiently as possible. Critical reading to evaluate the credibility of a published work does require analytical thinking, a process that usually takes more time than a quick skim will allow. Ultimately, though, you will be able to use the three-pass approach quickly and efficiently. As with any new procedure, the more you have practiced it, the more efficiently you will be able to do it— and the gain in insight will more than compensate for the additional time you spent initially.

Here is a form you can use to evaluate outside sources using the three-pass approach:

EVALUATING OUTSIDE SOURCES

Bibliographic Information

Author: _____

Title: _____

Publication Information (Publisher, Place, Date of Publication):

_____

Main Point: _____

Short Summary:

_____

_____

The Writer

Describe the expertise and motives of the writer.

Describe how the writer acknowledges the complexity of the topic.

The Quality of the Argument

Characterize the beliefs about the world implied in this argument.

Characterize the view of human nature that underlies this argument.

Summarize the evidence used to support this argument.

Analyze the use of language. Does it contribute to the credibility of the text?

EXERCISE: ARGUMENTS FOR ANALYSIS

Examine the following articles using the three-pass approach. Which articles do you find the most believable and trustworthy? Which arouse your suspicions? Why?

1. Mike Brake   "Needed: A License to Drink"

2. Rick Newcombe   "Put That in Your Pipe"

3. Peter Brimelow   "Thank You for Smoking . . . ?"

4. Vita Wallace   "Give Children the Vote"

Educating Tomorrow's Workers: Are We Ignoring Today's Girls?
Marcia Eldredge

Marcia Eldredge is the assistant editor of *National Business Woman,* in which this piece originally appeared (Summer 1992).

Are girls treated equally to boys in America's schools? Several recent develop- 1
ments in education throw into question the equity of our system for preparing today's students—tomorrow's workers—for their roles in the future. If America is to remain competitive, at home and abroad, it must begin by providing *all* of its future workers with the same foundation and the same competitive edge. One major development is the recent publication of "How Schools Shortchange Girls," by the American Association of University Women (AAUW) Educational Foundation. The report examines gender issues since passage of Title IX of the 1972 Education Amendments, which prohibits discrimination in educational institutions receiving federal funds. Like many acts passed to ensure equity for women and minorities, the rights won on Capitol Hill do not always translate into action for those they are designed to protect.

"How Schools Shortchange Girls" shows how educators have ignored one- 2
half of their students and how this affects not only young girls and women, but ultimately, America's work force. An equitable education for both girls and boys means a more equitable work force. The inequities detailed in the AAUW report range from unconscious attitudes of teachers, to gender-biased curriculums and tests, to the stereotyping of students. Reports on education are nothing new. In 1983, after the release of "A Nation at Risk," a report published by the U.S. Department of Education, an agenda was set to reform America's schools. Commissions, committees and special study groups were formed to learn why schools were failing America's children. Thirty-five reports issued from these groups were reviewed by the Wellesley College Center for Research on Women for AAUW to determine how much of the material dealt with gender and sex-equity issues. Most of the reports do not define the issues by gender, but four reports do include gender as a category in defining students at risk. Only one of the 35 reviewed addresses Title IX.

As in politics, government and corporate management, America needs more 3
women involved in the decisions that set the agendas and curriculums that are carried out in the nation's classrooms. The statistics show that, although teaching is still a women's field (72 percent of elementary and secondary school teachers are women), few women hold leadership positions. In 1990, women represented only 34 percent of the nation's school board members, 28 percent of principals and 5 percent of superintendents. In 1991, only nine of the 50

chief state school officers were women. Of the 35 commissions, committees and groups evaluating American education, only two had panels of at least 50 percent women.

Early Education

4 According to the AAUW report, there are few studies available of the varying effects of preschool environments on girls and boys. However, there is a common educational myth that suggests preprimary programs are more beneficial to girls than to boys. "How Schools Shortchange Girls" disputes this myth by noting that young girls often arrive in preschool having mastered impulse-control training, small-muscle development and language enhancement. Since these are considered important skills needed for success in early education, teachers turn their attention to the boys who have yet to master the skills. Because girls arrive at school proficient in these skills, one study suggests girls actually benefit less from the preschool experience.

5   According to the AAUW report, this is one of the first biases girls face as they begin their educational experience and, although girls may inherently be more proficient in some basic skills than boys, educators must establish a balanced curricula for preschoolers so that both sexes will benefit equally from their early education experience.

The Later Years and Self-Esteem

6 Upon high school graduation the self-esteem of girls is measurably lower than their male classmates. Although adolescence is a difficult time for both sexes, the report says it is a more difficult transition for girls. The report reminds readers that girls grow into young women in a society where they are both idealized and exploited and that school is only one place where they are reminded of their treatment as second-class citizens. In one report, research shows that being popular and well-liked is more important than being perceived as competent or independent among girls in grades six and seven. Boys, however, ranked being independent and competent as more important.

7   According to the AAUW report, both empirical and clinical studies, as well as public-opinion polls, show significant declines in girls' self-esteem and self-confidence as they move from childhood to early adolescence. The research surveyed in the report asserts that girls' significant drop in self-esteem between elementary school and middle school is due in part to the negative messages girls perceive about women's role in society. Another factor may be that girls experience puberty before boys and that puberty is often a more difficult time for girls than boys. Girls usually experience puberty while making a transition from one school to another, and this is an added stress for students who already are lacking in self-esteem. Research shows that girls' self-esteem benefits if they experience only one transition into high school as opposed to transitions from elementary school into a middle or junior high school and then again into high school.

As girls mature into late adolescence, their self-esteem continues to 8 decline. They are aware that marriage, family and employment are not equal situations for women and men. Although the report allows that schools are not responsible for the inequality women face in society, it holds educators and school administrators partially responsible by suggesting that inequality will not change until schooling changes.

Teen Pregnancy

The risk of pregnancy is an obstacle to success for adolescent girls. In the 9 reports reviewed for the AAUW study, the majority imply that teen pregnancy and dropping out of school are the only significant problems teenage girls face. Yet more than one-half of female drop-outs do so for reasons other than pregnancy. The reports also imply teen girls who give birth are a burden on society by increasing the number of female-headed households. There is no mention of the fathers who often offer little financial support to their children and the teen mothers. The AAUW report suggests that if teen pregnancy was seen as a systemic problem rather than an individual problem, and if policy initiatives focused on improving the educational system rather than girls' personal decisions, there might be fewer high school pregnancies.

Math and Science

In the past 15 years much research has concentrated on gender and math rela- 10 tionships. According to the AAUW report, the gender gap in math is small and declining. Both boys and girls take the same classes and do equally well until the later high school years, at which time boys outnumber girls in higher-level classes such as calculus. The girls who do enroll in these higher level math classes do as well or better in classroom work and tests; however, boys continue to score higher on the Scholastic Aptitude Test, the Advanced Placement Test and other national standardized tests.

According to the report, unlike math, the gender gap in science is not 11 decreasing but may be increasing. Since 1978, the gender gap has remained largest among 17-year-olds. Biology, traditionally the science with the most female representation, is the only field that has experienced a small decline in the gender gap. Again, girls perform the same or better in classroom work and tests, but score lower on national aptitude tests.

Although girls and boys are enrolled in the same science classes until later 12 high school years and express an equal interest in sciences, studies show they have different experiences. Girls tend to be exposed to more biology-related activities than to mechanical and electrical activities. With limited exposure to other fields, it should not be surprising that more females choose to pursue biology fields. When students make course selections in high school, boys tend to enroll in advanced physics and advanced chemistry classes; girls are found in the advanced biology classes. There are repercussions in higher education, too. With such a limited science background, high school girls, including those with exceptional academic preparation in math and science, are choosing math and science careers in disproportionately low numbers—careers that are high-paid, and will be increasingly in demand in our technological economy.

13   Janice Earle, of the National Science Foundation affirms that women are still not choosing the science careers that boys do. "It's not enough to say anyone can sign up for the class. Something more has to happen."

14   She attributes the lack of female science majors in college to girls' elementary and middle school science experience, where, she says, more emphasis on science is needed. Earle suggests that some elementary school teachers avoid science, because they are not prepared to teach it. Often science is an elective course in the master's elementary education discipline rather than a required course.

15   "The gross inequities [in schools] have been addressed, but the subtleties have not," Earle says. There are girls in higher level classes but there are still areas where they are not well represented, such as the advanced placement physics and calculus classes. With few role models for girls, their teachers, parents and peers must encourage them to participate at the advanced levels. It is through this encouragement that some of the subtleties of inequitable teaching will be addressed, she says.

Special Education

16 According to the AAUW report, more than two-thirds of students in special education classes are male. One explanation given for this difference is that boys are born more often with disabling conditions. The report then states that existing data does not, however, support this explanation. Medical reports on learning disabilities indicate that they occur almost equally in boys and girls. One 1988 survey revealed that 70 percent of learning-disabled students enrolled in special education classes were boys. Despite differing study results and contradictory statistics, one statement in the AAUW report suggests that some of the boys enrolled in special-education classes may have little more than behavioral problems. Girls who are more likely to sit quietly and less likely to misbehave, thus less likely to get the attention they deserve, are deprived of the specialized education they may need to develop fully.

Public Boys School Rejected

17 Despite the acts and amendments designed to protect discriminatory behavior in federally funded learning institutions, some administrators insist that girls and boys can get by on "separate but equal" educations. A recent example is the Detroit Board of Education, which, in February 1991, voted to establish three male public elementary schools to combat many of the problems young urban men face; problems such as high drop out rates, homicide, suspension, low grades and poor test scores, many of the same problems young urban girls also face.

18   On behalf of a mother who sought admission to the schools for her three daughters, the National Organization for Women (NOW) Legal Defense and Education Fund and the American Civil Liberties Union of Michigan filed a lawsuit.

According to the NOW Legal Defense and Education Fund, the suit argues 19 that separate educational environments for males suggest that girls are less in need of enhanced educational programs, a message to girls that their educational needs are inferior to those of boys; and that education demonstrating positive male-female interaction, not separation, is the best way to eliminate sexual harassment and anti-women attitudes, which hurt young women and young men.

In August 1991 a federal district court judge ruled that the Detroit Board of 20 Education must admit girls to the schools and issued a preliminary injunction against the school board ordering the development of a plan for admitting girls in the fall of that year.

Testing

Examinations of standardized tests also show bias favoring boys. The most obvi- 21 ous bias is when the number of references to one sex outnumber those of the other sex or if sexes are stereotypically portrayed. In the 1970s, test developers worked to equate the number of references to women and men and to exclude offensive items. Researchers analyzing tests given in 1984, however, showed twice as many references to men as to women, as well as more pictures of and references to boys than to girls. A study of the Scholastic Aptitude Test found references to 42 men and only three women in the reading comprehension passages of the four 1984–85 exams. Classroom tests given by teachers have not been researched and, according to the report, little can be generalized from such tests.

The full AAUW report contains many more examples of an inequitable U.S. 22 educational system. Many of the inequities discussed above are explored more thoroughly in the report and are supported by statistics and research notes. If the AAUW report is taken seriously by education administrators, and if school policy-makers decide girls in America's schools deserve the same education and first-class treatment as their male classmates, not only should girls' test scores and girls' self-esteem increase, the repercussions will extend far beyond primary and secondary schools. What is good for America's school girls will be better for higher education and could ultimately be great for America's competitive business edge.

QUESTIONS

1. What issue is Eldredge addressing in this essay? What is her stance on this issue?
2. What source materials does Eldredge cite? Does she cite from a variety of sources? Do they seem to be plausible authorities? Why or why not?
3. Do you find that you have witnessed a difference in the treatment of boys and girls in your own education? Describe and explain.
4. Can you find statements that sound like facts but that are really statements of opinion? How would you address this issue if you were to write a counterargument?

5. Is Eldredge's use of language stylistically trustworthy? What tone does she adopt for use in this argument?

6. Would this reading alone be enough for you to make a reasonable argument in response to this issue? Why or why not? What questions do you have that you feel must be answered before you can make a logical decision?

Needed: A License to Drink
Mike Brake

Mike Brake writes for the communication department at the Oklahoma State Department of Education. This article is from *Newsweek*
(March 14, 1994).

We buried my cousin last summer. He was 32 when he hanged himself from a 1
closet coat rack in the throes of alcoholism, the fourth of my blood relatives to
die prematurely from this deadly disease. If America issued drinking licenses,
those four men—including my father, who died at 54 of liver failure—might be
alive today.

Addiction to alcohol is one of the primary public-health problems in the 2
United States. It causes more than 19,000 auto fatalities each year, it is responsible for more than a third of deaths from drowning and fire. Booze is a central
factor in divorce. It can trigger incest, child and spousal abuse, suicide, homicide, assault and other crimes. It can kill by the liver, the kidneys, the heart, the
pancreas, the central nervous system. The total cost, from increased jail time to
workplace injuries and lost productivity, is impossible to measure, but a conservative estimate is as high as $90 billion per year. As ways to trim health-care
costs are considered we must recognize that alcoholism is a big contributor to
hospital admissions.

I spent two years working as a counselor in a chemical-dependency treat- 3
ment center and met these "statistics" on a daily basis. I remember the bright
young man who, because he passed out while smoking, lost both legs to terrible burns; the nurse with a master's degree who lost her license and became a
prostitute; and there was the cheerful grandmother dying of liver failure, with
only a few weeks to live. Their families cared about them but could do nothing.
I've seen the helplessness in my own family.

About two thirds of adolescent and adult Americans drink alcohol. Of 4
those, from 8 to 12 percent will become alcoholics or problem drinkers. Much
is being done to confront this huge public-health crisis as judges increasingly
sentence drunk drivers and other alcohol-related offenders to treatment programs and participation in Alcoholics Anonymous. I propose that a national system of licensing, with appropriate penalties, would do more.

Drivers are licensed by every state. There are licenses for fishing and for 5
hunting—hunters are often required to attend gun-safety classes before they
venture afield. These licenses are revocable: if you fail to keep to accepted
norms the state suspends your right to drive, hunt or fish and imposes criminal
penalties should you violate that suspension.

Although this might seem a farfetched idea, I believe drastic measures are 6
needed. Licensing drinking would acknowledge the growing medical consensus

that roughly one drinker in 10 has a genetic predisposition for addiction. In many cases, future alcoholics are dangerously unaware of their internal time bomb. They don't aspire to become drunks, but once trapped in the disease they can do enormous harm to others and themselves.

7   Because some potential alcoholics would not bother to apply for a drinking license, licensing would act as a screen—preventing a small percentage of the misery up-front. Those who do seek a license would follow a path similar to existing driver's licensing procedures.

8   Applicants would be required to study a manual containing basic information about alcohol and the law, much like the driver's manual we all memorized in high school. How many drinks will it take to intoxicate a 150-pound man? What is the penalty for drunk driving? Have any of your blood relatives been treated for alcoholism or chemical dependency? If they have, you need to know that you're at increased risk for developing addiction.

9   The next step would be to pass a written test. License holders would then be able to buy alcoholic beverages (including beer). A liquor store or bar caught selling to an unlicensed drinker would forfeit its license.

10   The 90 percent of us who do not have a problem with alcohol would simply show our licenses at the counter, bar or restaurant—in much the same way as driving to and from work each day with a driver's license.

11   Most of the problem 10 percent would at some point face arrest on an alcohol-related offense. Once convicted they'd lose their license. From that point on, attempting to buy or possess alcohol or being found with a detectable blood level of booze would subject them to a misdemeanor charge—with penalties comparable to those for drunk driving. Unlicensed drinkers who got drunk could be referred to treatment and to Alcoholics Anonymous.

12   Doctors are required to report cases of syphilis, gonorrhea, AIDS and tuberculosis as public-health hazards. They should also be required to report the medical diagnosis of alcoholism. If a patient is admitted to a chemical-dependency treatment center, his drinking license would be suspended. Physicians would report people who show signs of alcoholism after having their licenses rescinded, just as social agencies report parole violators. The objective would be treatment. If the offenders refuse to seek sobriety, they would be unable to get their licenses renewed.

13   A commonly accepted canon of civilized society is that when the public health is threatened, privacy rights must be compromised. Americans rarely die of typhoid, cholera or plague because we have identified their sources. Infectious carriers are quarantined when necessary and offered compassionate and lifesaving treatment.

14   The same criteria should apply to alcoholism, a disease that is the third leading cause of preventable death in this country. The costs inflicted by 18 million drunks, on themselves and on our social fabric, is unacceptable. Congress and the states should cooperate by instigating national drinking licenses, encouraging treatment for those afflicted and imposing firm penalties on violators. It's not such a crazy idea.

QUESTIONS

1. What is Brake's position on the issue of licensing alcohol? How does he use personal experience to support his position? Is this experience a useful entry into this debate? Is he a credible authority?
2. Brake compares licenses issued for driving with his own proposal for licenses issued for drinking. Is this a fair comparison? What would be the differences between driver's licenses and drinker's licenses? What would be the similarities?
3. Does Brake's proposal really address the problem of alcoholism? Is it consistent with what you believe is true of human behavior? Cite examples from the text.
4. Is the style of this essay trustworthy? Keeping in mind that Brake is an expert in communication, why do you think he chose this particular style to make his point?
5. What do you know about the publication this essay first appeared in? Does your knowledge (or lack of knowledge) about this publication change the way you approach this essay? What might you assume about the magazine on the basis of its title alone?
6. If you were to write an argumentative essay on this topic, what kind of material would you need to find to support it? How would you use this essay if it were one of your source materials?

Put That in Your Pipe
Rick Newcombe

This essay is from *Reason* (July 1994).

1   The end of the last century saw the birth of two Germans who are among the most famous individuals in history: Adolf Hitler, the bloodthirsty dictator, and Albert Einstein, the peace-loving scientific genius. Both men held strong views about smoking, and it is worth examining their opinions as we approach the end of the current century. This is especially true in light of the bills pending in Congress that would ban smoking in buildings open to the public, raise tobacco taxes by huge percentages, and regulate tobacco as a drug.

2   Hitler was a zealot about many things, so it is not surprising that he was an extremist on the subject of smoking, which he considered vile and disgusting. "Adolf Hitler was a fanatical opponent of tobacco," reports *Time*. He was fond of proclaiming that women of the Third Reich did not smoke, even though many of them did. In his fascinating book *Cigarettes Are Sublime*, Richard Klein, a professor of French literature at Cornell University, writes that Hitler was "a fanatically superstitious hater of tobacco smoke."

3   Einstein, on the other hand, was very passionate about his pipe smoking. During one lecture, he ran out of pipe tobacco and borrowed some cigarettes from his students so he could crumple the tobacco into his pipe. "Gentlemen," he said, "I believe we've made a great discovery!" He later decided that his conclusion was premature. He realized that cigarette tobacco lacks the aroma, the fullness, and the taste of pipe tobacco. But what appealed most to Einstein was the entire ritual of pipe smoking: carefully choosing from a variety of pipes and tobaccos, delicately loading the briar, puffing and tamping, and the associated contemplation. "I believe that pipe smoking contributes to a somewhat calm and objective judgment in all human affairs," he said in 1950 at age 71, when he became a lifetime member of the Montreal Pipe Smokers Club.

4   Fanatical intolerance, as opposed to moderation and consideration, is at the heart of the smoking debate in America today. The Occupational Safety and Health Administration wants to ban smoking in the workplace. Rep. Henry Waxman (D-Calif.) has proposed what he calls the Smoke-Free Environment Act, which would prohibit smoking in any building that is entered by 10 or more people at least one day a week (except residences, so far). What if the building is privately owned and its owner wants to smoke? Too bad. His private building will be classified as a "public facility." I am a successful entrepreneur who is responsible for sending millions of tax dollars to the state and federal governments each year—from my own taxes, from my company, from our shareholders, from our employees, from our clients, and from our vendors. This tax money finances politicians seeking to pass laws forbidding me to smoke a pipe in my own office.

In addition to the proposed smoking bans, the Clinton health plan would raise 5 the tax on certain cigars by more than 3,000 percent, on pipe tobacco by nearly 2,000 percent, and on chewing tobacco by more than 10,000 (!) percent. Supporters of these tax hikes should read some history. King James I of England, who hated smoking as much as Henry Waxman does, raised tobacco taxes by 4,000 percent. Instead of stamping out tobacco use, he created a huge black market.

David Kessler, head of the Food and Drug Administration, wants to regulate 6 tobacco as a drug, which under the agency's usual standards would probably mean banning it. (Can you imagine what our overcrowded prisons would be like if tobacco were banned?) *New York Times* columnist Anna Quindlen praises Kessler, as well as the "courageous" members of Congress who are eager to suspend the First Amendment by restricting tobacco advertising.

Smoking has been around for hundreds of years, and it won't go away, 7 regardless of legislation. The *Los Angeles Times* recently observed: "Russia once whipped smokers, Turkey beheaded them and India slit their noses. The Massachusetts colony outlawed public smoking in the 1630s, and Connecticut required smokers to have permits in the 1940s. At various times between 1893 and 1921, cigarette sales were banned in North Dakota, South Dakota, Washington, Iowa, Tennessee, Arkansas, Illinois, Utah, Kansas and Minnesota." Despite such efforts, about a billion people around the world continue to smoke.

As Klein, the Cornell professor, notes, there is a direct link between freedom 8 and the right to smoke. He writes: "Like other tyrants such as Louis XIV, Napoleon, and Hitler, James I despised smoking and demonized tobacco. The relation between tyranny and the repression of the right to grow, sell, use, or smoke tobacco can be seen most clearly in the way movements of liberation, revolutions both political and cultural, have always placed those rights at the center of their political demands. The history of the struggle against tyrants has been frequently inseparable from that of the struggle on behalf of the freedom to smoke."

Cigarette smokers are reluctant to speak out against anti-smoking measures. It is difficult to be a moderate cigarette smoker, and the typical cigarette 9 smoker is clearly at risk of suffering heart attacks, lung cancer, and emphysema. Despite these health hazards, adults have a right to continue smoking cigarettes. But I hope they will consider pipe smoking as an alternative. The difference between chainsmoking cigarettes and moderate pipe smoking is the difference between drinking a case of beer every day and having a glass of wine with lunch or dinner.

Pipe smoking is a fun hobby. It is relaxing. It tastes good. It feels good. It 10 helps us unwind. It helps us cope with stress. It enhances objectivity. It facilitates contemplation. People like Waxman and Kessler never mention these intangible benefits. They just want to know if the activity in question is "good for you" in a strict biological sense. If not, or if they think it is bad for you, they will attempt to outlaw it. This sort of reasoning would also support a ban on obesity, a requirement that all Americans exercise, the prohibition of junk food, limits on alcohol and caffeine consumption, and so on. The irony is that Waxman is, frankly, a little chubby, while Kessler used to be fat (and yo-yo dieting is quite unhealthy).

11   Compare these two with Arnold Schwarzenegger, who is as healthy as a horse and a dedicated cigar and occasional pipe smoker. I work out regularly myself. I have even trained with Arnold. In fact, I am something of a health nut. I go for a five-mile run at least once a week as part of my exercise program, which includes a minimum of four hours of strenuous workouts each week. I am in terrific physical condition. Yet I'm put on the defensive and treated as a pariah because I enjoy a pipe.

12   Our tax money is used to sponsor anti-smoking propaganda—official hate speech from the state. Anti-smoking billboards and TV commercials are aimed at encouraging the average citizen to loathe smoking and, by implication, smokers. Several days ago, I was standing on a street corner in Santa Monica waiting for the light to turn green. A city bus with an anti-smoking message on the side passed by, spewing filthy exhaust fumes. I crossed the street and entered the Tinder Box, a tobacco shop that was founded when Calvin Coolidge was president. The aroma was magnificent. I chatted with the store's founder, Ed Kolpin, who has come to work every day since 1928. He was puffing on his pipe, looking very contented. Ed attributes his good health and long life to the sense of peace that 65 years of relaxed and intelligent pipe smoking have given him.

13   Ed reminded me of a story about François Guizot, the French historian and statesman. A woman visited Guizot at his home one evening and found him absorbed in his pipe. She exclaimed, "What! You smoke, and yet have arrived at so great an age?" "Ah, madame," he said in reply, "if I had not smoked, I should have been dead 10 years ago." I believe we would have heard similar replies from many other famous pipe smokers who lived long and healthy lives, including Albert Schweitzer, Mark Twain, F. A. Hayek, Carl Sandburg, Bing Crosby, and Norman Rockwell.

QUESTIONS

1. What is Newcombe's purpose in this argument? What is his point? Is this point valid? Why or why not?
2. How is this article constructed? Can you outline it?
3. How does Newcombe use history in his argument? Is this historical perspective valuable? Why or why not?
4. Using the evaluating tips you've learned in this chapter, which points do you find most convincing? Why are they convincing? Which points are least convincing? Why?
5. Construct a counterargument in the academic genre. Note key points in Newcombe's essay where you do not feel he has fully addressed the issue at hand.
6. Compare this article to the piece by Brimelow. Which is more convincing? Why is it more convincing?

Thank You for Smoking . . . ?
Peter Brimelow

Peter Brimelow is a senior editor for *Forbes* magazine. This article is from *Forbes* magazine (July 4, 1994).

The hangperson's noose is unmistakably around the tobacco industry's neck. In Florida and Mississippi, state governments are attempting to force tobacco companies to pay some smoking-related health care costs. In Washington, D.C., the Environmental Protection Agency has claimed that "secondhand smoke" is a significant risk for nonsmokers and the Food & Drug Administration is making noises about regulating nicotine as a drug. And recently the American Medical Association agreed, reasserting that nicotine is addictive. Smokers have already been driven from many workplaces into the street for a furtive puff. But further legal harassment, to the point of what an industry spokesman calls "backdoor prohibition," seems unstoppable.   1

Lost in this lynching frenzy: the fact that smoking might be, in some small ways, good for you.   2

Hold on now! Let's be clear: *The Surgeon General has* indeed *determined that smoking is dangerous to your health.* Lung cancer and cardiovascular diseases are highly correlated with cigarette consumption. Annual smoking-related deaths are commonly said to be over 400,000 (although critics say the number is inflated).   3

But so is driving automobiles dangerous to your health (over 40,000 deaths a year). Yet people do it, because it has rewards as well as risk. And they judge, as individuals, that the reward outweighs the risk.   4

This is called freedom.   5

Well, what are the rewards of cigarette smoking? Apart from intangible pleasure, the most obvious is behavioral. A battery of studies, such as those by British researcher D.M. Warburton, show that cigarettes, whatever their other effects, really do stimulate alertness, dexterity and cognitive capacity.   6

And alertness, dexterity, etc. can be useful. Such as when driving. Or flying—as Congress recognized when it exempted airline pilots from the ban on smoking on domestic flights.   7

These behavioral benefits suggest an answer to the Great Tobacco Mystery: why almost a third of adult Americans continue to do something they are told, incessantly and insistently, is bad for them. (Duke University economist W. Kip Viscusi reported in his 1992 book, *Smoking: Making the Risky Decision,* that survey data show smokers, if anything, exaggerate the health danger of their habit.)   8

Smokers, according to numerous studies such as those by University of Michigan researchers Ovide and Cynthia Pomerleau, are different from nonsmok-   9 ers. They tend toward depression and excitability. Current understanding is that nicotine is "amphoteric"—that is, it can act to counter both conditions, depending on how it is consumed. (Quick puffs stimulate, long drags calm.)

10   The implication is fascinating: A large part of the population seems to be aware of its significant although not pathological personality quirks, and to have discovered a form of self-medication that regulates them.

11   Of course, this explanation for the stubbornness of smokers is not as satisfying as what Washington prefers to believe: mass seduction by the wicked tobacco companies and their irresistible advertising. Nor would it justify huge rescue operations by heroic politicians and bureaucrats.

12   Beyond its behavioral effects, smoking seems also to offer subtler health rewards to balance against its undisputed risks:

- *Parkinson's disease.* The frequency of this degenerative disorder of the nervous system among smokers appears to be half the rate among non-smokers—an effect recognized by the Surgeon General as long ago as 1964.

- *Alzheimer's disease.* Similarly, the frequency of this degenerative mental disorder has recently been found to be as much as 50% less among smokers than among nonsmokers—for example, by the 11 studies reviewed in the *International Journal of Epidemiology* in 1991.

- *Endometrial cancer.* There is extensive and long-standing evidence that this disease of the womb occurs as much as 50% less among smokers—as documented by, for example, a *New England Journal of Medicine* article back in 1985. The triggering mechanism appears to be a reduction in estrogen levels.

- *Prostate cancer.* Conversely, smoking seems to raise estrogen levels in men and may be responsible for what appears to be a 50% lower rate of prostate cancer among smokers, although this needs corroboration.

- *Osteoarthritis.* This degenerative disorder of bone and cartilage is up to five times less likely to occur among heavy smokers—as documented, for example, by the federal government's first Health and Nutrition Examination Survey.

- *Colon cancer, ulcerative colitis.* These diseases of the bowel seem to be about 30% and 50% less frequent among smokers—documented, for example, by articles in the *Journal of the American Medical Association* and in the *New England Journal of Medicine* in 1981 and 1983, respectively.

13   Other benefits that have been suggested for smoking: lower rates of sarcoidosis and allergic alveolitis, both lung disorders, and possibly even acne. Smokers are also lighter—ironic, because obesity is a leading cause of the cardiovascular disease that smoking is also supposed to exacerbate. So you could quit smoking and still die of a heart attack because of the weight you put on.

None of these health benefits is enough to persuade doctors to recommend 14
occasional cigarettes, in the way that some now occasionally recommend a
glass of wine.

But consider this theoretical possibility: Should 60-year-olds take up smok- 15
ing because its protection against Alzheimer's is more immediate than its potential damage to the lungs, which won't show up for 30 years if at all?

A theoretical possibility—and likely to remain theoretical. Research into 16
possible benefits of tobacco and nicotine is widely reported to be stymied by
the absolutist moral fervor of the antismoking campaign.

Under the Carter Administration, the federal government abandoned its 17
research into safer cigarettes in favor of an attack on all smoking. No effort is
made to encourage smokers to switch to pipes and cigars, although their users'
lung cancer and heart disease rates are five to ten times lower (somewhat offset
by minor increases in mouth and throat cancers). There is no current support
for studies of the marginal increase in danger for each cigarette smoked,
although it appears the human system can clear the effects of three to five of
the (much stronger) pre-1960 cigarettes, if dispersed across a day, with relatively little risk.

Instead, the extirpation of smoking has become another "moral equivalent 18
of war"—as President Carter called the energy crisis in the 1970s, and as price
and wage controls were viewed earlier. There is no role for tradeoffs, risk-
reward calculations or free choice.

Why don't tobacco companies point out the potential offsetting rewards of 19
smoking? Besides the usual corporate cowardice and bureaucratic inertia, the
answer may be another, typically American, disease—lawyers. Directing the
companies' defense, they apparently veto any suggestion that smoking has
benefits for fear of liability suits and of the possible regulatory implications if
nicotine is seen as a drug.

Which leaves smokers defenseless against a second typically American dis- 20
ease: the epidemic of power-hungry puritanical bigots.

QUESTIONS

1. This essay was originally published in *Forbes* magazine. What kind of
   magazine is *Forbes?* What would you expect this magazine to be about?
   If you don't know, how could you find out?
2. Do Brimelow's sources seem to be authoritative enough to support his
   argument? Is there sufficient information to make an informed decision
   as to their plausibility? Why or why not?
3. Identify the facts in this essay. Identify the opinions as well. Do they
   seem well balanced? Do the opinions arise from the discussion of the
   facts? Explain.
4. Brimelow feels that the political agenda concerning smoking forces us to
   disregard information that points to the contrary. What is your opinion?

Is the antismoking movement a political action or a health issue? What do you base your opinion on?

5. How are statistics used in this essay? Do you have enough information about the issue to determine their reliability? What questions would you like to ask about these statistical studies?

6. Having examined this essay, do you feel that moderate cigarette smoking should be encouraged in light of the beneficial side effects that Brimelow describes? Explain in detail.

Give Children the Vote
Vita Wallace

Vita Wallace, who was 16 when this article was published, lives in
Philadelphia. The essay originally appeared in *The Nation* (October
14, 1991).

I first became interested in children's rights two years ago, when I learned that   1
several states had passed laws prohibiting high school dropouts from getting
driver's licenses. I was outraged, because I believe that children should not be
forced to go to school or be penalized if they choose not to, a choice that is certainly the most sensible course for some people.

I am what is called a home schooler. I have never been to school, having   2
always learned at home and in the world around me. Home schooling is
absolutely legal, yet as a home schooler, I have had to defend what I consider to
be my right to be educated in the ways that make the most sense to me, and so
all along I have felt sympathy with people who insist on making choices about
how they want to be educated, even if that means choosing not to finish high
school. Now this choice is in jeopardy.

Since first learning about the discriminatory laws preventing high school   3
dropouts from getting driver's licenses that have been passed by some state legislatures, I have done a lot of constitutional and historical research that has convinced me that children of all ages must be given the same power to elect their
representatives that adults have, or they will continue to be unfairly treated and
punished for exercising the few legal options they now have, such as dropping
out of high school.

Most people, including children themselves, probably don't realize that   4
children are the most regulated people in the United States. In addition to all
the laws affecting adults, including tax laws, children must comply with school
attendance laws, child labor laws, and alcohol and cigarette laws. They are
denied driver's licenses because of their age, regardless of the dropout issue;
they are victims of widespread child abuse; and they are blatantly discriminated
against everywhere they go, in libraries, restaurants and movie theaters. They
have no way to protect themselves: Usually they cannot hire lawyers or bring
cases to court without a guardian, and they are not allowed to vote.

The child labor and compulsory schooling laws were passed by well-meaning   5
people to protect children from exploitation. Child labor laws keep children
from being forced to work, and compulsory schooling allows all children to get
an education. But the abolition of slavery in 1865 didn't end the exploitation of
black people. They needed the right to vote and the ability to bring lawsuits
against their employers. Children need those rights too. Without them, laws
that force children to go to school and generally do not allow them to work may

be necessary to prevent exploitation, but they also take away children's rights
as citizens to life, liberty and the pursuit of happiness. In my case, the compulsory education laws severely limited my right to pursue the work that is important to me (which is surely what "the pursuit of happiness" referred to in the
Declaration of Independence).

6   I am 16 now, still not old enough to vote. Like all children, then, the only
way I can fight for children's rights is by using my freedom of speech to try to
convince adults to fight with me. While I am grateful that I have the right to
speak my mind, I believe that it is a grave injustice to deny young people the
most effective tool they could have to bring about change in a democracy. For
this reason, I suggest that the right of citizens under 18 to vote not be denied or
abridged on account of age.

7   Many people argue that it would be dangerous to let loose on society a
large group of new voters who might not vote sensibly. They mean that children might not vote for the right candidates. The essence of democracy, however, is letting people vote for the wrong candidates. Democratic society has its
risks, but we must gamble on the reasonableness of all our citizens, because it
is less dangerous than gambling on the reasonableness of a few. That is why we
chose to be a democracy instead of a dictatorship in the first place.

8   As it is, only 36 to 40 percent of adults who are eligible to vote actually vote
in nonpresidential years, and about 25 percent of the population is under 18. As
you can see, our representatives are elected by a very small percentage of our citizens. That means that although they are responsible *for* all of us, they are responsible *to* only a few of us. Politicians usually do all they can to keep that few happy,
because both voters and politicians are selfish, and a politician's re-election
depends on the well-being of the voters. Large segments of society that are not
likely or not allowed to vote are either ignored or treated badly because of this
system. It would be too much to expect the few always to vote in the interests of
the many. Under these circumstances, surely the more people who vote the better, especially if they are of both sexes and of all races, classes and ages.

9   People also claim that children are irresponsible. Most of the teenagers
who act irresponsibly do so simply because they are not allowed to solve their
problems in any way that would be considered responsible—through the
courts or legislature. They fall back on sabotage of the system because they are
not allowed to work within it.

10   Some people believe that children would vote the way their parents tell
them to, which would, in effect, give parents more votes. Similarly, when the
Nineteenth Amendment was passed in 1920, giving women the vote, many people thought women would vote the way their husbands did. Now women are
so independent that the idea of women voting on command seems absurd. The
Nineteenth Amendment was a large part of the process that produced their
independence. I think a similar and equally desirable result would follow if children were allowed to vote. They are naturally curious, and most are interested
in the electoral process and the results of the elections even though they are
not allowed to vote. Lacking world-weary cynicism, they see, perhaps even

more clearly than their elders, what is going on in their neighborhoods and what is in the news.

Suffragist Belle Case La Follette's comment that if women were allowed to 11 vote there would be a lot more dinner-table discussion of politics is as true of children today. More debate would take place not only in the home but among children and adults everywhere. Adults would also benefit if politics were talked about in libraries, churches, stores, laundromats and other places where children gather.

People may argue that politicians would pander to children if they could 12 vote, promising for instance that free ice cream would be distributed every day. But if kids were duped, they would not be duped for long. Children don't like to be treated condescendingly.

Even now, adults try to manipulate children all the time in glitzy TV ads or, 13 for example, in the supposedly educational pamphlets that nuclear power advocates pass out in school science classes. Political candidates speak at schools, addressing auditoriums full of captive students. In fact, schools should be no more or less political than workplaces. Children are already exposed to many different opinions, and they would likely be exposed to even more if they could vote. The point is that with the vote, they would be better able to fight such manipulation, not only because they would have the power to do so but because they would have added reason to educate themselves on the issues.

What I suggest is that children be allowed to grow into their own right to 14 vote at whatever rate suits them individually. They should not be forced to vote, as adults are not, but neither should they be hindered from voting if they believe themselves capable, as old people are not hindered.

As for the ability to read and write, that should never be used as a criterion 15 for eligibility, since we have already learned from painful past experience that literacy tests can be manipulated to insure discrimination. In any case, very few illiterate adults vote, and probably very few children would want to vote as long as they couldn't read or write. But I firmly believe that, whether they are literate or not, the vast majority of children would not attempt to vote before they are ready. Interest follows hand in hand with readiness, something that is easy to see as a home schooler but that is perhaps not so clear to many people in this society where, ironically, children are continually taught things when they are not ready, and so are not interested. Yet when they are interested, as in the case of voting, they're told they are not yet ready. I think I would not have voted until I was 8 or 9, but perhaps if I had known I could vote I would have taken an interest sooner.

Legally, it would be possible to drop the voting-age requirements. In the 16 Constitution, the states are given all powers to set qualifications for voters except as they defy the equal protection clause of the Fourteenth Amendment, in which case Congress has the power to enforce it. If it were proved that age requirements "abridge the privileges or immunities of citizens of the United States" (which in my opinion they do, since people born in the United States or to U.S. citizens are citizens from the moment they are born), and if the states could not come up with a "compelling interest" argument to justify a limit at a particular age, which Justices Potter Stewart, Warren Burger and Harry Blackmun agreed they could not in *Oregon v. Mitchell* (the Supreme Court case challenging the 1970 amendment to the Voting Rights Act that gave 18-year-olds the vote), then age requirements would be unconstitutional. But it is not necessary that they be unconstitutional for the states to drop them. It is within the power of the states to do that, and I believe that we must start this movement at the state level. According to *Oregon v. Mitchell,* Congress cannot change the qualifications for voting in state elections except by constitutional amendment, which is why the Twenty-sixth Amendment setting the voting age at 18 was necessary. It is very unlikely that an amendment would pass unless several states had tried eliminating the age requirement and had good results. The experience of Georgia and Kentucky, which lowered their age limits to 18, helped to pass the Twenty-sixth Amendment in 1971.

17   Already in our country's history several oppressed groups have been able to convince the unoppressed to free them. Children, who do not have the power to change their situation, must now convince the adults who do to allow them that power.

QUESTIONS

1. Wallace was 16 years old when this essay was written (in 1991). Does her age influence your opinion of the essay? Do you feel that she's representative of most teenagers?

2. Is it appropriate to compare children's voting rights to the suffrage movement? Does the author account for any differences in this comparison?

3. What assumptions does Wallace make about children and their rights? Do these assumptions need further development?

4. When you were 16 could you have made an informed opinion about a political candidate? What kind of knowledge did you have at that age to base your opinions on?

5. Do you believe that children are oppressed by the American political system? Try using exploration questions (Chapter 3) to find your stance on this issue.

6. How does Wallace use her sources? Do the sources actively support her argument, or do they simply provide a context? Are the sources used convincingly?

Chapter 5

CONSIDERING YOUR AUDIENCE: ESTABLISHING CREDIBILITY

Because the purpose of an argumentative essay is to have an impact on an intended audience, it is important to think about who that audience might be and to anticipate how it is likely to react to you and your ideas. This chapter discusses several strategies for thinking about your audience and explains *Rogerian argument,* a form of argumentation that particularly depends on an understanding of audience. It also presents some techniques through which you can create a credible writing self within a text—that is, establish *ethos* by convincing an audience that you are trustworthy, knowledgeable, logical, and fair.

THE GENERAL AUDIENCE VERSUS THE TEACHER

Although all arguments are written to be read by an audience, it is sometimes difficult to define exactly who that audience actually is. If you think of *audience* as referring only to those who will actually read the essay, you may believe that your audience consists only of your teacher, or maybe your roommate. College essays, however, are not usually written for a specific person; usually, they are addressed to what is termed a "general audience," a vague concept that might be defined as *anyone with sufficient background in and concern for the subject who might choose to read the essay.*

Teachers may sometimes add to your confusion about audience by saying "consider your audience," without specifying what sort of audience you should consider. As a result, you may write your essay without thinking about audience at all, or if you do, you may think of it simply as your own teacher. Of course, your teacher is indeed someone who will be reading your essay, and it is certainly wise to consider your teacher's concerns and expectations. But it is not a good idea to think of audience only in this way. If you write only to your teacher, you may omit a lot of important information—explanations, definitions, or support—because you assume that the teacher is already familiar with the topic and will therefore not need very much background.

Another problem that results from confusion over the concept of audience is that you may inadvertently use an inappropriate tone or present only one side of an issue. A few of my students, for example, have written blatantly one-sided, aggressive, or often poorly reasoned harangues on a topic rather than the thoughtful, reasoned response appropriate to the genre of academic argument because they have not thought about the reaction of an audience. Remember that statements such as "Anyone who thinks this is just a racist" or "These ideas are hopelessly old-fashioned" are more likely to offend than to convince an audience and will therefore not contribute to the persuasiveness of your essay.

Being aware of audience and focusing on audience as ways of exploring the topic have the following advantages:

1. They help you keep in mind that the teacher is not the only audience for an argumentative essay.
2. They serve as means of generating ideas and of figuring out what additional information is needed.
3. They focus attention on the purpose of argumentative writing, to address a reader, not simply to express your own ideas.
4. They enable you to distinguish when it is appropriate to confront an opponent directly and when it is more appropriate to strive for change through mutual acceptance and understanding.
5. They help you decide what to emphasize.

Creating Your Audience

The well-known novelist John Updike claims that when he writes, he doesn't aim his work either for the sophisticated New York critics who will review his books nor for the crowds of city shoppers who will browse through them in bookstores. Rather, Updike claims that he directs his writing toward a spot "a little east of Kansas" where the books sit on library shelves without their jackets and where a "countryish teen-aged boy" will find them. Updike says that as he writes, he wants his books to speak particularly to that boy. Although this boy is not someone whom Updike knows personally, he conceives of him as the reader of his books. Updike thus "creates" an audience for his work that helps him focus his writing.

College writers can also find it helpful to think about a specific person toward whom the writing will be addressed, and, to a certain extent, to actually create that person. The technique called "character prompts" will help you create such a person and focus attention on your potential audience.

Using Character Prompts

Working with character prompts allows you to experiment with forms of writing usually associated with fiction or drama. To use this strategy, imagine that you are at a gathering (a party, a dinner, or a meeting, for example) where the subject of your assignment is being discussed. You listen to the conversation for a while and then notice someone who has a particularly strong opinion about it. Study this character and pay close attention to what he or she is saying. Try to gain insight into his or her values and ideas and to understand the feelings behind the words. Then answer the following:

1. What is this person's name, age, and profession? Describe this person's physical appearance.
2. What is this person's current attitude toward this topic?
3. How much does this person know about the topic?
4. Describe this person's value system.
5. How does this person's value system influence his or her attitude toward the topic?
6. Which aspect of the topic does this character find most disturbing?

In Chapter 2, I presented a scenario in which Brian, a college student, had decided to write a letter to his Uncle Stan about his decision to transfer from State to Northern College. In this hypothetical scenario, one would presume that Brian would know Uncle Stan quite well, so he would have no trouble "creating" his audience. Some of you may also "know" your audience; in fact, some instructors specify a particular audience for their students. But even if you think you know all about your audience, it is a good idea to write responses to these questions because the act of writing will lead to the discovery of new material. Here is how Brian "created" Uncle Stan as his audience.

1. Imagine this person with a name, an age, a profession, and a physical appearance:

Uncle Stan's name is Stan Rodgers. He is 67 years old and has no children. He is five-foot-nine, a little overweight, has thinning gray-brown hair, and a sort of wide face. He dresses pretty conservatively. He has a well-paying administrative position in a large company. He is not wealthy but is very comfortable.

2. What is this person's current attitude toward this topic?

Uncle Stan thinks that State College is a fantastic place. He went there as an undergraduate, loved getting involved in school sports as a spectator, and thought the business major was terrific preparation for getting a good job. He also loved the sports teams at State.

3. How much does this person know about the topic?

Actually, Uncle Stan may not know much about Northern College or about the program in environmental studies. (This information should probably be included in my letter.)

4. Describe this person's value system.

Uncle Stan is very concerned with success, and to him "success" means earning a fair amount of money. He is also concerned with being "up-to-date." He reads several newspapers every day to make sure he knows what's happening.

(The letter should probably stress that environmental studies is an up-and-coming field and that even people who work in business will have to know something about it.)

5. How does this person's value system influence his or her attitude toward the topic?

Uncle Stan thinks that making money is very important and that the best way to make money is to study business. (Maybe the letter can convince him that success means different things to different people?)

6. Which aspect of the topic does this character find most disturbing?

Uncle Stan definitely does not approve of studying a subject that does not lead to a good job after graduation. He's always talking about his nephew, Paul, who majored in creative writing and couldn't find any way of making money except by working in a fast food restaurant as a busboy. (The essay can explain that there are many jobs for environmentalists these days and that the courses the major requires include skills that can lead to a job. Actually, the math and computer requirement is even more rigorous than the one the Business School requires, something that should be included in the letter.)

You will note that as Brian responded to the prompts, his answers suggested new directions for investigation as well as information to include in his letter to Uncle Stan. Another way that character prompts can assist you is by influencing how you wish to present *yourself* in your essay. Personality is not static—to some extent, it changes according to whom we are with, which means that you are one person with your parents, another with your friends, another with your teachers, and so on. Realizing that there are many facets of the self, conscious writers *choose* who they wish to be when they write—in a sense, they *create themselves* as much as they create their audience, and that act of creation helps shape the text. Responding to character prompts thus will enable you to think about which aspect of yourself you wish to present in your essay.

UNDERSTANDING AUDIENCE THROUGH DIALOGUE

Conceiving of argumentation in terms of a **dialogue** or exchange about a topic is another strategy that can help you focus your ideas. Brian might find it useful to imagine himself having a dialogue with Uncle Stan in order to anticipate any points Uncle Stan might make about why Brian should remain at State College. Similarly, in writing argumentative essays for your college classes, you might find it useful to imagine a potential opponent, anticipate opposing points this opponent might make, and think about how you might refute them.

The idea that the genre of argument begins in dialogue is useful not only because it can help you develop ideas and strategies that can be used against a potential opposition, but also because it can highlight points of agreement between you and your reader. When writers acknowledge that they understand how their opponents might feel or believe, they present themselves as thoughtful and trustworthy because these points of agreement serve as a bridge or a link. If Brian can demonstrate that he understands Uncle Stan's point of view, Uncle Stan is more likely to trust Brian and to pay attention to Brian's ideas. It is as if Brian is saying, "I understand how you feel, and in fact there are many aspects of this topic about which the two of us agree. But here is where the two of us differ."

Writing a Dialogue

To utilize dialogue in the exploration of a topic, recall the character you created through character prompts. Then, assume that after listening to the character you have imagined, you decide to enter the discussion and engage in a dialogue with him or her. Script this exchange in a dialogue of one to two pages, remembering that both participants should be presented as polite and intelligent people. In this exchange, no one should make outrageous or insulting statements and no one should win. The aim is to generate an exchange of ideas, not to score points over an adversary.

Brian's Dialogue

BRIAN: Uncle Stan, I've been spending a lot of time thinking about where I ought to go to college.

UNCLE STAN: But you're already in college. Haven't you been enrolled at State since last September?

BRIAN: Yes, of course. And I've actually been pretty happy. I mean, State has a great business school and fantastic sports teams. It's pretty well known on a national level also. People are impressed when I say I go to State.

UNCLE STAN: That's right. Even when I went to State, its reputation was terrific. It was known nationally—even in Europe, people knew about it. And those teams. Boy, some of my happiest moments were spent cheering on the State Walruses. And I had a really excellent grounding in business, a really excellent grounding.

BRIAN: You know, Uncle Stan, I used to feel exactly the same way.

UNCLE STAN: What do you mean, "Used to feel"?

BRIAN: Well, this year I've done some serious investigation into job opportunities. And the jobs for people with straight business degrees just aren't there anymore.

UNCLE STAN: Is that so?

BRIAN: Right. Nowadays, with tight economic conditions, the jobs are for people in newer fields. People who get the jobs are those who have all of the training that used to be associated with business—lots of math and computer experience, for example—but they also know about some of the newer fields.

UNCLE STAN: What fields are you talking about?

BRIAN: Well, like environmental studies, for example. I took a geography course last semester, and I learned about all sorts of job opportunities in environmental policy, jobs involving field work, government jobs, lots of possibilities.

UNCLE STAN: It sounds like that's what you plan to major in at State.

BRIAN: Well, not exactly. You see, State doesn't have a major in environmental policy. But there is a terrific program at Northern College.

UNCLE STAN: Northern? That's a smaller school, isn't it? It certainly didn't have much of a reputation when I went to State. In fact, the kids who went to Northern were the ones who didn't get into State.

BRIAN: That's all changed now, Uncle Stan. Northern's reputation has really come up. It's still true that Northern is smaller than State, but that means the classes are smaller and that you get more attention from the teachers. For me, that's really important. I learned so much from just talking with my geography teacher after class—in a way, I learned more in those conversations than I did in class.

UNCLE STAN: And you say that there are job opportunities in environmental studies?

BRIAN: Yes. I've even got a list of jobs that graduates in environmental policy have gotten right after graduation. It looks like they're doing okay.

UNCLE STAN: Well, it looks as if you know what you're doing. At least you did your homework. So you want to transfer to Northern?

BRIAN: Oh, yes, Uncle Stan. Environmental policy is such an interesting field. I can see all sorts of possibilities in it for me. I know this is the right choice.

This dialogue, of course, presumes that Uncle Stan is a reasonable person and will not simply shout, "I went to State. You're going to State. That's all there is to it." If Brian thought that Uncle Stan was someone like that, there would be no point in trying to convince him of anything. So one of the functions of writing dialogue is to enable you to envision your audience as reasonable, an audience who will listen to convincing reasons supported by credible evidence.

EXERCISE

Choose a partner and role-play Brian's dialogue. Then answer the following questions:

1. How did Brian indicate that he understood Uncle Stan's position on the topic?
2. List the arguments that Brian made to convince Uncle Stan. Why did he choose this particular order of presentation?
3. If Brian had presented his arguments in a different order, would it have made any difference?
4. What role did Brian create for himself in this dialogue?

Josh's Dialogue

In his composition course, Josh, a college freshman, selected the topic of high school prerequisites for athletes. He decided that he wanted to argue the following position:

In 1985, in an effort to increase the graduation rates of college athletes, the NCAA passed Proposition 48, which raised entry requirements for incoming freshmen. In order for a freshman athlete to compete, he must have a 2.0 grade point average and a score of 700 on the SAT. In 1990, Proposition 48 was amended to raise the minimum GPA requirement to 2.7, and many people feel that this increase will help the graduation rate. However, although many people feel that these standards will increase the graduation rate, this new requirement has not helped African-Americans and in fact is keeping some of them from getting to attend college. It is for this reason that Proposition 48 should be reconsidered.

Josh's Use of Character Prompts

1. What is this person's name, age, and profession? Describe this person's physical appearance.

Chuck Wilson, age 32, height six-foot-eight, weight 245 pounds, is a professional basketball player who has played in the NBA for eight years. He graduated from an NCAA Division 1 school before Proposition 48 was implemented. Chuck grew up in a poor family. His parents were not educated, which made it hard for him to receive help on his school work. They did understand the importance of an education, though, and encouraged Chuck to work hard in school so that he would be eligible for an athletic scholarship. Chuck was drafted by an NBA team after his junior year but went back during the next few summers to complete his degree.

2. What is this person's current attitude toward this topic?

Chuck feels that he worked hard to get where he is and that it is because of his hard work that he is so successful. He also knows that none of his teammates in college made it into the league and that only a few actually graduated. He thinks that the higher standards might be a good thing because he has seen how poorly prepared some of his teammates were.

3. How much does this person know about the topic?

Chuck knows a lot from his own experience, but he doesn't realize that a lot of the tests used to admit students into college are not always reliable, and that sometimes they are testing students on skills that don't directly affect their ability to succeed in college. He also doesn't realize that college athletics provide an important way for African-Americans to obtain higher education.

4. Describe this person's value system.

Chuck believes in the importance of hard work. He thinks that high school grades reflect hard work and that only those with high grades deserve to be admitted on athletic scholarship. He is also interested in promoting the interests of African-Americans.

5. How does this person's value system influence his or her other attitude toward the topic?

Because Chuck values hard work, he believes in high standards.

6. Which aspect of the topic does this character find most disturbing?

Chuck worries that a reconsideration of the standards will not be helpful for African-Americans in that it will perpetuate stereotypes.

After describing Chuck, Josh wrote the following hypothetical dialogue:

JOSH: What are your feelings about the higher standards for admission to college on an athletic scholarship?

CHUCK: I think they're a good thing because I know that being an athlete in college requires a lot of hard work. If you don't know how to study in the first place, you're going to be in big trouble and you won't graduate, so what's the point?

JOSH: You were obviously successful. But did you know a lot of people who had this kind of trouble?

CHUCK: That's right. I know so many guys who didn't have a clue about what college was about and how you have to study just to keep up. You need to admit people who know what they're doing so they can graduate.

JOSH: I understand your concern for the graduation rate. But if you raise the standards, aren't you leaving out a lot of people who might really benefit from an opportunity to go to college?

CHUCK: What kind of opportunity is that if no one gets to graduate?

JOSH: Well, suppose that, instead of changing the requirements, the NCAA required colleges to provide better academic help once students got in.

CHUCK: I suppose if it helped them graduate, it would be okay.

JOSH: For some athletes, college is the only way out of the ghetto. By preventing them from getting in, the NCAA is taking away an important chance for them.

CHUCK: I guess if the school made sure they were getting a quality education, it could help the graduation rate.

EXERCISE

With a partner, role-play Josh's dialogue. Then discuss the following questions:

1. How did Josh indicate that he understood Chuck's position on the topic?

2. List the arguments that Josh made to convince Chuck. Why did he choose this particular order of presentation?

3. If Josh had presented his arguments in a different order, would it have made any difference?

WRITING ASSIGNMENT

Read "Dress Codes and Uniforms in Urban Schools" and think about your position on this subject. Then consider this scenario:

At Madison High School, located in a large American city, Principal Martin Blair has drafted a memo to the Board of Education arguing in favor of requiring all students to wear school uniforms beginning next year. Principal Blair is concerned primarily with the issue of safety, and he feels that the uniform requirement will protect children from attacks by gang members. He also believes that requiring all students to dress alike will focus their attention on their studies rather than on their clothes. The president of the Parent-Teacher Association, Beverly Woodson, however, opposes the uniform requirement and thinks that whether or not a child wears a uniform to a public school should be the parents' and even the child's choice. President Woodson feels that schools should not be allowed to dictate personal decisions regarding clothing and that the imposition of such a requirement would stifle children's creativity.

How do you feel about the issue of school uniforms? Were you required to wear a uniform when you attended school? If so, how did you feel about it? Do you perhaps have children of your own who are required to wear a uniform to school? If so, are you in favor of such a policy? If not, do you wish schools had such a requirement?

Choose a position in this controversy and write a dialogue between yourself and either Principal Blair or President Woodson discussing this issue.

THE ROLE OF AUDIENCE IN ROGERIAN ARGUMENT

The concept of audience is especially important in a form of argumentation known as "Rogerian argument," which takes its name from the psychologist Carl Rogers. In working with his patients, Rogers noted that although reason is an important component of making a point or instituting change, many people are not convinced by reasons alone—often people need to feel understood before they can even contemplate changing their ideas. Rogers thus postulates a defensive, fearful audience, resistant to any new position, an audience that does not easily tolerate differences in opinion but that can be swayed if it does not feel threatened. Rogerian argument is not used very much within the genre of argument, but it can focus a writer's attention on the psychological factors that influence the effect of an argument on an audience.

Writers who utilize Rogerian argument understand that they will not impact their audience if they simply present their ideas and cite their reasons because for some audiences, a direct statement of a new idea might generate hostility. Given this idea of a threatened, fearful audience, Rogerian argument maintains that it is preferable first to engender empathy in the audience by indicating that the writer understands its position, delaying the thesis statement until the audience is comfortable. It is as if the writer is saying: "I understand your view very well. Here is a restatement of it, and here are all the aspects of it that I agree with." Then, after the writer has gained the audience's confidence, he or she can then present a claim or position and perhaps move the audience to consider alternative viewpoints.

The Structure and Tone of Rogerian Argument

An argument based entirely on Rogers's model differs considerably from other models used in the genre of argument. Where the writer of traditional argument may assume an assertive tone, stating the thesis directly in the first or second paragraph, the writer of Rogerian argument begins by communicating understanding and empathy and often waits until further along in the essay to indicate points of disagreement. One may also see differences in the conclusion. In traditional argument, the writer aims for agreement or at least serious consideration, so the conclusion may reaffirm the writer's claim. In Rogerian argument, all the writer can hope for is that the audience will acknowledge that the writer's view is worth considering or perhaps allow for the existence of alternative possibilities. The conclusion may therefore call for further discussion or exchange of ideas.

Whether or not you ever write a true Rogerian argument, Rogers's concept of empathy can be applied to all forms of argumentative writing because it defines an attitude that can influence the writer's tone. If you are aware of the importance of empathy and of assuming a sufficiently judicious and qualified tone, you will be more likely to win the trust of your audience, whatever form your actual text may assume.

EXERCISE

1. Do you agree with Rogers that people find it difficult to change? Can you recall an issue about which you have changed your opinion?
2. Read "What Is the Point of Working?" by Lance Morrow. How does the author project a tone of empathy and indicate his awareness of the opposing viewpoint? Where in the essay does the author state his main point?

WRITING ASSIGNMENT

1: Write a brief Rogerian argument responding to one of the following scenarios. Use small groups to discuss your strategy.

A: A mother is worried about sending her 12-year-old son to summer camp. Write a Rogerian argument to help her understand that the child would benefit from the experience.

B: Your roommate does (or doesn't) want to join a sorority or fraternity. Write a Rogerian argument to help him or her understand the opposing position.

C: One of your friends says that he or she will never use a computer. He or she says that writing by hand and then typing has worked well in the past and can continue to do so in the future. You suspect that for some reason, he or she is afraid to use a computer. Write a Rogerian argument helping him or her understand that it is important to know how to use a computer.

2: For the essay you wrote in Chapter 2 about the appropriateness of fairy tales in a nursery school, write a Rogerian argument to help a worried mother understand that fairy tales are not likely to traumatize her four-year-old daughter. You can use Teeanna's essay as a model. Note how she indicates awareness of her audience's position and the placement of the thesis.

Are Fairy Tales Still Relevant?

Every day you read about it—violence in the streets, dysfunctional families, sexual harassment—and you see it everywhere in our society. What has been done to our children? How can we teach the next generation that certain behaviors are not acceptable? Can old-fashioned fairy tales, which are filled with vicious actions and harmful sexual stereotypes, possibly hold anything useful for today's child? Or will they simply make matters worse?

The most disturbing problem in society is that of violence, and unfortunately, most violent acts are committed by young people. We can blame TV and gangs, but the fact remains that somehow along the line, today's children are missing something in their education or upbringing that makes them able to cope with everyday stresses that ultimately explode into violence. Can anything be done to make our young people less violent? Can education in early childhood have an impact on how young people learn to cope with anger and frustration?

The psychologist Bruno Bettelheim, in The Uses of Enchantment, states that young children need to work through anger and hostility through the imagination and that old-fashioned fairy tales, which contain many violent elements, are extremely helpful in enabling children to express these feelings vicariously. This doesn't mean that fairy tales are some kind of cure-all for juvenile delinquents, but maybe if some of our violent teenagers had read fairy tales when they were young, they could have learned to express anger or frustration using their imagination rather than a gun.

Sexism is another problem in society that is difficult to solve because it involves bucking a system that has existed almost as long as we have history. We work hard to erase sexist terms and imagery in all areas of our lives, and especially in the lives of our children. We hope that if we teach our children these lessons early enough, they will be comfortable being loving fathers, involved in their children's lives, and confident women, capable of earning equal respect (and income) in the workplace. And yet, so little progress has been made and so many stereotypes still exist. Doesn't it seem likely that if we expose children to traditional fairy tales we will only make matters worse?

Of course, traditional fairy tales do contain unflattering portraits of both men and women. Some of the women are depicted as passive characters, who wait for Prince Charming to show up on a white horse and rescue them. Others are evil, witchlike creatures who perpetrate nasty deeds on one another out of jealousy. Moreover, a number of the fathers in fairy tales are not heroes, either. Many are depicted as uninvolved or even absent from their families. It doesn't seem possible that fairy tales with all of these terrible stereotypes will help children avoid harmful views of both sexes. Isn't it more likely that if we teach our children that all people are equal, and they carry that lesson with them as they read fairy tales, that the fairy tales themselves will destroy what we have taught?

In response to this concern, Bruno Bettelheim argues that fairy tales can help children understand the importance of struggling against great difficulties, even those caused by age-old sexist stereotypes. Bettelheim points out that fairy tales are stories about characters who are good overcoming characters who are evil and powerful, and he maintains that if children read fairy tales in that way, they will be encouraged to succeed, regardless of their sex. In deciding whether or not to include traditional fairy tales in early childhood education, then, the answer must be "yes." Although fairy tales contain elements we no longer find acceptable, they are still useful to children because fairy tales allow children to learn how to express themselves and to empower themselves.

ESTABLISHING CREDIBILITY

A writer with an established reputation for reliability and integrity is more likely to have an impact on an audience. But as a college writer, you are probably not an expert on your topic, and, therefore, you will have to establish credibility or trustworthiness through the text itself. This section discusses several strategies that you can use to appear credible to your readers, in particular:

1. by demonstrating that you have done a lot of work and are knowledgeable about the topic
2. by creating trustworthiness through tone and style
3. by using shared assumptions between you and your audience to establish connections

The Role of Ethos

The classical rhetoricians recognized that an audience would be more likely to accept a claim made by a speaker if that speaker were perceived as trustworthy and credible. In his *Rhetoric,* Aristotle maintained that *ethos,* or the credibility of the speaker, is most effectively established from the speech itself; he believed that credibility is created when the audience thinks of the speaker as a person of intelligence, moral integrity, and good intentions. In written argument, too, these three characteristics are important in establishing the credibility of the writer—that is:

1. The writer must convince the audience that he or she is knowledgeable about the subject.
2. The writer must indicate awareness and understanding of the ideas of others by presenting a balanced perspective on the topic.
3. The writer must use language in such a way as to appear truthful and fair.

Credibility and Knowledge

Although you are probably not an expert on the topic you are writing about, you can demonstrate that you have researched your topic adequately and provide a lot of pertinent and appropriate information in support of your position. To be a credible writer, you must support your statements with examples, statistics, and references to reliable authority, demonstrating that you are someone who has "done your homework." Your work indicates that you have thought carefully about the topic and have located sufficient and appropriate information to strengthen your position.

Adequate information on a researchable topic is a key determiner of a writer's credibility. Following are two paragraphs, one that lacks sufficient supporting material and one that uses it effectively. Note the differences between them in terms of the use of supporting information.

John's Paragraph

> To my understanding, exams, in many cases, do not promote learning. They exert pressure on students and result only in cramming, not in real education. Many students stay up all night studying and then find that their minds have blacked out before the test because of lack of sleep and too much input of information all at once. Often the effort put into studying throughout the year is not reflected in how well a person does on an exam. Sometimes, all the information learned before an exam is forgotten in one week.

The claim in John's paragraph is that exams do not promote learning but instead result in all-night cramming that neither guarantees a high performance on a test nor reflects how much the student has actually learned. John's claim is clearly stated, but John does not appear credible because his topic is so broad that he could not research it adequately and because he does not use supporting material that would strengthen his position. In his reference to college exams, John did not specify what sort of exams or college courses he means. Does he believe that all exams are useless and that there is no exam that can measure student learning? Would he advocate the elimination of licensing exams for doctors and lawyers? How about exams for licensing drivers? Most people would not feel comfortable consulting an unlicensed doctor or lawyer or hiring an unlicensed driver, so it is important that John define more specifically what he means by useless exams.

Discerning readers know that one cannot be an "expert" on a topic that is too broad and that one cannot research a broad topic adequately—therefore, John cannot be knowledgeable on the effectiveness of all exams in all college courses. In fact, because John has not adequately narrowed his subject, his paragraph sounds more like a student complaining about all the studying he has to do than someone who has carefully researched the topic.

The other reason that John does not appear credible is that his claim is based solely on his own experience. Although personal experience can often provide relevant support for many subjects, readers of academic argument usually expect additional support—having a strong view on a topic can be an advantage, but it is a disadvantage if you have nothing else. John's paragraph would have been a great deal stronger if he had cited studies or reliable authorities concerning the relationship of particular exams to learning. In its current form, the paragraph does not indicate that John has "done his homework," and he therefore does not appear credible.

Naomi Wolf's Paragraph

In contrast to John's paragraph, examine the following paragraph from Naomi Wolf's recent book, *The Beauty Myth:*

> Every generation since about 1830 has had to fight its version of the beauty myth. "It is very little to me," said the suffragist Lucy Stone in 1855, "to have the

right to vote, to own property, etcetera, if I may not keep my body, and its uses, in my absolute right." Eighty years later, after women had won the vote, and the first wave of the organized women's movement had subsided, Virginia Woolf wrote that it would still be decades before women could tell the truth about their bodies. In 1962, Betty Friedan quoted a young woman trapped in the *Feminine Mystique:* "Lately, I look in the mirror, and I'm so afraid I'm going to look like my mother." Eight years after that, heralding the cataclysmic second wave of feminism, Germaine Greer described "the Stereotype": "To her belongs all that is beautiful, even the very word beauty itself . . . she is a doll . . . I'm sick of the masquerade." In spite of the great revolution of the second wave, we are not exempt.

Wolf's claim is that every generation since 1830 has had to contend with some version of what she refers to as "the beauty myth," meaning the necessity for women to conform to some standard of beauty and to be overly concerned with the way they look. She then supports that claim by citing representative women from several generations—the suffragist Lucy Stone, the writer Virginia Woolf, and the feminists Betty Friedan and Germaine Greer. Although Wolf may indeed have personal experience that pertains to her topic (she, herself, may be overly concerned with beauty, or she may have friends who are), she provides support for her claim by citing the opinions of well-known feminists from several representative eras. Wolf thus appears credible, someone who has "done her homework."

EXERCISE

In small groups, read aloud each of the following paragraphs, noting how the writer establishes credibility. Which writer is more credible? Which features of the text contribute to the writer's credibility?

Debbie's Paragraph

Many of today's problems are blamed on the disintegration of the family. Yet, what often remains unacknowledged is the fact that the well-being of the family is strongly influenced by economic factors. During the post-World War II period, a time of economic prosperity, there were many jobs available, and it was possible for a father's single income to support the entire family. Now times have changed dramatically. One income is usually not enough for the family to sustain itself on, so both fathers and mothers have to work. Moreover, a large percentage of families consist of only one parent, with the increase in single mothers, teenage mothers, or divorced families. As David Eggebeen points out in an issue of Generations, "the ability of families to survive economically has been further exacerbated by the fact that an increasingly larger percentage of them are single-parent families—by definition dependent on one income" (45). Thus, in both one-parent and two-parent households, parents are busy trying to support their children and are unable to spend as much time with them as might be desirable. The U.S. Bureau of Child

Development reports that fewer than 40 percent of children are cared for by a parent after school. Moreover, "a recent Children's Defense Fund Report notes that 31 states and the District of Columbia had waiting lists for child care with up to 30,000 names and projected waiting periods of over a year" (Kagan 5).

Jason's Paragraph

Today we are living in a very violent society in which even young children and teenagers are committing crimes. Every night on the news we hear of gang-related incidents in which very young children commit murders and don't even seem to feel guilty about it. What seems pretty obvious, though, is that this increase in violence in society is strongly influenced by television and that television is having a severely negative effect on the morals and values of our society. Elementary school children watch over 40 hours of television a week, and a lot of what is on television is extremely violent and immoral. Even if children don't actually imitate what they see on television, watching violence continuously on their favorite shows desensitizes children to violence and confuses them about what is morally right. If educators and lawmakers are looking for the cause of our increasingly violent society, they should examine the impact of television.

Credibility and Tone

Tone is another factor that determines whether your audience will perceive you as credible. Although *tone* is difficult to define, it may be viewed in terms of two factors: your approach to the topic and the word choices you make.

THE ROLE OF BALANCE
IN ARGUMENTATION

The genre of argument presumes that a writer will have a balanced approach to a topic. Although you may feel strongly about a position, you must also acknowledge that on complex, controversial topics, people differ in their opinions. Because academic argument is concerned with topics about which people disagree, credible writers show respect for their audience by aiming for a thoughtful, qualified approach, or, as Joseph Williams phrases it in his book, *Style: Ten Lessons in Clarity and Grace,* a writer should try to avoid sounding like either "an uncertain milquetoast or a smug dogmatist" (82).

Rationale for Qualification

Writers of academic argument prefer a qualified approach because the "truth" or a clear concept of right and wrong concerning complex, controversial topics is difficult to "know" with absolute certainty. In fact, most topics for academic argument are, by definition, those about which even concerned, intelligent, informed, and well-meaning people have long had difficulty making decisions. Writing about most areas involving human interaction often involves navigating between extreme positions, acknowledging the difficulty of making definitive predictions or absolute value judgments, and developing a compromise position because the writer is aware of other perspectives. An intelligent statement about human beings suggests implicitly that it is always possible that events (or policies or results) may take an unusual turn or that people may not behave admirably or according to expectation. Therefore, because human nature is complex and often unpredictable, a great deal of academic writing in the humanities and social sciences is characterized by *qualification*—writers may predict consequences or present an analysis of particular conditions or events, but they may also indicate the tentativeness of their observations by using words such as *seems, suggests, indicates, to some degree,* or *to a certain extent.* For an example of how qualifying words indicate the writer's awareness of the complexity of human behavior, read the following paragraph, concerned with predicting a potential outcome of the decision to send American troops to Somalia in 1992:

> Less than two years after Africa's last colony—Namibia—gained its independence, the United Nations may have taken the first step on a slippery slope leading to de facto re-colonization of collapsing African states. And the United States, which seemed to be on the verge of abandoning Africa, may soon find itself more deeply engaged in the continent's affairs than ever before.
>
> Michael Clough, "The Heart of the Matter," *Los Angeles Times* (December 6, 1992)

In the preceding paragraph, note the use of the word *may* in two instances as well as the word *seemed.* These words indicate not that the author knows with certainty what is going to happen, but rather that his article is an educated appraisal based on his expertise in African policy.

Here is another example from an article titled "When Parents Are Not in the Best Interests of the Child," which takes the controversial stance that sometimes living in an institutional setting is better for children from troubled homes than living in an intimate family environment. Because our culture is so strongly in favor of family living, even under troubled circumstances, the writer is careful to qualify her statements so as to acknowledge the opposing viewpoint.

> Life without parents is a difficult sentence to pronounce upon a child, but it's happening more and more often. "Sometimes children have gone beyond the opportunity to go back and capture what needed to be done between the ages of three and eight," says Gene Baker, the chief psychologist at *The Children's Village.* "Sometimes the thrust of intimacy that comes with family living is more than they can handle. Sometimes the requirement of bonding is more than they have the emotional equipment to give. As long as we keep pushing them back into what is our idealized fantasy of family, they'll keep blowing it out of the water for us."
>
> Mary-Lou Weisman, *Atlantic Monthly,* July 1994

In this paragraph, Mary-Lou Weisman has anticipated an audience that feels strongly about keeping children in a family environment as much as possible, an audience that distrusts institutionalization except under the most extreme circumstances. Therefore, Weisman acknowledges her audience's reaction at the beginning of the paragraph and repeatedly uses the word *sometimes* to qualify her statements.

Approaching a Topic Judiciously

Qualifying words indicate that the writer has respect for the reader and is aware of the complexity of the issue under consideration. No reader is going to be persuaded by your claim if you simply proclaim that "you are absolutely wrong, and I am absolutely right"—that approach rarely works under any circumstances, as most of us know from our own lives and as the psychologist Carl Rogers has pointed out. After all, if someone says, "Let me show you how wrong you are about this issue, and then I'll tell you how you can improve your thinking," you are likely to resist and hold on even more tightly to your own position. For most people, a dogmatic approach is more likely to engender hostility than agreement. You will be more successful, then, if you approach your subject politely and judiciously, indicate that you understand the complexity of the subject, and qualify your discussion to allow for the possibility of compromise.

Qualification Enables Negotiation

A qualified thesis on a topic suitable for argumentation enables the writer to *negotiate* a compromise position with the reader so that the reader moves a bit further toward the writer's position than he or she was situated before. Your message to your reader should be "I understand how you feel, and here are the points on which both of us agree. But here is where I differ from you, based on the following reasons." Usually, whether we are listening to a speech or reading an essay, we are more likely to pay attention to what someone has to say if we feel that he or she understands our own point of view.

Examine the following excerpt from Stanley Fish's article "How the Pot Got to Call the Kettle Black," which makes the case that although programs favoring minorities seem to be unfair, in reality they are not. In this excerpt, note how Fish anticipates and acknowledges criticism from his readers:

> When all is said and done, however, one objection to affirmative action is unanswerable on its own terms, and that is the objection of the individual who says, "Why me? Sure, discrimination has persisted for many years, and I acknowledge that the damage done has not been removed by changes in the law. But why me? I didn't own slaves; I didn't vote to keep people on the back of the bus. I didn't turn water hoses on civil-rights marchers. Why, then, should I be the one who doesn't get the job or who doesn't get the scholarship or who gets bumped back to the waiting list?"

I sympathize with this feeling, if only because in a small way I have had the experience that produces it. I was recently nominated for an administrative post at a large university. Early signs were encouraging, but after an interval I received official notice that I would not be included at the next level of consideration, and subsequently I was told unofficially that at some point a decision had been made to look only in the direction of women and minorities. Although I was disappointed, I did not conclude that the situation was "unfair," because the policy was obviously not directed at me—at no point in the proceedings did someone say, "let's find a way to rule out Stanley Fish." Nor was it directed even at persons of my race and sex—the policy was not intended to disenfranchise white males. Rather the policy was driven by other considerations, and it was only as a by-product of those considerations—not as the main goal—that white males like me were rejected. Given that the institution in question has a high percentage of minority students, a very low percentage of minority faculty, and an even lower percentage of minority administrators, it made perfect sense to focus on women and minority candidates, and within that sense, not as the result of prejudice, my whiteness and maleness became disqualifications.

I can hear the objection in advance: "What's the difference? Unfair is unfair: you didn't get the job; you didn't even get on the short list." The difference is not in the outcome but in the ways of thinking that led up to the outcome. It is the difference between an unfairness that befalls one as the unintended effect of a policy rationally conceived and an unfairness that is pursued as an end in itself.

"How the Pot Got to Call the Kettle Black," *Atlantic Monthly*, November 1993

In these three paragraphs, Fish indicates that he is sympathetic to his opposition. He acknowledges that white males are sometimes overlooked in favor of women and minorities. In fact, he admits that he, himself, lost an administrative position because of preferential hiring policies. But then he points out that although he was not happy about the situation, he could not, logically, claim that the policy was unfair, and he distinguishes this type of discrimination from the discrimination that existed in the past. Readers are thus inclined to trust Fish's opinion because he devotes considerable space in the text to anticipating and acknowledging his readers' objections.

Qualification Enhances Credibility

Qualification thus enhances your credibility because it indicates that you are a thoughtful person who is aware of the complexity of the topic. It indicates that you are someone who has adequately examined the topic so as to be aware of alternate possibilities, someone whom the reader can respect and trust. It does not, however, mean that you are uncommitted to your topic or that you do not feel strongly about it. An effective piece of writing is both committed and qualified. It combines a thoughtful presentation with intensity of feeling, maximizing the chances that the essay will accomplish its purpose. If you indicate that you are aware of multiple perspectives and acknowledge points of agreement and disagreement, it does not mean that you are undecided.

Terms That Indicate Qualification

Qualification is usually achieved by words that linguists term "hedges." Hedges enable writers to soften their stance and make exceptions. Here are some of the more common hedges:

COMMON HEDGES

usually, often, sometimes, almost, virtually, possible, perhaps, apparently, seemingly, in some ways, to a certain extent, sort of, for the most part, may, might, can, could, seem, tend, try, attempt, seek, hope

---

The opposite of qualifying words are those that underscore the writer's point. These are called "emphatics." Emphatics are words that tell the reader that the writer believes strongly in his or her ideas. Here are some common emphatics:

EMPHATICS

as everyone knows, it is generally agreed that, it is quite true that, it's clear that, it is obvious that, the fact is, as we can plainly see, literally, clearly, obviously, undoubtedly, invariably, certainly, always, of course, indeed

---

EXERCISE

1: Rephrase the following thesis statements so that they express a qualified view of the topic. Then, in small groups discuss the impact that qualification would have on the credibility and effectiveness of each statement.

A: The recent laws passed on college campuses to institutionalize political correctness are a naked attempt at repression of free speech.

B: The homeless are a shiftless, lazy group who prefer to beg for money rather than work for it honestly.

C: The distribution of birth control devices in the schools will undermine the efforts of parents to institute moral values in their children.

D: Television news presents a distorted picture of violence in the inner city.

E: Being a vegetarian is the only humane way of dealing with the suffering that animals undergo when they are raised for food.

2: The following selection was taken from Walter I. Williams's essay, "The Relationship between Male-Male Friendship and Male-Female Marriage" from *Men's Friendships* (Sage Publications, 1992). Williams argues that Americans suffer from alienation and a lack of emotional support because our culture prohibits intimate friendships between members of the same sex. He feels that the real culprit is our idealization of romantic love—we expect our spouses to be our "sexual playmate, economic partner, kinship system, best friend, and everything else," but this ideal often "only leads to grief."

Read through the selection. Then, in small groups discuss how Williams presents and qualifies his argument. Can you find the hedges and the emphatics?

Strong extended family kinship networks have often not been able to survive the extensive geographical mobility characteristic of modern America. Relatives are separated as the capitalist job market has forced many people to migrate to other locations. Under these pressures, "the family" has been reduced from its original extended form (the most common type of family among humans) to a mere nuclear remnant of parents and children. In modern America, a person's "significant other" has now become practically the sole person with whom he or she can be intimate. For many couples, this is too much to ask of their relationships, as the significant other is expected simultaneously to be sexual playmate, economic partner, kinship system, best friend, and everything else. Because of the dictatorship of the romantic ideal, many Americans expect their spouse to meet all their emotional needs. That is doubly difficult to do while both partners are also holding down full-time employment outside the home.

As more American marriages become households where both spouses have jobs outside the home, there is less energy left for being emotionally supportive of one's partner. Even these rump nuclear family marriages are, therefore, in increasing numbers of cases, falling apart. The flip side of the American ideal of individual freedom and progress is thus often a legacy of individual alienation and loneliness.

In contrast, by not expecting the marriage relationship to fulfill all of a person's needs, many other cultures allow people more emotional closeness to same-sex friends. To take one example, in some cultures, families are not often broken up over the issue of homosexuality. In such a situation, in fact, there is not as much emotional need for homosexually inclined individuals to construct a separate homosexual identity. There will, of course, still be a certain percentage of people who erotically prefer a same-sex partner, but that inclination may be fulfilled within the friendship bond. There is no social pressure for persons to leave their marriage just because they desire same-sex erotic contacts. Sexual desires may have little to do with family bonding because the marriage is not assumed to be sexually exclusive.

Same-sex friendships need not, of course, include a sexual component, but as far as the society is concerned, the important factor is the friendship rather than the sexual behavior. The person might be sexually involved with a same-sex friend while also being heterosexually married. Both forms of bonding occur and a person does not have to choose one over the other. This flexibility resolves to the advantage of society and the individual. There is a looseness and an adaptiveness that allow for close intimate interaction with both sexes within the dual bonds of marriage and friendship.

QUESTIONS

1. What is the controversy associated with this topic? Why is it worthwhile to examine?
2. What tone does Williams adopt in this argument? Based on this tone, what kind of audience do you think he was writing for?
3. Note where Williams uses qualifiers in the essay. What are the arguments against his position that these hedges are meant to disarm?
4. If Williams were writing for a more specific audience—a friend going through a divorce, for example—would he make changes in this argument? What kind of changes?

3: Read the following selection from Stephen Carter's book, *Reflections of an Affirmative Action Baby* (Basic Books, 1991). Then, in small groups discuss the following:

A: What is Carter's main point?

B: What ideas is he refuting?

C: How does Carter acknowledge and disarm his opposition?

I got into law school because I am black.

As many black professionals think they must, I have long suppressed this truth, insisting instead that I got where I am the same way everybody else did. Today I am a professor at the Yale Law School. I like to think that I am a good one, but I am hardly the most objective judge. What I am fairly sure of, and can now say without trepidation, is that were my skin not the color that it is, I would not have had the chance to try.

For many, perhaps most, black professionals of my generation, the matter of who got where and how is left in a studied and, I think, purposeful ambiguity. Some of us, as they say, would have made it into an elite college or professional school anyway. (But in my generation, many fewer than we like to pretend, even though one might question the much-publicized claim by Derek Bok, the president of Harvard University, that in the absence of preferences, only 1 percent of Harvard's entering class would be black.) Most of us, perhaps nearly all of us, have learned to bury the matter far back in our minds. We are who we are and where we are, we have records of accomplishment or failure, and there is no rational reason that anybody—employer, client, whoever—should care any longer whether racial preference played any role in our admission to a top professional school.

When people in positions to help or hurt our careers do seem to care, we tend to react with fury. Those of us who have graduated professional school over the past fifteen to twenty years, and are not white, travel career paths that are frequently bumpy with suspicions that we did not earn the right to be where we are. We bristle when others raise what might be called the qualification question—"Did you get into school or get hired because of a special program?"—and that prickly sensitivity is the best evidence, if any is needed, of one of the principal costs of racial preferences. Scratch a black professional with the qualification question, and you're likely to get a caustic response, such as this one from a senior executive at a major airline: "Some whites think I've made it because I'm black. Some blacks think I've made it only because I'm an Uncle Tom. The fact is, I've made it because I'm good."

Given the way that so many Americans seem to treat receipt of the benefits of affirmative action as a badge of shame, answers of this sort are both predictable and sensible. In the professional world, moreover, they are very often true: relatively few corporations are in a position to hand out charity. The peculiar aspect of the routine denial, however, is that so many of those who will bristle at the suggestion that they themselves have gained from racial preferences will try simultaneously to insist that racial preferences be preserved and to force the world to pretend that no one benefits from them.

QUESTIONS

1. Is Carter's opening line effective? Does it influence what we expect from the rest of the essay? How?
2. Does Carter use qualifications to enable negotiation? Give examples.
3. How does Carter establish his credibility? Why should we consider him knowledgeable about this topic?
4. If you were to have a dialogue with Stephen Carter on the issue of affirmative action, what would you ask him? What issues would you like to see him discuss that aren't addressed in this short reading?

Dress Codes and Uniforms in Urban Schools

Velma LaPoint, Lillian Holloman, and Sylvan I. Alleyne

The authors collaborated on this piece while at Howard University, Washington, D.C. The essay was originally condensed from the *NASSP Bulletin* (October 1992) and was published as it appears here in *Education Digest* (March 1993).

In recent years, many large urban public school systems have experienced problems that relate to students' appearance. Attendance, attention to instruction, and grades suffer when appearance is overemphasized. 1

Some youngsters will delay or not purchase books and supplies, instead using their money for clothing, accessories, or hairstyling. Others may skip school or work long hours after school—or worse, become involved in illegal activities—to finance fashionable wardrobes. Some educators feel that many young people view school as a major arena in which to display their latest fashions. 2

Competition over appearance can result in verbal taunts, fights, and thefts. Such behavior occurs not only among enrolled students but also among non-enrolled peers, who can instigate problems relating to appearance. Certain types of clothing and accessories have come to symbolize lifestyles relating to drugs, violence, and disrespect for authority. 3

Schools can play a major role in developing strategies to address problems related to appearance. Many public schools have established dress codes that prescribe or prohibit certain clothing or grooming practices. Others have begun to require that students wear uniforms. 4

Public school policies regarding dress codes and uniforms vary from district to district. The Baltimore (Maryland) City Public School System is explicit in setting standards, while public schools in Chicago, Atlanta, and Washington, D.C., defer decisions regarding appearance to individual school principals, teachers, students, and parents. It appears that these systems want to maximize participatory governance as well as avoid litigation that alleges violation of students' rights. 5

Although such differences exist, public schools in major urban areas agree on their positions in certain areas. Some specific items are banned: athletic shoes, gold chains, gold teeth, leather and fur coats, mini- and tight-fitting skirts, and other items that distract or invite antisocial behavior. 6

A number of public schools in large urban areas use or are exploring the use of uniforms. Advocates of uniforms indicate several advantages: 7

- Uniforms can serve as a symbol or representation of the organization, certify the individual as a legitimate member of the organization, and conceal status. They can promote a feeling of "oneness" among students and can reduce the difference between the "haves" and "have-nots."

■ Uniforms promote conformity to organizational goals. A Maryland junior high school principal and his colleagues observed an increase in honor-roll students after the school implemented a uniform policy. Another principal noted a significant decrease in the number of disputes among students and an increase in positive student interaction.

■ Uniforms can reduce the money young people and their parents spend for clothing. An initial modest outlay is required for uniform purchase and routine care.

8   Reasons for opposition to uniforms include restriction of student and parental rights to freedom of expression in appearance; restriction of youth to engage in normal developmental tasks of identity experimentation using clothing or other bodily adornment; intrusion into the private lives of students and parents; and lack of research to show relationships between academic achievement, positive social behavior, and youth appearance in schools. Furthermore, policies on uniforms may not be seen as a priority because other major social problems are increasing in the schools.

9   Principals must consider several issues:

■ The right of youth to express their identity through adornment practices and choices within schools where student health and safety needs must be met;

■ The right and responsibility of educational leaders to make policies in schools when various human rights organizations, such as the American Civil Liberties Union, seek to protect the rights of students to look as they desire;

■ The right and responsibility of parents to socialize their children in accord with their values, which may conflict or compete with educational policies;

■ The role and responsibility of manufacturers, retailers, and advertisers to make and sell clothing and other products which may be questionable and undesirable in educational and other settings.

10   In the past, the primary socialization agents of youth were families, schools, and churches. Several educators, psychologists, social workers, and health providers have suggested that today's youth are increasingly being socialized by peers and by the popular culture—television, movies, popular music, sports, and "the streets." The fashion and advertising industries can be added to this list. They have capitalized on characteristics and conditions that drive many youth to desire, obtain, and use products that may contribute to problems in schools and other settings.

11   Since problems related to youth appearance in schools are multifaceted, solutions also must be broad-based. Principals, other policymakers, and teachers must work in partnership with students and their families to resolve problems related to youth appearance.

Students and parents should help develop and implement policies regard- 12
ing dress codes and uniforms. Parents must actively manage and monitor how
youth obtain and wear clothing and accessories. In one community, students,
school personnel, parents, and community members designed and sold their
own athletic shoes. This was a fund raiser and means to promote positive
behavior by having shoes with the school's emblem and colors. It also was an
alternative to expensive athletic shoes that cause competition and other negative behavior.

Many principals show leadership in confronting problems relating to 13
appearance among youth in public schools. However, not all school systems
and/or individual schools confront problems relating to appearance among
youth; other major social problems may take priority. Therefore, principals must
individualize their analysis and response to events in their specific schools.

Research is needed to provide information about relationships between 14
appearance and behavior among youth in public schools. Published studies are
virtually nonexistent; yet, anecdotal reports indicate positive changes in student
achievement and behavior when dress codes and uniforms are used. There is
also need to collect and exchange information about the impact of dress codes
and uniforms to establish a basis from which policies can be generated.

There is a need to recognize the cultural and subcultural influences on 15
appearance among youth. Policies and practices should be sensitive to both
cultural and subcultural influences. Finally, there is need to actively involve
youth, parents, community leaders, business leaders, and education experts in
analyzing the problems and developing solutions.

QUESTIONS

1. Was there a dress code in the schools you attended as a child? Did the
   dress code (or lack of dress code) influence your school experience?
   How?
2. Are the points offered by the authors valid? Do the points seem logical
   and within common experience for most people?
3. Can you situate this essay within the "conversation" of school dress
   codes? Do you feel you know enough to enter into this dialogue com-
   fortably? Why do you feel this way?
4. Do the authors seem trustworthy? How do the tone and structure of this
   essay reflect your opinion of their reliability?
5. How do the authors use construction to emphasize key concepts?
   Could they have accomplished the same thing using a different construction? Explain.
6. Do you believe that the evidence cited in this essay could be used to
   write a similar argument against school dress codes? Give it a try!

What Is the Point of Working?
Lance Morrow

Lance Morrow is a writer and journalist whose essays appear fre-
quently in *Time.* His books include *Heart: A Memoir* (1995) and
America: A Rediscovery (1987). This essay is reprinted from *100
Essays from Time* (1992).

01 When God foreclosed on Eden, he condemned Adam and Eve to go to work.
Work has never recovered from that humiliation. From the beginning, the
Lord's word said that work was something bad: a punishment, the great stone
of mortality and toil laid upon a human spirit that might otherwise soar in the
infinite, weightless playfulness of grace.

2   A perfectly understandable prejudice against work has prevailed ever since.
Most work in the life of the world has been hard, but since it was grindingly
inevitable, it hardly seemed worth complaining about very much. Work was
simply the business of life, as matter-of-fact as sex and breathing. In recent
years, however, the ancient discontent has grown elaborately articulate. The
worker's usual old bitching has gone to college. Grim tribes of sociologists have
reported back from office and factory that most workers find their labor
mechanical, boring, imprisoning, stultifying, repetitive, dreary, heartbreaking.
In his 1972 book *Working,* Studs Terkel began: "This book, being about work,
is, by its very nature, about violence—to the spirit as well as to the body." The
historical horrors of industrialization (child labor, Dickensian squalor, the dark
satanic mills) translate into the 20th century's robotic busywork on the line,
tightening the same damned screw on the Camaro's fire-wall assembly, going
nuts to the banging, jangling Chaplinesque whirr of modern materialism in
labor, bringing forth issue, disgorging itself upon the market.

3   The lamentations about how awful work is prompt an answering wail from
the management side of the chasm: nobody wants to work any more. As American productivity, once the exuberant engine of national wealth, has dipped to an
embarrassingly uncompetitive low, Americans have shaken their heads: the
country's old work ethic is dead. About the only good words for it now emanate
from Ronald Reagan and certain beer commercials. Those ads are splendidly
mythic playlets, romantic idealizations of men in groups who blast through
mountains or pour plumingly molten steel in factories, the work all grit and grin.
Then they retire to flip around iced cans of sacramental beer and debrief one
another in a warm sundown glow of accomplishment. As for Reagan, in his pres-
idential campaign he enshrined work in his rhetorical "community of values,"
along with family, neighborhood, peace and freedom. He won by a landslide.

4   Has the American work ethic really expired? Is some old native eagerness to
level wilderness and dig and build and invent now collapsing toward a deca-
dence of dope, narcissism, income transfers and aerobic self-actualization?

The idea of work—work as an ethic, an abstraction—arrived rather late in the history of toil. Whatever edifying and pietistic things may have been said about work over the centuries (Kahlil Gibran called work "love made visible," and the Benedictines say, "To work is to pray"), humankind has always tried to avoid it whenever possible. The philosophical swells of ancient Greece thought work was degrading; they kept an underclass to see to the laundry and other details of basic social maintenance. That prejudice against work persisted down the centuries in other aristocracies. It is supposed, however, to be inherently un-American. Edward Kennedy likes to tell the story of how, during his first campaign for the Senate, his opponent said scornfully in a debate: "This man has never worked a day in his life!" Kennedy says that the next morning as he was shaking hands at a factory gate, one worker leaned toward him and confided, "You ain't missed a goddamned thing."   5

The Protestant work ethic, which sanctified work and turned it into vocation, arrived only a few centuries ago in the formulations of Martin Luther and John Calvin. In that scheme, the worker collaborates with God to do the work of the universe, the great design. One scholar, Leland Ryken of Illinois' Wheaton College, has pointed out that American politicians and corporate leaders who preach about the work ethic do not understand the Puritans' original, crucial linkage between human labor and God's will.   6

During the 19th century industrialization of America, the idea of work's inherent virtue may have seemed temporarily implausible to generations who labored in the mines and mills and sweatshops. The century's huge machinery of production punished and stunned those who ran it.   7

And yet for generations of immigrants, work was ultimately availing; the numb toil of an illiterate grandfather got the father a foothold and a high school education, and the son wound up in college or even law school. A woman who died in the Triangle Shirtwaist Co. fire in lower Manhattan had a niece who made it to the halcyon Bronx, and another generation on, the family went to Westchester County. So for millions of Americans as they labored through the complexities of generations, work worked, and the immigrant work ethic came at last to merge with the Protestant work ethic.   8

The motive of work was all. To work for mere survival is desperate. To work for a better life for one's children and grandchildren lends the labor a fierce dignity. That dignity, an unconquerably hopeful energy and aspiration—driving, persisting like a life force—is the American quality that many find missing now.   9

The work ethic is not dead, but it is weaker now. The psychology of work is much changed in America. The acute, painful memory of the Great Depression used to enforce a disciplined and occasionally docile approach to work— in much the way that older citizens in the Soviet Union do not complain about scarce food and overpopulated apartments, because they remember how much more horrible everything was during the war. But the generation of the Depression is retiring and dying off, and today's younger workers, though sometimes laid off and kicked around by recessions and inflation, still do not keep in dark   10 storage that residual apocalyptic memory of Hoovervilles and the Dust Bowl and banks capsizing.

11   Today elaborate financial cushions—unemployment insurance, union benefits, welfare payments, food stamps and so on—have made it less catastrophic to be out of a job for a while. Work is still a profoundly respectable thing in America. Most Americans suffer a sense of loss, of diminution, even of worthlessness, if they are thrown out on the street. But the blow seldom carries the life-and-death implications it once had, the sense of personal ruin. Besides, the wild and notorious behavior of the economy takes a certain amount of personal shame out of joblessness; if Ford closes down a plant in New Jersey and throws 3,700 workers into the unemployment lines, the guilt falls less on individuals than on Japanese imports or American car design or an extortionate OPEC.

12   Because today's workers are better educated than those in the past, their expectations are higher. Many younger Americans have rearranged their ideas about what they want to get out of life. While their fathers and grandfathers and great-grandfathers concentrated hard upon plow and drill press and pressure gauge and tort, some younger workers now ask previously unimaginable questions about the point of knocking themselves out. For the first time in the history of the world, masses of people in industrially advanced countries no longer have to focus their minds upon work as the central concern of their existence.

13   In the formulation of Psychologist Abraham Maslow, work functions in a hierarchy of needs: first, work provides food and shelter, basic human maintenance. After that, it can address the need for security and then for friendship and "belongingness." Next, the demands of the ego arise, the need for respect. Finally, men and women assert a larger desire for "self-actualization." That seems a harmless and even worthy enterprise but sometimes degenerates into self-infatuation, a vaporously selfish discontent that dead-ends in isolation, the empty face that gazes back from the mirror.

14   Of course in patchwork, pluralistic America, different classes and ethnic groups are perched at different stages in the work hierarchy. The immigrants—legal and illegal—who still flock densely to America are fighting for the foothold that the jogging tribes of self-actualizers achieved three generations ago. The zealously ambitious Koreans who run New York City's best vegetable markets, or boat people trying to open a restaurant, or chicanos who struggle to start a small business in the *barrio* are still years away from est and the Sierra Club. Working women, to the extent that they are new at it, now form a powerful source of ambition and energy. Feminism—and financial need—have made them, in effect, a sophisticated-immigrant wave upon the economy.

15   Having to work to stay alive, to build a future, gives one's exertions a tough moral simplicity. The point of work in that case is so obvious that it need not be discussed. But apart from the sheer necessity of sustaining life, is there some inherent worth in work? Carlyle believed that "all work, even cotton spinning, is noble; work is alone noble." Was he right?

16   It is seigneurial cant to romanticize work that is truly detestable and destructive to workers. But misery and drudgery are always comparative. Despite the

sometimes nostalgic haze around their images, the preindustrial peasant and the 19th century American farmer did brutish work far harder than the assembly line. The untouchable who sweeps excrement in the streets of Bombay would react with blank incomprehension to the malaise of some $17-an-hour workers on a Chrysler assembly line. The Indian, after all, has passed from "alienation" into a degradation that is almost mystical. In Nicaragua, the average 19-year-old peasant has worked longer and harder than most Americans of middle age. Americans prone to restlessness about the spiritual disappointments of work should consult unemployed young men and women in their own ghettos: they know with painful clarity the importance of the personal dignity that a job brings.

Americans often fall into fallacies of misplaced sympathy. Psychologist 17 Maslow, for example, once wrote that he found it difficult "to conceive of feeling proud of myself, self-loving and self-respecting, if I were working, for example, in some chewing-gum factory . . ." Well, two weeks ago, Warner-Lambert announced that it would close down its gum-manufacturing American Chicle factory in Long Island City N.Y.; the workers who had spent years there making Dentyne and Chiclets were distraught. "It's a beautiful place to work," one feeder-catcher-packer of chewing gum said sadly. "It's just like home." There is a peculiar elitist arrogance in those who discourse on the brutalizations of work simply because they cannot imagine themselves performing the job. Certainly workers often feel abstracted out, reduced sometimes to dreary robotic functions. But almost everyone commands endlessly subtle systems of adaptation; people can make the work their own and even cherish it against all academic expectations. Such adaptations are often more important than the famous but theoretical alienation from the process and product of labor.

Work is still the complicated and crucial core of most lives, the occupation 18 melded inseparably to the identity; Freud said that the successful psyche is one capable of love and of work. Work is the most thorough and profound organizing principle in American life. If mobility has weakened old blood ties, our coworkers often form our new family, our tribe, our social world; we become almost citizens of our companies, living under the protection of salaries, pensions and health insurance. Sociologist Robert Schrank believes that people like jobs mainly because they need other people; they need to gossip with them, hang out with them, to schmooze. Says Schrank: "The workplace performs the function of community."

Unless it is dishonest or destructive—the labor of a pimp or a hit man, 19 say—all work is intrinsically honorable in ways that are rarely understood as they once were. Only the fortunate toil in ways that express them directly. There is a Renaissance splendor in Leonardo's effusion: "The works that the eye orders the hands to make are infinite." But most of us labor closer to the ground. Even there, all work expresses the laborer in a deeper sense: all life must be worked at, protected, planted, replanted, fashioned, cooked for, coaxed, diapered, formed, sustained. Work is the way that we tend the world, the way that people connect. It is the most vigorous, vivid sign of life—in individuals and in civilizations.

QUESTIONS

1. Is this essay in a Rogerian essay form? How can you tell? Provide details.
2. What is the controversy presented by this article? State the main thesis.
3. What audience do you think Morrow is writing for? Can you tell what role he himself is assuming in this text?
4. What kind of assumptions does Morrow make about the kind of knowledge he expects his audience to have? What are these tidbits of knowledge? Are there any you do not understand?
5. Do you believe that the essay presents a balanced approach? Does he include a rationale for his position? Does he employ any qualifications in the argument?
6. Does Morrow use enough support to lend credibility to his argument? What kind of authorities does he cite? Make a list of these supporting details.

Chapter 6

TYPES OF SUPPORT

Sitting in the student cafeteria, you might have the following conversation with a friend:

You: My roommate, Sylvester, is impossible to live with.
Friend: Why?
You: Because he's sloppy and inconsiderate.

Your friend might then nod in sympathy, convinced that Sylvester is indeed impossible to live with. But suppose you were trying to convince the members of the Housing Bureau on your campus that you need to change roommates. In that case, you might construct your position more formally as an enthymeme:

Enthymeme: My roommate, Sylvester, is difficult to live with because he is sloppy and inconsiderate.

Or you might analyze your claim as follows:

Claim: My roommate, Sylvester, is difficult to live with.

Reasons: He is sloppy.
            He is inconsiderate.

Warrant: Sloppy, inconsiderate people are difficult to live with.

However, although the reasons cited would probably be sufficient for your friend in a casual conversation, some members of the Housing Bureau might require additional support for your reasons, raising questions such as "In what way is he sloppy? How is he inconsiderate? Can you give examples of his sloppiness and lack of consideration?" Or they might raise a question about your warrant such as "Why do his sloppiness and lack of consideration make him impossible to live with?" In other words, you may have to provide further support in order for your audience to be convinced.

Support is a key component in the genre of argument. Sometimes you may need additional support for your reasons; at other times, you may need to bolster your underlying assumptions or warrants as well. This chapter is concerned with various strategies for providing support, in particular, statements from experts, examples, statistics, and information from surveys and interviews.

DEFENDING YOUR WARRANT

The claim "My roommate, Sylvester, is difficult to live with" was supported by the warrant "Sloppy, inconsiderate people are difficult to live with," an assumption that many people probably share. Not everyone, however, will accept this warrant as absolutely true. Learning of Sylvester's irritating habits, some members of the Housing Bureau might say, "As far as I'm concerned, sloppiness and lack of consideration cause only minor difficulties. A grouchy, angry roommate with a foul temper—now these are more serious problems. But if Sylvester is cheerful and pleasant, his sloppiness and lack of consideration should be regarded as only minor character flaws."

In this case, if you wished to convince the Housing Bureau that Sylvester should be exchanged for another roommate, someone you found easier to live with, you would have the obligation to defend your warrant. You might then decide to provide the additional support that college students are particularly disadvantaged when they must contend with sloppy, inconsiderate people. This additional support might be stated as follows:

For college students, people who are sloppy and inconsiderate are especially difficult to live with because **their habits interfere with study.**

This additional information would provide additional support for your warrant because it specifies that sloppiness and lack of consideration interfere with an important component of education—the ability to study—thereby establishing that such qualities are particularly unsuitable for a college roommate. Phrased as a syllogism, this additional support might appear as follows:

Major premise: People whose habits interfere with study are unsuitable roommates for college students.

Minor premise: Sylvester's habits interfere with study (he is sloppy and inconsiderate).

Conclusion: Sylvester is an unsuitable roommate.

The claim that a roommate's habits interfere with your ability to study would then probably be regarded as serious by members of the Housing Bureau and might indeed get Sylvester out of your room. It is therefore important for you to scrutinize your warrants as well as your reasons to decide whether or not you need to provide additional support.

Supporting Your Reasons

Additional support might occur in the form of examples or specific details that lend specificity and concreteness to your writing and help the reader understand your ideas more clearly. For example, support for reason 1 (Sylvester is sloppy) might consist of the following examples:

1. Sylvester throws his dirty clothes everywhere. His filthy socks and dirty underwear are draped over chairs, on the beds, and all over the floor. His stuff is draped all over my own desk, making it hard for me to keep my notes organized.
2. Sylvester never throws away his own trash—all available surfaces in the room are littered with pizza boxes, containers from McDonald's, candy bar wrappers, and so forth. The mess in the room upsets me so much that I have difficulty concentrating on my work.
3. Sylvester never cleans up any mess he makes. If he spills soda, the spill remains until the ants get to it. There's always something sticky on the dresser because Sylvester has knocked something over. Once he spilled soda all over a paper I was writing.

Support for reason 2 (Sylvester is inconsiderate) might consist of the following:

1. Sylvester plays his music loudly until very late at night, even when I am studying.
2. Sylvester invites his noisy friends in every night to argue, sing, and party until the early hours of the morning so that I can't get any sleep.
3. Sylvester's idea of a joke is to sneak up on my pet canary, Tweety, and scare her half to death. In fact, Tweety has become so traumatized that she has started to pluck her own feathers. I have had to spend time taking Tweety to the vet, taking time away from my studies.

These examples substantiate the reasons you cited in support of the claim "Sylvester is difficult to live with," and they significantly strengthen your argument because they are specific and concrete. Certainly the members of the Housing Bureau would be more likely to take your complaint against Sylvester seriously if you cited these specific examples of his difficult behavior.

EXERCISE

For a situation in your own life, write a claim supported by at least two reasons. Then, for each reason, cite evidence that provides support. If you have difficulty thinking of claims, here are some ideas you can use:

1. My parents are very old-fashioned because they think _____.
2. My children are unappreciative of whatever they have because they complain that _____.
3. Mr. Gradgrind is a terrible teacher because _____.
4. _____ is a film worth seeing because _____.
5. My roommate is difficult to live with because _____.
6. My (husband, wife, sister, brother, mother, father) is difficult to live with because _____.

For each claim, indicate the warrant on which it was based.

EXAMPLES AS EVIDENCE

Examples provide an important form of support. If you wish to argue that some children's toys reinforce gender stereotypes, you might cite the example of the "Talking Barbie" who says, "Math class is hard." If you wish to argue that a particular business charges extremely high prices, you can cite numerous examples to indicate that this is so. If you are examining the trend of many motorists to equip their cars as if they were homes and offices, you can cite examples of people who have not only phones and fax machines in their cars, but also video cameras, television sets, changes of clothes, and coffee makers. In her essay at the end of this chapter, "Talking from 9 to 5," Deborah Tannen uses the example of the university president who gives indirect orders to her assistant to illustrate an important theme in her essay—that women frequently speak differently than men do, even when they are in a position of power.

In selecting examples, be sure to use those that are concrete and pertinent; you should also make sure to include enough of them to be convincing. The following paragraph has little impact because it cites only a few general examples:

Working parents are concerned about a number of problems associated with child care. Often child-care facilities are dirty and poorly supervised.

More-specific examples and additional information, however, can improve this paragraph:

Working parents are concerned about a number of problems associated with child care. Day care is hard to find, difficult to afford, and often of distressingly poor quality. Having toured over a dozen facilities, one working mother tells appalling stories of what she found. In one place the children all were lined up in front of the TV like a bunch of zombies. In another, the place was so filthy that she was unable to find a clean spot in which to seat her child during the interview. Because of the scarcity of good facilities, waiting lists for established day-care centers are so long that parents apply for a spot months before their child is born, and, in some cases, before the child is even conceived.

Extended Examples

Sometimes it is useful to develop one example fully rather than to use several, as in the following paragraph:

> Child care has always been an issue for the working poor. Traditionally, they have relied on neighbors or extended family and, in the worst of times, have left their children to wander in the streets or tied to the bedpost. In the mid-19th century, the number of wastrels in the streets was so alarming that charity-minded society ladies established day nurseries in cities around the country. A few were sponsored by employers. Gradually, local regulatory boards began to discourage infant care, restrict nursery hours and place emphasis on a kindergarten or Montessori-style instructional approach. The nurseries became nursery schools, no longer suited to the needs of working mothers.
>
> Claudia Wallis, from "The Child-Care Dilemma: Millions of U.S. Families Face a Wrenching Question—Who's Minding the Kids?" *Time,* June 22, 1987

In this example, the main idea, "Child care has always been an issue for the working poor," is supported with a historical narrative of various problems existing in the past. Although the narrative contains a series of events, it really functions as an extended example of the first idea. Extended examples can be especially effective when you are recounting a personal experience.

Hypothetical Examples

Real examples or examples from your own life can be effective, but you can also cite hypothetical examples if they seem sufficiently illustrative of the point you are attempting to develop. For example, an illustration I have heard used in favor of bilingual education is as follows:

Suppose you were planning to visit another country for a long period of time. Certainly, you would find it easier to maneuver in that country if you had access to someone in the country who spoke your own language, could answer your questions, and provide an overview of what you would need to know. Now imagine what it would be like if you did not have access to such a person. Without that form of assistance, your adjustment to your new country would most likely take much longer.

Hypothetical examples can be especially useful if the concept you are explaining is difficult to understand or abstract. The essay "The Case for Torture" points out that in some instances, torture would be considered a moral act, and it uses the example of a terrorist who has refused to reveal the whereabouts of a deadly virus that will destroy civilization unless found immediately. The essay points out that in this instance, the use of torture might be considered morally justifiable.

AUTHORITY AS SUPPORT

Statements from authorities in the field provide another important form of support within the genre of argument. Even in casual conversation, the question "Who says so?" is frequently posed when someone offers an unsupported opinion, and the strength of your position will be greatly enhanced if you can say, "Several authorities on this subject say so" or perhaps, "I myself am an expert on this topic, and I say so."

The Authority of Personal Experience

Personal experience or the experiences of people you know can be an important source of support. For the topic of whether fairy tales are helpful or harmful for children, for example, most, if not all, of you will be able to recall fairy tales from your childhood, remember some of the feelings they evoked in you, and use these recollections to support your position on this topic. Many other topics also lend themselves to support through personal observation. If you were writing a paper about the role of resident advisors in college dorms, you might discuss the role your own advisor played in helping you adjust to college life. If you were writing about the necessity for public schools to provide after-school care, you might cite difficulties you have had finding adequate after-school activities for your own children. Topics relating to school, work, or travel are particularly likely to be within the realm of your personal experience that can be used to support your position.

PERSONAL EXPERIENCE AND APPEAL TO THE READER (PATHOS)

Short narratives and descriptions based on personal experience can be very appealing to readers, enabling them to share experiences with you that serve as support for your ideas. L. Christopher Awalt in his essay "Brother, Don't Spare a Dime" uses an example from his own experience to help readers understand how he arrived at his position on helping the homeless:

> One person I worked with is a good example. He is an older man who has been on the streets for about ten years. The story of his decline from respectability to alcoholism sounded believable and I wanted to help. After buying him toiletries and giving him clothes, I drove him one night to a Veterans Administration hospital, an hour and [a] half away, and put him into a detoxification program. I wrote him monthly to check on his progress into his program and attempted to line up a job for him when he got out. Four months into his program, he was thinking and speaking clearly and talking about plans he wanted to make. At five months, he expressed concern over the life he was about to lead. During the sixth month, I called and was told that he had checked himself out and returned home. A month later I found him drunk again, back on the streets.

> L. Christopher Awalt, "Brother, Don't Spare a Dime," *Newsweek,* September 30, 1991

When you read about Awalt's fruitless efforts to help this man, you may find yourself agreeing with him that it is often impossible to help the homeless. On the other hand, you may be wondering if this example is really representative of all or even of most of the homeless, which raises the important issue of when personal experience is appropriate to use in the genre of argument. Unfortunately, there is no hard and fast rule about this, but my recommendation is based on how typical it might be and how relevant it is to the topic. The well-known writer Richard Rodriguez, for example, used his own experience as the major source of evidence in his book, *Hunger of Memory.* Rodriguez recounts his experience with learning English and with adjusting to American society to argue against bilingual education policies; in essence, Rodriguez is claiming that his own experience has greater validity than the claims of the "experts" in the field of language acquisition who may not have actually gone through the experience of learning a second language as a child.

Personal experience, then, can enhance your own credibility (ethos) and have an impact on your reader (pathos). Keep in mind, however, that the genre of argument requires you to supplement personal experiences with material from other sources, so you should not plan to base your essay solely on your own experiences, even if they are typical and representative. Moreover, it is also possible that your own experiences may be neither typical nor representative. As the best-selling fiction writer John Irving observes,

> It's a myth that because it's your own experience you can't get it wrong. I find personal experience and memory are not necessarily a fiction writer's friends. You can make lots of mistakes and have many . . . misperceptions about what has been your own experience. The most outrageous of those being that since it was your experience it must be universal.
>
> *Los Angeles Times Book Review,* September 4, 1994

WRITING ASSIGNMENT

In a one- to two-page narrative, recount an experience you have had since you have enrolled at your college. The experience may be concerned with registration, an incident occurring in a class, the cafeteria, a club or team, and so forth. Then read your narrative aloud to a group of three classmates. Do they feel that your experience is typical? Would you be able to use this experience as an example in an argumentative essay?

AUTHORITIES FROM PUBLISHED WORKS

Even if you have had a great deal of personal experience with your topic, the inclusion of acknowledged authorities will enhance your credibility. Those who have published books and articles about the topic bring the weight of publication to their assertions and may have familiarity with aspects of the topic you may not have thought of; sometimes, they have been involved in the controversy a long time and can provide a historical perspective that you cannot have. Remember, though, that the publication of a book or article on an issue does not make that person an "authority." As a critical thinker, you should find out as much as possible about the author so that you can assess whether to include him or her in your essay.

Opinions of authorities can be included in a number of ways, such as:

■ to support a statement of yours, thus enhancing your authority
■ to contradict someone else's opinion
■ to indicate that an example you have cited is typical
■ to provide another example
■ to interpret facts
■ to analyze the causes of a problem
■ to offer a solution
■ to predict a consequence

Note the use of information from an authority in the following paragraph:

> Over the past several years, many American parents are being forced to make room for their adult children, who are returning to the nest in increasing numbers. "There is a naive notion that children grow up and leave home when they're 18, and the truth is far from that," says Sociologist Larry Bumpass of the University of Wisconsin in Madison. "Today, according to the U.S. Census Bureau, 59% of men and 47% of women between 18 and 24 depend on their parents for housing, some living in college dorms, but most at home."
>
> Anastasia Toufexis, "Show Me the Way to Go Home: Expected Numbers of Young Adults Are Living with Their Parents," *Time,* May 4, 1987

In this paragraph, the use of the sociologist and the citation of statistics from the U.S. Census Bureau indicate that the tendency of adult children to return home is typical. It thus helps establish the credibility of the writer who is examining this trend.

EXERCISE

Read Deborah Tannen's essay "Talking from 9 to 5" and note how she cites authorities in the fields of linguistics and anthropology to substantiate her thesis that "women and men are both indirect, but in addition to differences associated with their backgrounds—regional, ethnic and class—they tend to be indirect in different situations and in different ways."

In small groups discuss how Tannen's citations from authorities contribute to the author's credibility.

OTHER TYPES OF EVIDENCE

In addition to examples and the statements of authorities, two other effective forms of support within the genre of argument are *analogies* and *evidence provided by statistics.*

Analogy as Evidence

An analogy is an extended comparison between two "things" (processes, ideas, actions, etc.), a strategy that is especially useful for helping readers understand something unfamiliar by presenting it in terms of a parallel, more-familiar case. When used appropriately, analogy can be a helpful device for convincing an audience that if two things, or ideas, or policies are similar in one way, then they are also similar in other ways and that what is true for one is therefore true for the other.

In the following paragraph, Alfee Enciso uses an analogy to make his point that America tends to deny that it is racist:

> America's denial of its racism is tantamount to an alcoholic refuting his illness. And like an addict, if my students, city, or country continue to insist on being "colorblind" or judging all people by the content of their character, then the specter of racism will continue to rear its terrifying head.
>
> Alfee Enciso, "Living under 'a Veil of Denial,'" *Los Angeles Times,* December 1992

The analogy here attempts to establish that if America continues to deny that it is a racist country, it will never be able to improve, as is the case when an alcoholic denies his alcoholism.

Sometimes, however, an analogy may seem to strengthen a position, but when scrutinized more carefully, it breaks down. For example, look at the following paragraph, which uses an analogy to argue in favor of mandatory drug testing:

> Any of us who has ever gone for a medical examination has had to submit to a blood test. Blood tests are required for many jobs, entrance into schools, and even marriage licenses, and even if we think that they represent an invasion of privacy, we recognize their necessity because we feel that they are good for society. Drug testing, which involves the testing of urine, is similarly used for the good of society. However, many people object to mandatory drug testing because they consider it an invasion of privacy. But if we allow blood testing, surely we can allow urine testing for drugs, because drug abuse is such a tremendous societal problem.

In this paragraph, the writer is arguing by analogy that blood testing is similar to urine testing in that both may be considered invasions of privacy, but both are necessary for the good of society. However, if you examine this analogy carefully, you will see that in certain ways it doesn't completely support the case for mandatory drug testing because of the purposes for which these tests are used. Blood tests are used to diagnose diseases that usually can be cured, and thus the tests are used *for* the benefit of the person being tested. Urine tests for drug abuse are usually used to identify a drug user to his or her employer, and the information is often used *against* the person being tested. Moreover, people usually choose to have blood tests voluntarily as part of routine physical examinations, whereas urine tests for drugs are usually mandatory. The effectiveness of the analogy, then, is undercut by some of these differences.

Statistics

Showing what statistics indicate is another forceful way of supporting a position. However, statistics can also be misleading if they are not current, if they are not typical of the population they are intended to describe, or if they do not reflect what the author claims they reflect. Moreover, statistics are problematic not only for the average person, but also sometimes even for those who are familiar with statistical methods. In deciding on the credibility of a source that uses statistics, the three-pass approach to critical thinking can help you figure out if the writer has a particular agenda that he or she is using statistics to support. Pay particular attention to the following:

FACTORS TO CONSIDER IN EXAMINING STATISTICS

the source of the information

the size and representativeness of the sample

percentages versus actual figures

associative versus causal connections

The Source of the Information

In deciding whether or not to include statistical information, examine the source of the information and try to figure out how the numbers were obtained. Did the information come from a study that used a questionnaire? If so, do you have access to the sorts of questions that were asked, and do you feel that these questions elicited the information that they claim they did? Would people be likely to misrepresent, either intentionally or unintentionally?

The most reliable reports are those that are published in peer-reviewed journals. A particularly reliable source of statistics is a government organization because the government is unlikely to award money for research without seriously evaluating its importance.

The Size and Representativeness of the Sample

For a statistic to be valid, it should mean what the author says it means, and thus it should be representative of the population of which it is a sample. Yet, often a sample is drawn from only a small segment of the population, and it may not be representative at all. For instance, if you asked men in a pet store if they like dogs and cats and most answered "yes," it would not be valid to conclude that most men like dogs and cats because the population was self-selecting. Similarly, if you stood outside the student cafeteria with a sign reading, "please use this form to express your feelings about the food," it is likely that only students who feel very strongly about the food would bother to respond—probably the students who dislike the food would respond most frequently. You might then conclude that most of the students dislike the food when that might not be the case at all. Some studies are actually conducted in this way, but in examining their results, you should think carefully about how the information was obtained.

Percentages versus Actual Figures

The other point is to notice whether the statistic cites percentages or actual numbers and to reflect on the significance of what is being claimed. Both percentages and actual figures may not be significant if the number is fairly small, as in the following examples:

Twice as many college women are looking to marriage as their major goal in life, a study conducted at the University of Crockerville suggests. When questioned about their plans after college, 40 percent of respondents indicated that their primary goal after graduation was to find a husband, as opposed to only 20 percent of respondents questioned two years ago.

Of course, this paragraph does not state that only 20 women participated in the study. A critical reader might also ask who conducted the study and how the question was phrased.

Here is another example of how statistics can misrepresent information:

More college men expect their wives to stay at home and take care of the house in 1992 than they did in 1985, a study conducted at the University of Crockerville suggests. Whereas in 1985, only 500 college men responded in a survey that they expected their wives to stay at home, in 1992, 750 college men answered the same survey in the affirmative.

This paragraph does not state how many people were questioned, nor does it mention that the enrollment at the University of Crockerville increased extremely rapidly during these years, from 2,000 students in 1985 to 20,000 students in 1992. Therefore, the figure cited may actually indicate a *decline* in the proportion of college men who say that they expect their wives to stay at home.

Associative versus Causal Connections

An important point to keep in mind when deciding whether or not to include statistics is that a link between two events or situations does not necessarily imply cause and effect. For example, an article might claim that there is an association between the number of television sets in a region and death rates from heart attacks. But that doesn't mean that the television sets, themselves, caused the heart attacks. Instead, the association might mean that people who watch television a great deal get little exercise or perhaps eat fattier foods, both of which might be responsible for the increase in coronaries.

If you are writing about social issues, which are commonly used as subject matter in the genre of argument, it is particularly difficult to use statistics to make definitive statements because human behavior tends to be imprecise and difficult to measure. For example, one of the difficulties of assessing the effect of new educational programs in a classroom is that the effect of a particular teacher's personality cannot be measured definitively, and thus the success or failure of a particular program might be due to the teacher, not to the program itself. Similarly, in measuring the success of programs teaching basic skills such as reading and writing, improvement sometimes is not readily reflected on tests and often does not manifest itself immediately after instruction. The worth of any particular educational program is thus extremely difficult to assess objectively.

INTERVIEWS, SURVEYS, AND QUESTIONNAIRES

An additional source of evidence for essays in the genre of argument are interviews or surveys that you have conducted yourself. Interviews can be especially useful because they not only provide expert opinion and important information, but also can help you understand alternative or opposing viewpoints. The important point to remember about conducting an interview, though, is that you should plan for it carefully. Before the interview, find out as much as you can about the person you will be interviewing and be prepared to explain the interview's purpose. It is also a good idea to write out your questions in advance so that you don't waste time trying to formulate them during the interview. Of course, it goes without saying that you will receive a more favorable reception if you are punctual, courteous, and respectful. Do not argue with the people you are interviewing, even if you strongly disagree with them. Remember that the purpose of the interview is for you to gain material for your argumentative essay, not to engage in a debate.

In recording information from an interview, it is a good idea to tape it. If that is not possible, be sure to take good notes. Then as soon as the interview is over, rewrite your notes while the information is fresh in your mind.

An informal survey can also be an effective use of evidence. At a local school, an enterprising member of the PTA polled 86 parents about whether they wanted an after-school program for the children of working parents and whether they would be willing to contribute a small amount to it. Overwhelmingly, the response was positive, and as a result the school now has an afternoon child-care facility.

Questionnaires also provide useful information, but developing and distributing them are more tricky than writing an informal survey. In fact, those who write questionnaires as part of their research—social scientists, for example—must take special courses to learn how to do it properly. Writing a questionnaire may seem simple on the surface, but if the questions are confusingly worded or if the possibilities for response do not allow for enough flexibility, the questionnaire will bias the response and not provide accurate information. If you plan to write a questionnaire, you should include the following activities:

WORKING WITH A QUESTIONNAIRE

1. Explain its purpose.
2. Keep your questions simple.
3. Try it out on a friend to work out problematic sections before making multiple copies.
4. Make sure it is neatly typed and easy to read.

ANTICIPATING THE OPPOSITION: THE NEED FOR ADDITIONAL REASONS

The final support strategy I will discuss involves anticipating the objections your audience might have to your reasons and then supporting those reasons with other reasons. For example, Brian, the college student who wishes to change his major, might make the following argument:

Students should major in subjects that interest them.

Environmental studies interest me.

Therefore, I should major in environmental studies.

This line of thinking, however, might not be sufficient to convince his Uncle Stan, who might then pose the following objection to Brian's claim:

I don't believe that students should major in a subject just because it interests them. I, myself, am interested in a lot of things, like sports, for example. That doesn't mean that I should have been a recreational studies major or tried to become a professional baseball player. Your cousin majored in creative writing because it interested him, but now he can't earn a living. Choosing a major just out of interest is a luxury that only wealthy people can afford, and you, Brian, aren't wealthy.

Having considered Uncle Stan's objections, Brian might then respond with the qualification that people should major in subjects that interest them, provided that these subjects lead to employment after college. He could then point out the professional opportunities that exist in the field. Anticipating Uncle Stan's objections, Brian could also point out the differences between pursuing a sport such as baseball and majoring in a subject like environmental studies. He could argue that baseball is a highly competitive sport, at which only a few talented athletes succeed, whereas environmental studies is a growing field that requires students to learn many transferable skills such as statistics and mathematics and that is likely to provide diverse career opportunities in the future. By anticipating Uncle Stan's objections, Brian would thus be able to provide additional support.

EXERCISE: THE USE OF EVIDENCE IN A PUBLISHED ESSAY

To examine how evidence is used in a published essay, read "The Sex-Bias in Medicine" by Dr. Andrew Kadar. Dr. Kadar's thesis is that contrary to anecdotal evidence and widespread belief that American health-care delivery and research benefit women at the expense of men, the truth appears to be exactly the opposite. Read the essay carefully, noting Dr. Kadar's extensive use of evidence. In particular, pay attention to the following:

1. How does Dr. Kadar introduce his topic?
2. Where does Dr. Kadar state his claim?
3. Where does Dr. Kadar anticipate the opposition?
4. Note all the places where Dr. Kadar uses statistics. Do you find these statistics convincing? Why or why not?
5. What function does the conclusion play in this essay?
6. This essay does not use endnotes or footnotes. But *Atlantic Monthly* is known for its scrupulous examination of quoted material. Do you find this essay convincing even without these notes? Would you prefer that these notes had been included?

Talking from 9 to 5
Deborah Tannen

Deborah Tannen is University Professor of Linguistics at Georgetown University. This piece appeared in an altered form in her book *Talking from 9 to 5* (1994).

A university president was expecting a visit from a member of the board of trustees. When her secretary buzzed to tell her that the board member had arrived, she left her office and entered the reception area to greet him. Before ushering him into her office, she handed her secretary a sheet of paper and said: "I've just finished drafting this letter. Do you think you could type it right away? I'd like to get it out before lunch. And would you please do me a favor and hold all calls while I'm meeting with Mr. Smith?" 1

When they sat down behind the closed door of her office, Mr. Smith began by telling her that he thought she had spoken inappropriately to her secretary. "Don't forget," he said. "*You're* the president!" 2

Putting aside the question of the appropriateness of his admonishing the president on her way of speaking, it is revealing—and representative of many Americans' assumptions—that the indirect way in which the university president told her secretary what to do struck him as self-deprecating. He took it as evidence that she didn't think she had the right to make demands of her secretary. He probably thought he was giving her a needed pep talk, bolstering her self-confidence. 3

I challenge the assumption that talking in an indirect way necessarily reveals powerlessness, lack of self-confidence or anything else about the character of the speaker. Indirectness is a fundamental element in human communication. It is also one of the elements that varies most from one culture to another, and one that can cause confusion and misunderstanding when speakers have different habits with regard to using it. I also want to dispel the assumption that American women tend to be more indirect than American men. Women and men are both indirect, but in addition to differences associated with their backgrounds—regional, ethnic and class—they tend to be indirect in different situations and in different ways. 4

At work, we need to get others to do things, and we all have different ways of accomplishing this. Any individual's ways will vary depending on who is being addressed—a boss, a peer or a subordinate. At one extreme are bald commands. At the other are requests so indirect that they don't sound like requests at all, but are just a statement of need or a description of a situation. People with direct styles of asking others to do things perceive indirect requests—if they perceive them as requests at all—as manipulative. But this is often just a way of blaming others for our discomfort with their styles. 5

6   The indirect style is no more manipulative than making a telephone call, asking "Is Rachel there?" and expecting whoever answers the phone to put Rachel on. Only a child is likely to answer "Yes" and continue holding the phone—not out of orneriness but because of inexperience with the conventional meaning of the question. (A mischievous adult might do it to tease.) Those who feel that indirect orders are illogical or manipulative do not recognize the conventional nature of indirect requests.

7   Issuing orders indirectly can be the prerogative of those in power. Imagine, for example, a master who says "It's cold in here" and expects a servant to make a move to close a window, while a servant who says the same thing is not likely to see his employer rise to correct the situation and make him more comfortable. Indeed, a Frenchman raised in Brittany tells me that his family never gave bald commands to their servants but always communicated orders in indirect and highly polite ways. This pattern renders less surprising the finding of David Bellinger and Jean Berko Gleason that fathers' speech to their young children had a higher incidence than mothers' of both direct imperatives like "Turn the bolt with the wrench" *and* indirect orders like "The wheel is going to fall off."

8   The use of indirectness can hardly be understood without the cross-cultural perspective. Many Americans find it self-evident that directness is logical and aligned with power while indirectness is akin to dishonesty and reflects subservience. But for speakers raised in most of the world's cultures, varieties of indirectness are the norm in communication. This is the pattern found by a Japanese sociolinguist, Kunihiko Harada, in his analysis of a conversation he recorded between a Japanese boss and a subordinate.

9   The markers of superior status were clear. One speaker was a Japanese man in his late 40's who managed the local branch of a Japanese private school in the United States. His conversational partner was a Japanese-American woman in her early 20's who worked at the school. By virtue of his job, his age and his native fluency in the language being taught, the man was in the superior position. Yet when he addressed the woman, he frequently used polite language and almost always used indirectness. For example, he had tried and failed to find a photography store that would make a black-and-white print from a color negative for a brochure they were producing. He let her know that he wanted her to take over the task by stating the situation and allowed her to volunteer to do it: (This is a translation of the Japanese conversation.)

> On this matter, that, that, on the leaflet? This photo, I'm thinking of changing it to black-and-white and making it clearer. . . . I went to a photo shop and asked them. They said they didn't do black-and-white. I asked if they knew any place that did: They said they didn't know. They weren't very helpful, but anyway, a place must be found, the negative brought to it, the picture developed.

10   Harada observes, "Given the fact that there are some duties to be performed and that there are two parties present, the subordinate is supposed to assume that those are his or her obligation." It was precisely because of his

higher status that the boss was free to choose whether to speak formally or informally, to assert his power or to play it down and build rapport—an option not available to the subordinate, who would have seemed cheeky if she had chosen a style that enhanced friendliness and closeness.

The same pattern was found by a Chinese sociolinguist, Yuling Pan, in a 11 meeting of officials involved in a neighborhood youth program. All spoke in ways that reflected their place in the hierarchy. A subordinate addressing a superior always spoke in a deferential way, but a superior addressing a subordinate could either be authoritarian, demonstrating his power, or friendly, establishing rapport. The ones in power had the option of choosing which style to use. In this spirit, I have been told by people who prefer their bosses to give orders indirectly that those who issue bald commands must be pretty insecure; otherwise why would they have to bolster their egos by throwing their weight around?

I am not inclined to accept that those who give orders directly are really 12 insecure and powerless, any more than I want to accept that judgment of those who give indirect orders. The conclusion to be drawn is that ways of talking should not be taken as obvious evidence of inner psychological states like insecurity or lack of confidence. Considering the many influences on conversational style, individuals have a wide range of ways of getting things done and expressing their emotional states. Personality characteristics like insecurity cannot be linked to ways of speaking in an automatic, self-evident way.

Those who expect orders to be given indirectly are offended when they 13 come unadorned. One woman said that when her boss gives her instructions, she feels she should click her heels, salute, and say "Yes, boss!" His directions strike her as so imperious as to border on the militaristic. Yet I received a letter from a man telling me that indirect orders were a fundamental part of his military training. He wrote:

> Many years ago, when I was in the Navy, I was training to be a radio technician. One class I was in was taught by a chief radioman, a regular Navy man who had been to sea, and who was then in his third hitch. The students, about 20 of us, were fresh out of boot camp, with no sea duty and little knowledge of real Navy life. One day in class the chief said it was hot in the room. The students didn't react, except perhaps to nod in agreement. The chief repeated himself: "It's hot in this room." Again there was no reaction from the students.
>
> Then the chief explained. He wasn't looking for agreement or discussion from us. When he said that the room was hot, he expected us to do something about it—like opening the window. He tried it one more time, and this time all of us left our workbenches and headed for the windows. We had learned. And we had many opportunities to apply what we had learned.

This letter especially intrigued me because "It's cold in here" is the stan- 14 dard sentence used by linguists to illustrate an indirect way of getting someone to do something—as I used it earlier. In this example, it is the very obviousness and rigidity of the military hierarchy that makes the statement of a problem sufficient to trigger corrective action on the part of subordinates.

15   A man who had worked at the Pentagon reinforced the view that the burden of interpretation is on subordinates in the military—and he noticed the difference when he moved to a position in the private sector. He was frustrated when he'd say to his new secretary, for example, "Do we have a list of invitees?" and be told, "I don't know; we probably do" rather than "I'll get it for you." Indeed, he explained, at the Pentagon, such a question would likely be heard as a reproach that the list was not already on his desk.

16   The suggestion that indirectness is associated with the military must come as a surprise to many. But everyone is indirect, meaning more than is put into words and deriving meaning from words that are never actually said. It's a matter of where, when and how we each tend to be indirect and look for hidden meanings. But indirectness has a built-in liability. There is a risk that the other will either miss or choose to ignore your meaning.

17 On Jan. 13, 1982, a freezing cold, snowy day in Washington, Air Florida Flight 90 took off from National Airport, but could not get the lift it needed to keep climbing. It crashed into a bridge linking Washington to the state of Virginia and plunged into the Potomac. Of the 79 people on board, all but 5 perished, many floundering and drowning in the icy water while horror-stricken bystanders watched helplessly from the river's edge and millions more watched, aghast, on their television screens. Experts later concluded that the plane had waited too long after de-icing to take off. Fresh buildup of ice on the wings and engine brought the plane down. How could the pilot and co-pilot have made such a blunder? Didn't at least one of them realize it was dangerous to take off under these conditions?

18   Charlotte Linde, a linguist at the Institute for Research on Learning in Palo Alto, Calif., has studied the "black box" recordings of cockpit conversations that preceded crashes as well as tape recordings of conversations that took place among crews during flight simulations in which problems were presented. Among the black box conversations she studied was the one between the pilot and co-pilot just before the Air Florida crash. The pilot, it turned out, had little experience flying in icy weather. The co-pilot had a bit more, and it became heartbreakingly clear on analysis that he had tried to warn the pilot, but he did so indirectly.

19   The co-pilot repeatedly called attention to the bad weather and to ice building up on other planes:

> Co-pilot: Look how the ice is just hanging on his, ah, back, back there, see that?
> . . .
> Co-pilot: See all those icicles on the back there and everything?
> Captain: Yeah.

20   He expressed concern early on about the long waiting time between de-icing:

> Co-pilot: Boy, this is a, this is a losing battle here on trying to de-ice those things, it [gives] you a false feeling of security, that's all that does.

21   Shortly after they were given clearance to take off, he again expressed concern:

Co-pilot: Let's check these tops again since we been setting here awhile.
Captain: I think we get to go here in a minute.

When they were about to take off, the co-pilot called attention to the 22
engine instrument readings, which were not normal:

Co-pilot: That don't seem right, does it? [three-second pause] Ah, that's not
right. . . .
Captain: Yes, it is, there's 80.
Co-pilot: Naw, I don't think that's right. [seven-second pause] Ah, maybe it is.
Captain: Hundred and twenty.
Co-pilot: I don't know.

The takeoff proceeded, and 37 seconds later the pilot and co-pilot exchanged 23
their last words.

The co-pilot had repeatedly called the pilot's attention to dangerous condi- 24
tions but did not directly suggest they abort the takeoff. In Linde's judgment, he
was expressing his concern indirectly, and the captain didn't pick up on it—
with tragic results.

That the co-pilot was trying to warn the captain indirectly is supported by 25
evidence from another airline accident—a relatively minor one—investigated
by Linde that also involved the unsuccessful use of indirectness.

On July 9, 1978, Allegheny Airlines Flight 453 was landing at Monroe County 26
Airport in Rochester, when it overran the runway by 728 feet. Everyone survived.
This meant that the captain and co-pilot could be interviewed. It turned out that
the plane had been flying too fast for a safe landing. The captain should have realized this and flown around a second time, decreasing his speed before trying to
land. The captain said he simply had not been aware that he was going too fast. But
the co-pilot told interviewers that he "tried to warn the captain in subtle ways, like
mentioning the possibility of a tail wind and the slowness of flap extension." His
exact words were recorded in the black box. The crosshatches indicate words
deleted by the National Transportation Safety Board and were probably expletives:

Co-pilot: Yeah, it looks like you got a tail wind here.
Captain: Yeah.
[?]: Yeah [it] moves awfully # slow.
Co-pilot: Yeah the # flaps are slower than a #.
Captain: We'll make it, gonna have to add power.
Co-pilot: I know.

The co-pilot thought the captain would understand that if there was a tail 27
wind, it would result in the plane going too fast, and if the flaps were slow, they
would be inadequate to break the speed sufficiently for a safe landing. He
thought the captain would then correct for the error by not trying to land. But
the captain said he didn't interpret the co-pilot's remarks to mean they were
going too fast.

Linde believes it is not a coincidence that the people being indirect in these 28
conversations were the co-pilots. In her analyses of flight-crew conversations

she found it was typical for the speech of subordinates to be more mitigated—
polite, tentative or indirect. She also found that topics broached in a mitigated
way were more likely to fail, and that captains were more likely to ignore hints
from their crew members than the other way around. These findings are evidence that not only can indirectness and other forms of mitigation be misun-
derstood, but they are also easier to ignore.

29   In the Air Florida case, it is doubtful that the captain did not realize what the
co-pilot was suggesting when he said, "Let's check these tops again since we been
setting here awhile" (though it seems safe to assume he did not realize the gravity
of the co-pilot's concern). But the indirectness of the co-pilot's phrasing certainly
made it easier for the pilot to ignore it. In this sense, the captain's response, "I
think we get to go here in a minute," was an indirect way of saying, "I'd rather
not." In view of these patterns, the flight crews of some airlines are now given
training to express their concerns, even to superiors, in more direct ways.

30   The conclusion that people should learn to express themselves more
directly has a ring of truth to it—especially for Americans. But direct communication is not necessarily always preferable. If more direct expression is better
communication, then the most direct-speaking crews should be the best ones.
Linde was surprised to find in her research that crews that used the most mitigated speech were often judged the best crews. As part of the study of talk
among cockpit crews in flight simulations, the trainers observed and rated the
performances of the simulation crews. The crews they rated top in performance had a higher rate of mitigation than crews they judged to be poor.

31   This finding seems at odds with the role played by indirectness in the examples of crashes that we just saw. Linde concluded that since every utterance
functions on two levels—the referential (what it says) and the relational (what
it implies about the speaker's relationships), crews that attend to the relational
level will be better crews. A similar explanation was suggested by Kunihiko
Harada. He believes that the secret of successful communication lies not in
teaching subordinates to be more direct, but in teaching higher-ups to be more
sensitive to indirect meaning. In other words, the crashes resulted not only
because the co-pilots tried to alert the captains to danger indirectly but also
because the captains were not attuned to the co-pilots' hints. What made for
successful performance among the best crews might have been the ability—or
willingness—of listeners to pick up on hints, just as members of families or
longstanding couples come to understand each other's meaning without anyone being particularly explicit.

32   It is not surprising that a Japanese sociolinguist came up with this explanation; what he described is the Japanese system, by which good communication
is believed to take place when meaning is gleaned without being stated
directly—or at all.

33 While Americans believe that "the squeaky wheel gets the grease" (so it's best to
speak up), the Japanese say, "The nail that sticks out gets hammered back in" (so
it's best to remain silent if you don't want to be hit on the head). Many Japanese

scholars writing in English have tried to explain to bewildered Americans the ethics of a culture in which silence is often given greater value than speech, and ideas are believed to be best communicated without being explicitly stated. Key concepts in Japanese give a flavor of the attitudes toward language that they reveal—and set in relief the strategies that Americans encounter at work when talking to other Americans.

Takie Sugiyama Lebra, a Japanese-born anthropologist, explains that one of 34 the most basic values in Japanese culture is *omoiyari*, which she translates as "empathy." Because of *omoiyari*, it should not be necessary to state one's meaning explicitly; people should be able to sense each other's meaning intuitively. Lebra explains that it is typical for a Japanese speaker to let sentences trail off rather than complete them because expressing ideas before knowing how they will be received seems intrusive. "Only an insensitive, uncouth person needs a direct, verbal, complete message," Lebra says.

Sasshi, the anticipation of another's message through insightful guesswork, 35 is considered an indication of maturity.

Considering the value placed on direct communication by Americans in 36 general, and especially by American business people, it is easy to imagine that many American readers may scoff at such conversational habits. But the success of Japanese businesses makes it impossible to continue to maintain that there is anything inherently inefficient about such conversational conventions. With indirectness, as with all aspects of conversational style, our own habitual style seems to make sense—seems polite, right and good. The light cast by the habits and assumptions of another culture can help us see our way to the flexibility and respect for other styles that is the only best way of speaking.

QUESTIONS

1. What is Tannen's claim? What is her warrant, and how does she support it?
2. Define what Tannen means by the term "indirect speaking." Based on the opening anecdote, what kind of value judgment does she think American society makes about this manner of communication?
3. Does Tannen use analogies effectively? Are there important differences between her analogies and her topic? Explain.
4. What kind of evidence is Tannen using to support her argument? Do you believe it is effective? Why or why not?
5. Tannen describes a specific type of verbal exchange: a simple statement meant to elicit a response in a subordinate. Think about your own life, in school, at work, at home. Have you experienced this indirect form of address? When? Where? With whom?
6. Do you believe that an indirect manner of speaking or writing has a place in your school or professional career? Write a dialogue between yourself and a superior (either at school or work) in which you are trying to correct a mistake he/she has made.

The Sex-Bias Myth in Medicine
Andrew Kadar, M.D.

Dr. Andrew Kadar is an anesthesiologist at Cedars Sinai Hospital in Los Angeles. This essay was published in *Atlantic Monthly* (August 1994).

1   "When it comes to health-care research and delivery, women can no longer be treated as second-class citizens." So said the President of the United States on October 18, 1993.

2   He and the First Lady had just hosted a reception for the National Breast Cancer Coalition, an advocacy group, after receiving a petition containing 2.6 million signatures which demanded increased funding for breast-cancer prevention and treatment. While the Clintons met with leaders of the group in the East Room of the White House, a thousand demonstrators rallied across the street in support. The President echoed their call, decrying the neglect of medical care for women.

3   Two years earlier Bernadine Healy, then the director of the National Institutes of Health, charged that "women have all too often been treated less than equally in . . . health care." More recently Representative Pat Schroeder, a co-chair of the Congressional Caucus for Women's Issues, sponsored legislation to "ensure that biomedical research does not once again overlook women and their health." Newspaper articles expressed similar sentiments.

4   The list of accusations is long and startling. Women's-health-care advocates indict "sex-biased" doctors for stereotyping women as hysterical hypochondriacs, for taking women's complaints less seriously than men's, and for giving them less thorough diagnostic workups. A study conducted at The University of California at San Diego in 1979 concluded that men's complaints of back pain, chest pain, dizziness, fatigue, and headache more often resulted in extensive workups than did similar complaints from women. Hard scientific evidence therefore seemed to confirm women's anecdotal reports.

5   Men more often than women undergo angiographies and coronary-artery-bypass-graft operations. Even though heart disease is the No. 1 killer of women as well as men, this sophisticated, state-of-the-art technology, critics contend, is selectively denied to women.

6   The problem is said to be repeated in medical research: women, critics argue, are routinely ignored in favor of men. When the NIH inventoried all the research it had funded in 1987, the money spent on studying diseases unique to women amounted to only 13.5 percent of the total research budget.

7   Perhaps the most emotionally charged disease for women is breast cancer. If a tumor devastated men on a similar scale, critics say, we would declare a state of national emergency and launch a no-cost-barred Apollo Project–style program to cure it. In the words of Matilda Cuomo, the wife of the governor of

New York, "If we can send a woman to the moon, we can surely find a cure for breast cancer." The neglect of breast-cancer research, we have been told, is both sexist and a national disgrace.

Nearly all heart-disease research is said to be conducted on men, with the 8 conclusions blindly generalized to women. In July of 1989 researchers from the Harvard Medical School reported the results of a five-year study on the effects of aspirin in preventing cardiovascular disease in 22,071 male physicians. Thousands of men were studied, but not one woman: women's health, critics charge, was obviously not considered important enough to explore similarly. Here, they say, we have definite, smoking-gun evidence of the neglect of women in medical research—only one example of a widespread, dangerous phenomenon.

Still another difference: pharmaceutical companies make a policy of giving 9 new drugs to men first, while women wait to benefit from the advances. And even then the medicines are often inadequately tested on women.

To remedy all this neglect, we need to devote preferential attention and 10 funds, in the words of the *Journal of the American Medical Women's Association,* to "the greatest resource this country will ever have, namely, the health of its women." Discrimination on such a large scale cries out for restitution—if the charges are true.

In fact one sex does appear to be favored in the amount of attention devoted to 11 its medical needs. In the United States it is estimated that one sex spends twice as much money on health care as the other does. The NIH also spends twice as much money on research into the diseases specific to one sex as it does on research into those specific to the other, and only one sex has a section of the NIH devoted entirely to the study of diseases afflicting it. That sex is not men, however. It is women.

In the United States women seek out and consequently receive more med- 12 ical care than men. This is true even if pregnancy-related care is excluded. Department of Health and Human Services surveys show that women visit doctors more often than men, are hospitalized more often, and undergo more operations. Women are more likely than men to visit a doctor for a general physical exam when they are feeling well, and complain of symptoms more often. Thus two out of every three health-care dollars are spent by women.

Quantity, of course, does not guarantee quality. Do women receive second- 13 rate diagnostic workups?

The 1979 San Diego study, which concluded that men's complaints more 14 often led to extensive workups than did women's, used the charts of 104 men and women (fifty-two married couples) as data. This small-scale regional survey prompted a more extensive national review of 46,868 office visits. The results, reported in 1981, were quite different from those of the San Diego study.

In this larger, more representative sample, the care received by men and 15 women was similar about two thirds of the time. When the care was different, women overall received more diagnostic tests and treatment—more lab tests, blood-pressure checks, drug prescriptions, and return appointments.

16   Several other, small-scale studies have weighed in on both sides of this issue. The San Diego researchers looked at another 200 men and women in 1984, and this time found "no significant differences in the extent and content" of workups. Some women's-health-care advocates have chosen to ignore data from the second San Diego study and the national survey while touting the first study as evidence that doctors, to quote once again from the *Journal of the American Medical Women's Association,* do "not take complaints as seriously" when they come from women: "an example of a double standard influencing diagnostic workups."

17   When prescribing care for heart disease, doctors consider such factors as age, other medical problems, and the likelihood that the patient will benefit from testing and surgery. Coronary-artery disease afflicts men at a much younger age, killing them three times as often as women until age sixty-five. Younger patients have fewer additional medical problems that preclude aggressive, high-risk procedures. And smaller patients have smaller coronary arteries, which become obstructed more often after surgery. Whereas this is true for both sexes, obviously more women fit into the smaller-patient category. When these differences are factored in, sex divergence in cardiac care begins to fade away.

18   To the extent that divergence remains, women may be getting better treatment. At least that was the conclusion of a University of North Carolina/Duke University study that looked at the records of 5,795 patients treated from 1969 to 1984. The most symptomatic and severely diseased men and women were equally likely to be referred for bypass surgery. Among the patients with less-severe disease—the ones to whom surgery offers little or no survival benefit over medical therapy—women were less likely to be scheduled for bypass surgery. This seems proper in light of the greater risk of surgical complications, owing to women's smaller coronary arteries. In fact, the researchers questioned the wisdom of surgery in the less symptomatic men and suggested that "the effect of gender on treatment selection may have led to more appropriate treatment of women."

19   As for sophisticated, pioneering technology selectively designed for the benefit of one sex, laparoscopic surgery was largely confined to gynecology for more than twenty years. Using viewing and manipulating instruments that can be inserted into the abdomen through keyhole-sized incisions, doctors are able to diagnose and repair, sparing the patient a larger incision and a longer, more painful recuperation. Laparoscopic tubal sterilization, first performed in 1936, became common practice in the late 1960s. Over time the development of more-versatile instruments and of fiber-optic video capability made possible the performance of more-complex operations. The laparoscopic removal of ectopic pregnancy was reported in 1973. Finally, in 1987, the same technology was applied in gallbladder surgery, and men began to enjoy its benefits too.

20   Years after ultrasound instruments were designed to look inside the uterus, the same technology was adapted to search for tumors in the prostate. Other pioneering developments conceived to improve the health care of women include mammography, bone-density testing for osteoporosis, surgery to allevi-

ate bladder incontinence, hormone therapy to relieve the symptoms of menopause, and a host of procedures, including in vitro fertilization, developed to facilitate impregnation. Perhaps so many new developments occur in women's health care because one branch of medicine and a group of doctors, gynecologists, are explicitly concerned with the health of women. No corresponding group of doctors is dedicated to the care of men.

So women receive more care than men, sometimes receive better care than men, and benefit more than men do from some developing technologies. This hardly looks like proof that women's health is viewed as secondary in importance to men's health. 21

The 1987 NIH inventory did indeed find that only 13.5 percent of the NIH research budget was devoted to studying diseases unique to women. But 80 percent of the budget went into research for the benefit of both sexes, including basic research in fields such as genetics and immunology and also research into diseases such as lymphoma, arthritis, and sickle-cell anemia. Both men and women suffer from these ailments, and both sexes served as study subjects. The remaining 6.5 percent of NIH research funds were devoted to afflictions unique to men. Oddly, the women's 13.5 percent has been cited as evidence of neglect. The much smaller men's share of the budget is rarely mentioned in these references. 22

As for breast cancer, the second most lethal malignancy in females, investigation in that field has long received more funding from the National Cancer Institute than any other tumor research, though lung cancer heads the list of fatal tumors for both sexes. The second most lethal malignancy in males is also a sex-specific tumor: prostate cancer. Last year approximately 46,000 women succumbed to breast cancer and 35,000 men to prostate cancer; the NCI spent $213.7 million on breast cancer research and $51.1 million on study of the prostate. Thus although about a third more women died of breast cancer than men of prostate cancer, breast-cancer research received more than four times the funding. More than three times as much money per fatality was spent on the women's disease. Breast cancer accounted for 8.8 percent of cancer fatalities in the United States and for 13 percent of the NCI research budget; the corresponding figures for prostate cancer were 6.7 percent of fatalities and three percent of the funding. The spending for breast-cancer research is projected to increase by 23 percent this year, to $262.9 million; prostate-research spending will increase by 7.6 percent, to $55 million. 23

The female cancers of the cervix and the uterus accounted for 10,100 deaths and $48.5 million in research last year, and ovarian cancer accounted for 13,300 deaths and $32.5 million in research. Thus the research funding for all female-specific cancers is substantially larger per fatality than the funding for prostate cancer. 24

Is this level of spending on women's health just a recent development, needed to make up for years of prior neglect? The NCI is divided into sections dealing with issues such as cancer biology and diagnosis, prevention and control, 25 etiology, and treatment. Until funding allocations for sex-specific concerns became a political issue, in the mid-1980s, the NCI did not track organ-specific spending data. The earliest information now available was reconstructed retroactively to 1981. Nevertheless, these early data provide a window on spending patterns in the era before political pressure began to intensify for more research on women. Each year from 1981 to 1985 funding for breast-cancer research exceeded funding for prostate cancer by a ratio of roughly five to one. A rational, nonpolitical explanation for this is that breast cancer attacks a larger number of patients, at a younger age. In any event, the data fail to support claims that women were neglected in that era.

26   Again, most medical research is conducted on diseases that afflict both sexes. Women's-health advocates charge that we collect data from studies of men and then extrapolate to women. A look at the actual data reveals a different reality.

27   The best-known and most ambitious study of cardiovascular health over time began in the town of Framingham, Massachusetts, in 1948. Researchers started with 2,336 men and 2,873 women aged thirty to sixty-two, and have followed the survivors of this group with biennial physical exams and lab tests for more than forty-five years. In this and many other observational studies women have been well represented.

28   With respect to the aspirin study, the researchers at Harvard Medical School did not focus exclusively on men. Both sexes were studied nearly concurrently. The men's study was more rigorous, because it was placebo-controlled (that is, some subjects were randomly assigned to receive placebos instead of aspirin); the women's study was based on responses to questionnaires sent to nurses and a review of medical records. The women's study, however, followed nearly four times as many subjects as the men's study (87,678 versus 22,071), and it followed its subjects for a year longer (six versus five) than the men's study did. The results of the men's study were reported in the *New England Journal of Medicine* in July of 1989 and prompted charges of sexism in medical research. The women's-study results were printed in the *Journal of the American Medical Association* in July of 1991, and were generally ignored by the nonmedical press.

29   Most studies on the prevention of "premature" (occurring in people under age sixty-five) coronary-artery disease have, in fact, been conducted on men. Since middle-aged women have a much lower incidence of this illness than their male counterparts (they provide less than a third as many cases), documenting the preventive effect of a given treatment in these women is much more difficult. More experiments were conducted on men not because women were considered less important but because women suffer less from this disease. Older women do develop coronary disease (albeit at a lower rate than older men), but the experiments were not performed on older men either. At most the data suggest an emphasis on the prevention of disease in younger people.

30   Incidentally, all clinical breast-cancer research currently funded by the NCI is being conducted on women, even though 300 men a year die of this tumor. Do studies on the prevention of breast cancer which specifically exclude males

signify a neglect of men's health? Or should a disease be studied in the group most at risk? Obviously, the coronary-disease research situation and the breast-cancer research situation are not equivalent, but together they do serve to illustrate a point: diseases are most often studied in the highest-risk group, regardless of sex.

What about all the new drug tests that exclude women'? Don't they prove 31 the pharmaceutical industry's insensitivity to and disregard for females?

The Food and Drug Administration divides human testing of new medicines 32 into three stages. Phase 1 studies are done on a small number of volunteers over a brief period of time, primarily to test safety. Phase 2 studies typically involve a few hundred patients and are designed to look more closely at safety and effectiveness. Phase 3 tests precede approval for commercial release and generally include several thousand patients.

In 1977 the FDA issued guidelines that specifically excluded women with 33 "childbearing potential" from phase 1 and early phase 2 studies; they were to be included in late phase 2 and phase 3 trials in proportion to their expected use of the medication. FDA surveys conducted in 1983 and 1988 showed that the two sexes had been proportionally represented in clinical trials by the time drugs were approved for release.

The 1977 guidelines codified a policy already informally in effect since the 34 thalidomide tragedy shocked the world in 1962. The births of armless or otherwise deformed babies in that era dramatically highlighted the special risks incurred when fertile women ingest drugs. So the policy of excluding such women from the early phases of drug testing arose out of concern, not out of disregard, for them. The policy was changed last year, as a consequence of political protest and recognition that early studies in both sexes might better direct testing.

Throughout human history from antiquity until the beginning of this cen- 35 tury men, on the average, lived slightly longer than women. By 1920 women's life expectancy in the United States was one year greater than men's (54.6 years versus 53.6). After that the gap increased steadily, to 3.5 years in 1930, 4.4 years in 1940, 5.5 in 1950, 6.5 in 1960, and 7.7 in 1970. For the past quarter of a century the gap has remained relatively steady: around seven years. In 1990 the figure was seven years (78.8 versus 71.8).

Thus in the latter part of the twentieth century women live about 10 percent 36 longer than men. A significant part of the reason for this is medical care.

In past centuries complications during childbirth were a major cause of 37 traumatic death in women. Medical advances have dramatically eliminated most of this risk. Infections such as smallpox, cholera, and tuberculosis killed large numbers of men and women at similar ages. The elimination of infection as the dominant cause of death has boosted the prominence of diseases that selectively afflict men earlier in life.

Age-adjusted mortality rates for men are higher for all twelve leading causes 38 of death, including heart disease, stroke, cancer, lung disease (emphysema and pneumonia), liver disease (cirrhosis), suicide, and homicide. We have come to accept women's longer life span as natural, the consequence of their greater biological fitness. Yet this greater fitness never manifested itself in all the millennia of human history that preceded the present era and its medical-care system—the same system that women's-health advocates accuse of neglecting the female sex.

39   To remedy the alleged neglect, an Office of Research on Women's Health was established by the NIH in 1990. In 1991 the NIH launched its largest epidemiological project ever, the Women's Health Initiative. Costing more than $600 million, this fifteen-year program will study the effects of estrogen therapy, diet, dietary supplements, and exercise on heart disease, breast cancer, colon cancer, osteoporosis, and other diseases in 160,000 postmenopausal women. The study is ambitious in scope and may well result in many advances in the care of older women.

40   What it will not do is close the "medical gender gap," the difference in the quality of care given the two sexes. The reason is that the gap does not favor men. As we have seen, women receive more medical care and benefit most from medical research. The net result is the most important gap of all: seven years, 10 percent of life.

QUESTIONS

1. What kind of argument format is Kadar using? Is his structure effective? Why?
2. How is statistical data used in this argument? Would more information about the genesis of studies cited be helpful to determine their accuracy? What else would you like to know?
3. After reviewing the data Kadar offers, do you come to the same conclusions he has? Why or why not?
4. Do you feel Kadar has successfully anticipated negative responses? Explain and give details.

Chapter 7

ORGANIZING AND INCORPORATING OUTSIDE INFORMATION

Imagine a college student emerging from the library, her backpack stuffed with all sorts of potentially useful materials she has found in articles and books. She walks jauntily, pleased with the success of her visit to the library, and when she arrives home she fixes herself a snack, sits down at her desk, and piles all of her materials around her, ready to begin to work. But then she looks at all the "stuff" she has found, and her euphoria suddenly evaporates. "Now that I have found it, what do I do now?" she thinks to herself. "How can I learn all the information in these materials? What should I do to understand it? How should I organize it so that I will really be able to use it in my essay? How much of it should I use? How can I create order out of all of this chaos?"

Gathering information from the library is an important part of the research and writing process. But after you have found materials you can use, you need to be able to take notes, figure out how you might use the information you have found to support your thesis, and incorporate it smoothly into your essay using proper documentation conventions—in other words, to "create order out of chaos." Organizing, synthesizing, and documenting information are particularly important in the genre of argument because it is important to demonstrate to your reader that you have thoroughly researched and considered necessary information, background, and viewpoints. Whereas personal information is sufficient for some genres, such as a personal narrative or an exploratory essay on a personal topic, academic argument requires you to gain a breadth of perspective on your topic.

This chapter is concerned with various strategies for managing information. It discusses methods for taking notes, including summaries and direct quotations, and suggestions for organizing and incorporating information smoothly into your text.

BEING ACTIVE IN THE RESEARCH PROCESS

To thoroughly engage with your topic, it is important to assume an active role in all stages of the research process. Before you even begin to search for sources, it is a good idea to do some preliminary exploration of the topic or even to write a rough draft of your essay so that you can jot down a possible thesis. With at least some idea of your thesis, you will be more focused in searching for information, although it is likely that your ideas will change, at least somewhat, as you discover new possibilities.

As you read and take notes, you should not simply be trying to "learn" or memorize; rather, you should be thinking about how new information or a particular perspective corresponds to what you already know about the topic, whether or not you are convinced by it, and how you might be able to use it in your essay. If you simply record information mechanically, without thinking much about it, or if you photocopy many articles and selections from books and then sit down with a highlighter, skimming and underlining mechanically, you may be spending a great deal of time photocopying, waiting to use the copy machine, and underlining. But when you have finished, you may not have reflected deeply on what you have read.

If this describes your own method of working with information, you might consider whether your method really is saving you time. On the surface, it appears quite easy and efficient, but unless you become involved with what you read, either by taking notes or by writing comments in the margin, you can breeze through an entire essay without really reading it at all—you simply cast your eye over the page and move your highlighter deftly over what seem to be important sentences. But then, when you are in the process of actually writing your essay and want to incorporate information from outside sources, you may discover that you have forgotten completely what these sources are about and that you are unable to remember where a piece of information you want to use is located. Then you will have to spend considerable time rereading. In many instances, the quick highlighting job is not really efficient at all.

The Role of Outside Sources

The genre of argument uses information from published works to support the thesis and to indicate that the writer has thoroughly researched the topic. Because you are probably not an authority on the topic you are writing about, your argument needs the support of credible experts who have worked and/or published in the field. For example, in the following excerpt from an essay supporting the death penalty, Steve cites statistics he found in an article by Frank Kelly published in the *New York State Bar Journal:*

> For the death penalty to work as a deterrent, it must be allowed to instill fear in the criminals. As of now, that threat does not exist because "any punishment, including death, will cease to be an effective deterrent if it is recognized as mostly bluff" (Kelly 62). As an article published in the New York State Bar Journal points out, "from 1976 to 1990, there have been only 134 executions in the 14 participating states" (Kelly 62).

Because Steve could not know these statistics on the basis of his own experience, he obtained them from the *New York State Bar Journal,* a reputable journal that carefully reviews its submissions. Statistics published in such a source are examined and verified, ensuring a high degree of accuracy. Moreover, although the idea that "no punishment is likely to be effective if it is perceived as mainly bluff" is logical and convincing on its own, the fact that a contributor to the *New York State Bar Journal* has stated it lends additional credibility to Steve's thesis and strengthens Steve's argument.

Common Knowledge

In working with information obtained from outside sources, students often are confused about what kind of information should be documented. Some kinds of information are considered "common knowledge." This is information that most people know and therefore does not require a reference. For instance, the statement that the Los Angeles riots occurred in the spring of 1992 is common knowledge, but any commentary on that incident—for instance, the number of arrests or the extent of the damage—would require a reference. Similarly, the fact that Malcolm X was a civil rights leader who was assassinated is common knowledge; however, if you refer to a social historian who claimed that Malcolm X did not condone racial violence, as is commonly assumed, then it is important that you acknowledge that point of view through a citation. Sometimes it is difficult to determine whether something is common knowledge because for someone it may be new information. In general, though, well-known facts are considered common knowledge; opinions and observations on these facts must be documented.

Distinguishing between
Primary and Secondary Sources

When you are citing your sources, you need to be aware that there is a difference between primary and secondary sources. A primary source provides firsthand or "primary" knowledge of your topic. It is the original work or document upon which your paper is based. Primary sources would include such items as the Declaration of Independence or a novel or poem. If you are writing about a particular person, a statement made by that person would constitute a primary source, and it is possible for you to obtain primary source material from interviews published in the newspaper.

A secondary source is any type of commentary on the primary source. For instance, an article that analyzes the Declaration of Independence is a secondary source. A critical commentary on a work of literature is a secondary source. A statement made about the person who is the subject of your paper is a secondary source. For instance, if you are writing a paper about the president's economic views, his own statements about proposed tax increases are a primary source, but newspaper articles commenting on his statements would be a secondary source.

It is important to differentiate between primary and secondary sources so that you do not misrepresent or distort in any way. For instance, the following sentence was written by an observer and is therefore a secondary source:

The president was obviously concerned by the latest allegations in the Whitewater case.

This statement reflects the opinion of someone who observed the president, and it may only indicate that to the observer, the president appeared to be concerned. However, the phrase "obviously concerned" is also interpretive because it suggests that the president may have something to hide or is guilty in some way. All secondary sources are interpretive to some degree, and it is important to be aware of that when you decide to use them in your essay.

In contrast, an actual statement made by the president is a primary source. If you were listening to the president speak, and he said, "I am concerned about these latest allegations because it will take up more of my time," his statement is a primary source.

How Many Sources to Use?
How Do These Sources Function within the Essay?

You may be under the impression that the more sources you use, the better your papers will be. However, it is the *quality*, rather than the number of sources, that is important, and it is the *function* that these sources fulfill within the text that determines an essay's quality. In deciding to use a source, the main consideration, after assessing its quality, is what role it will play in your essay. Sources can be used as **examples,** as a **source of factual data,** as **expert support,** or as a representation of the **opposition** against which the essay will then argue.

In trying to decide how many sources to use, you should include enough to show that you have "done your homework." However, if you include too many sources, the paper will read like a long list of quotations, and your own position will be overwhelmed. The key is to use enough sources to support your position, but not so many that your own perspective is lost.

A SUGGESTED METHOD FOR
TAKING NOTES: USING WORK SHEETS

In order to work with information effectively and efficiently, it is important to construct a method of taking notes that works for you. Many students have been taught to use index cards for this purpose, and if you have been successful in using them, you should continue. No particular system of note-taking is best for everyone.

However, some people find that a note card does not leave enough space to write on and that when they fragment ideas, they lose the sense of the main point of the article or book selection as a whole. Those who prefer to take notes in the context of the whole work or those who like to take a lot of notes and jot down ideas for using them as they occur may prefer to use work sheets, pads of paper, or the computer. If you are interested in using note sheets rather than note cards for the purpose of recording information from outside sources, I suggest that you create note sheets from a long pad of lined paper or make copies of the sheets included in this chapter. You can also replicate the form of this sheet on your computer. Then, I suggest that you use the following procedure:

SUGGESTIONS FOR TAKING NOTES

1. Select your sources
Using the three-pass approach, select those sources you want to read for the purpose of taking notes. If possible, photocopy each selection that you think will be particularly useful so that you will be able to refer to it again. When you photocopy, be sure to include the page that contains the bibliographical information because this can be a valuable resource for locating additional material if you need it.

2. Record bibliographical information at the top of a note sheet
At the top of a note sheet, copy down all relevant bibliographical information—the author's name, the title of the book or article, the copyright or journal information, and the page numbers of the selection. Even if you have a photocopy of the material, it is still important to record this information in your notes because you do not want to lose track of your sources. All of us who write have had the experience of rereading our notes and finding a statement that we really want to use, but for which we cannot locate the source. Many a frantic last-minute scramble around the library has been due to carelessness about recording a source.

3. Briefly summarize the main point of the selection at the top of the sheet
After recording the bibliographical information at the top of the sheet, try to get an overview of the work so that you can write a summary of it (introductory paragraphs, abstracts, and book introductions are useful for this). A summary of the selection or article will help you understand your notes more fully when you look them over at a later time. Without that summary, you may not remember how the notes you took fit into the author's main idea, and they will then be less meaningful to you. Of course, you may not be able to discern the main point of the selection as a whole until you have read it through, so leave a few lines blank for this purpose.

(continued)

(continued from the previous page)

4. Record notes

Read the selection carefully, and when you come upon an idea that you think is important or that you may want to use in your essay, **write down the number of the page** on which it occurs and then either copy the quotation directly, using quotation marks, or summarize or paraphrase the ideas it expresses. As you write down your notes, ideas may come to you about how you would like to use that note in your essay. As they occur, write these ideas down so that you don't forget them, and mark each one with a symbol such as an asterisk (*) so that it will attract your attention later when you reread your notes.

To illustrate how this method can be used to write an actual essay, let us look at how Tyrone took notes for his essay, which is concerned with potential dangers associated with genetic research. The article he took notes on was titled "Genetics and Human Malleability," published in *The Hastings Center Report,* January/February 1990, 67-73. The author was W. French Anderson. Here is how Tyrone recorded some information from that article using a note sheet:

EXAMPLE OF A NOTE SHEET

Bibliographical Information:

Anderson, W. French. "Genetics and Human Malleability," *The Hastings Center Report,* January/February 1990, 67–73.

Summary:

The article distinguishes between *somatic* cell gene therapy used to cure diseases and *enhancement* genetic engineering, which would enable scientists to engineer away characteristics that those in power consider abnormal or undesirable. The main position of the article is that genetic engineering should be restricted to medical therapy.

Notes:

  * Information provided on W. French Anderson, who has pioneered research on gene therapy. Shows his credibility.

68 ". . . successful somatic cell gene therapy also opens the door for enhancement genetic engineering, that is, for supplying a specific characteristic that individuals might want for themselves (somatic cell engineering) or their children (germline engineering) which would not involve the treatment of a disease."

  * Use in defining differences between somatic and enhancement therapy.

70 Raises a number of ethically questionable scenarios.

"Should a pubescent adolescent whose parents are both five feet tall be provided with a growth hormone gene on request?"

  * Could be used as an example of possible dangers of unrestricted genetic testing.

This example also raises the question about how to distinguish a serious disease from a "minor" disease from cultural "discomfort."

Important to make this distinction.

In this example of a note sheet, the author's last name appears first in the bibliographic information, enabling Tyrone to alphabetize his sheets very easily when he is compiling his bibliography. Notice that Tyrone has distinguished direct quotations from paraphrase by enclosing the direct quotation in quotation marks and that he used an ellipsis in the first note (marked with three spaced dots like this: . . .) to show that some of the quotation was left out. Distinguishing direct quotation from paraphrase or summary is very useful when you reread your notes because it will enable you to document properly if you decide to include that particular note in your paper. If you take notes on the computer, you will be able to paste them directly into your essay, saving you some time. Note also that Tyrone has made notes for himself about how he might want to use information from this article in his paper.

RECORDING INFORMATION IN THE FORM OF DIRECT QUOTATION

In recording information on a note sheet, there are many instances in which you would prefer direct quotation rather than paraphrase or summary. These may be summarized as follows:

1. Use direct quotation if the style is so unusual that you wish to retain its flavor. Here is an example:

One of the most famous scenes in the history of film is the moment in *Gone with the Wind* when Rhett says to Scarlett, "Frankly, my dear, I don't give a damn."

It would be much less effective if this were summarized, as in the following example:

One of the most famous scenes in the history of film is the moment in *Gone with the Wind* when Rhett tells Scarlett that he is completely indifferent to what happens to her.

2. Use direct quotation if the passage was spoken by a particular authority or famous person, and you wish to use the actual words of that authority to support your own position.
For example:

The well-known physician Lewis Thomas argues that "the only solid piece of scientific truth about which I feel really confident is that we are profoundly ignorant about nature" (321).

3. Use direct quotation if you are discussing someone's firsthand experience, and you wish to capture that immediacy by using the speaker's or writer's actual words.

For example:

John Burns, eyewitness to the accident, said that "the Mercedes was speeding down the street at about 70 miles an hour."

In this instance, the use of direct quotation enhances the reliability of the statement.

Punctuating Direct Quotations in Your Text

If you decide to quote your source directly using direct quotation, be sure to enclose all quoted material within quotation marks and punctuate as follows:

1. Place commas and periods *inside* quotation marks. Thus:

On the astrology page of the *Star Gazette,* the well-known astrologist Fifi Moonbeam stated that "Jupiter will ally itself with Mars in two weeks" and that "the Moon will be in its seventh house."

However, if you are including a page reference in parentheses, then the comma or period goes after the quotation marks. Thus:

On the astrology page of the *Star Gazette,* the well-known astrologist Fifi Moonbeam stated that "Jupiter will ally itself with Mars in two weeks" (7) and that within the month "the Moon will be in its seventh house" (8).

2. Place semicolons and colons outside of the quotation marks. For example, here is a passage from a book by Roland Smith about the habits of cats:

Many cats sleep at least sixteen hours a day, their favorite spot usually being a chair or some place relatively high off the ground such as an ironing board. Even a comfortable fluffy rug will not usually attract them because it lies on the floor.

Roland Smith, *The Lion at the Hearth: The Way of the Cat*

If you wish to quote from this passage in a sentence that has a semicolon, this is how you would do it:

Smith discusses the tendency that cats have of sleeping "relatively high off the ground"; he notes that they will avoid even a soft, fluffy rug because it "lies on the floor" (49).

If you wish to quote from this passage in a sentence that has a colon, this is how you would do it:

Smith notes two favorite sleeping places for cats: "a chair or some place relatively high off the ground" (49).

3. Question marks and exclamation marks are kept **within** quotation marks if they are part of the original quotation. For example:

Speaking to his nephew, Uncle Stan asked, "What's so interesting about environmental studies?"

Because the question mark is part of the original quotation, the question mark is kept inside. However, when the sentence itself is in the form of a question, the question mark is placed **outside** the quotation marks, as in the following example:

Didn't the nephew have an answer prepared when Uncle Stan asked what is "so interesting about environmental studies"?

Because the question mark is part of the whole sentence, it is placed outside of the quotation marks.

4. Single quotation marks are placed inside double quotation marks for a quote within a quote:

The nephew said, "I needed some more time to respond to Uncle Stan's question about what is 'so interesting about environmental studies.' "

5. If you omit part of a quotation, use an ellipsis (three spaced dots). For example, here is a paragraph from Roland Smith's book about cats:

The cat remains a mysterious animal. Although it is a popular domestic pet, it never really loses its wildness, and one can always sense the throb of the jungle behind an inscrutable pair of cat eyes. Watch a cat as it stalks its prey, its body motionless, its whole being intent on the chase, and it is clear that the deep feline nature of the lion lies just beneath the skin of even the most domesticated tabby sleeping by a fire.

Roland Smith, *The Lion at the Hearth: The Way of the Cat,* 57

Here is an example of a sentence that quotes directly from this paragraph using an ellipsis:

Roland Smith maintains that the cat "never really loses its wildness and . . . that the deep feline nature of the lion lies just beneath the skin of even the most domesticated tabby" (57).

6. Use brackets whenever you need to substitute or add words to a quotation. For example:

Roland Smith maintains that when a cat "stalks its prey, its body [becomes] motionless [and] its whole being [becomes] intent on the chase" (57).

WRITING A SUMMARY

A summary, defined as a restatement of a piece of writing in a compact form, is an important strategy for working with information because it helps you to understand the major point, important ideas, and structure of a source. Summaries are very useful for condensing a longer piece of writing and help you gain a clear sense of the author's purpose and the major direction of the piece.

The Purpose of a Summary

The type of summary you write depends on the purpose for which it is intended. If you are writing the summary for yourself, and you have retained the full copy of the text, the summary can be much shorter and less detailed than one written for a reader who has not read the original and has no access to it. But whether you write a summary for yourself or for someone else, it is important to note the author and/or the article's title and to include sufficient details so that any reader, including you at a later time, will be able to understand it without confusion.

If you are writing the summary for yourself (in a note sheet, for example) you would write a shortened version of the information contained in the book or article without necessarily mentioning the author or title in the actual summary. If you plan to incorporate the summary into your essay, you should include the author's name and the title. To illustrate the differences between these types of summary, read the following passage from Michael Crichton's "Introduction" to his novel *Jurassic Park* and note the two summaries that follow.

Original Passage

But the biotechnology revolution differs in three important respects from past scientific transformations.

First, it is broad-based. America entered the atomic age through the work of a single research institution, at Los Alamos. It entered the computer age through the efforts of about a dozen companies. But biotechnology research is now carried out in more than two thousand laboratories in America alone. Five hundred corporations spend five billion dollars a year on this technology.

Second, much of the research is thoughtless or frivolous. Efforts to engineer paler trout for better visibility in the stream, square trees for easier lumbering, and injectable scent cells so you'll always smell of your favorite perfume may seem like a joke, but they are not. Indeed, the fact that biotechnology can be applied to the industries traditionally subject to the vagaries of fashion, such as cosmetics and leisure activities, heightens concern about the whimsical use of this powerful new technology.

Third, the work is uncontrolled. No one supervises it. No federal laws regulate it. There is no coherent government policy, in America or anywhere else in the world. And because the products of biotechnology range from drugs to farm crops to artificial snow, an intelligent policy is difficult.

But most disturbing is the fact that no watchdogs are found among scientists themselves. It is remarkable that nearly every scientist in genetics research is also engaged in the commerce of biotechnology. There are no detached observers. Everybody has a stake.

A summary for oneself might be written as follows:

The biotechnology revolution differs from past scientific transformations in three important respects. First, it is more "broad-based." Second, it sometimes is geared toward unimportant areas of investigation and often follows the "vagaries of fashion," and third, it is not subject to consistent government regulation. But what is of most concern is that there are no "watchdogs" among the scientists themselves because most have commercial affiliations (Crichton *Jurassic Park*).

Note that in this summary, neither the title nor the author are mentioned. The information is simply replicated in a shorter form.

In contrast, a summary that includes the author and the title indicates the distinction between the writer of the summary and the author of the passage. Here is an example:

In his "Introduction" to *Jurassic Park,* Michael Crichton notes three ways in which the current biotechnology differs from "past scientific transformations." The first is that it is "broad-based" in that it is conducted in over 2,000 laboratories. The second is that it sometimes is geared toward unimportant areas of investigation and often follows the "vagaries of fashion," and the third is that it is not subject to consistent government regulation. But what Crichton identifies as of most concern is that there are no "watchdogs" among the scientists themselves because most have a commercial stake in their research.

In this summary, emphasis is placed on the author and source. Note that in both summaries, quotation marks are used whenever the author's exact words are included. This is very important to remember in order to avoid inadvertent plagiarism.

Writing the Summary: Some Suggestions

Writing a summary means understanding the overall meaning of the text and making decisions about what is important. Here are some steps you might find helpful for writing a summary:

1. *Scan for the main point.* A summary represents the essence of a book or article, and it is therefore necessary to understand the main point that the author is trying to make before you write. To find this main point, scan the first paragraph or two because this is often where the main argument or thesis may be found. Then look over the conclusion, where you may find an overview of the results or a rephrasing of the main ideas in the text. After you feel that you understand the main point, look for subpoints that might be related to it.

2. *Determine the structure.* By locating subpoints, you will gain insight into the structure of the text. If you are working with a photocopy of the work you are summarizing, underline the subpoints and be sure to include them in your summary. Try to distinguish main points from examples. Decide whether you need to include any examples in your summary.

3. *Condense lists and eliminate extraneous detail.* Most published works have at least some repetition and superfluous detail. In selecting material to eliminate, look for repetition and unnecessary elaboration. Pay attention to words or even whole paragraphs that may simply repeat previously stated information or link two paragraphs together.

4. *Use synonyms and rephrase.* Finding synonyms and rephrasing can help you understand what you read and can develop your writing style. Avoid copying too much material from the text, particularly if you plan to include it in your essay.

5. *Rewrite the summary so that it reads well.* Particularly if you plan to include the summary in your essay, you should rewrite it so that it reads well.

EXERCISE

Choose one of the following passages and write a summary of it:

Today, huge television audiences watch surgical operations in the comfort of their living rooms. Moreover, thanks to the animated cartoon, the geography of the digestive system has become familiar territory even to the nursery school set, and the satisfaction of curiosity about almost all matters is a national pastime. Obviously, then, the secrecy surrounding embalming can, surely, hardly be attributed to the inherent gruesomeness of the subject.

Adapted from Jessica Mitford, "Behind the Formaldehyde Curtain," *The American Way of Death*

The koala, all 10 to 30 pounds and two to three feet of it (there is an amazing range in size among adults), is a beast of tall trees. Koalas live most of their lives high up in any one of 35 species of eucalyptus, or gum tree. They subsist on eucalyptus leaves, which they can't digest on their own. They rely on microorganisms in their digestive tract to do it for them. They can also handle some mistletoe leaves and some leaves from a tree known as the box.

Roger Caras, "What's a Koala?"

As much as America is joined in a common culture, Americans are reluctant to celebrate the process of assimilation. We pledge allegiance to diversity. America was born Protestant and bred Puritan, and the notion of community we share is derived from a seventeenth-century faith. Presidents and the pages of ninth-grade civics readers yet proclaim the orthodoxy: We are gathered together—but as individuals with separate pasts, distinct destinies. Our society is as paradoxical as a Puritan congregation: We stand together, alone.

Richard Rodriguez, "Does America Still Exist?"

My concern is that, at this point in the development of our culture's scientific expertise, we might be like the young boy who loves to take things apart. He is bright enough to disassemble a watch, and maybe even be bright enough to get it back together again so that it works. But what if he tries to "improve" it? Maybe put on bigger hands so that the time can be read more easily. But if the hands are too heavy for the mechanism, the watch will run slowly, erratically, or not at all. The boy can understand what is visible, but he cannot comprehend the precise engineering calculations that determined exactly how strong each spring should be, why the gears interact in the ways that they do, etc. Attempts on his part to improve the watch will probably only harm it. We are now able to provide a new gene so that a property involved in a human life would be changed, for example a growth hormone gene. If we were to do so simply because we could, I fear we would be like that young boy who changed the watch's hands. We, too, do not really understand what makes the object we're tinkering with tick. . . .

W. French Anderson, "Genetics and Human Malleability," *The Hastings Center Report,* January/February 1990, 67–73

EXERCISE

Read "How Far Should We Go?" by Gail Vines. Write a summary of this article and use a note sheet to take notes on it.

Sample Sheet for Taking Notes

Bibliographical Information:

Summary:

Page Number: Note:

AVOIDING PLAGIARISM

The term *plagiarism* is derived from the Latin word *plagiarius,* meaning "kidnapper," and to plagiarize means to steal, to take what is not yours. In current usage, to plagiarize is to take the ideas of another writer and to pass them off as one's own. It is the unacknowledged borrowing of sources.

Today, plagiarism is considered a serious academic offense (often resulting in a failing grade, or worse), but in earlier times the unacknowledged borrowing of sources was not considered a problem. In fact, in the Middle Ages, to mimic or echo another author's ideas, style, or actual words was considered the highest compliment. Originality was not valued, nor were authors considered the owners of their work. Shakespeare never even published his own plays, and those who did felt free to amend them as they wished (at one point *King Lear* was even given a happy ending!). It was not until the eighteenth century that an author's writing was seen as a personal expression, and thus a personal possession.

In using information from published works in the genre of argument, an author's words and ideas are considered a form of permanent property that must be acknowledged, even if these words were downloaded directly from a Web page. When you use another writer's words or ideas and acknowledge that you have used them, it is as if you are borrowing that property. But if you use another writer's words or ideas and do not acknowledge your source, it is as if you are stealing something that does not belong to you. And the theft of words and ideas in the genre of argument is regarded very seriously. At the present time, when so much information is readily available via the Internet, people are paying very close attention to the acknowledgement of sources. It is therefore very important that you learn to document the information you have found in outside sources.

The two types of documentation style that are most commonly used are the MLA (Modern Language Association) and the APA (American Psychological Association), and the style of documentation varies according to discipline, both of which are discussed in the Appendix. Some useful manuals that can be found in your library include:

MLA Handbook for Writers of Research Papers. 3rd ed. (New York: MLA, 1995)

This explains the MLA system, which is preferred in most disciplines in the humanities, including philosophy, religion, and history.

Publication Manual of the American Psychological Association. 4th ed. (Washington, D. C.: APA, 1994)

This outlines the APA system, which is preferred in most disciplines in the social sciences, including sociology, political science, and economics.

The Chicago Manual of Style. 14th ed. (Chicago: University of Chicago Press, 1993)

This method uses a system of footnotes inserted into the text. It is often required for research papers in history and for some humanities publications.

Before deciding which system you should use, check with your instructor.

WRITING ASSIGNMENTS

Assignment 1 (this assignment was created by Jennifer Welsh at the University of Southern California):

Our culture's attitude toward science and technology has its roots in the Enlightenment, a period in which reason and observable fact were believed to hold the answers to any questions we could think up. Being steeped in these beliefs, we have difficulty imagining any other way of thinking: Questions about the limitations and risks of scientific knowledge seem to threaten our most fundamental principle that to know more is always better. But the controversies surrounding new discoveries and technological developments, from the atomic bomb to gene splicing, from computers to threshing machines, suggest that we are not as comfortable with this principle as we thought. Certainly, in the introduction to *Jurassic Park,* Michael Crichton suggests the need for scientists to be monitored. He points out that a major problem with current research in biotechnology is that there are no "watchdogs" among the scientists themselves because most have a commercial stake in their research.

Writing Topic

Choose one area of scientific research that has the potential for having a profound impact on humanity (genetic engineering and prenatal testing lend themselves well to this topic). Use the library and, if possible, the Internet, to find out more information about it. Then write a four- to six-page argument essay that addresses the following question:

Are there dangers inherent in this type of research that scientists ought to consider?

Assignment 2 (this assignment was created by Jennifer Oguma at the University of Southern California):

Choose two movies that use the theme of science or technology running amok: *Terminator II, Frankenstein, Back to the Future, The Fly* and, of course, *Jurassic Park* are good possibilities. Examine the attitude toward scientific research expressed in these movies and note that in all of them, the "creator" is blamed or holds himself responsible, at least in part, for the ensuing events. Then write an argumentative essay of four to six pages addressing the following topic:

Should scientists be responsible for the consequences of their work?

Sample Student Paper Using Information from Outside Sources

Tyrone Emery   Genetic Testing

Genetic testing is the fastest-growing area in medical research and can be
used to diagnose illnesses in children and adults. Researchers have
already found genes associated with Alzheimer's disease, Huntington's
chorea, and colon cancer, and it is a realizable possibility that tests based
on these and other discoveries might be able to warn people that they are
at risk for these diseases. Used with therapies that replace defective
genes with working ones, genetic tests could lead to cures. However, the
rapid growth of genetic testing is raising ethical questions for which
there are no simple answers. Some of the information obtained from this
research can easily be misinterpreted and lead to discriminatory employment and insurance practices. Moreover, the potential danger that genetic
testing will lead to genetic "improvements" cannot be overlooked.

   Genetic illness is often understood in terms of the single-gene model,
in which a defect in a gene causes a particular health effect. Some diseases work this way (such as sickle-cell anemia and Tay-Sachs disease),
and interpretations of the single-gene model invite people to think that
genes equal fate. However, it is now recognized that because many conditions arise from both genetic and environmental factors, this model is
turning out to be an oversimplification. No more than three percent of all
human diseases are caused by defects in a single gene (Rennie), and for
most illnesses, genetic tests can never by themselves predict the course
of a patient's health.

   Moreover, the misperception that genes determine health on a one-to-
one ratio can have serious social and ethical repercussions. In fact,
screening programs aimed at detecting genetic diseases in large groups of
people have already been attempted with often less than desirable
results. In the early 1970s the federal government funded a screening
program to detect carriers of the sickle-cell gene, which is prevalent in
the African-American community. Characteristics of the disease, for
which there is no cure, include fever, anemia, and pain in the joints and
abdomen (Harkavy). However, instead of providing insight into the dis-

ease, the testing became a weapon to justify long-standing prejudices. Some insurance companies began to deny coverage to black carriers on the grounds that they had a preexisting medical condition or that their children were bad risks. Some scientists even suggested that the best solution to the anemia problem would be for blacks carrying the gene not to breed. Eventually, this misinformation was corrected and the test began to be useful, but the problems caused by widespread testing for sickle-cell anemia indicate the potential harm that could arise from uncritical use of genetic screening.

Of course, in some instances, genetic screening has done a great deal of good, as is the case involving screening for Tay-Sachs disease, which is prevalent among Jews of eastern European descent. Children born with this disease suffer from a gradual deterioration leading to mental retardation, paralysis, and blindness, usually dying before the age of four (Harkavy). However, with the advent of genetic testing, couples who both are carriers of the mutation can choose to have preimplantation genetic testing, which enables scientists to analyze the DNA of cells taken from pre-embryos and to implant in the mother those genes that do not carry the deadly Tay-Sachs disease (Rennie). The tests set at ease the minds of fearful couples who might otherwise never risk having children.

Unlike the screening for sickle-cell anemia, the Tay-Sachs program was always voluntary, which means that people had the opportunity to prepare for the consequences of the testing. Genetic testing should always be voluntary, and the results should be kept confidential to prevent misuse. Moreover, patients undergoing such testing should be provided with access to genetic counseling, so that they can understand the results and their implications.

Much of the potential harm associated with genetic testing concerns discrimination by insurance companies. Community rating is a system in which a customer's premiums are determined by the health profile of his or her community. Genetic information about individuals does not matter. Insurers claim that individual risk rating serves the public welfare more equitably at less expense and that therefore genetic information is needed to set fair rates for all policy holders. It would be wrong, they argue, to make healthy people pay higher premiums because they had been lumped in with those at higher risk (Rennie). The problem, however, is that everybody is genetically defective in some way. According to most estimates, everyone carries at least 5 to 10 genes that could make that person sick under the wrong circumstances or could adversely affect children (Rennie). The ability of insurers and others to interpret genetic information wisely is questionable, and as the circumstances surrounding the testing for sickle-cell anemia suggest, such information has the potential to fuel discrimination.

Moreover, an additional potentially harmful issue associated with genetic testing concerns the difficulty of distinguishing between a genetic disease and an undesirable trait. As genetic researcher W. French Anderson points out,

> . . . successful somatic cell gene therapy also opens the door for enhancement genetic engineering, that is, for supplying a specific characteristic that individuals might want for themselves (somatic cell engineering) or their children (germline engineering) which would not involve the treatment of a disease. (68)

Scientists are showing that genes influence many aspects of human behavior such as intelligence, alcoholism, overeating, anger, and murderous aggression (Horgan). Would it be ethically appropriate to use genetic testing and genetic therapies to enhance height or intelligence? Suppose a memory-enhancing gene were discovered—on what basis would a decision be made "to allow one individual to receive the gene but not another" (Anderson 70)? Although some argue that all scientific discoveries are useful and that research should not be inhibited, we need to ask ourselves a question: Will we know what to do with all this information about a human's genetic map?

Presuming technological feasibility, parents may someday be able to select their children's sex, height, or other cosmetic features, and the consequences of those choices may be hard to predict. In order to minimize its potentially adverse effects, genetic testing should be restricted to those conditions for which there is some urgency and for which some beneficial intervention is possible, either as therapy or as reproductive planning. We should try to stay out of those areas where genetic diseases and undesirable traits are blurred and focus on those that can prevent illnesses and death.

Works Cited

Anderson, W. French. "Genetics and Human Malleability." The Hastings Center Report, January/February 1990, 67–73.

Harkavy, Michael. The American Spectrum Encyclopedia. Uitgeverij Het Spectrum B.V, 1991.

Horgan, John. "Eugenics Revisited." Scientific American (June 1993): 122–128+.

Kolata, Gina. "If Tests Hint Alzheimer's, Should a Patient Be Told?" New York Times. 24 October 1995: A11.

Rennie, John. "Grading the Gene Tests." Scientific American (June 1994): 88–92.

Siebert, Charles. "At the Mercy of Our Genes." New York Times. 5 January 1996: A11.

Vines, Gail. "How Far Should We Go?" New Scientist (February 1994): 12–13.

EXERCISE

The preceding student paper incorporates outside sources for a variety of purposes, and each instance in which sources have been used has been highlighted. Note each instance and then in small groups discuss the form each one has taken (quotation or summary) and the purpose of each one within the essay.

How Far Should We Go?
Gail Vines

Gail Vines has published numerous articles on scientific topics and is the author of *Raging Hormones: Do They Rule Our Lives?* (1994). This article first appeared in *New Scientist* (February 12, 1994).

On 5 October 1992, a young German woman on her way home from work 1 drove her car into a tree, smashing her skull. She was 13 weeks pregnant.

The woman was flown by helicopter to the university hospital in Erlangen, 2 Bavaria, and put on life support. Doctors declared her brain dead but, when they asked her parents to agree to organ donation, they refused. The doctors then decided to try to keep her body alive until March the following year, when they hoped to deliver the child by Caesarean section. Nobody knew who the father was, and he never came forward. The woman's parents agreed to this plan, although they later told a national newspaper that they consented only under pressure from doctors. On 16 November, the fetus spontaneously aborted, and died. The German press criticised the doctors' actions, portraying the case as a grisly experiment that destroyed the dignity of the woman's death, and called for tighter controls over clinical practice.

More recently, in Britain, a similar press furore followed the news of the 3 birth of twins to a woman of 59 on Christmas Day, and the prospect of babies being born from fetal eggs. Scientists and doctors worried that a critical media could generate a public backlash ending in some forms of research and clinical practice being banned.

One response to these concerns are "ethics committees," which are already 4 commonplace in Europe and North America, to supplement the professional "self-regulation" of medicine. Most doctors and scientists have welcomed the chance to present at least their research proposals to committees, if only to reassure the public. But are these committees effective? And how good are the controls over what scientists and doctors can do to people?

Most ethics committees in Britain are based at universities and hospitals, 5 and assess local research proposals, most of which are trials of drugs in patients or healthy volunteers. There are more than 200 of these local research ethics committees in Britain, although the shake-up of the NHS has put the future of some in doubt.

Guidelines on what these committees should do, and who should be on 6 them, have been issued by the Department of Health, the Royal College of Physicians and the Medical Research Council, among others. But there is no statutory requirement to stick to any of these guidelines, or to submit research to a committee.

The health department says the job of the committees includes ensuring 7 that the scientific benefit of a study outweighs the cost to subjects in the trial, that any hazards are minimal and can be coped with, that subjects have given informed consent, and to check on the inducements offered to doctors, nurses, patients or volunteers for taking part in the study.

8   However, hardly any ethics committees concern themselves with issues of everyday clinical practice, such as when a doctor wants to try out a drug in a new way or a new surgical technique that he or she does not consider to be research.

9   One exception to this rule is a new ethics committee led by Claire Rayner, the agony aunt and former pediatric nurse, at Northwick Park Hospital in London. It plans to consider all manner of issues affecting patients' health, including the procedures used for selecting employees.

10   Great Ormond Street Hospital in London is also setting up a committee where staff can talk over worries they have about clinical practice. "There should be many more such committees," says Rabbi Julia Neuberger, chairman of Camden and Islington Community Health Services NHS Trust.

11   At a national level, the Human Fertilisation and Embryology Authority (HFEA), which licenses IVF clinics and research that falls within its remit, does concern itself with clinical practice. But even its well-funded review system is not foolproof. Simon Fishel, an embryologist at the University of Nottingham, says the authority approved his proposal to use a new fast-freeze technique to store embryos without realising that it was new. "Several babies had been born by the time they told me they had made an error, and could I please stop using the technique," he says.

12   According to a report Neuberger produced in 1992 for the King's Fund, an independent centre in London that focuses on health policy issues, most local ethics committees are seriously under-resourced. She found that performance varies widely and that most committees have little power to enforce decisions. Because doctors and scientists are not required to submit research for ethical review, "there is the worry that if they [committees] are too fierce, research won't be sent to them," Neuberger says.

13   "Bad research is unethical in itself," she adds. Yet most committees are unable to judge the quality of research, partly because there is "a shocking lack of statisticians on these committees." Moreover, few committees monitor research to ensure that it is carried out as agreed.

14   The health department recommends that committees should be made up of between eight and twelve members, including doctors, nurses and at least two lay members. Neuberger found more than a third of these bodies have no or only one lay person, and most are dominated by hospital doctors.

Poorly Trained

15 Committees need to be properly funded and staffed, says Neuberger, with at least one full-time worker. "Now, at best, the committee is one-eighth of someone's job," and most members work on a voluntary basis.

16   Committees now deal with a throughput that is "absolutely enormous," says Richard Nicholson, editor of the *Bulletin of Medical Ethics*. At least one com-

mittee reviews 500 proposals a year. "You're talking about six weeks of unpaid work a year if you're going to do it properly," he says. Some committees vet 30 proposals in two hours. "That cannot be a proper review," says Nicholson.

Even the best local ethics committees can only react to research proposals [17] presented to them. Debating broader issues and thinking ahead are often left to ethical committees linked to professional organisations, such as the British Medical Association, which represents most British doctors. "It is a very good thing that the BMA has an ethics committee," says philosopher John Harris, research director of the Centre for Social Ethics and Policy at the University of Manchester, and a member of the BMA's ethics committee. "The problem is with the way it works."

Last year the BMA ethics committee ruled that there was nothing wrong in [18] principle with parents availing themselves of sperm-sorting technologies to choose the sex of their children. But at the association's annual meeting, the rank and file overturned the committee's ruling. "I don't see much point in an organisation having an ethics committee, deliberating these issues with expert advice, if they are going to be overturned by a show of hands by the proverbial GP with his 3-litre Rover, one rainy afternoon in Margate or wherever," says Harris. He argues that the members should have presented their reasons to the ethics committee for further deliberation.

But Britain's time-honoured way of deciding whether advances in science [19] and medicine need special controls is to set up ad hoc committees of inquiry, such as the Warnock Committee into embryo research and fertility treatment, which greatly influenced the 1990 act that lays down the law in these areas. But this piecemeal approach inevitably leads to delays in decision-making and a lack of continuity.

To avoid these problems, France set up a national committee in 1983. So far, [20] Britain has not followed suit. In 1991, the Nuffield Foundation set up its bioethics council to fill the gap in Britain, but only after soundings made it clear that the government "was satisfied with ad hoc inquiries," says Patrick Nairne, now chairman of the Nuffield Council on Bioethics. Bioethics is too important to be left to scientists, doctors and academics, he says. "It is on the agenda for all of us."

The council sees its function as defining ethical questions raised by medical [21] and biological advances and anticipating public concern. Through its reports, it hopes to stimulate public debate. The first fruit of its labours arrived last December—a report on genetic screening which urged a moratorium on the use of genetic information by insurance companies. The Nuffield Foundation has agreed to continue funding for another three years but, says David Shapiro, executive secretary of the council, "If the government were to change its mind and set up a standing Royal Commission on Bioethics, it would represent the ultimate aim of those who came to the foundation in 1988."

Harris, however, has misgivings about the ultimate value of national ethics [22] committees: "These are usually a group of worthies and are relatively conservative bodies." They tend, he argues, to look at issues from the point of view of "what you think you could get the public to find acceptable, as the Warnock committee did, rather than what ought to be acceptable." Instead, he says, they should work out what they think is right and try to persuade people through education.

23   "The real trouble with ethics committees is that they tend to encourage the habit of mind that says, 'we've referred it to them, the ethics is now sorted, now we can just get on with the business.' " This is not the right approach, Harris argues. "Ethics committees should be the start of the national debate."

Public Participation

24 But successful attempts to involve the public in making ethical decisions are few and far between. In a move in this direction, the HFEA recently produced a "consultation document" on the prospect of transferring eggs taken from cadavers or fetuses into women who want to have children. It encouraged the public to send in comments by 1 June. But these exercises may do little to reveal the public's real feelings: the authority's first consultation document on sex selection prompted only a few hundred responses from the public.

25   To stimulate public debate, the Danes and the Dutch have devised special "consensus conferences," in which a dozen or so lay people meet for several weekends to read and discuss the issues. They can call on expert witnesses from a wide range of disciplines. The event culminates in a large public meeting over several days in which the lay panel's conclusions are aired.

26   "It is a good way of opening up debate," says Nicholson. In Denmark, the reports of the panels go to parliament where they carry considerable influence (*This Week*, 3 October 1992). But the process is also expensive, running to about £50 000 per conference.

27   Nonetheless, the Agricultural and Food Research Council announced in November that it is to fund a series of consensus conferences on aspects of biotechnology. The first, at the end of this year, will concentrate on plant biotechnology and genetically engineered food.

28   Meanwhile, the Danish Council of Ethics is hosting an international conference on "ethical debate and public participation" in Copenhagen this April, "to clarify how the interaction between scientists, politicians and the public can be managed."

29   "We envy the Danes," says Shapiro. "It is very impressive the way they can reach out into the community. The chair of their ethics council can call in the editors of the 20 largest newspapers and say 'we are going to have a debate.' Here, you'd be lucky if you could assemble even three features editors from Fleet Street."

QUESTIONS

1. Identify Vines's use of primary sources. Identify the use of secondary sources. Is Vines directing our understanding of these materials?
2. What are the key points in this essay? Identify and restate in your own words.

3. What are the ethical issues that Vines feels need to be addressed? Can you construct a theoretical model of an ethics committee that would address these points?
4. What are the possible dangers involved in the scientific breakthroughs that Vines mentions? In what ways could they prove damaging to individuals? Society? The medical industry?
5. This article focuses on the British scientific community. Are there parallels between their problems and problems we face in the United States? Look for a source detailing a medical ethical question here in the States. Summarize it and compare it to Vines's essay.
6. Do you agree that the "consensus conferences" offered by the Danes and the Dutch enable the layperson to make an educated decision about the ethics of new scientific practices? What would the layperson need to know to make an informed decision?

Chapter 8

THE FUNCTION OF FORM

When you are assigned to write argumentative essays in college, many of your teachers will expect a particular essay structure that has been in existence since the time of the ancient Greeks. Because this structure continues to dominate most academic writing, you should become familiar with it, understand how it contributes to the development of your ideas, and utilize that understanding in your writing. This chapter discusses how form functions within the genre of argument and examines how a number of factors—your teacher's expectations, the conventions of a particular discipline, and, of course, your own purpose and the knowledge you have of your audience—influence the structure of an argumentative essay.

THE RELATIONSHIP OF FORM TO CONTENT

In thinking about the concept of "form," it is important to be aware that the value of any formal features of an argumentative essay depends on the extent to which they help achieve the essay's purpose—that is, to have an impact on a rational audience. The form of any essay does not consist simply of a set of slots into which appropriate content is poured because mechanical adherence to any form stifles creative thought and results in a boring, ineffective essay. Rather, the structure of your essay should reflect careful thinking about the relationship between form and function. Although it is important to be comfortable with the text structures that characterize the genre of argument, you should not think of form as an end in itself.

Nevertheless, awareness of form is important, particularly the classical form of argumentation, which is very often expected in college classes.

THE CLASSICAL FORM OF ARGUMENTATION

The classical argumentative form consists of an **introduction,** which states the thesis or claim, a **body,** which supports that claim and addresses the opposing viewpoint, and a **conclusion,** which sums up the main ideas and perhaps restates the thesis. The components of this form, which are probably familiar to you, may be summarized as follows:

Introduction

In this section, which may consist of only one or two paragraphs, you indicate your topic, establish briefly why it is controversial and significant, and present your thesis or claim. The introduction may also include relevant background material. In some instances, it might summarize a viewpoint that the body of the essay will refute.

Body

The body of the essay consists of the following components:

- The nature of the controversy: This explains the conflict or problem and summarizes various viewpoints to indicate that you understand the ideas of others and have researched the topic thoroughly. This section might also define important key terms and include personal experience that is relevant to the topic.
- Support for your thesis: This is usually the longest and most substantive section of the essay. It supports the thesis with compelling reasons and evidence that might include facts, statistics, data, statements by authorities, and illustrative examples. It may also establish common ground between you and your intended readers.
- Anticipation and refutation of opposing viewpoints: In this section, you indicate areas where your opponent will probably agree with your thesis and then demonstrate that you are aware of areas where you are likely to disagree. After you have indicated that you understand your opponent's point of view, you can show how your own point of view is superior.

Conclusion

This section summarizes your main argument and perhaps suggests what action, if any, the reader ought to take. It also gives the reader a sense of closure by restating the main thesis or postulating potential implications or consequences.

THE ADVANTAGES OF A THESIS-FIRST STRUCTURE

Most of you have probably had experience with essays that use the form I have just outlined. In fact, some of you may feel you *must* use that form for school writing assignments, no matter what sort of writing you are doing, but you may never have thought about why this should be the case. Has this form lasted simply because it was used in the past? Has it simply become a formula? Or are there sound reasons for using it that go beyond the constraints of tradition?

One reason that the classical structure continues to be used is that its placement of the thesis toward the beginning of the essay offers significant advantages to both writer and reader. A thesis with "because" clauses enables the writer to view the entire argument in miniature, enabling him or her to predict and create structure. Placing the thesis up front also enables the writer to establish credibility, outline the controversy, and establish his or her position within that controversy right from the beginning, involving the reader immediately. For the reader, too, the thesis-first model has advantages because it facilitates the efficient processing of information. By getting a clear sense of the main point of the essay and an overview of its structure, the reader will be able to understand immediately what direction the essay is likely to take and to engage the issues with relative ease.

Ironically, although the classical form has been around for a long time, it is particularly well suited to modern life, when many readers cannot afford the time to "hunt" for the main point in a text. Many of today's readers, both in college and in the business world, are overwhelmed by the amount of reading they have to do and consequently welcome the convenience of being able to predict where the thesis and main points in an essay will be located. An essay that does not establish its position and purpose early is sometimes frustrating to read. "Get to the point," readers are tempted to say.

Thesis-first writing is especially effective in composition programs that require students to prepare a portfolio of their work for evaluation at the end of the semester. Portfolio grading has many advantages for both students and teachers, but the process of grading many portfolios usually requires evaluators to do a great deal of reading in a short period of time and to understand what an essay is about very quickly. If your argument essays are going to be evaluated in this way, it is usually a good idea to utilize a thesis-first structure because it facilitates efficient reading.

The other advantage of the classical form is that it provides a well-defined structure for the presentation of the writer's reasons and the support provided for those reasons. It thus provides a sense of order and expectation for both writer and reader because the body of the essay contains "slots" that help determine the placement of information.

The advantages of the established "thesis-first" form may be summed up as follows:

ADVANTAGES OF THE THESIS-FIRST PLACEMENT

1. It enables the reader to know right away what the essay is about, thus facilitating the efficient processing of information.
2. It enables the writer to present an overview of the essay as a whole.
3. It provides the writer with an opportunity to address the opposing viewpoint and thus to grapple with the complexity of the topic.

Alternatives in the Placement of the Thesis

The advantages just cited make the classical form of argumentation a useful model, but there are times when you might wish to delay the presentation of your thesis until later in the essay. For some topics and some audiences, you might wish to capture the audience's attention before you make your position known. For example, you may be writing to an audience that is likely to be resistant to your point of view, in which case you may wish to establish your credibility about the topic and indicate your understanding of the audience's position before presenting your main point. For such an audience, you may wish to write a Rogerian argument in which you first sketch out your audience's position and indicate that you understand it before you state points of disagreement. You might then place your thesis toward the end of the essay, rather than at the beginning.

Generally, though, it is easier to write essays using the thesis-first classical form than it is to use the Rogerian model. So if you are unsure of your writing abilities, I suggest using that form unless you have clear reasons for choosing an alternative.

SOME SUGGESTIONS FOR INTRODUCTIONS AND CONCLUSIONS

The Introduction

Some students have difficulty writing introductions because they have not clarified for themselves what they want to say. If you are having trouble—that is, your waste basket is filled with crumpled-up pieces of paper, or you find yourself rephrasing the same sentence over and over without making any progress—I suggest that you leave the introduction for later on and begin working on the middle of your paper, the place where you develop your supporting points and cite your evidence. Usually, after you have involved yourself sufficiently in the topic by developing several main points about it, the introduction will not be difficult to write.

Following are several suggestions you might find useful for writing an introduction:

1. Establish that a "problem" exists that is serious enough to need solving. The problem may take the form of an ongoing situation, a plan that has failed, a proposal that is inadequate, and so forth. Your thesis or claim will then present another perspective. For example:

   One can sympathize with the Cruzan family's distress concerning their daughter Nancy's medical condition for the past decade. But a Missouri court's Dec. 14 decision that her food and water could be withheld, causing her to starve and dehydrate within two weeks, has ominous implications.

   D.I. Cuddy, "Society Should Not Decide Life's End," *USA Today,* December 19, 1990

2. Establish that a controversy exists. Your thesis or claim will then indicate your position in the controversy. For example:

At the Parent-Teacher Association meeting last week, a dispute broke out over whether all the children in the school should be required to wear school uniforms. Several of the parents were adamantly opposed to the idea, claiming that uniforms stifle children's creativity and self-expression. Others felt that uniforms actually promote creativity because they eliminate children's preoccupation with clothing, leaving their minds free to explore other subjects. Although it is probably impossible to determine whether uniforms stifle or promote creativity, they have an important advantage that neither group addressed adequately: Uniforms protect children from being mistaken for gang members, thus contributing to their safety. For this reason, school uniforms should be required for all students at the local high school.

3. Present the background of the topic, defining relevant terms, if necessary. For example:

"The one absolutely certain way of bringing this nation to ruin, of preventing all possibility of its continuing to be a nation at all, would be to permit it to become a tangle of squabbling nationalities." So warned Teddy Roosevelt in 1915.

We have avoided that danger here—which Canada has not. We have avoided it in part because of the common use of English by all of the immigrants that make up America: Adopting the English language has always been part of becoming American. Relative ease of communication in a single language has provided a kind of national glue, a common thread to the creation and development of a nation that is spread over a wide area and harbors diverse interests, beliefs and national origins.

But a threat to that thread is emerging in the increasingly strident political campaign for separate Spanish teaching.

Howard Banks, "Bilingualism: Do We Want Quebec Here?" *Forbes*, June 11, 1990

4. Attract your reader with a thought-provoking or attention-getting statement or anecdote.

5. Briefly summarize the viewpoint that you wish to refute. Your thesis then is based on the distinction between your point of view and the point of view you are refuting.

The beginning of the essay "Stop Banning Things at the Drop of a Rat" illustrates strategies 4 and 5:

In 1959, the nation experienced its first food related cancer scare: An official said that a chemical used on cranberries caused cancer in rodents. Panic ensued. Cranberry products were destroyed.

In 1989, a movie star and an environmental group announced Alar on apples caused cancer. Panic ensued. Apple products were destroyed across the land. And in between these two events, artificial sweeteners, hair dyes, bacon, muffin mix and more were targeted because they had "cancer-causing agents."

The common link: the animal test and the assumption that any chemical which at megadoses causes cancer in rodents must be assumed to cause cancer in humans, even at minuscule levels of exposure.

This has no basis in science. There is not a shred of evidence that the barely measurable levels of these much-maligned chemicals cause any cancer in humans.

Elizabeth M. Whelan, *USA Today,* October 19, 1990

These strategies can be helpful if you are having trouble getting started on an introduction. Keep in mind, though, that an introduction can utilize more than one strategy (as in the preceding example) and that information you have about your reader can also influence the type of introduction you decide to write.

The Introduction and the "Although" Statement

Beginning with the ideas of an author whose position you wish to refute enables you to introduce your position using an "although" statement. That statement functions as a transitional sentence that distinguishes the writer's main idea from ideas that have already been proposed or that are generally believed. The "although" statement, which was also discussed in Chapter 1, is used when the writer states an existing point of view or proposal and then raises an objection to it, using the word *although,* which naturally leads up to the thesis statement. In its essence, the "although" statement says the following:

Although something (another idea or proposal) may appear to be true (or good or beneficial or inevitable), the truth is actually something else—the writer's point.

The word *although* indicates to the reader that what the writer has to say is superior to what has been said before.

EXERCISE

In small groups, discuss the strategies used in the following introductions:

For 70 years, it has been public school organizing principle No. 1: Each grade has high-track students, middle level students, and some version of the Sweathogs on "Welcome Back Kotter." While some discuss Voltaire in class, others are in metal shop. Some make the algebra-readiness cut, some do not. It's the American way.

Now a growing number of educators—most of whom, it is safe to say, never took metal shop—are convinced that it's the wrong way. Their cause is "detracking," the dismantling of the sorting mechanisms that American schools rely upon. Pressing arguments of efficacy or equity or both, they are trying to convince Americans that stratification in school hurts some and helps none.

Laura Masnerus, "Should Tracking Be Derailed?" *New York Times,* November 1, 1992

Multiculturalism—the notion that ethnic and cultural groups in the United States should preserve their identities instead of fusing them in a melting pot—

has become a byword in education in Los Angeles and other cities. But now, educators at the elementary, secondary, and university levels are rethinking that idea—and worrying that past efforts to teach multiculturalism may have widened the ethnic divisions they were meant to close.

Sharon Bernstein, "Multiculturalism: Building Bridges or Burning Them?" *Los Angeles Times,* November 30, 1992

The problem lay buried, unspoken, for many years in the minds of American women. It was a strange stirring, a sense of dissatisfaction, a yearning that women suffer in the middle of the twentieth century in the United States. Each suburban housewife struggled with it alone. As she made the beds, shopped for groceries, matched slip-cover material, ate peanut butter sandwiches with her children, chauffeured Cub Scouts and Brownies, lay beside her husband at night—she was afraid to ask even of herself the silent question—"Is this all?"

Betty Friedan, *The Feminine Mystique* (New York: Norton, 1963)

Last December a man named Robert Lee Willie, who had been convicted of raping and murdering an 18-year-old woman, was executed in the Louisiana state prison. In a statement issued several minutes before his death, Mr. Willie said: "Killing people is wrong. . . . It makes no difference whether it's citizens, countries, or governments. Killing is wrong." Two weeks later in South Carolina, an admitted killer named Joseph Carl Shaw was put to death for murdering two teenagers. In an appeal to the governor for clemency, Mr. Shaw wrote: "Killing is wrong when I did it. Killing is wrong when you do it. I hope you have the courage and moral strength to stop the killing."

It is a curiosity of modern life that we find ourselves being lectured on morality by cold-blooded killers. Mr. Willie previously had been convicted of aggravated rape, aggravated kidnapping, and the murders of a Louisiana deputy and a man from Missouri. Mr. Shaw committed another murder a week before the two for which he was executed, and admitted mutilating the body of the 14-year-old girl he killed. I can't help wondering what prompted these murderers to speak out against killing as they entered the deathhouse door. Did their newfound reverence for life stem from the realization that they were about to lose their own?

Life is indeed precious, and I believe the death penalty helps to affirm this fact. Had the death penalty been a real possibility in the minds of these murderers, they might well have stayed their hand. They might have shown moral awareness before their victims died, and not after. Consider the tragic death of Rosa Velez, who happened to be home when a man named Luis Vera burglarized her apartment in Brooklyn. "Yeah, I shot her," Velez admitted. "She knew me, and I knew I couldn't go to the chair."

Edward I. Koch, "The Death Penalty Is Justice," *The New Republic,* 1985

The Conclusion

Like introductions, conclusions can be problematic, particularly because writers sometimes lose patience by the time they get to the conclusion and are tempted to say, "Okay, I'm finished. This is all I have to say." Don't give in to that temptation, though, because conclusions are important, too. In fact, aside from the introduction, the conclusion is often what readers remember best. The conclusion is the place where you can direct the readers' attention back to the central problem discussed at the beginning of the paper, sum up your main thesis, and tie things together. Strong conclusions are usually concise and sometimes can be memorable, particularly if you can think of a thought-provoking or dramatic last sentence. Drama, though, is not the main requirement of the conclusion, so don't be concerned if you can't think of punchy concluding lines. Here are some suggestions you might find useful in writing a conclusion:

1. *Return to the problem you discussed earlier.* Because your thesis is likely to be concerned with a particular issue or problem, it is sometimes useful to return to that problem in the conclusion to refocus your reader's attention on it. Perhaps you began with a specific example or a personal reference—if so, mention it again in the conclusion as a way of tying the essay together. Returning to something mentioned in your introduction can provide unity to your essay. In an essay titled "Owls Are Not Threatened, Jobs Are," Randy Fitzgerald begins his essay by referring to a man named Donald Walker, Jr., who received a letter from an environmental group forbidding him to cut down a single tree on his 200 acres of Oregon timberland. He then concludes his essay by referring to that example:

Spotted owls and logging are not incompatible—and Congress must take this controversy away from the courts and carve out a compromise that serves the national interest. "The reign of terror against private landowners must end," says Donald Walker, Jr. "Loggers need their jobs back, the Alaska Widows need their husbands, and the nation needs the renewable resource that this group of hard-working Americans provides."

Randy Fitzgerald, "Owls Are Not Threatened, Jobs Are," *Reader's Digest,* November 1992

2. *Summarize your main points.* Conclusions frequently contain a summary of your main points, connecting them to your thesis. This is the place where you can restate your ideas, without having to provide additional explanation, because the body of the essay has already done that. Readers often find it helpful for an essay to conclude with a summary of main points because it helps them remember what the essay was about. In an essay titled " 'To Hell with Shakespeare,' or the Great Color Purple Hoax," Gerald Graff uses his conclusion to reiterate his main point that contrary to what some scholars have asserted, the classics of Western civilization are not disappearing from college reading lists:

My point in producing statistics is not to minimize the changes that have been taking place in the teaching of the humanities, changes we will soon examine more closely. The exposés of political correctness have exaggerated and misrepresented the phenomenon, but they have not made it up. There are those who disregard the norms of democratic debate and seek to turn the entire curriculum into an extension of a radical social agenda, with compulsory re-education workshops thoughtfully provided for the unenlightened. There are those who justify turning their courses into consciousness raising sessions on the ground that all teaching is inevitably political anyway. This authoritarian behavior is indeed disturbing, and it has been making enemies out of potential friends of the reform movement. But this is hardly an excuse for the critics' apocalyptic descriptions.

Gerald Graff, *Beyond the Culture Wars: How Teaching the Conflicts Can Revitalize American Education,* (New York: Norton, 1992)

3. *Direct your reader's attention to the implications and potential consequences of your ideas.* You might conclude your essay by showing how the issue you have discussed will impact society as a whole, thus widening the context of your discussion. A paper arguing in favor of bilingual education, for example, might conclude with a statement showing that the United States cannot afford to reduce a whole segment of society to a life of poverty because it is unable to speak English.

4. *Use an illustrative anecdote.* The significance of your thesis might be reinforced for your reader if you conclude with an illustrative anecdote or description. In an essay titled "The New Immigrants," which argues against the idea that bilingual education will prevent young people from adjusting to American culture, James Fallows concludes with a reference to a young man originally named "Ramon" who, after having participated in a bilingual education program, wished his name to be spelled "Raymond," showing that Americanization occurs in spite of bilingual education. Here is how Fallows concludes his essay:

Most of the young people I met—the rank and file, not the intellectuals who espouse a bilingual society—seemed fully willing to give what in Fuchs's view the nation asks. I remember in particular one husky Puerto Rican athlete at Miami Senior High School who planned to join the Navy after he got his diploma. I talked to him in a bilingual classroom, heard his story, and asked his name. He told me, and I wrote "Ramon." He came around behind me and looked at my pad. "No, no!" he told me. "You should have put R-A-Y-M-O-N-D."

James Fallows, "The New Immigrants," *Atlantic Monthly,* 1983

STRATEGIES FOR CREATING STRUCTURE

Using an Outline

Some writers create structure by writing a formal outline before beginning to write, complete with multilayered subheadings down to the smallest detail, and if that system works for you, by all means continue to use it. Other writers object to the idea of a preplanned outline, claiming that the imposition of a formal structure is unrealistic because writers often discover ideas as they write; moreover, they feel that too much planning inhibits the creative impulse. Such writers do little planning on paper—after they know what their preliminary thesis is, they simply begin to write and see what develops, creating a concept of structure as they go along.

Unless you have already developed a system that works for you, my recommendation is to take the middle ground—that is, after you have a fairly clear idea of what position you wish to develop, then write down your main points and jot down possible examples and supporting pieces of evidence, thus giving yourself something to refer to as you write. Creating an informal outline such as this will give you an opportunity to think through your main ideas before actually beginning to write and to gain a sense of the preliminary structure of your paper, enabling you to see what may be weak, missing, or disproportionately emphasized. After you have created an outline, it can serve as a guideline for proceeding and can indicate to you where your paper might need additional research, development, or balance. However, because it involves only noting ideas, it will not absorb as much time as creating a formal outline.

Organizing Your Main Points

Most writers prefer to organize subsections of their essays so as to parallel the overall structure of the essay as a whole—that is, they use a deductive structure for each of their major points, stating a point, supporting that point, stating the next point, supporting that point, and so forth. On the other hand, for creating variation and for calling attention to a point you wish to emphasize, you may wish to use an inductive structure, presenting facts or observations and leading your readers to make discoveries for themselves.

When considering possibilities for arrangement, one possibility is to consider which of your points is most important or compelling and to discuss that point first. Readers often pay most attention to points presented at the beginning of a text, and if you present your most significant point first, it is likely to have the most profound impact on your reader. You can then develop your major points in descending order of importance, ultimately reminding your reader of your most important point when you refute the opposition and perhaps when you present your conclusion as well.

Alfee Enciso's essay about racism in America (at the end of this chapter) develops his position through the following main points:

1. Racism is promoted through magazines, television shows, and billboards.
2. Racism is implicit in the ideal of beauty that young men and women adopt as a standard.
3. Racism is implicit in a number of ways, such as confusing two people for the same one, assuming that two black people know each other, believing that all black people share the same ideology, viewing black people as unfortunate, or suspecting black students of being thieves.

His main point, though, is that racism is everywhere because it is promoted through the media; therefore he presents that point as his first one.

Sometimes you might wish to save your most important point for last. In an essay titled "Four-Letter Words Can Hurt You" Barbara Lawrence makes the point that the reason that four-letter words are considered taboo is not simply because of sexual hang-ups, but because they refer to women as body parts, thereby denying them their humanity. However, before she makes that point, she discusses the origin of many of these forbidden words, and therefore establishes their origin in violent, sadistic acts. In that essay, the author has built up to her most important point, saving it for last.

Signposting Ideas

No matter what order of presentation you decide on, your essay will not hold together unless you link each point to your main thesis by signposts or, as my colleague Jack Blum refers to them, "cueing devices." Signposts remind your reader of how each point supports the main point of the essay, review where the essay has been, indicate where it is going, and keep the reader from getting lost. Most readers can focus on only a limited amount of information at any one time; therefore, signposts or cueing devices help readers understand how the essay is structured so that they will not become confused.

The simplest method of signposting is to say simply, "this is my first point; this is my second; etc." Less obvious signposts do not announce their presence so explicitly, but instead smooth the transition between ideas. Alfee Enciso uses a signpost by beginning his fourth paragraph with a reference back to the main idea of his third paragraph, as follows:

> *Despite my race-relations credentials,* none of these particulars, whether isolated or bunched together, can stand up to one undeniable fact: I am an American, born and raised. To be an American is to be racist.

Signposting can be achieved through transitional words and phrases such as *however, nonetheless, therefore, moreover, additionally, nevertheless,* and many others. Here are some transitional devices that are frequently used for signposting:

- to establish cause and effect—*therefore, thus, as a result, consequently*
- to show similarity—*similarly, in the same way*
- to show difference—*however, on the contrary, but, despite that*
- to elaborate—*moreover, furthermore, in addition, finally*
- to explain or present examples—*for example, for instance, such as, in particular*

Signposting can also be achieved through transitional paragraphs that act as a link between two ideas and prepare the reader for a new topic or indicate a forthcoming order of ideas. Here is an example of a transitional paragraph:

> But too many of those who wave the flag for multiculturalism have let enthusiasm outrun reason. In particular, I believe four major issues deserve more

debate and consideration before we embrace the brave new world of multicultural education.

Kenneth T. Jackson, "Too Many Have Let Enthusiasm Outrun Reason"

In this paragraph, Jackson refers to four issues, which he explains further in subsequent paragraphs.

USING A FUNCTION OUTLINE

A useful way to ensure that your essay is well structured is to analyze a text using a "function outline." A function outline consists of brief statements about how each paragraph functions within an essay in terms of its relationship either to the thesis or to one of its supporting points; the outline's purpose is to focus on thesis development and coherence and to initiate revision. Function outlines may be written either on a separate sheet of paper, such as a function outline work sheet, or in the margins of the text itself.

Here is an example of how a function outline could be used to analyze the essay "Brother, Don't Spare a Dime."

FUNCTION OUTLINE WORK SHEET

Steps for Writing a Function Outline:

1. Number all the paragraphs in your essay.
2. Highlight or underline the thesis statement. Write the thesis statement below.

Thesis Statement: The group most responsible for the homeless being the way they are is the homeless themselves.

3. Skim the essay, highlighting the main supporting points. Briefly summarize these points below.

First Main Point: There are many people who are only temporarily homeless. They work hard to get off the street and are usually homeless only for a short time.

Second Main Point: The real problem is the homeless who actually choose the streets. They "enjoy the freedom and consider begging a minor inconvenience." These people may suffer from mental illness, alcoholism, poor education, or laziness.

Third Main Point: Cites the example of a man the author tried to help. Despite the best of help, the man was back on the street a month later.

Fourth Main Point: Suggests that those who don't believe him offer work to those who are begging.

Fifth Main Point: The solution to homelessness must include some notion of self-reliance and individual responsibility.

4. Go through the essay, paragraph by paragraph, noting how each one functions to support the main point of the essay. Does the paragraph develop a main supporting point? Does it provide background material? Is it an example? Does it present a counterargument? Locate specific words or cueing devices in the paragraph that refer back to the thesis and remind the reader of the main point to be developed. If cueing devices do not appear, think about what material you might want to add.

Paragraph 1 establishes that homelessness is a problem, a danger to public safety.

Paragraph 2 discusses various explanations for homelessness and establishes thesis.

Paragraph 3 establishes the credibility of the writer, based on his own experience.

Paragraph 4 qualifies that not every homeless person is on the street because he or she wants to be. There are exceptions.

Paragraph 5 establishes that the homeless who try to get off the street are not the real problem.

Paragraph 6 makes the point that many of the homeless actually prefer to be on the street.

Paragraph 7 cites example of the man he tried to help.

Paragraph 8 refers to his example to emphasize his point that society was not to blame for this man's failure. He had only himself to blame.

Paragraph 9 anticipates objection that his experience was merely anecdotal. Advises readers to try to offer a homeless person work.

Paragraph 10 points out that solutions are not easy. Indicates the implications of the thesis—any solution must include some notion of self-reliance and individual responsibility.

Paragraph 11 _____

_____

5. Are there places in the paragraph that seem to head in another, perhaps related, direction? If so, can these sections be refocused, or do you wish to modify the thesis to accommodate a potential new direction?

The author skips over the effect that drug and alcohol addiction and mental illness can have on a person's ability to take responsibility for him or herself. The idea of blame usually is associated with that of choice. These people may not really have a choice.

6. Having worked through the entire essay, note which areas of the paper need modification or elaboration. Do you feel that the thesis statement should be modified in any way? If so, what new cueing and support would be needed?

The author needs to define more carefully what he means by "blame." He also should discuss the problems posed by alcohol and drug addiction as well as mental illness. Basing the argument on only one example also weakens the argument.

FUNCTION OUTLINE WORK SHEET

A function outline consists of brief statements about how each paragraph functions within an essay in terms of its relationship either to the thesis or to one of its supporting points; the purpose of writing a function outline is to focus attention on thesis development and coherence and to initiate revision. Function outlines may be written either in the margins of the essay itself or on a separate sheet of paper, such as the function outline work sheet below:

Steps for Writing a Function Outline:

1. Number all the paragraphs in your essay.
2. Highlight or underline the thesis statement. Write the thesis statement below.

Thesis Statement: _____

_____

3. Skim the essay, highlighting the main supporting points. Briefly summarize these points below.

First Main Point: _____

_____

Second Main Point: _____

_____

Third Main Point: _____

_____

Fourth Main Point: _____

_____

Fifth Main Point: _____

_____

4. Go through the essay, paragraph by paragraph, noting how each one functions to support the main point of the essay. As you read, think about the following questions: Does the paragraph develop a main supporting point? Does it provide background material? Is it an example? Does it present a counterargument? Locate specific words or cueing

devices in the paragraph that refer back to the thesis and remind the reader of the main point to be developed. If cueing devices do not appear, think about what material you might want to add.

Other questions to consider: Are there places in the paragraph that seem to head in another, perhaps related, direction? If so, can these sections be refocused, or do you wish to modify the thesis to accommodate a potential new direction?

In the space below, indicate the function of each paragraph in your essay.

Paragraph 1 _____

_____

Paragraph 2 _____

_____

Paragraph 3 _____

_____

Paragraph 4 _____

_____

Paragraph 5 _____

_____

Paragraph 6 _____

_____

Paragraph 7 _____

_____

Paragraph 8 _____

_____

Paragraph 9 _____

_____

Paragraph 10_____

_____

Paragraph 11_____

_____

5. Having worked through the entire essay, note which areas of the paper
   need modification or elaboration. Do you feel that the thesis statement
   should be modified in any way? If so, what new cueing and support
   would be needed?

EXERCISE: ANALYZING A TEXT USING A FUNCTION OUTLINE

A well-known document that adheres almost perfectly to the classical form of argumentation is the Declaration of Independence. Use a function outline to analyze that text. Then respond to the following questions:

1. What is the thesis or claim?
2. How does Jefferson establish credibility?
3. Which form of reasoning is used?
4. In which sections does Jefferson address the opposing viewpoint?

THE USE OF NARRATIVE AND DESCRIPTION IN THE GENRE OF ARGUMENT

Narrative and description are not usually considered important in argumentation because they are more often associated with fiction. However, if you consider the goal of argumentative writing, you will recognize that narrative and description can also be used to fulfill an argumentative purpose. Certainly, when you are writing a formal argument, you can use narrative and description to enliven your writing and to attract the attention of your reader. Specific narrative examples and lively descriptions provide far more interesting reading than do broad generalizations.

Narrative or descriptive examples are particularly useful for introducing a topic. Remember, though, to link such examples firmly to your thesis and to do so within the first few paragraphs. Anticipate the reaction of impatient readers who might be tempted to say, "Okay. Get to the point already." Do not become so enthralled with the narrative itself that you forget about establishing and supporting a position.

Using "I"

In some disciplines, students are absolutely forbidden to use the pronoun *I* in formal argumentation, and this restriction may pertain to the writing you do for many of your college courses. You may, in fact, be under the impression that the rule is absolute.

The rule against using *I,* however, sometimes produces some pretty convoluted, awkward writing, and over the past few years, some departments and disciplines have become more flexible, accepting the use of the first person when it enhances the effectiveness of the argument. If you are including narrative or descriptive examples as a means of introducing or explaining your argument, the use of the first person can lend vividness and immediacy to your writing by enabling the reader to experience the incident through your own eyes. You might also want to use the first person if you are writing about a subject in which your own firsthand experience renders you an expert. Topics concerned with the experiences of a college student, for example, are often based on personal experience, so it would be perfectly appropriate for you to use the first person in writing about them. If you decide to use the first person, be able to explain your reason for doing so. Do not, for example, use it in your thesis statement by stating simply, "I do not think this is right" or "In my opinion, this idea is false." A reader might respond by saying, "Why should I listen to your opinion?" or "Why should I care what you think?" Unless you are an expert on your topic because you, yourself, have firsthand experience that supports your main point, the fact that you have a particular opinion or endorse a particular idea will have little impact on a reader.

Here is an example of how first-person narrative can be used to introduce a topic and establish the writer's credibility. In this case, the writer has had direct personal experience that renders him qualified to use it:

> I am the enemy! One of those vilified, inhumane physician-scientists involved in animal research. How strange, for I have never thought of myself as an evil person. I became a pediatrician because of my love for children and my desire to keep them healthy. During medical school and residency, however, I saw many children die of leukemia, prematurity, and traumatic injury—circumstances against which medicine has made tremendous progress, but still has far to go. More important, I also saw children, alive and healthy, thanks to advances in medical science such as infant respirators, potent antibiotics, new surgical techniques and the entire field of organ transplantation. My desire to tip the scales in favor of the healthy, happy children drew me to medical research.
>
> My accusers claim that I inflict torture on animals for the purpose of career advancement. My experiments supposedly have no relevance to medicine and are easily replaced by computer simulation. Meanwhile, an apathetic public barely watches, convinced that the issue has no significance, and publicity-conscious politicians increasingly give way to the demands of the activists.
>
> Ron Karpati, "I Am the Enemy," *Newsweek,* 1989

EXERCISE: INFORMAL VERSUS FORMAL ARGUMENTATION

Using the first person, write an informal two-page essay about some aspect of college life that you think needs to be changed (some suggestions: the registration system, the computer facilities, the food in the cafeteria, the condition of the residence halls). Then rewrite your essay as a formal argument addressed to a university official. What differences can you detect between the two essays in terms of narrative and description?

EXERCISE: COMPARING TWO STRUCTURES

The classical argumentative structure is applicable to a variety of disciplines and writing tasks. But there are times when such a structure may not be as effective as one that employs techniques from fiction, such as narrative and description. Following is an essay titled "The Iguana" by Isak Dinesen, followed by a rewrite of that essay using an argumentative structure. Read both versions and answer the questions that follow. Discuss your responses in small groups. What facets of argumentation are shared by both versions?

The Iguana
Isak Dinesen

Isak (Karen) Dinesen (b. 1885) spent most of her life living in Africa
and writing about her experiences there. This selection was first published in her book *Out of Africa* (1937).

1   In the Reserve, I have sometimes come upon the Iguana, the big lizards, as they
were sunning themselves upon a flat stone in a riverbed. They are not pretty in
shape, but nothing can be imagined more beautiful than their coloring. They
shine like a heap of precious stones or like a pane cut out of an old church window. When as you approach, they swish away, there is a flash of azure, green
and purple over the stones, the color seems to be standing behind them in the
air, like a comet's luminous tail.

2   Once I shot an Iguana. I thought that I should be able to make some pretty
things from his skin. A strange thing happened then, that I have never afterwards
forgotten. As I went up to him, where he was lying dead upon his stone, and actually while I was walking the few steps, he faded and grew pale, all color died out
of him as in one long sigh, and by the time that I touched him he was grey and
dull like a lump of concrete. It was the live impetuous blood pulsating within the
animal, which had radiated out all that glow and splendor. Now that the flame
was put out, and the soul had flown, the Iguana was as dead as a sandbag.

3   Often since I have, in some sort, shot an Iguana, and I have remembered the
first one of the Reserve. Up at Meru I saw a young Native girl with a bracelet on, a
leather strap two inches wide, and embroidered all over with very small turquoise-
colored beads which varied a little in color and played in green, light blue and
ultramarine. It was an extraordinarily live thing; it seemed to draw breath on her
arm, so that I wanted it for myself, and made Farah buy it from her. No sooner had
it come upon my own arm than it gave up the ghost. It was nothing now, a small,
cheap, purchased article of finery. It had been the play of colors, the duet between
the turquoise and the "negre"—that quick, sweet, brownish black, like peat and
black pottery, of the Native's skin—that had created the life of the bracelet.

4   In the Zoological Museum of Pietermaritzburg, I have seen, in a stuffed
deep-water fish in a showcase, the same combination of coloring, which there
had survived death; it made me wonder what life can well be like, on the bottom of the sea, to send up something so live and airy. I stood in Meru and
looked at my pale hand and at the dead bracelet, it was as if an injustice had
been done to a noble thing, as if truth had been suppressed. So sad did it seem
that I remembered the saying of the hero in a book that I had read as a child: "I
have conquered them all, but I am standing amongst graves."

5   In a foreign country and with foreign species of life one should take measures to find out whether things will be keeping their value when dead. To the
settlers of East Africa I give the advice: "For the sake of your own eyes and
heart, shoot not the Iguana."

Rewrite of "The Iguana"

Some things are beautiful only in their natural state. Their beauty is part of their environment or culture. If we remove something from its natural environment, its beauty may die. It is important for us to recognize the value of such things and to respect them. Although we may appreciate the beauty of a thing or a place, we cannot possess it because, if we try, we will lose the very thing we admire.

A good example is the East African iguana. The animal itself is not very pretty, but its skin is beautiful: blue-green and purple, shining like gem stones. If you kill one to make something out of its skin, though, the colors seem to fade. It loses its beauty and becomes gray and dull like rock. Its natural beauty seems to come from its life.

Another example of this phenomenon may be seen when a beautiful cultural object is removed from its native environment. In the African town of Meru, the women wear bracelets made of leather strips embroidered with turquoise colored beads that look lovely on the African women. The bracelets seem alive and gemlike as they glisten against the women's dark skin. But against anyone else's skin, the bracelets look gray and dead, as if the life has gone out of them. Meru's women are a part of the East African environment, and the jewelry they wear is a part of their culture. We can buy their jewelry, but we cannot buy the culture that gives it beauty.

Sometimes the brilliance of natural colors does survive death, as can be seen in a stuffed deep-water fish displayed in a showcase in the Zoological Museum of Pietermaritzburg. Looking at this beautiful creature, one wonders what life can be like at the bottom of the sea to send up something that seems so alive. Nevertheless, the fish, like the dead leather bracelet, seems like an injustice done to a noble thing. It reminds one of the saying of the hero in a children's book, "I have conquered them all, but I am standing amongst graves."

People who travel to foreign countries and among foreign species should find out whether things will keep their value after they are dead. It is important to realize that removing something from its natural environment can destroy its beauty.

QUESTIONS (PLEASE PROVIDE EXPLANATIONS FOR YOUR ANSWERS)

1. What is the thesis of essay 1?

_____

2. Did you find essay 1 easy to understand?
1. _____ (difficult)
2. _____ (neither easy nor difficult)
3. _____ (easy)

Please explain your response. What made essay 1 easy or difficult for you to understand?

_____

3. Do you think that essay 1 is well structured?
1. _____ (poorly structured)
2. _____ (moderately well structured)
3. _____ (well structured)

Which features of the text influenced your response?

_____

4. Do you think that essay 1 was well written?
1. _____ (poorly written)
2. _____ (moderately well written)
3. _____ (well written)

Which features of the text influenced your response?

_____

5. Do you think that essay 1 is likely to have an impact on its readers?
1. _____ (no impact)
2. _____ (moderate impact)
3. _____ (considerable impact)

Why or why not?

_____

_____

6. What is the thesis of essay 2?

_____

7. Did you find essay 2 easy to understand?
1. _____ (difficult)
2. _____ (neither easy nor difficult)
3. _____ (easy)

Please explain your response. What made essay 2 easy or difficult for you to understand?

_____

8. Do you think that essay 2 is well structured?
1. _____ (poorly structured)
2. _____ (moderately well structured)
3. _____ (well structured)

Which features of the text influenced your response?

_____

9. Do you think that essay 2 was well written?
1. _____ (poorly written)
2. _____ (moderately well written)
3. _____ (well written)

Which features of the text influenced your response?

_____

10. Do you think that essay 2 is likely to have an impact on its readers?
1. _____ (no impact)
2. _____ (moderate impact)
3. _____ (considerable impact)

Why or why not?

_____

_____

11. Which essay did you like better: essay 1 or essay 2?
essay 1 _____   essay 2 _____

Please explain why you liked one essay over the other.

_____

_____

_____

WRITING ASSIGNMENT

Read "A Culture of Cruelty" and "Brother, Don't Spare a Dime" and decide which point of view you agree with most. Then respond to the following questions:

1. What strategies for introducing the topic are used in each essay?
2. What strategies for concluding are used in each essay?
3. Write an argumentative essay of three to five pages that responds to one of these essays. In your introduction, you might lead into your thesis by referring to the position with which you *disagree*.

Brother, Don't Spare a Dime
L. Christopher Awalt

L. Christopher Awalt is a writer/editor from Austin, Texas. This piece
is from *Newsweek* (September 1991).

1   Homeless people are everywhere—on the street, in public buildings, on the
evening news and at the corner parking lot. You can hardly step out of your
house these days without meeting some haggard character who asks you for a
cigarette or begs for "a little change." The homeless are not just constant symbols of wasted lives and failed social programs—they have become a danger to
public safety.

2   What's the root of the homeless problem? Everyone seems to have a scapegoat: advocates of the homeless blame government policy; politicians blame the
legal system; the courts blame the bureaucratic infrastructure; the Democrats
blame the Republicans; the Republicans, the Democrats. The public blames the
economy, drugs, the "poverty cycle" and "the breakdown of society." With all
this finger-pointing, the group most responsible for the homeless being the way
they are receives the least blame. That group is the homeless themselves.

3   How can I say this? For the past two years I have worked with the homeless, volunteering at the Salvation Army and at a soup kitchen in Austin, Texas. I
have led a weekly chapel service, served food, listened, counseled, given time
and money and shared in their struggles. I have seen their response to troubles,
and though I'd rather report otherwise, many of them seem to have chosen the
lifestyles they lead. They are unwilling to do the things necessary to overcome
their circumstances. They must bear the greater part of the blame for their man-
ifold troubles.

4   Let me qualify what I just said. Not everyone who finds himself out of a job
and in the street is there because he wants to be. Some are victims of tragic circumstances. I met many dignified, capable people during my time working
with Austin's homeless: the single father struggling to earn his high-school
equivalency and to be a role model for his children; the woman who fled a good
job in another city to escape an abusive husband; the well-educated young man
who had his world turned upside down by divorce and a layoff. These people
deserve every effort to help them back on their feet.

5   But they're not the real problem. They are usually off the streets and resum-
ing normal lives within a period of weeks or months. Even while "down on
their luck," they are responsible citizens, working in the shelters and applying
for jobs. They are homeless, true, but only temporarily, because they are eager
to reorganize their lives.

6   For every person temporarily homeless, though, there are many who are
chronically so. Whether because of mental illness, alcoholism, poor education,

drug addiction or simple laziness, these homeless are content to remain as they are. In many cases they choose the streets. They enjoy the freedom and consider begging a minor inconvenience. They know they can always get a job for a day or two for food, cigarettes and alcohol. The sophisticated among them have learned to use the system for what it's worth and figure that a trip through the welfare line is less trouble than a steady job. In a society that has mastered dodging responsibility, these homeless prefer a life of no responsibility at all.

Waste of time: One person I worked with is a good example. He is an older 7 man who has been on the streets for about 10 years. The story of his decline from respectability to alcoholism sounded believable and I wanted to help. After buying him toiletries and giving him clothes, I drove him one night to a Veterans Administration hospital, an hour and a half away, and put him into a detoxification program. I wrote him monthly to check on his progress and attempted to line up a job for him when he got out. Four months into his program, he was thinking and speaking clearly and talking about plans he wanted to make. At five months, he expressed concern over the life he was about to lead. During the sixth month, I called and was told that he had checked himself out and returned home. A month later I found him drunk again, back on the streets.

Was "society" to blame for this man? Hardly. It had provided free medical 8 care, counseling and honest effort. Was it the fault of the economy? No. This man never gave the economy a chance to solve his problems. The only person who can be blamed for his failure to get off the streets is the man himself. To argue otherwise is a waste of time and compassion.

Those who disagree will claim that my experience is merely anecdotal and 9 that one case does not a policy make. Please don't take my word for it. The next time you see someone advertising that he'll work for food, take him up on it. Offer him a hard day's work for an honest wage, and see if he accepts. If he does, tell him you'll pay weekly, so that he will have to work for an entire week before he sees any money. If he still accepts, offer a permanent job, with taxes withheld and the whole shebang. If he accepts again, hire him. You'll have a fine employee and society will have one less homeless person. My guess is that you won't find many takers. The truly homeless won't stay around past the second question.

So what are the solutions? I will not pretend to give ultimate answers. But 10 whatever policy we decide upon must include some notion of self-reliance and individual responsibility. Simply giving over our parks, our airports and our streets to those who cannot and will not take care of themselves is nothing but a retreat from the problem and allows the public property that we designate for their "use" to fall into disarray. Education, drug and alcohol rehabilitation, treatment for the mentally ill and job training programs are all worthwhile projects, but without requiring some effort and accountability on the part of the homeless for whom these programs are implemented, all these efforts do is break the taxpayer. Unless the homeless are willing to help themselves, there is nothing anyone else can do. Not you. Not me. Not the government. Not anyone.

QUESTIONS

1. Where is Awalt's thesis placed in this essay? Does its placement affect its impact? How?
2. How is this essay structured? Could you devise a different structure using the strategies offered in this chapter? Rewrite the essay using one of these strategies.
3. Does Awalt's use of personal narrative lend credence to his claim? Why or why not?
4. Locate the counterargument in this piece. Is it fully developed? Has Awalt fully addressed the arguments against his position? Elaborate on this.
5. Is Awalt telling us that we do not need social services for the homeless? Is it possible to determine whether someone is a good candidate for social services? What might those services be?
6. Imagine that you are homeless. Describe what your day would be like. Remember that you do not have available the conveniences we take for granted (restroom, money, bed, etc.).

The Culture of Cruelty
Ruth Conniff

Ruth Conniff is the associate editor of *The Progressive,* where this article first appeared (September 1992).

Not long ago I was on a morning radio show talking about welfare, when an   1
irate caller from Milwaukee got on the line and introduced himself as "that
most hated and reviled creature, the American taxpayer." He went on to vent
his spleen, complaining about freeloading welfare mothers living high on the
hog while he goes to work each day. "A whiff of starvation is what they need,"
he said.

I was chilled by the hatred in his voice, thinking about the mothers I know   2
on welfare, imagining what it would be like for them to hear this.

One young woman I've met, Karetha Mims, recently moved to Wisconsin,   3
fleeing the projects in Chicago after her little boy saw a seven-year-old playmate
shot in the head. Mims is doing her best to make a better life for her son, a shy
third-grader named Jermain. She volunteers at his elementary school, and worries about how he will fit in. The Mimses have received a cold welcome in Wisconsin, where the governor warns citizens that welfare families spilling across
the border from Illinois will erode the tax base and ruin the "quality of life."

Of course, even in Wisconsin, life on welfare is no free ride. The average   4
family of three receives about $500 a month in Aid to Families with Dependent
Children—barely enough to pay the rent. Such figures are widely known. So is
the fact that each state spends a small amount—about 3.4 per cent of our taxes,
or a national total of $22.9 billion annually—on welfare. In contrast, we have
now spent $87 billion—about $1,000 per taxpaying family—to bail out bank
presidents at failed savings-and-loans.

But neither the enraged taxpayer nor my host on the radio program wanted   5
to hear these dry facts. "What ever happened to the work ethic in this country?" the host demanded. "What about the immigrants who came over and
worked their way up?"

I had the feeling I was losing my grasp on the conversation. I could see my   6
host getting impatient, and the more I said the more I failed to answer her central question: *What's wrong with those people on welfare?*

The people on welfare whom I know have nothing wrong with them. They   7
live in bad neighborhoods; they can't find safe, affordable child care; often, they
are caught in an endless cycle of unemployment and low-wage work—quitting
their jobs when a child gets sick, losing medical insurance when they go back
to their minimum-wage jobs. They don't have enough money to cover such
emergencies as dental work or car repairs. In short, they are poor. They are
struggling hard just to make it, in the face of extreme hardship and in an
increasingly hostile environment.

8   Meanwhile, rhetoric about lazy welfare bums is taking the country by storm. Policy experts keep coming up with new theories on the "culture of poverty" and its nameless perpetrators, members of a socially and morally deformed "underclass." "Street hustlers, welfare families, drug addicts, and former mental patients," political scientist Lawrence Mead calls them.

9   "It's simply stupid to pretend the underclass is not mainly black," adds Mickey Kaus in his much-acclaimed new book *The End of Equality.* Kaus and fellow pundit Christopher Jencks, who wrote his own book this year— *Rethinking Social Policy: Race, Poverty, and the Underclass*—are two of the most recent riders on the underclass bandwagon. But the essence of their work is uncomfortably familiar. Both writers start by asking the question: *What's wrong with the underclass?,* and both proceed to talk about the depravity of poor black people, devoting large though inconclusive sections to such ideas as genetic inferiority and "Heredity, Inequality, and Crime."

10   Kaus paints a lurid picture of young black men who sneer at the idea of working for the minimum wage, which he says they deride as "chump change." (It's not clear where Kaus gets this information, since he doesn't cite any interviews with actual poor blacks.)

11   Why don't poor black people just get jobs and join the mainstream of society? Kaus asks rhetorically. While many African-Americans have moved up to the middle class, he writes, the important question is "what enabled some of them, a lower-class remnant, to stay behind in the ghetto? And what then allowed them to survive in the absence of legitimate sources of income?"

12   The answer, of course, is welfare. Kaus compares black people's attachment to poverty with a junkie's addiction to a drug. Welfare is the "enabling" force that indulges ghetto residents' propensity for living in squalor. When they stopped working hard and learned they could collect welfare while living in the ghetto, Kaus theorizes, poor black people's values eroded and they became a blight on society.

13   Kaus's solution to the "underclass problem," then, relies largely on such motivational initiatives as instilling a work ethic in lazy black youth through hard labor and "military-style discipline." Likewise, he proposes cutting benefits to mothers who have more than one child, creating an example for their neighbors, who, he says, would "think twice" before becoming pregnant.

14 To his credit, J. Anthony Lukas, the writer who reviewed *The End of Equality* for *The New York Times.* noted near the end of his essay that Kaus had forgotten to talk to anyone on welfare in the course of writing his book. But Lukas detected no prejudice in Kaus's prescriptions for an overhaul of the underclass, and he found a touching note of "compassion" in Kaus's assurance that under his plan, "no one would starve."

15   What I want to know is how Kaus came to be considered even remotely qualified to analyze the psychology and motivations of poor black mothers and their sons. Kaus's whole program rests on a faith in his own ability to do exactly that: to surmise what ghetto residents are thinking and why they behave the way they do.

Kaus and Jencks show little interest in learning about the real lives or day- 16
to-day difficulties of people who are poor. Rather, in the grand tradition of
underclass theory, they invent hypothetical characters with demeaning little
names.

"Phyllis may not be very smart," writes Jencks, in a revised version of 17
underclass theorist Charles Murray's famous "Harold and Phyllis" scenario. "But
if she chooses AFDC over Harold, surely that is because she expects the choice
to improve the quality of her family life. . . ." Furthermore, says Jencks, "If Phyllis does not work, many—including Sharon—will feel that Phyllis should be
substantially worse off, so that there will be no ambiguity about Sharon's virtue
being rewarded."

On the strength of the projected feelings of the fictitious Sharon, Jencks 18
goes on to recommend a welfare system in which single mothers don't get too
much money.

Incredibly, this sort of work then gets translated into concrete public policy. 19

Under the Family Support Act, states are now running a number of experi- 20
ments designed to tinker with the motivations and attitudes of poor people—
despite data that demonstrate such tinkering will have no positive effect. There
is no evidence, or example, to back up one of the popular notions Kaus sub-
scribes to—that "most" poor women would stop having babies if benefits were
cut. Women who live in states with higher benefits do not have more babies.
They do not have fewer babies in Alabama or Mississippi (or Bangladesh, for
that matter), where benefits are shockingly low. Yet Wisconsin, California, and
New Jersey are now cutting AFDC payments to women who have more than
one child. Likewise, theories about the underclass have inspired initiatives to
teach poor people job skills and "self-esteem"—despite the fact that in many of
the areas where the training is done, no jobs are available.

The results of these policies are often disastrous for the poor. As more and 21
more states treat poverty as an attitude problem, legislatures justify slashing the
safety net and cutting back social programs that help poor people survive. The
situation is particularly dire for the "extra" children of women on welfare, who
are punished just for being born.

But in Kaus's estimation, the suffering of children is nothing next to the 22
social benefits he thinks will accrue from causing pain to their mothers. "If we
want to end the underclass, remember, the issue is not so much whether working or getting two years of cash will best help Betsy Smith, teenage high-school
dropout, acquire the skills to get a good private sector job *after* she's become a
single mother. It is whether the prospect of having to work will deter Betsy
Smith from having an out-of-wedlock child in the first place. . . . The way to
make the true costs of bearing a child out of wedlock clear is to let them be felt
when they are incurred—namely, at the child's birth."

The callousness and immorality of such thinking, I believe, are part of a pathol- 23
ogy that is spreading throughout our society. We might call it a "culture of cruelty."

Such theorists as Kaus and Jencks build the rational foundation beneath our 24
national contempt for the poor. They lend legitimacy to the racist and misogynist

stereotypes so popular with conservative politicians and disgruntled taxpayers who feel an economic crunch and are looking for someone to blame. Understanding the roots of the culture of cruelty, and trying to determine how, through the adoption of decent social values, we might overcome it, would be far more useful than any number of volumes of speculation by upper-class white experts on the attitudes and pathologies of the "underclass."

25   Underclass theory as promoted by Kaus and Jencks has four main characteristics:

26   It is extremely punitive, appealing to a desire to put poor black people, especially women, in their place.

27   It is based on prejudice rather than fact, full of stereotypical characters and flippant, unsupported assertions about their motivations and psychology.

28   It is inconsistent in its treatment of rich and poor. While poor people need sternness and "military-style discipline," to use Kaus's words, the rich are coddled and protected. This third characteristic is particularly important, since treating the "underclass" as alien and inhuman permits the prescription of draconian belt-tightening that one would never impose on one's own family or friends.

Finally, there is the persistent, faulty logic involved in claims that we can
29 "end the cycle of poverty" by refusing aid to an entire generation of children. These children are thus punished for their mothers' sins in producing them, and, if such programs persist, they will soon have no hope of getting out from under the weight of belonging to a despised lower caste.

30 In his book *Savage Inequalities,* Jonathan Kozol describes visiting a wealthy public school, where he talks to some students who argue that giving equal funding to the schools in poorer districts wouldn't make a difference. Poor children "still would lack the motivation," they say, and "would probably fail in any case because of other problems." Racial integration would cause too many problems in their own school, they say. "How could it be of benefit to us?"

31   "There is a degree of unreality about the whole exchange," Kozol writes. "The children are lucid and their language is well chosen and their arguments well made, but there is a sense that they are dealing with an issue that does not feel very vivid, and that nothing that we say about it to each other really matters since it's 'just a theoretical discussion.' To a certain degree, the skillfulness and cleverness that they display seem to derive precisely from this sense of unreality. Questions of unfairness feel more like a geometric problem than a matter of humanity or conscience. A few of the students do break through the note of unreality, but, when they do, they cease to be so agile in their use of words and speak more awkwardly. Ethical challenges seem to threaten their effectiveness. There is the sense that they were skating over ice and that the issues we addressed were safely frozen underneath. When they stop to look beneath the ice they start to stumble."

32   Kaus and Jencks remind me of nothing so much as precocious sophomores, dominating the class discussion, eager to sound off about the lives and motivations of people they have never met.

This is particularly true of Kaus, since he is even less interested in empirical 33
data than Jencks. Kaus postulates a problem: the loss of a work ethic among
lower-class blacks. Then he deftly applies a solution: "military-style discipline."
Voilà, the problem is solved. This virtuoso performance might earn an A in
academia. But when it becomes the basis for real-world public policy, we are,
indeed, on thin ice.

Kaus's ideas are not all unpleasant. In the first half of *The End of Equality*, 34
he conjures up images of a new civic America with public squares, clean
libraries, parades, and a wonderful, pervading sense of fraternity and equal citizenship. But loose reasoning and a wishful premise—that economic inequality
is not the real problem in our society; the real problem is that people aren't trying hard enough to be nice to each other and get along—lead to some remark-
ably loony claims. For instance, Kaus proposes that being poor doesn't bother
people so much in Los Angeles, because the roads are good, and everyone can
equally enjoy driving on them. (There must have been a little forehead-slapping
among the editors and publishers at Basic Books when *The End of Equality*
came out in the wake of the L.A. riots.)

The real trouble starts when Kaus gets down to specifics. When it comes to 35
social programs for the poor, Kaus poisons the well, deriding "Money Liberals"
for their tiresome whining about economic justice. Money-based solutions are
too simplistic for a creative thinker like Kaus.

Kaus wants to create a massive "neo-WPA" program, with guaranteed jobs 36
for everyone. But the jobs, he says, should be "authoritarian, even a little militaristic," and they should pay less than the minimum wage. The program would
not raise anyone out of poverty, since there would be no opportunity for
advancement within it. We can't have a class of workers dependent on the state
for permanent employment, Kaus reasons. Instead, once people have gained
work "skills" through his jobs program, Kaus says, the transition to a job in the
private sector will "take care of itself." Never mind the recession, the thousands
of former middle-class workers who are now out of work, or the fact that even
in the best of times we do not have a full-employment economy.

Anyway, Kaus never explains why the poor black men he talks about 37
would abandon employment in the illegal economy to work in labor gangs, for
even less than "chump change." Nor does he note that there is already an
extensive discipline-dispensing institution for black men: our ever-expanding
prison system.

(Jencks, for his part, declares that we don't have enough prisons: "We 38
claim that crime will be punished, but this turns out to be mostly talk. Building
prisons is too expensive. . . ." It is hard to know what Jencks is talking about,
since America's prison population doubled in the last decade. Prisons were the
second fastest-growing item in state budgets last year, behind Medicaid. And the
United States far surpasses the country with the next largest rate of incarceration, South Africa.)

It seems that Americans are insatiable gluttons for punishment when it 39
comes to punishing the "underclass." But locking people up has not stemmed

the tide of crime, and Jencks is right that it is extremely expensive. Nonetheless, our policy experts, along with our politicians, keep calling for more punishment and incarceration.

40   Perhaps because Kaus senses, on some level, that he cannot compete in getting hold of black men and disciplining them, he focuses most of his wrath on women, who are more vulnerable anyway since they get pregnant and have young children who depend on them.

41 When Kaus turns to his plans for poor women and children, he reaches the absolute shallow end of his thinking. Mothers should be forced out of the home to do a job—any job—rather than be allowed to stay home with their children, Kaus says. The state should be prepared to invest a great deal of money in creating such jobs. "Even a leaf-raking job rakes leaves," he reasons. "If that's all someone's capable of doing, does that mean she shouldn't be paid for doing it? The alternative, remember, is to pay her to stay home and raise children."

42   Kaus takes his contempt for child-rearing to its logical extreme. First, the state must deny benefits to women who have more than one child, and insist that mothers go to work. Then, we must be on the lookout for signs of neglect when poor parents fail to provide a proper home for their children. "The long answer, then, is that society will also have to construct new institutions, such as orphanages. . . ."

43   So much for family values.

44   While Kaus deplores the "female-headed household" and the breakdown of the family as a central problem of the "underclass," his grand solution is to warehouse the children of the poor in vast institutions, away from love and nurturing care. Perhaps the state could also hire appropriate role models to come in and deliver speeches to the kids on the value of work. Kaus seems to think that's all they need.

45   Work, in Kaus's book, is supposed to become the value that binds society together. Work—at menial tasks for poverty-level wages—is supposed to give poor people a sense of citizenship and social equality. Work is even supposed to bring the family back together, since, without AFDC, "soon enough ghetto women will be demanding and expecting that the men in their lives offer them stable economic support." And children will want to work "because they will have grown up in a home where the rhythms and discipline of obligation pervade daily life."

46   You would think Kaus was talking about a group of people who had it too easy. He fails to consider the fact that AFDC already does not pay enough to live on. And he ignores the fact—a fact even Jencks points out—that most people on welfare *already* work. Because AFDC payments are not enough to support a family, almost everyone who receives AFDC does some sort of labor. Many do not report it, since the Government docks a dollar of benefits for every dollar a welfare recipient earns.

47   A front-page story in *The New York Times,* part of a series entitled "Rethinking Welfare," recently highlighted the irony of saying there is something wrong

with people who stay on AFDC. The subject of the article was Linda Baldwin, a young woman who gave up welfare for minimum-wage work and is now making $169 less each month.

"While no one knows how many women on welfare would work if the financial rewards were greater," the article states, "most analysts agree it takes an especially motivated woman like Ms. Baldwin when there are no financial rewards at all." *Motivated* hardly seems the appropriate term here. Motivation usually implies some potential for upward motion, rather than submissiveness to life below the poverty level and a future of dead-end work. 48

Furthermore, while Kaus sees only moral turpitude in welfare mothers' efforts to care for their children by staying home, the more "moral" option— stashing the kids and taking a low-wage job, often means abandoning a sick child. Even free medical care and Kaus's offhand promise to provide day care for everyone (something the Family Support Act also promised, and failed to produce) are unlikely to lead to safe, nurturing environments for kids. This may not be a primary concern for Kaus, but it is for mothers who love their children. 49

Interestingly, Jencks points out all of these problems in his last chapter, when he finally comes into contact with some real-life welfare recipients. Through interviews conducted by his colleague, Kathryn Edin, Jencks discovers that concrete obstacles connected with poverty—as opposed to vague problems of immorality—account for the troubles these women face. He ends the chapter by making a series of fairly benign policy recommendations—better access to health care, tax credits for low-income housing—ideas that have nothing to do with race, the "underclass," or the rest of his book. 50

Kaus, on the other hand, holds firmly to the principle that the uppity attitude of the "underclass," not poverty, is our most salient social problem. 51

The solutions he comes up with, although he says they will be good for the poor, are really mostly good for the readers he addresses. Many wealthy suburbanites will undoubtedly agree that "foul-smelling" people in the library and the post office, a general lack of "civility," and poor black people who are not eager to labor and to serve present major difficulties to whites who want to lead lives of comfortable privilege in clean and pleasant communities. 52

But Kaus certainly doesn't intend to make his own children, or the children of affluent suburbanites, clean up the streets and subway stops or work at raking leaves. 53

Privilege and economic hierarchy are carefully preserved in Kaus's "civic liberal" dream. The rich must be bribed and coddled and persuaded to permit a modicum of integration (which would not extend to full integration of the public schools), Kaus says. 54

As an incentive toward integration, he offers tax advantages to the rich. Income and property taxes could be cut, he says, and regressive taxes which disproportionately affect the poor—the sales tax, for example—could be raised to pay for the schools. In addition, tracking within the school system might soften the blow of integration for wealthy people who do not want their chil- 55 dren tainted by coming into contact with the poor. (Kaus says he would not want his own child to go to school with the children of welfare recipients, because they might absorb some damaging "underclass culture.")

56   In any case, Kaus says, integration of the schools must be a very gradual process—nothing to get alarmed about. You can almost hear his suburban readers letting out a collective sigh of relief.

57   Kaus feels so sympathetic toward the rich that, in another bit of virtuoso reasoning, he discovers a noble motive in the suburbanite's flight from the city (a trend he himself blames for much of the decline of civic life). "We don't like to act superior to people we actually come into contact with in daily life, so we set things up so we don't have to come into contact with people who might provoke such feelings," Kaus deduces. "One reason Americans must stratify themselves is that they aren't such natural snobs at all."

58   Segregated neighborhoods and schools, for Kaus, prove a secret yearning for social egalitarianism.

59   Among the poor, in contrast, Kaus roots out the most vile and despicable motives behind such activities as being poor and being a mother.

60   Kaus just can't fathom the idea that not having money could seriously affect people's lives. He places arch quotation marks around the word "homeless," as if it strains credulity to imagine that someone in America might not have a place to live. Perhaps all those cardboard shanties, those families sleeping in bus stations and subway cars, are part of an elaborate put-on sponsored by the Money Liberals, who, it seems, will go to almost any length to drain the tax dollars and try the patience of the professional class.

61   *The End of Equality* is a particularly scary piece of work because it drags bigotry into the daylight and presents it as egalitarianism, making disdain for the poor safe for liberals. In a way, Kaus brings the hidden agenda of underclass theory to fruition. He shifts the blame for a range of social ills—from crime to poverty and unemployment to segregation—onto the disenfranchised. This is the very heart of the culture of cruelty: Blame and punishment replace compassion and justice. Unburdened of the archaic principles of civil rights, Kaus says it proudly: The underclass means black people, and what blacks need is to be brought to heel.

62   Rather than addressing the inequities in our society—segregated schools, unjust wages, inadequate health care, things that social policy could actually fix—Kaus throws away the whole idea of economic injustice. He replaces it with a new villain—the "underclass," whom he blames not only for the problems of poor people on welfare, but for the problems of our society as a whole. Suddenly, the middle-class taxpayer, the politician, and the wealthy upper class are all victims. United in having been wounded by the "underclass," they are all innocent of any responsibility in society. Ominously, Kaus declares that it is only by gathering together and dealing with the "underclass problem" that we can make America a good place to live.

While Kaus bills his book as a manual for reform of the Democratic Party, a 63
new platform that will give the liberal reputation a boost, the Democrats have
already discovered much of Kaus's prescription—though few are quite so bald-
faced about emphasizing its more punitive aspects. "Personal responsibility,"
not Government aid for the poor, has become the rallying cry of Democratic
politicians from Senator Daniel Patrick Moynihan to candidate Bill Clinton.

There is a lively market these days for political theories that defend the rich 64
and disparage the poor. The poor are a perfect scapegoat. After all, as Kaus
points out, it is the suburbanites who vote. "Throwing money at the problem
won't solve anything," is the old conservative mantra, chanted in exclusive
clubs and suburban living rooms all over America.

Meanwhile, the cities seethe.   65

QUESTIONS

1. Compare the topic of this essay with the topic of Awalt's essay. What are
   the similarities? What are the differences? Are they really talking about
   the same thing?
2. Describe how Conniff evaluates the source materials she uses.
3. Conniff notes that the cause-and-effect relationship espoused by her
   opposition doesn't really apply to the reality of poverty in the United
   States. Does she use any cause-and-effect arguments in her article? What
   are they, and are they compelling?
4. There are two social issues at stake when discussing the problem of Aid
   to Families with Dependent Children (AFDC): Should mothers stay
   home with their young children, or should they go to work to get off
   welfare? Which of these things do you consider more important? Why
   do you feel that way?
5. What are the four characteristics of the "underclass theory" posited by
   Mickey Kaus and Christopher Jencks? How (and where) does Conniff
   respond to these characteristics?
6. What is the tone that Conniff uses in her argument? Is it effective? Why
   or why not?

Living under "a Veil of Denial"
Alfee Enciso

Alfee Enciso teaches English at Palms Junior High School in Los Angeles. He previously taught at Markham Intermediate School in Watts.
This essay is from the *Los Angeles Times* (December 1992).

1   Stacy Koon, one of the officers involved in the Rodney King beating case,
referred to King as "Mandingo" and feared him because he is black, but insists
he is "not a racist." My students, in post-unrest discussions, framed their comments with the tired "I'm not a racist but . . ." and my colleagues bend over
backward trying to show me how liberal they are. No one, it seems, wants to
admit to our country's deeply racist roots.

2   America's denial of its racism is tantamount to an alcoholic refuting his illness. And like an addict, if my students, city or country continues to insist on
being "colorblind" or judging all people by the content of their character, then
the specter of racism will continue to rear its terrifying head.

3   To belie my own racism would be quite easy. I worked in Watts for 8½ years; I
even asked the school district to place me there. I also hail from an oppressed
minority—Mexican-American—and suffered discrimination. In fact, I even remember being called a n----- during my formative years in Glendale. My chess-playing
buddies Gene, Eddie, Vince and Charlie are all, like my wife, African-American. So
how could I possibly be prejudiced or racist? Shall I bend my back some more?

4   Despite my race-relations credentials, none of these particulars, whether
isolated or bunched together, can stand up to one undeniable fact: I am an
American, born and raised. To be an American is to be racist. Anyone can see
this, with their eyes closed—or can they?

5   After a few years of teaching in Watts, I developed a keener insight into the
dynamics of racism or, as Malcolm X called it, Americanism. In supermarkets, I
noticed the images of wealth, beauty, happiness and success in the magazines
at the checkout stands. With the exception of sports magazines, where a few
African-Americans—namely Michael (Jordan) and Magic (Johnson)—dominated the covers, I realized that blacks, Latinos or Asians rarely achieved front-
page status. The print media's message rings loud and clear. Success is fair skin,
blue eyes and a European figure. No African butts, slanted eyes or greasy hair
allowed. My awareness didn't stop there. Billboards, radio and television all
spoke the same message every day, "If it's dark or foreign, you're not welcome
in the glamour of America's home." Even trying to find solace in a pool hall, I
discovered that the eight-ball, the darkest ball in the rack, was the last to go in
the pocket, leaving only the white ball to roam the green felt.

6   I asked my students how they could watch television and not be insulted
by the images that brainwashed them. Outraged by such a claim, they balked.
So, to prove my point, I asked the males in my class, "What's the first thing you

guys do when you're together discussing a 'freak' or a 'fox'? You ask, 'Hey, what she look like? . . . Oh, man! She's real fine, man. She's light-skinned,' " at which the class got quiet and smiled. Then a young girl said, "He's right. . . ." while the rest of the students giggled, easing the embarrassment of being "moded."

Awareness of my Eurocentric society made me realize how my own atti- 7
tudes shaped my preferences. As a child, I proudly announced to my older sister that my choice of girlfriend, when I got old enough, would be blond and
blue-eyed. And through my formative years I would constantly look in the mirror, dreaming of blond locks and a surfer face, something I couldn't readily
describe but tangible enough for me to know I didn't possess.

Walking among my students in Watts, exposed to a people from whom I'd 8
been sheltered, I viewed American society in a different light. I started asking
questions. Who had kept this rich, beautiful, African-American culture from my
consciousness? Why had I never even thought of my own Latinas as gorgeous or
goddess-like? And why weren't these the faces that spill out on the pages of
magazines or the myriad television commercials that ingrain our preferences
and desires? But despite these questions and revelations, I realized how much
of America I personally swallowed.

Like a fugue in a G minor, my own Americanism played itself out in a variety 9
of ways. There were the obvious ones: confusing two people for the same one,
assuming two black people knew each other or believing that all of my African-
American colleagues shared the same political ideology. In addition, the liberal
paternalism with which my mother raised me—the "Oh, these poor black people have had such a hard life," attitude—prevailed not only in me, but in many of
my white colleagues. In class I would often accuse students of stealing my things
only to find out I had merely misplaced them. And in college, I manifested a
superiority over my own Mexican people. Apparently, I believed the constant
refrain my Anglo friends intoned: "You're Mexican, but not really." As one of my
African-American teammates pointed out, "You think you're better than me."

These attitudes and beliefs, since changed, nonetheless existed, a part of 10
my upbringing that subconsciously incorporated itself into my American psyche. Upon reflection of this American culture and my own experience in the
inner city, I realized how incredibly powerful this disease is that brainwashed
me, and how tightly its insidious grip steers the conscious and subconscious
behavior of most citizens in this country.

While my experiences may be unique, the outcome—my being made 11
aware of and sensitive to the racist world I live in—should not.

Anyone willing to question themselves and the system in which we live will 12
hopefully come to one conclusion—the truth; much better than the current veil
of denial under which most Americans live.

QUESTIONS

1. How is this essay structured? Does this structure enhance the essay?
   Explain.

2. What kind of evidence does Enciso use to illustrate his perception of racism in America? How effective is his use of personal observation?

3. What is your perception of racial difference? Does the phrase "I'm not a racist, but . . ." come up in your own reflections on this topic? Do you think this is a fair statement? Why or why not?

4. Is Enciso asking the public simply to examine its attitudes toward racial differences? What would the ramifications be of such an examination?

5. Take an informal survey of the media images you come into contact with. How many are of minorities? In what contexts do you find minority representations? Does your survey support Enciso's findings, or does it contradict them?

6. Are the issues that Enciso is concerned with important? How much impact do they have on our day-to-day lives?

The Declaration of Independence

Thomas Jefferson, who became the third president of the United States, was chosen to draft the Declaration of Independence when he was a delegate to the Continental Congress. This document uses many principles associated with the genre of argument to challenge the concept of the divine right of kings, a basic assumption of that time.

When in the Course of human events, it becomes necessary for one people to 1
dissolve the political bands which have connected them with another, and to assume among the powers of the earth, the separate and equal station to which the Laws of Nature and of Nature's God entitle them, a decent respect to the opinions of mankind requires that they should declare the causes which impel them to the separation.—

We hold these truths to be self-evident, that all men are created equal, that 2
they are endowed by their Creator with certain unalienable rights, that among these are Life, Liberty and the pursuit of Happiness.—

That to secure these rights, Governments are instituted among Men, deriv- 3
ing their just powers from the consent of the governed,—

That whenever any Form of Government becomes destructive of these 4
ends it is the Right of the People to alter or to abolish it, and to institute new Government, laying its foundation on such principles and organizing its powers in such form, as to them shall seem most likely to effect their Safety and Happiness. Prudence, indeed, will dictate that Governments long established should not be changed for light and transient causes; and accordingly all experience hath shown, that mankind are more disposed to suffer, while evils are sufferable, than to right themselves by abolishing the forms to which they are accustomed. But when a long train of abuses and usurpations, pursuing invariably the same Object evinces a design to reduce them under absolute Despotism, it is their right, it is their duty, to throw off such Government, and to provide new Guards for their future security.—

Such has been the patient sufferance of these Colonies; and such is now the 5
necessity which constrains them to alter their former Systems of Government. The history of the present King of Great Britain is a history of repeated injuries and usurpations, all having in direct object the establishment of an absolute Tyranny over these States. To prove this, let Facts be submitted to a candid world.—

He has refused his Assent to Laws, the most wholesome and necessary for 6
the public good.—

He has forbidden his Governors to pass Laws of immediate and pressing 7
importance, unless suspended in their operation till his Assent should be obtained; and when so suspended, he has utterly neglected to attend to them.—

He has refused to pass other Laws for the accommodation of large districts 8
of people, unless those people would relinquish the right of Representation in the Legislature, a right inestimable to them and formidable to tyrants only.—

9   He had called together legislative bodies at places unusual, uncomfortable, and distant from the depository of their public Records, for the sole purpose of fatiguing them into compliance with his measures.—

10   He has dissolved Representative Houses repeatedly, for opposing with manly firmness his invasions on the rights of the people.—

11   He has refused for a long time, after such dissolutions, to cause others to be elected; whereby the Legislative powers, incapable of Annihilation, have returned to the People at large for their exercise; the State remaining in the mean time exposed to all the dangers of invasion from without, and convulsions within.—

12   He had endeavoured to prevent the population of these States; for that purpose obstructing the Laws for Naturalization of Foreigners; refusing to pass others to encourage their migrations hither, and raising the conditions of new Appropriations of Lands.—

13   He has obstructed the Administration of Justice, by refusing his Assent to Laws for establishing Judiciary powers.—

14   He has made Judges dependent on his Will alone, for the tenure of their offices, and the amount and payment of their salaries.—

15   He has erected a multitude of New Offices, and sent hither swarms of Officers to harrass our people, and eat out their substance.—

16   He has kept among us in times of peace, Standing Armies without the Consent of our legislatures.—

17   He has affected to render the Military independent of and superior to the Civil power.—

18   He has combined with others to subject us to a jurisdiction foreign to our constitution, and unacknowledged by our laws; giving his Assent to their Acts of pretended Legislation:—

19   For quartering large bodies of armed troops among us:—

20   For protecting them, by a mock Trial, from punishment for any Murders which they should commit on the Inhabitants of these States:—

21   For cutting off our Trade with all parts of the world:—

22   For imposing Taxes on us without our Consent:—

23   For depriving us in many cases, of the benefits of Trial by Jury:—

24   For transporting us beyond Seas to be tried for pretended offences:—

25   For abolishing the free System of English Laws in a neighbouring Province, establishing therein an Arbitrary government, and enlarging its Boundaries so as to render it at once an example and fit instrument for introducing the same absolute rule in these Colonies:—

26   For taking away our Charters, abolishing our most valuable Laws, and altering fundamentally the Forms of our Governments:—

27   For suspending our own Legislatures, and declaring themselves invested with power to legislate for us in all cases whatsoever.—

28   He has abdicated Government here, by declaring us out of his Protection and waging War against us.—

29   He has plundered our seas, ravaged our Coasts, burnt our towns, and destroyed the lives of our people.—

He is at this time transporting large Armies of foreign Mercenaries to com- 30 pleat the works of death, desolation and tyranny, already begun with circumstances of Cruelty & perfidy scarcely paralleled in the most barbarous ages, and totally unworthy the Head of a civilized nation.—

He has constrained our fellow Citizens taken Captive on the high Seas to 31 bear Arms against their Country, to become the executioners of their friends and Brethren, or to fall themselves by their Hands.—

He has excited domestic insurrections amongst us, and has endeavoured to 32 bring on the inhabitants of our frontiers, the merciless Indian Savages, whose known rule of warfare, is an undistinguished destruction of all ages, sexes and conditions.—

In every stage of these Oppressions We have Petitioned for Redress in the 33 most humble terms: Our repeated Petitions have been answered only by repeated injury. A Prince, whose character is thus marked by every act which may define a Tyrant, is unfit to be the ruler of a free people.—

Nor have We been wanting in attentions to our British brethren. We have 34 warned them from time to time of attempts by their legislature to extend an unwarrantable jurisdiction over us. We have reminded them of the circumstances of our emigration and settlement here. We have appealed to their native justice and magnanimity, and we have conjured them by the ties of our common kindred to disavow these usurpations, which, would inevitably interrupt our connections and correspondence. They too have been deaf to the voice of justice and of consanguinity. We must, therefore, acquiesce in the necessity, which denounces our Separation, and hold them, as we hold the rest of mankind, Enemies in War, in Peace Friends.—

We, therefore, the Representatives of the united States of America, in Gen- 35 eral Congress, Assembled, appealing to the Supreme Judge of the world for the rectitude of our intentions, do, in the Name, and by Authority of the good People of these Colonies, solemnly publish and declare, That these United Colonies are, and of Right ought to be, Free and Independent States; that they are Absolved from all Allegiance to the British Crown, and that all political connection between them and the State of Great Britain, is and ought to be totally dissolved; and that as Free and Independent States, they have full Power to levy War, conclude Peace, contract Alliances, establish Commerce, and to do all other Acts and Things which Independent States may of right do.—

And for the support of this Declaration, with a firm reliance on the protec- 36 tion of divine Providence, we mutually pledge to each other our Lives, our Fortunes and our sacred Honor.

QUESTIONS

1. What is the thesis of the Declaration? Can you state it as an enthymeme?
2. What reasons are cited for the thesis in the Declaration?
3. How do the authors of the Declaration establish credibility?
4. How is the Declaration similar to the classical form of argumentation? How is it different?

Chapter 9

TWO IMPORTANT STRATEGIES IN ARGUMENTATION: ESTABLISHING CAUSALITY AND DEFINING TERMS

Although essays written in the genre of argument address controversial issues of all sorts, these issues frequently involve cause and effect. For example, in the 1996 California election, those people in favor of Proposition 209 claimed that affirmative action policies that favor women and minorities have caused unfair hiring practices, whereas those opposed to the proposition claimed that such policies cause the hiring process to be more fair. Similarly, educators advocating required school uniforms for high school students claim that the uniforms will cause greater concentration on school work. Those opposed argue that school uniforms would detract from students' need to express their individuality. If you chose to write about either of these topics, you would have to address the issue of causality in developing your position.

Another concept that is extremely important to the genre of argument is that of definition. Whenever you support an idea with a value-laden word such as *fair, just, sexist,* or *appropriate,* you need to define what you mean because what is considered "fair," "just," "sexist," or "appropriate" in one context may not be so in another. Because causality and definition are so important in argumentation, this chapter will explore possibilities for including these strategies in your essay.

THE NATURE OF CAUSAL ARGUMENTS

Statements that are concerned with cause and effect claim that a particular event, condition, or situation is going to *cause* a specific effect or effects, or that a particular effect or effects were *caused* by a particular event, condition, or situation. Here are some examples:

- An increase in the minimum wage will *cause* harm to small business.
- Eating genetically enhanced vegetables will *not cause* harmful side effects.
- Violence in children is an *effect* of watching violent cartoons.

Causation is an important strategy in the genre of argument because it often addresses the cause or effect of existing or potential societal problems, such as immigration, crime, technology, or racism and sexism. In dealing with topics such as these, an argumentative essay will frequently identify a problem and then

- examine its causes
- call attention to potential consequences or effects
- suggest possibilities for solving it, based on what predicted effects are likely to be

Causal arguments are based on a relationship between one event or situation and another. If high school student Farley decides not to study for his math final, and he then receives a failing grade on it, the *cause* is his failure to study, and the *effect* is his failing grade. If his failing grade on the test causes him to fail the course, the poor grade on the test then becomes the cause of his failure. Thus, an event or situation can be both a cause and an effect, depending on *when* it occurs. Causes come *before* effects; effects come *after* causes.

Causation involving physical actions is usually easy to determine. If Bart Simpson throws a brick at a window and the window breaks, it is obvious that the breakage was caused by the brick, no matter what excuse Bart might offer. But causation as a topic for argumentative writing is usually concerned with more complex human behavior than breaking a window with a brick (and if you try to figure out *why* Bart decided to throw the brick, this action becomes more complex as well). For example, one might ask why Farley didn't study for his math final. Was it simply laziness or lack of interest? Did something happen in Farley's personal life that so distracted him that he couldn't study? Was Farley so intimidated by math that he felt that he had no chance of passing? Maybe Farley has a full-time job that leaves him no time to study. These questions (and I'm sure you can think of several others) about what seems to be a simple issue, the failing of a math exam, show how difficult it is to determine causality, especially when you are writing about political, social, and ethical issues.

Causality is difficult to understand because human behavior often seems inexplicable and unpredictable. For example, it is generally acknowledged that children raised in poverty in the inner city are often educationally disadvantaged. Yet, there are a number of instances in which some of these children rise above their circumstances and become quite successful students. Why can some children accomplish this, whereas others cannot? Some factors, such as family stability, offer a partial explanation, but they don't explain everything. Conversely, it is also true that not all educationally advantaged children succeed in school. The literature is stuffed with possible explanations for why this might be so, but no one can either predict or explain human behavior with absolute certainty.

Immediate versus Remote Causality

Causality is often discussed in terms of a chain, which means that one cause leads to an effect, which becomes the cause of another effect, and so on. The *immediate cause* is the one that is closest in time to the event or situation being analyzed. *Remote causes* are those that occurred in the past.

To distinguish between immediate and remote causes, note the following example:

1. Farley did not study for the math exam.
2. Farley failed the math exam.
3. Farley's failing grade on the math exam caused him to fail the math course.
4. Farley's failure of the math course caused him to drop out of school.
5. Because Farley did not have a high school diploma, he could not get a job to support himself.
6. Farley's failure to get a job caused him to become unable to meet his expenses.
7. Unable to meet his expenses, Farley began shoplifting small items from the supermarket.
8. Farley then began stealing items from department stores.
9. Farley eventually met an underworld character named Felix, a notorious cat burglar, who stole expensive jewelry from hotel rooms.
10. Felix made Farley his apprentice.
11. Eventually Farley became an internationally known jewel thief.

In this admittedly absurd example, Farley's meeting Felix and becoming his apprentice are the *immediate causes* of his becoming a notorious jewel thief. But as in most instances, a number of earlier events or factors led to the one in the present—Farley's dropping out of school and being unable to get a job, for example, are certainly important factors. Sometimes, though, it is difficult to determine the role that remote causes play in contributing to a present event. It would be nonsensical, for example, for someone to claim that Farley's career as a jewel thief was caused by his failure to study for a math exam in high school. But every causal event can be traced backward through the chain into the past, often indefinitely. Philosophers know that it is difficult, if not impossible, to determine the first cause of anything.

EXERCISE

1. Choose an event or condition in your own life and trace as many causes for it as possible. What causes have contributed, for example, to the fact that you are reading this book?

2. In small groups, choose a problematic situation in your school and trace as many causes for it as possible.

Precipitating versus Contributing Cause

Similar to the distinction between an immediate and a remote cause is that between a *precipitating* and a *contributing* cause. A precipitating cause is an

event or situation that triggers a particular effect. A contributing cause is a condition that gives rise to the precipitating cause. For example, Farley may have
had poor experiences in math classes all of his life, and these poor experiences
are the contributing causes of Farley's failure to study for his math exam. But
then, in his junior year in high school, Farley had a particularly poor math
teacher, Mr. Smith, who came to class unprepared and gave Farley the impression that he would never succeed in math no matter how hard he tried. Mr.
Smith's poor teaching, then, might have been the precipitating cause of Farley's
failure to study for his math final.

The Danger of Oversimplification

A common mistake of writers who address causality is to assume that there is
only one cause for a particular consequence. Because human nature is complex, most issues suitable for argumentation can be traced to multiple causes,
so in writing an argumentative essay that deals with causality, you should be
careful not to oversimplify. It would be ridiculous to claim, for example, that if
Farley had only not had Mr. Smith for math, he would never have become a
notorious jewel thief.

EXERCISE

Working in small groups, identify the immediate cause, remote cause, precipitating cause, and contributing cause for the following events or situations:

1. why a particular television program is popular
2. how you chose the college you are attending
3. how you chose your major
4. why women tend to earn lower salaries than men
5. why computers have become so important
6. why certain brands of running shoes are so popular
7. why a particular sport is popular

Typical Weaknesses of the Causation Argument

Arguments that address causality typically can be weakened by the following
features:

1. Oversimplification
    In analyzing causation, it is tempting to try to find one discrete cause
when, in reality, most events or situations have many causes. If you are analyzing why a candidate lost an election, the loss was most likely due to a number
of factors, not to just one. Certainly, complex social problems, such as an
increase in crime, unemployment, or divorce, must be analyzed in terms of
multiple causes.

2. Mistaking correlation for causation

When one event occurs immediately after another, they are correlated, but not necessarily connected. The fallacy known as "false cause" assumes causal connections where none may exist. The increase in crime in big cities has been paralleled by the growth of the television industry, but that doesn't necessarily mean that watching television causes people to commit crimes.

CAUSATION IN THE PROPOSAL ARGUMENT

Determining causality and predicting consequences are particularly important in arguments that may loosely be labeled "proposal arguments." Proposal arguments analyze a problem, often in terms of causation, and suggest solutions based on predicted consequences or effects. Writers who argue in favor of speech codes on campus, for example, predict that such codes will have the effect of eliminating racist or sexist speech. Writers who argue against speech codes on campus predict that such codes will have the effect of stifling free speech.

The proposal argument consists of two main components:

1. identifying that a problem exists
2. showing that the proposal represents a reasonable solution or a way of addressing the problem

To demonstrate to your readers that a problem exists, you may need to discuss its background or to cite evidence, such as examples or statistics. To convince them that they should accept your perspective on the problem, you will have to cite reasons and evidence, just as you would in any argumentative essay.

Policy or Action Proposals

Proposal arguments may be concerned either with questions of policy or with specific actions or behaviors. *Policy* proposals aim to address major social, political, or economic problems, such as allocating resources within the population, controlling crime, or providing equal opportunity in education and employment. Frequently, they are broad in scope and may be based on philosophical and ethical concerns. The other type of proposal, sometimes designated the *action* proposal, advocates a specific action to solve a particular problem and is usually more narrow and concrete. Proposals to change the registration system at your university or to institute recycling in a particular community are examples of an action proposal.

Often, proposal arguments will address both policy and action because the justification for a particular action may be based on philosophical and ethical values. A policy providing maternity leave for both mothers and fathers, for example, is based on the idea that both parents need to bond with a child and that the early months of a child's life are when this important bonding occurs. On the other hand, a policy that provides maternity leave only for the mother is based on the idea that mothers should assume the primary responsibility for caring for a newborn and that the father should provide monetary support. In the course of your professional and academic life, you will probably write proposals of both kinds.

The Structure of Proposal Arguments

Proposal arguments usually consist of three parts: 1) describing the problematic situation and convincing the audience that the problem is important, 2) proposing a way of addressing or solving the problem (predicting consequences), and 3) indicating why your proposal is better than other possibilities. Here is a suggestion for structuring a proposal argument:

Introduction	■ introduces the problem or controversy concerning a person, situation, issue, or concept
	■ provides relevant background
	■ indicates why the problem or controversy is important to address
	■ presents the writer's proposal for addressing or solving the problem
Body:	■ examines the cause or causes of the problem
	■ presents justification for the proposal
	■ shows that the proposal can help solve the problem
	■ provides evidence in support of the proposal
	■ acknowledges that the problem is complex and may not be easily solved (particularly in policy proposals)
	■ indicates awareness of alternative viewpoints
	■ refutes the opposing viewpoint
Conclusion:	■ sums up argument
	■ reiterates importance of accepting the proposal

CONVINCING YOUR AUDIENCE THAT A PROBLEM EXISTS: ARGUING FROM PRECEPT, EFFECT, AND SIMILARITY

Because proposal arguments aim to solve or at least to address a problem, an important goal for you is to convince the audience that a problem exists. Many readers are surprisingly unaware of the major problems in society—many people are so busy with their own lives that they simply do not know about them. Others deliberately avoid thinking about anything that will disturb their concept of a safe and ordered world. If your readers do not understand that there is a problem, or if they believe that the problem is not serious enough to warrant concern or change, they will be unlikely to pay much attention to your proposal. To convince your readers to recognize that a problem exists or to consider the problem seriously, you might wish to present it in terms of one or all of three useful strategies: precept, effect, and similarity. All of these strategies have the goal of persuading your audience to pay attention to the problem you are addressing through an appeal to emotion and values. Here is an example of how precept, effect, and similarity might be used in a proposal argument:

Proposal: The university should not mandate political correctness.

Arguing from precept:	because political correctness is a form of censorship (Censorship is a precept that most people condemn.)
Arguing from effect:	because laws mandating political correctness cannot control sexist or racist thinking and can lead to a repressive environment on campus
Arguing from similarity:	because laws that mandate political correctness are like mind control in the novel *1984*

Arguments Based on Precept

Arguing on the basis of a precept involves showing that a particular situation or policy is either wrong or right according to a generally accepted value, principle, definition, or belief that your reader is likely to take seriously. For example, one common argument against the use of racial quotas in the workplace is that they are "unfair." This strategy argues from the principle that "unfairness" means that something is "bad," and it presumes that most readers would reject racial quotas on that basis. Of course, someone in favor of racial quotas might argue that they are not "unfair" at all but are, in actuality, aimed at redressing the unfairness that occurred in the past. This person might feel that racial quotas actually contribute to "fairness" in the workplace. Similarly, a popular argument against school policies that mandate political correctness is that they are actually a form of censorship, which in the United States is considered "bad." An opponent to this claim, however, might argue that the laws against censorship never were designed to include offensive racial or sexist slurs and that controlling this form of speech cannot be considered censorship.

Arguments Based on Effect

Proposal arguments can also claim that if a problem is not solved or a problematic situation is not addressed, then an undesirable effect or consequence will occur. You might argue, for example, that unless affirmative action policies are enacted, women and minorities will not be given a fair chance. Or you might make the claim that unless political correctness laws are passed on campus, students will make racist remarks that will result in a hate-obsessed, divided university community. On the other hand, you might also argue that political correctness mandates do not solve the problem at all, but rather might cause other undesirable effects, such as discouraging students from engaging in honest debate on emotionally charged issues.

Arguments Based on Similarity

A writer who argues from similarity will compare the situation that he or she is addressing with another situation that an audience might relate to with greater force or emotion. The aim of this strategy is to transfer the audience's attitude from one emotionally charged topic to another. For example, if you were arguing that there should be serious penalties for plagiarism, you might discover that many people do not view plagiarism as a serious crime. You might then compare plagiarism with stealing, which your readers would probably view more gravely. Similarly, a proposal to institute stronger penalties for littering in the local park might argue that destroying the environment is like burning down your own house. If you decide to argue from similarity, it is important to remember its function—that is, to generate a strong response in your reader and to call attention to the seriousness of the issue you are addressing. Similarities that don't produce this impact will not enhance the effectiveness of your essay.

EXERCISE

Working in small groups, think of potential support for each of the following claims, using one of the three methods of justification just noted—precept, effect, and similarity. If possible, use "because" clauses to indicate the kind of support you would provide. Here is an example:

Claim: Teenagers should be required to do community service.

Precept: because doing community service is an unselfish act

Effect: because community service will help teenagers become concerned citizens

Similarity: because living in a community without taking any interest in it is like living in a house about which you have no concern. You are unlikely to do anything to improve it.

1. All college students should be required to take a money management course.

Precept: because taking a money management course is _____

Effect: because taking a money management course will have the effect of _____

Similarity: because taking a money management course is like

_____

2. Smoking should be forbidden in restaurants.

Precept: because smoking in restaurants is _____

Effect: because smoking in restaurants will have the effect of

_____

Similarity: because smoking in restaurants is like _____

3. Grading in composition courses should be eliminated.

Precept: because grading in composition classes is _____

Effect: because grades in composition classes can have the effect of

_____

Similarity: because grades in composition classes are like _____

Qualification in the Proposal Argument

In writing the proposal argument, it is especially important to use qualifying words and to acknowledge the existence of alternative viewpoints because the topics for a proposal argument are often concerned with complex problems that are extremely difficult, if not impossible, to solve easily. Although you may feel strongly that your proposal is superior to others, and although you may predict that only the most positive consequences will result, you will appear more credible to your audience if you acknowledge the possibility that events may take an unusual turn or that people may behave unpredictably. Indicate your awareness of these possibilities by using qualifying terms such as *seems, suggests, indicates, to some degree,* or *to a certain extent.* See Chapter 6 for further discussion on the importance of qualification.

WRITING ASSIGNMENT

Working either individually or in small groups, make a list of problems affecting your community or society as a whole. Then choose one and write an argumentative essay of four to six pages in which you 1) identify the problem, 2) indicate why it is a problem that ought to be addressed, 3) propose a solution or a way of addressing the problem, and 4) indicate your awareness of the complexity of this problem by discussing alternative perspectives. If appropriate, use one or more of the strategies discussed in this chapter: precept, effect, and similarity.

Use the following exploration questions to generate material for this topic:

1. Is there a controversy associated with this problem?
2. Is this a problem that you were aware of when you were growing up?
3. Is this a problem that has affected you personally in some way?
4. Can you think of at least two people who hold differing views about this problem? If so, describe these people and summarize what you believe were their points of view.
5. Has your opinion about this problem changed in any way? Why or why not?
6. Do you think that this problem is important for people to think about? Why or why not?

ADDITIONAL QUESTIONS IN THINKING ABOUT CAUSALITY

1. What is the cause of this problem?
2. Who is affected by this problem?
3. Who has the power to do something about this problem?
4. Why hasn't it been addressed or solved until now?
5. Why would it be useful to address or solve this problem?
6. What costs would be incurred by addressing or solving this problem?
7. Who would pay for these costs?
8. Have other solutions to this problem been proposed?
9. Why is your solution better than others?

Student Proposal Essay

Read the following essay, noting how cause and effect are used. Compare the structure of this essay with the structure discussed earlier.

Los Angeles Must Conserve Water

Los Angeles continues to struggle with the overwhelming problem of water shortage. The two main reasons for water shortage in Los Angeles are 1) Los Angeles is a desert, and 2) Los Angeles has an ever-increasing population. These two reasons for water shortage are not going to change; therefore, our system must. Most of our water comes from natural reservoirs such as the Owens Valley River, the Colorado River, and Mono Lake. These natural suppliers depend on one thing to get their water: rainfall (including water runoff from mountains). For the past 40 years southern California has had low rainfall, but within the past 10 years rainfall has been decreasing the most. Because Californians cannot continue to use water at a faster rate than our natural resources can replenish it, the local government should regulate the production of water utilities so that only "low-flow" utilities are produced.

Government officials have recently stated that as a result of last year's abundant rainfall Los Angeles is no longer in a drought. Maybe at the present moment this is true, but according to a Los Angeles Times editorial, "Ground water supplies are a long way from being replenished and key reservoirs remain unfilled" (April 8, 1991, B4). Even if several more storms hit, about 50 more inches of rain and snow must fall to replace the losses from preceding drought years. We are not out of a drought, and the slightest heat wave could put us right back where we were before all the recent rain. For this reason, it is necessary to install some system of water conservation.

For those of us who live in Los Angeles, a hot desert area, water is perhaps our most precious natural resource. Yet, the public negligently continues to waste it. A Los Angeles Times editorial asserts, "the average city resident uses 180 gallons of water a day (Feb. 6, 1991, B6). The 180 gallons is divided into several areas of use: drinking water, cooking, cleaning, lawns and agriculture, and industry. What this 180 gallons exemplifies is that people use water negligently in everyday life. For instance, many people take showers to relax and to daydream when showers should be, as conventionally thought, for cleaning one's body.

Many people also allow the water to run when they are brushing their teeth. Another infuriating example of excessive use is when people wash off their driveways with the hose. These few, yet very common, examples of excessive water usage continue to deplete our water supply.

There are many ways to decrease the amount of water that each Los Angeles resident uses on a daily basis. Sitting on the table are four major proposals on how to do so: the "use more, pay more" plan, recycling, desalination, and installing a "low-flow" water utilities system. Installing "low-flow" water utilities is the best because each of the other options has severe drawbacks.

Implementing higher rates on a "use more, pay more" basis is the plan presently existing. The top-to-bottom rate overhaul rewards residential and business customers who use less of this region's most precious commodity (by lowering their water bills) and penalizes those who use more by charging them extra (Los Angeles Times, Sept. 4, 1992, B6).

"Use more, pay more" is a good start and has been somewhat effective in decreasing water usage by 22.8 percent (Los Angeles Times, Sept. 4, 1992, B6). But it does not absolutely restrict the amount of water the average person can use because it benefits the wealthy. Someone who makes $100,000 a year is less likely to be seriously affected by higher water rates than someone who makes $30,000. As a result, the wealthier individual might be more inclined to continue using a larger amount of water. Moreover, under this plan, the wealthier individual is not absolutely restricted from using the average 180 gallons of water and so might choose to use more without thought of the consequences. Thus, although this plan reduces usage, it is not enough.

Another plan that also looks to be very positive, recycling water, would involve building plants that take used water from industry and housing and that filter it so that it could be used over and over. Considering that our natural lakes, rivers, and other inland water suppliers would be saved, this is an excellent idea. The only problem is that the entire system would have to be restructured to pull in used water and flush cleaned water back into the system, a plan that would cost millions of dollars more than is currently available.

It is also argued that the best way to solve the entire problem of water shortage is desalination. Desalination involves pumping water from the world's largest water resource, the ocean (98 percent of the earth's water) and converting it to drinking water or "freshwater." The desalination process reduces the salt and other seawater ingredients down to a level at which the water can be used for agriculture, drinking, and all other facets of freshwater usage. Desalination is quite expensive. It costs "$4.00 for every 1000 gallons" of water (Abselon 1289). Desalination has worked quite well in Malta, but Malta has considerably fewer people than Los Angeles. With 13 million people in the city, each of whom uses 180 gallons a day, the cost of desalination would be far too great.

The most effective way to reduce the amount of water used in Los Angeles and to continue reducing it with the growing population is to implement laws stating that only "low-flow" water utilities be used and produced. "Low-flow" water utilities greatly reduce the amount of water used, without forcing people to make great sacrifices or attempting to change their water-use habits. For example, "the difference between a 5-minute shower under a conventional shower head and one under a low-flow shower head is 27.5 gallons" (Los Angeles Times, Feb. 6, 1991, B6). "Low-flow" faucets and shower heads have smaller-diameter holes through which the water flows, allowing less water through while maintaining a high-pressure water stream, thus creating the same power as that of the conventional faucet or shower head. Considerable water savings—"up to 10,000 gallons a year—are coming from each low-flush toilet that replaces older models" (Los Angeles Times, April 8, 1991, B4). "Low-flush" toilets reduce the amount of water used, from seven gallons to six gallons, by reducing the flow of water into the toilet after every flush, thus reducing the amount used the next time. Conserving water with "low-flow" utilities can save millions of gallons a day, and it is relatively effortless.

Another benefit of the "low-flow" system is that it will expand to help conserve water in the future. With the vastly growing population of Los Angeles, construction of new houses, apartment buildings, condominiums, factories, office buildings, and any other type of structure is inevitable. Therefore, installation of "low-flow" utilities in all new construction would automatically conserve water for the people who will occupy them.

Not only will the "low-flow" system grow with the future, but it will also not put on future generations any burden of saving to conserve water. Conservation will be a subconscious way of life that will occur whether people think about it or not. It will even occur with continuous bad habits. This is not to say that future generations should not attempt to conserve, but whether they attempt to or not, they will automatically with "low-flow" utilities. A "low-flow" system is a sure-fire way of making sure that conservation of water would be a subconscious way of life for everyone now and in the future.

Two things must be done in order to start a "low-flow" conservation system. First, companies that produce water faucets, shower heads, and other forms of water utilities must be restricted by law to making only "low-flow" products. One might argue that government interference should not be allowed and that companies should not be restricted from producing things, but just as GM was forced to put smog-control devices on cars, so should the water utility industry be forced to produce only "low-flow" products.

Another law should be enacted requiring that within three years all existing conventional faucets, shower heads, and toilets be replaced with "low-flow" products. After the three years, the Department of Water and Power should check every company and household, including condominiums and apartments, to make sure that low-flow utilities have been installed. For those people who have not installed them, a fine should be charged, and for each impending month, the fine should go up.

One might oppose this entire plan by stating that in order for the government to put such a system into effect, a lot of money is needed— money that Los Angeles does not have. Yes, money is needed so that the Department of Water and Power can hire people to make routine checks on water utility companies and enforce the laws, but, unlike opponents might think, no money is necessary for subsidizing these companies. Every year, water utility companies come up with different product lines of faucets, shower heads, and toilets. Therefore, it would not be a problem or cost the companies any money to start producing new "low-flow" product lines. Even so, some money is necessary to make the "low-flow" system work. For this reason, even with some of the problems created with the "use more, pay more" plan, we should continue it and use the money gained to start the "low-flow" system.

Due to its desert location, Los Angeles needs a lot of water for its fast-growing population. The water we use every day comes from decreasing natural reservoirs. The only way to ensure water for the future, save our natural resources, and keep up with a fast-growing population is to install a "low-flow" water conservation system. Producing and installing only "low-flow" water utilities not only save water now, but also will help to save water in the future. With every person who grows up under this system and buys a new house, water conservation will automatically be a part of life. Los Angeles is not out of the drought, and we should install a "low-flow" system in order to continue conserving with a growing population.

References

Abelson, Philip. 1991. "Desalination of Brackish and Rain Water." <u>Science Magazine.</u>

"Use More—Pay More." Editorial. <u>Los Angeles Times</u>. September 4, 1992, B6.

"Water Conservation—a Saving Grace." Editorial. <u>Los Angeles Times</u>. April 8, 1991, B4.

QUESTIONS

1. Note all instances in the essay "Los Angeles Must Conserve Water" that address causality. How does causality support the thesis of this essay?
2. How does this essay acknowledge an opposing viewpoint?

THE IMPORTANCE OF DEFINING TERMS

Whether your argumentative essay is concerned with causality or with other themes, it is important that you define your terms so that the reader will understand their meaning. For example, in statements such as

"Affirmative action programs are not *fair*."

"That movie is not *suitable* for children."

the terms *fair* and *suitable* require definition because what is "right," "good," "fair," or "suitable" for one person may not be for another and may depend a great deal on the context. Similarly, if you decide to support a particular candidate for president of the student government because he or she is a "good leader," it will be necessary for you to define what you mean by "good leader." Or if you have decided that a particular television program is not "appropriate" for children, you would have to define what you mean by "appropriate."

Types of Definitions

Ordinary versus Stipulative

There are a number of ways that a term may be defined. One common method is to define a word in terms of its ordinary or customary usage; often the source of that definition will be a dictionary. A "hero," for example, is defined in several ways by *The American Heritage Dictionary:*

1. In mythology and legend, a man, often of divine ancestry, who is endowed with great courage and strength, celebrated for his bold exploits and favored by the gods.
2. A man noted for feats of courage or nobility of purpose—esp one who has risked or sacrificed his life: *a war hero.* 3. A man noted for his special achievements in a particular field: *the heroes of medicine* 4. The principal male character in a novel, poem or dramatic presentation. 5. (Slang) A large sandwich consisting of a roll that is split lengthwise and contains a variety of fillings, as lettuce, tomatoes, onions, meats and cheese.

If you were writing an essay in which the term *hero* was important, you might wish to clarify for your reader that you conceived of a hero in terms of its customary usage as defined in a dictionary. Or you might wish to cite the customary or ordinary definition in order to show that a public figure or celebrity wasn't really a hero at all.

Another form of definition that you might wish to use in an argumentative essay is the *stipulative definition,* which involves assigning a term a special or particular meaning that limits the way it will be defined within a specific context. In his essay titled "From Hero to Celebrity," Daniel Boorstin stipulates the following definition:

> The traditional heroic type included figures as diverse as Moses, Ulysses, Aeneas, Jesus, Caesar, Mohammed, Joan of Arc, Shakespeare, Washington, Napoleon, and Lincoln. For our purposes it is sufficient to define a hero as a human figure—real or imaginary or both—who has shown greatness in some achievement. He is a man or woman of great deeds.

In this stipulative definition, Boorstin has indicated how he is defining the term *hero,* and he cites the attributes that he feels are most important. For Boorstin, a hero is a human figure, one who has reached greatness in some achievement, someone who has performed great deeds. He also indicates that a hero can be either a man or a woman, and in this way he distinguishes his definition from that in the dictionary, which uses the term to refer only to a man.

Here is another example of a stipulative definition:

> Although a child who has a roomful of expensive toys is sometimes referred to as "spoiled," that child may not exhibit the behavior of a spoiled child. A child who is spoiled is one who believes that he or she is better than other children, is generally rude and inconsiderate, demands that his or her every wish be granted, and sulks if this does not happen. Thus the term *spoiled* is more indicative of an attitude and mode of behavior than it is of the possession of material goods.

EXERCISE

Working in small groups, create a stipulative definition of the following terms:

1. a good dog
2. a satisfying job
3. an effective teacher
4. a car worth buying
5. a computer for daily use
6. a worthwhile profession

Essential versus Incidental Characteristics of a Definition

The simplest way to define a term is to provide either a dictionary definition or a synonym and then to present those characteristics that make the term what it is. The definition of a vest, for example, is stated in the dictionary as "a short sleeveless collarless garment, either open or fastening in front, worn over a shirt or blouse and often under a suit coat or jacket." This definition is stated in the most common format, which places the term within the next-larger class or category and then cites the particular features that distinguish it from other terms in the same category. Thus, a vest is first of all an article of clothing.

However, in defining terms, it is also important to distinguish characteristics that are essential from those that are merely incidental. Essential characteristics are those that must be present in order for the article to be what it is. Incidental characteristics are those that may be present but that are not absolutely necessary. An essential characteristic of a vest, for example, is that it is sleeveless; otherwise, it would be considered a blouse or a shirt. Therefore, the characteristic "sleeveless" is essential for defining the term *vest*. However, although current fashion suggests that a vest be worn over a shirt or a blouse, it is sometimes worn on its own and yet would still be considered a vest. In this instance, then, the characteristic "being worn over a shirt or blouse" would be considered incidental, meaning that it is not absolutely essential to the definition.

EXERCISE

Find the dictionary definition of the following terms or formulate your own. Then, working in groups, examine the definition of each term and decide which characteristics are essential and which are incidental.

1. salad
2. party
3. pet
4. sandwich
5. game
6. computer nerd
7. nosy person
8. best friend

STRATEGIES OF DEFINITION

Many words can be defined fairly easily by noting their essential characteristics or by providing a synonym. The word *honor*, for example, may be defined as "homage," "reverence," or "deference." Terms used in academic argument, however, often require a more expanded definition beyond a simple one-word or one-sentence explanation. Strategies that are useful for this purpose are the following: defining by example, defining by negation, defining by classification, and defining by operation.

Defining by Example

It is often useful to provide an illustration or example to help your reader understand what you mean. If you are discussing an educational television program that you think is suitable for young children, you might mention *Sesame Street*. If you refer to a "suspenseful" book, it would be useful for you to illustrate that concept by mentioning a few titles. Citing examples, however, does not provide a complete definition, so it is important to include other methods of definition as well. The following passage concerned with defining a leader begins with a simple definition and then uses several examples for clarification:

> Great leaders are always great simplifiers, who cut through argument, debate, and doubt to offer a solution everybody can understand and remember. Churchill warned the British to expect "blood, toil and sweat"; FDR told Americans that "the only thing we have to fear is fear itself"; Lenin promised the war-weary Russians peace, land and bread. Straightforward but potent messages.
>
> Michael Korda, "How to Be a Leader," *Newsweek,* January 5, 1981

Defining by Negation

Defining by negation means explaining what something *is* by showing what it *is not.* Some examples of this strategy are as follows: "Freedom of speech" does not mean "permission to make racist remarks," "liberty" does not mean "license," "a greeting card rhyme" is not "poetry." Related to this method of definition is that of defining by contrast—that is, a particular thing or concept is defined by contrasting it with something else.

In the following paragraphs, the expression *taken advantage of* is contrasted with the word *rape* in order to show that the expression has the effect of trivializing a terrible crime:

A recent article in a local newspaper referred to a woman who was raped as having been "taken advantage of," a phrase that trivializes a terrible crime and does a disservice to its victims. The word *taken* implies only a mild intrusion, most likely involving a possession of some sort, as in "his wallet was taken out of his dresser drawer," and the term *advantage* suggests winning a competition or game, another mild association. For example, in the game of tennis, a player who is one point from winning a game is referred to as having an "advantage."

The word *rape,* however, conjures up images of violence and violation, agony and shame. According to the police, a rape is a "sexual assault," meaning a violent act of unwanted sex perpetrated against an unwilling person, words with extremely disturbing connotations. The phrase *taken advantage of,* however, does not embody the concepts of either "unwanted" or "sexual" in the picture it creates. It is a euphemism that should not be used to mean the act of "rape."

Defining by Classification

When you define by classification, you situate the term within a class of things—people, animals, tools, subjects, ideas, and so forth—and then indicate how that term differs from other terms in that class. In the following excerpt, Patty McEntee situates the word *obscenity* within the class of pornography in order to show that obscenity is not protected by the First Amendment:

> "Pornography" is a generic term that includes both hard-core and soft-core porn. "Obscenity" is the legal term for "hard-core pornography," and obscenity is not protected by the First Amendment. . . . According to the U.S. Supreme

Court, materials or performances are "obscene" if: a) taken as a whole, they appeal to the prurient interest; b) depict or describe in a patently offensive manner sexual conduct specifically defined; or c) taken as a whole, lack serious literary, artistic, political and scientific value. Obscenity may apply to magazines, videos, dial-a-porn, cable-porn or live performances.

Patty McEntee, "Is Pornography a Matter of Free Expression?" *America,* August 10, 1991

Defining by Operation or Function

An effective way to define is to state what something does or to explain how it works. The word *debate* can be defined as "a formal contest of argumentation in which two opposing teams defend and attack a given idea." A *tutor* may be defined as "a private instructor who gives additional, special, or remedial instruction." A *writing center* may be defined as "a facility where writers of all kinds can receive individualized assistance in writing through the help of a knowledgeable, well-trained tutor."

EXERCISES

1: Working in small groups, write a definition for the following terms. Try to include all of the strategies noted earlier: synonym, example, negation, classification, and operation.

A: competition

B: political correctness

C: "working out"

D: sports car

E: guilt

F: sexual harassment

G: stress

H: a worthwhile college course

2: Write a definition of a term from a profession, sport, or hobby that you know a great deal about but that may be unfamiliar to most people. Use at least one of the strategies discussed earlier.

THE ESSAY OF DEFINITION

In some instances, the entire premise of an argumentative essay may be based on a problem involving definition—that is, the purpose of the essay is to establish that a problematic situation, concept, or issue either does or does not fit a particular definition. For example, the famous case of Rodney King that became the catalyst for the Los Angeles riots in 1992 involved the question of whether the police were guilty of brutality or whether they were just "doing their jobs." If you were to write an essay with the goal of establishing that the police were, indeed, guilty of brutality to Rodney King, you would first have to define *brutality,* establish criteria for labeling an action "brutal," and then show how the actions of the police on that day fit that definition.

Because most definitions are not straightforward, argumentative essays that focus on definition contain the implicit question "To what extent?" or "To what degree?" Here are some examples of how the element of "degree" or "extent" helps shape the definition essay:

Topic	Question
heroism	To what extent is a particular action "heroic"?
marriage	To what extent is marriage for women a form of slavery?
political correctness	To what extent is political correctness a form of repression?
after-school sports	To what extent is participation in after-school sports educationally beneficial?

Characteristics of the Definition Essay

An argumentative essay that focuses on a definition retains the primary characteristics of the genre of argument—that is,

1. It focuses on a problem or controversy concerned with whether a particular person, situation, issue, or concept fits a definition; for example, whether the incidence of crimes committed by inner-city young people should be considered a state "emergency," whether current unemployment figures should be considered a national "crisis," or whether a particular sports figure should be considered a "hero."

2. It aims to move readers to think about the criteria for the definition and to acknowledge that the person, situation, issue, or concept either does or does not possess these necessary criteria; for example, whether the crime situation in the inner city possesses the necessary criteria to be considered a state "emergency," whether the current state of unemployment possesses the necessary criteria to be considered a "crisis," or whether Michael Jordan fits the characteristics of a "hero."

3. It explores its subject in sufficient depth so as to acknowledge an opposing viewpoint—that is, it recognizes that the person, situation, issue, or concept may have characteristics that confound easy definition and so is not easily classified. For example, in considering what is meant by a state "emergency," some people might define it as being of greater severity than the current crime statistics would warrant. In defining what is meant by a "hero," some people may feel that a sports figure cannot be considered a hero just because he or she is popular. For them, a sports figure would not be considered a hero unless he or she had performed heroic deeds. A compelling definition essay would consider both sides of a controversy.

4. It presents convincing evidence utilizing a variety of support strategies.

Structure in the Definition Essay

The structure of the definition essay similarly retains the generic components of academic argument. Here is a model you can apply:

Introduction:	■ introduces the problem or controversy concerning a person, situation, issue, or concept
	■ provides relevant background
	■ indicates that the problem or controversy is concerned with definition
	■ states position, thesis, or claim
Body:	■ presents the definition in terms of necessary and sufficient criteria
	■ illustrates the definition using a variety of strategies
	■ establishes that the person, situation, issue, or concept possesses the necessary criteria for the definition
	■ addresses the opposing viewpoint by acknowledging that the person, situation, issue, or concept may have characteristics that confound easy definition, making it difficult to classify
	■ refutes the opposing viewpoint
Conclusion:	■ sums up argument

WRITING ASSIGNMENTS

Causality

1. Read "Why Johnny Can't Read, But Yoshio Can" at the end of this chapter, which discusses three characteristics of Japanese schools that seem to be responsible for their students' superior performance. Then write an argumentative essay of four to six pages responding to the following question:

Should these characteristics be adopted in American schools?

In responding to this question, you might also wish to include those characteristics that you wouldn't like to see adopted.

2. Read "The Debate over Placing Limits on Racist Speech Must Not Ignore the Damage It Does to Its Victims" and " 'Speech Codes' and Free Speech." Then write an argumentative essay in which you address the following question:

To what extent are speech codes helpful or harmful on a college campus?

Definition: The Topic of Heroism

Background: Read "Is a Hero Really Nothing But a Sandwich?" and "Where Have You Gone, Joe DiMaggio?" and "Have We Outgrown the Age of Heroes?"

1. Using the culture with which you are most familiar, choose a contemporary figure who might be considered heroic. Write an argumentative essay of five to six pages discussing how and why this person ought to be considered a hero. Be sure to formulate a clear definition on which to base your argument.

2. Develop a clear definition of a "hero" and write an argumentative essay addressing the following question:

Do you think it is possible for a hero to exist in modern society?

3. Read the following scenario (This assignment was created by the Freshman Writing Program at the University of Southern California):

In the city of Evansby, Indiana, Russell Brown, a young police officer, succeeded in apprehending a murderer/rapist who had claimed the lives of over 25 young women over a six-month period. During those six months, a virtual "reign of terror" had been imposed on Evansby, and no one felt safe after dark in the once-peaceful town.

Brown worked indefatigably to bring the criminal into custody, and, in several instances, he even risked his own life. In fact, due to his willingness to be lowered from the roof of a building, he was able to save the life of an 11-year-old girl who was being held terrorized at knife point, and, in the resulting struggle, Brown himself suffered several debilitating injuries.

In gratitude, the people of Evansby wish to issue a plaque to be installed in the town square, hailing Russell Brown as a hero. Unfortunately, however, the publicity surrounding Brown has brought to light several less-than-flattering aspects of his life and personality. It turns out that in the course of several marriages, Brown has fathered several children, none of whom he acknowledges or supports, and he is also known to be an active member of a racially biased organization that has been implicated in terrorizing minorities. In fact, it was largely because Brown presumed that the criminal was a member of a minority group that he worked so tirelessly in bringing the culprit to justice.

In an argumentative essay of five to six pages, discuss whether or not Brown ought to be honored as a hero. Read the articles on the topic included in this chapter and take into account the following issues:

- the definition of a hero
- the distinction between a hero and a person who merely performs a heroic act
- the role of intention in determining who is a hero
- the relationship between private vice and public heroism
- whether it is possible for anyone to be a hero in the modern world

ADDITIONAL QUESTIONS TO FOCUS YOUR THINKING

To access some additional ideas on this topic, write responses to the questions that follow. You might also wish to discuss these questions in small groups.

1. Should any person who performs a heroic deed be considered a hero? Or is it important to separate the deed from the person who performed it?
2. Does the intention count in defining a hero—that is, if a soldier is running away from a battle and, in the course of doing so, discovers a hidden mine field, thereby saving thousands of men, is he a hero?
3. Does a hero have to be perfect?
4. Does the private life of a hero have a bearing on whether that person can be considered heroic?
5. Is it possible for anyone to be a hero in the modern world, in which intense media scrutiny reveals every flaw?
6. How would you distinguish a hero from a celebrity?

Why Johnny Can't Read, but Yoshio Can
Richard Lynn

Richard Lynn teaches in the psychology department at the University
of Ulster, Northern Ireland. This essay was taken from his book *Educational Achievement in Japan* (1988) and appeared in its current
form in *National Review* (October 28, 1988).

1   There can be no doubt that American schools compare poorly with Japanese
schools. In the latter, there are no serious problems with poor discipline, violence, or truancy; Japanese children take school seriously and work hard. Japanese educational standards are high, and illiteracy is virtually unknown.

2   The evidence of Japan's high educational standards began to appear as long
ago as the 1960s. In 1967 there was published the first of a series of studies of
educational standards in a dozen or so economically developed nations, based
on tests of carefully drawn representative samples of children. The first study
was concerned with achievement in math on the part of 13- and 18-year-olds.
In both age groups the Japanese children came out well ahead of their coevals
in other countries. The American 13-year-olds came out second to last for their
age group; the American 18-year-olds, last. In both age groups, European children scored about halfway between the Japanese and the Americans.

3   Since then, further studies have appeared, covering science as well as
math. The pattern of results has always been the same: the Japanese have generally scored first, the Americans last or nearly last, and the Europeans have
fallen somewhere in between. In early adolescence, when the first tests are
taken, Japanese children are two or three years ahead of American children; by
age 18, approximately 98 percent of Japanese children surpass their American
counterparts.

4   Meanwhile, under the Reagan Administration, the United States at least
started to take notice of the problem. In 1983 the President's report, *A Nation
at Risk,* described the state of American schools as a national disaster. A follow-
up report issued by the then-secretary of education, Mr. William Bennett, earlier this year claims that although some improvements have been made, these
have been "disappointingly slow."

5   An examination of Japan's school system suggests that there are three factors responsible for its success, which might be emulated by other countries: a
strong national curriculum, stipulated by the government; strong incentives for
students; and the stimulating effects of competition between schools.

6   The national curriculum in Japan is drawn up by the Department of Education. It covers Japanese language and literature, math, science, social science,
music, moral education, and physical education. From time to time, the Department of Education requests advice on the content of the curriculum from representatives of the teaching profession, industry, and the trade unions. Syllabi

are then drawn up, setting out in detail the subject matter that has to be taught at each grade. These syllabi are issued to school principals, who are responsible for ensuring that the stipulated curriculum is taught in their schools. Inspectors periodically check that this is being done.

The Japanese national curriculum ensures such uniformly high standards 7 of teaching that almost all parents are happy to send their children to the local public school. There is no flight into private schools of the kind that has been taking place in America in recent years. Private schools do exist in Japan, but they are attended by less than 1 percent of children in the age range of compulsory schooling (six to 15 years).

This tightly stipulated national curriculum provides a striking contrast with 8 the decentralized curriculum of schools in America. Officially, the curriculum in America is the responsibility of school principals with guidelines from state education officials. In practice, even school principals often have little idea of what is actually being taught in the classroom.

America and Britain have been unusual in leaving the curriculum so largely 9 in the hands of teachers. Some form of national curriculum is used throughout Continental Europe, although the syllabus is typically not specified in as much detail as in Japan. And now Britain is changing course: legislation currently going through Parliament will introduce a national curriculum for England and Wales, with the principal subjects being English, math, science, technology, a foreign language, history and geography, and art, music, and design. It is envisioned that the new curriculum will take up approximately 70 percent of teaching time, leaving the remainder free for optional subjects such as a second foreign language, or extra science.

Under the terms of the new legislation, schoolchildren are going to be 10 given national tests at the ages of seven, 11, 14, and 16 to ensure that the curriculum has been taught and that children have learned it to a satisfactory standard. When the British national curriculum comes into effect, America will be left as the only major economically developed country without one.

To achieve high educational standards in schools it is necessary to have 11 motivated students as well as good teachers. A national curriculum acts as a discipline on teachers, causing them to teach efficiently, but it does nothing to provide incentives for students, an area in which American education is particularly weak.

One of the key factors in the Japanese education system is that secondary 12 schooling is split into two stages. At the age of 11 or 12, Japanese children enter junior high school. After three years there, they take competitive entrance examinations for senior high schools. In each locality there is a hierarchy of public esteem for these senior high schools, from the two or three that are regarded as the best in the area, through those considered to be good or average, down to those that (at least by Japanese standards) are considered to be poor.

The top schools enjoy national reputations, somewhat akin to the famous 13 English schools such as Eton and Harrow. But in England the high fees exacted by these schools mean that very few parents can afford them. Consequently there are few candidates for entry, and the entrance examinations offer little incentive to work for the great mass of children. By contrast, in Japan the elite senior high schools are open to everyone. While a good number of these schools are private (approximately 30 percent nationwide, though in some major cities the figure is as high as 50 percent), even these schools are enabled, by government subsidies, to keep their fees within the means of a large proportion of parents. The public schools also charge fees, but these are nominal, amounting to only a few hundred dollars a year, and loans are available to cover both fees and living expenses.

14   Thus children have every expectation of being able to attend the best school they can qualify for; and, hence, the hierarchical rankings of senior high schools act as a powerful incentive for children preparing for the entrance examinations. There is no doubt that Japanese children work hard in response to these incentives. Starting as early as age ten, approximately half of them take extra tuition on weekends, in the evenings, and in the school holidays at supplementary coaching establishments known as *juku,* and even at that early age they do far more homework than American children. At about the age of 12, Japanese children enter the period of their lives known as *examination hell:* during this time, which lasts fully two years, it is said that those who sleep more than five hours a night have no hope of success, either in school or in life. For, in addition to conferring great social and intellectual status on their students, the elite senior high schools provide a first-rate academic education, which, in turn, normally enables the students to get into one of the elite universities and, eventually, to move into a good job in industry or government.

15   Although Japanese children are permitted to leave school at the age of 15, 94 percent of them proceed voluntarily to the senior high schools. Thus virtually all Japanese are exposed in early adolescence to the powerful incentive for academic work represented by the senior-high-school entrance examinations. There is nothing in the school systems of any of the Western countries resembling this powerful incentive.

16   The prestige of the elite senior high schools is sustained by the extensive publicity they receive from the media. Each year the top hundred or so schools in Japan are ranked on the basis of the percentage of their pupils who obtain entry to the University of Tokyo, Japan's most prestigious university. These rankings are widely reported in the print media, and the positions of the top twenty schools are announced on TV news programs, rather like the scores made by leading sports teams in the United States and Europe. At a local level, more detailed media coverage is devoted to the academic achievements of all the schools in the various localities, this time analyzed in terms of their pupils' success in obtaining entry to the lesser, but still highly regarded, local universities.

17   Thus, once Japanese 15-year-olds have been admitted to their senior high schools, they are confronted with a fresh set of incentives in the form of entrance examinations to universities and colleges, which are likewise hierarchically ordered in public esteem. After the University of Tokyo, which stands at

the apex of the status hierarchy, come the University of Kyoto and ten or so other highly prestigious universities, including the former Imperial Universities in the major provincial cities and the technological university of Hitosubashi, whose standing and reputation in Japan resembles that of the Massachusetts Institute of Technology in the United States.

Below these top dozen institutions stand some forty or so less prestigious 18 but still well-regarded universities. And after these come numerous smaller universities and colleges of varying degrees of standing and reputation.

To some extent the situation in Japan has parallels in the United States and 19 Europe, but there are two factors that make the importance of securing admission to an elite university substantially greater in Japan than in the West. In the first place, the entire Japanese system is geared toward providing lifelong employment, both in the private sector and in the civil service. It is practically unheard of for executives to switch from one corporation to another, or into public service and then back into the private sector, as in the United States and Europe. Employees are recruited directly out of college, and, needless to say, the major corporations and the civil service recruit virtually entirely from the top dozen universities. The smaller Japanese corporations operate along the same lines, although they widen their recruitment net to cover the next forty or so universities in the prestige hierarchy. Thus, obtaining entry to a prestigious university is a far more vital step for a successful career in Japan than it is in the United States and Europe.

Secondly, like the elite senior high schools, the elite universities are meri- 20 tocratic. The great majority of universities are public institutions, receiving substantial government subsidies. Again, as with the senior high schools, fees are quite low, and loans are available to defray expenses. In principle and to a considerable extent in practice, any young Japanese can get into the University of Tokyo, or one of the other elite universities, provided only that he or she is talented enough and is prepared to do the work necessary to pass the entrance examinations. Knowing this, the public believes that *all* the most talented young Japanese go to one of these universities—and, conversely, that anyone who fails to get into one of these schools is necessarily less bright. Avoiding this stigma is, of course, a further incentive for the student to work hard to get in.

The third significant factor responsible for the high educational standards 21 in Japan is competition among schools. This operates principally among the senior high schools, and what they are competing for is academic reputation. The most prestigious senior high school in Japan is Kansei in Tokyo, and being a teacher at Kansei is something like being a professor at Harvard. The teachers' self-esteem is bound up with the academic reputation of their schools—a powerful motivator for teachers to teach well.

In addition to this important factor of self-esteem, there is practical neces- 22 sity. Since students are free to attend any school they can get into, if a school failed to provide good-quality teaching, it would no longer attract students. In business terms, its customers would fade away, and it would be forced to close. Thus the essential feature of the competition among the Japanese senior high schools is that it exposes the teachers to the discipline of the free-enterprise system. In the case of the public senior high schools, the system can be regarded as a form of market socialism in which the competing institutions are state-owned but nevertheless compete against each other for their customers. Here the Japanese have been successfully operating the kind of system that Mikhail Gorbachev may be feeling his way toward introducing in the Soviet Union. The Japanese private senior high schools add a further capitalist element to the system insofar as they offer their educational services more or less like firms operating in a conventional market.

23   The problem of how market disciplines can be brought to bear on schools has been widely discussed in America and also in Britain ever since Milton Friedman raised it a quarter of a century or so ago, but solutions such as Friedman's voucher proposal seem as distant today as they did then. Although the proposal has been looked at sympathetically by Republicans in the United States and by Conservatives in Britain, politicians in both countries have fought shy of introducing it. Probably they have concluded that the problems of getting vouchers into the hands of all parents, and dealing with losses, fraud, counterfeits, and so forth, are likely to be too great for the scheme to be feasible.

24   The Japanese have evolved a different method of exposing schools to market forces. Subsidies are paid directly to the schools on a per-capita basis in accordance with the number of students they have. If a school's rolls decline, so do its incomes, both from subsidies and from fees. This applies to both the public and private senior high schools, although the public schools obviously receive a much greater proportion of their income as subsidies and a smaller proportion from fees.

25   A similar scheme is being introduced in Britain. The Thatcher government is currently bringing in legislation that will permit public schools to opt out of local-authority control. Those that opt out will receive subsidies from the central government on the basis of the number of students they have. They will then be on their own, to sink or swim.

26   There is little doubt that this is the route that should be followed in America. The exposure of American schools to the invigorating stimulus of competition, combined with the introduction of a national curriculum and the provision of stronger incentives for students, would work wonders. Rather than complaining about Japanese aggressiveness and instituting counterproductive protectionist measures, Americans ought to be looking at the source of Japan's power.

QUESTIONS

1. What would you say, based on reading this essay, is the main reason American students aren't performing as well as their Japanese counterparts? Do you feel that the cause-and-effect relationship that Lynn assumes tells the whole story, or would you like more information on some points?

2. Is the Japanese system too rigorous for American students? Would it work for American students? Write a cause-and-effect model of such a system in American schools: What would happen if we tried to use that system here?
3. How does Lynn define *education?*
4. Are there cultural differences between Japanese society and American or European societies that would make the Japanese school system unfeasible elsewhere? Make a list of the cultural differences.
5. Does this essay follow a definitional structure? Is that structure effective for the academic argument genre?
6. How do you feel about your education? Do you feel you were challenged? Were you bored? Did you learn enough to function well in society?

The Debate over Placing Limits
on Racist Speech Must Not Ignore
the Damage It Does to Its Victims
Charles R. Lawrence III

Charles R. Lawrence III is a professor of law at Stanford University.
This article was adapted from a speech Lawrence delivered before
the American Civil Liberties Union and appeared in the *Chronicle of
Higher Education* (1989).

1   I have spent the better part of my life as a dissenter. As a high school student, I
was threatened with suspension for my refusal to participate in a civil-defense
drill, and I have been a conspicuous consumer of my First Amendment liberties
ever since. There are very strong reasons for protecting even racist speech. Perhaps the most important of these is that such protection reinforces our society's
commitment to tolerance as a value, and that by protecting bad speech from
government regulation, we will be forced to combat it as a community.

2   But I also have a deeply felt apprehension about the resurgence of racial violence and the corresponding rise in the incidence of verbal and symbolic assault
and harassment to which blacks and other traditionally subjugated and excluded
groups are subjected. I am troubled by the way the debate has been framed in
response to the recent surge of racist incidents on college and university campuses and in response to some universities' attempts to regulate harassing
speech. The problem has been framed as one in which the liberty of free speech
is in conflict with the elimination of racism. I believe this has placed the bigot on
the moral high ground and fanned the rising flames of racism.

3   Above all, I am troubled that we have not listened to the real victims, that
we have shown so little understanding of their injury, and that we have abandoned those whose race, gender, or sexual preference continues to make them
second-class citizens. It seems to me a very sad irony that the first instinct of
civil libertarians has been to challenge even the smallest, most narrowly framed
efforts by universities to provide black and other minority students with the
protection the Constitution guarantees them.

4   The landmark case of *Brown* v. *Board of Education* is not a case that we
normally think of as a case about speech. But *Brown* can be broadly read as
articulating the principle of equal citizenship. *Brown* held that segregated
schools were inherently unequal because of the *message* that segregation con-
veyed—that black children were an untouchable caste, unfit to go to school
with white children. If we understand the necessity of eliminating the system
of signs and symbols that signal the inferiority of blacks, then we should hesi-
tate before proclaiming that all racist speech that stops short of physical violence must be defended.

University officials who have formulated policies to respond to incidents of 5
racial harassment have been characterized in the press as "thought police," but
such policies generally do nothing more than impose sanctions against inten-
tional face-to-face insults. When racist speech takes the form of face-to-face
insults, catcalls, or other assaultive speech aimed at an individual or small group
of persons, it falls directly within the "fighting words" exception to First
Amendment protection. The Supreme Court has held that words which "by
their very utterance inflict injury or tend to incite an immediate breach of the
peace" are not protected by the First Amendment.

If the purpose of the First Amendment is to foster the greatest amount of 6
speech, racial insults disserve that purpose. Assaultive racist speech functions
as a preemptive strike. The invective is experienced as a blow, not as a prof-
fered idea, and once the blow is struck, it is unlikely that a dialogue will follow.
Racial insults are particularly undeserving of First Amendment protection
because the perpetuator's intention is not to discover truth or initiate dialogue
but to injure the victim. In most situations, members of minority groups realize
that they are likely to lose if they respond to epithets by fighting and are forced
to remain silent and submissive.

Courts have held that offensive speech may not be regulated in public 7
forums such as streets where the listener may avoid the speech by moving on,
but the regulation of otherwise protected speech has been permitted when the
speech invades the privacy of the unwilling listener's home or when the unwilling listener cannot avoid the speech. Racist posters, fliers, and graffiti in dor-
mitories, bathrooms, and other common living spaces would seem to clearly
fall within the reasoning of these cases. Minority students should not be
required to remain in their rooms in order to avoid racial assault. Minimally,
they should find a safe haven in their dorms and in all other common rooms
that are a part of their daily routine.

I would also argue that the university's responsibility for ensuring that these 8
students receive an equal educational opportunity provides a compelling justification for regulations that ensure them safe passage in all common areas. A
minority student should not have to risk becoming the target of racially assault-
ing speech every time he or she chooses to walk across campus. Regulating vil-
ifying speech that cannot be anticipated or avoided would not preclude
announced speeches and rallies—situations that would give minority-group
members and their allies the chance to organize counterdemonstrations or
avoid the speech altogether.

The most commonly advanced argument against the regulation of racist 9
speech proceeds something like this: We recognize that minority groups suffer
pain and injury as the result of racist speech, but we must allow this hate mon-
gering for the benefit of society as a whole. Freedom of speech is the lifeblood of
our democratic system. It is especially important for minorities because often it
is their only vehicle for rallying support for the redress of their grievances. It
will be impossible to formulate a prohibition so precise that it will prevent the

racist speech you want to suppress without catching in the same net all kinds of speech that it would be unconscionable for a democratic society to suppress.

10   Whenever we make such arguments, we are striking a balance on the one hand between our concern for the continued free flow of ideas and the democratic process dependent on that flow, and, on the other, our desire to further the cause of equality. There can be no meaningful discussion of how we should reconcile our commitment to equality and our commitment to free speech until it is acknowledged that there is real harm inflicted by racist speech and that this harm is far from trivial.

11   To engage in a debate about the First Amendment and racist speech without a full understanding of the nature and extent of that harm is to risk making the First Amendment an instrument of domination rather than a vehicle of liberation. We have not all known the experience of victimization by racist, misogynist, and homophobic speech, nor do we equally share the burden of the societal harm it inflicts. We are often quick to say that we have heard the cry of the victims when we have not.

12   The *Brown* case is again instructive because it speaks directly to the psychic injury inflicted by racist speech by noting that the symbolic message of segregation affected "the hearts and minds" of negro children "in a way unlikely ever to be undone." Racial epithets and harassment often cause deep emotional scarring and feelings of anxiety and fear that pervade every aspect of a victim's life.

13   *Brown* also recognized that black children did not have an equal opportunity to learn and participate in the school community if they bore the additional burden of being subjected to the humiliation and psychic assault contained in the message of segregation. University students bear an analogous burden when they are forced to live and work in an environment where at any moment they may be subjected to denigrating verbal harassment and assault. The same injury was addressed by the Supreme Court when it held that sexual harassment that creates a hostile or abusive work environment violates the ban on sex discrimination in employment of Title VII of the Civil Rights Act of 1964.

14   Carefully drafted university regulations would bar the use of words as assault weapons and leave unregulated even the most heinous of ideas when those ideas are presented at times and places and in manners that provide an opportunity for reasoned rebuttal or escape from immediate injury. The history of the development of the right to free speech has been one of carefully evaluating the importance of free expression and its effects on other important societal interests. We have drawn the line between protected and unprotected speech before without dire results. (Courts have, for example, exempted from the protection of the First Amendment obscene speech and speech that disseminates official secrets, that defames or libels another person, or that is used to form a conspiracy or monopoly.)

15   Blacks and other people of color are skeptical about the argument that even the most injurious speech must remain unregulated because, in an unregulated marketplace of ideas, the best ones will rise to the top and gain acceptance. Our experience tells us quite the opposite. We have seen too many

demagogues elected by appealing to America's racism. We have seen too many good liberal politicians shy away from the issues that might brand them as being too closely allied with us.

Whenever we decide that racist speech must be tolerated because of the 16 importance of maintaining societal tolerance for all unpopular speech, we are asking blacks and other subordinated groups to bear the burden for the good of all. We must be careful that the ease with which we strike the balance against the regulation of racist speech is in no way influenced by the fact that the cost will be borne by others. We must be certain that those who will pay that price are fairly represented in our deliberations and that they are heard.

At the core of the argument that we should resist all government regulation of 17 speech is the ideal that the best cure for bad speech is good, that ideas that affirm equality and the worth of all individuals will ultimately prevail. This is an empty ideal unless those of us who would fight racism are vigilant and unequivocal in that fight. We must look for ways to offer assistance and support to students whose speech and political participation are chilled in a climate of racial harassment.

Civil-rights lawyers might consider suing on behalf of blacks whose right to 18 an equal education is denied by a university's failure to ensure a nondiscrimina-tory educational climate or conditions of employment. We must embark upon the development of a First Amendment jurisprudence grounded in the reality of our history and our contemporary experience. We must think hard about how best to launch legal attacks against the most indefensible forms of hate speech. Good lawyers can create exceptions and narrow interpretations that limit the harm of hate speech without opening the floodgates of censorship.

Everyone concerned with these issues must find ways to engage actively in 19 actions that resist and counter the racist ideas that we would have the First Amendment protect. If we fail in this, the victims of hate speech must rightly assume that we are on the oppressors' side.

QUESTIONS

1. What is the cause-and-effect relationship of racist language, according to Lawrence? Does he take into consideration both immediate cause and remote cause?
2. What strategies does Lawrence use to define racism?
3. Lawrence focuses his argument mostly on racist speech in school. Can you find other examples of racist speech in other areas of society? Do they follow the same kind of causality?
4. How do you define the First Amendment? Consider the excerpt on obscenity in this chapter: Do you feel you really understand what is obscene based on this explanation? Could you write a similar statement concerning racist language? How useful would that be?
5. Is this a proposal argument? Explain.
6. Does Lawrence's use of personal experience contribute to the defining process in this essay? Why or why not?

"Speech Codes" and Free Speech
Nat Hentoff

Nat Hentoff is a columnist for the *Village Voice* and the *Washington Post*. He is also an associate professor of music at New York University. This essay is from *The Progressive* (1989).

1   During three years of reporting on anti-free-speech tendencies in higher education, I've been at more than twenty colleges and universities—from Washington and Lee and Columbia to Mesa State in Colorado and Stanford.

2   On this voyage of initially reverse expectations—with liberals fiercely advocating censorship of "offensive" speech and conservatives merrily taking the moral high ground as champions of free expression—the most dismaying moment of revelation took place at Stanford.

3   In the course of a two-year debate on whether Stanford, like many other universities, should have a speech code punishing language that might wound minorities, women, and gays, a letter appeared in the *Stanford Daily*. Signed by the African-American Law Students Association, the Asian-American Law Students Association, and the Jewish Law Students Association, the letter called for a harsh code. It reflected the letter and the spirit of an earlier declaration by Canetta Ivy, a black leader of student government at Stanford during the period of the grand debate. "We don't put as many restrictions on freedom of speech," she said, "as we should."

4   Reading the letter by this rare ecumenical body of law students (so pressing was the situation that even Jews were allowed in), I thought of twenty, thirty years from now. From so bright a cadre of graduates, from so prestigious a law school would come some of the law professors, civic leaders, college presidents, and maybe even a Supreme Court justice of the future. And many of them would have learned—like so many other university students in the land— that censorship is okay provided your motives are okay.

5   The debate at Stanford ended when the president, Donald Kennedy, following the prevailing winds, surrendered his previous position that once you start telling people what they can't say, you will end up telling them what they can't think. Stanford now has a speech code.

6   This is not to say that these gags on speech—every one of them so overboard and vague that a student can violate a code without knowing he or she has done so—are invariably imposed by student demand. At most colleges, it is the administration that sets up the code. Because there have been racist or sexist or homophobic taunts, anonymous notes or graffiti, the administration feels it must *do something*. The cheapest, quickest way to demonstrate that it cares is to appear to suppress racist, sexist, homophobic speech.

7   Usually, the leading opposition among the faculty consists of conservatives—when there is opposition. An exception at Stanford was law professor

Gerald Gunther, arguably the nation's leading authority on constitutional law. But Gunther did not have much support among other faculty members, conservative or liberal.

At the University of Buffalo Law School, which has a code restricting 8 speech, I could find just one faculty member who was against it. A liberal, he spoke only on condition that I not use his name. He did not want to be categorized as a racist.

On another campus, a political science professor for whom I had great 9 respect after meeting and talking with him years ago has been silent—students told me—on what Justice William Brennan once called "the pall of orthodoxy" that has fallen on his campus.

When I talked to him, the professor said, "It doesn't happen in my class. 10 There's no 'politically correct' orthodoxy here. It may happen in other places at this university, but I don't know about that." He said no more.

One of the myths about the rise of PC is that, coming from the Left, it is pri- 11 marily intimidating conservatives on campus. Quite the contrary. At almost every college I've been to, conservative students have their own newspaper, usually quite lively and fired by a muckraking glee at exposing "politically correct" follies on campus.

By and large, those most intimidated—not so much by the speech codes 12 themselves but by the Madame Defarge-like spirit behind them—are liberal students and those who can be called politically moderate.

I've talked to many of them, and they no longer get involved in class dis- 13 cussions where their views would go against the grain of PC righteousness. Many, for instance, have questions about certain kinds of affirmative action. They are not partisans of Jesse Helms or David Duke, but they wonder whether progeny of middle-class black families should get scholarship preference. Others have a question about abortion. Most are not pro-life, but they believe that fathers should have a say in whether the fetus should be sent off into eternity.

Jeff Shesol, a recent graduate of Brown, and now a Rhodes scholar at 14 Oxford, became nationally known while at Brown because of his comic strip. *Thatch,* which, not too kindly, parodied PC students. At a forum on free speech at Brown before he left, Shesol said he wished he could tell the new students at Brown to have no fear of speaking freely. But he couldn't tell them that, he said, advising the new students to stay clear of talking critically about affirmative action or abortion, among other things, in public.

At that forum, Shesol told me, he said that those members of the Left who 15 regard dissent from their views as racist and sexist should realize that they are discrediting their goals. "They're honorable goals," said Shesol, "and I agree with them. I'm against racism and sexism. But these people's tactics are obscuring the goals. And they've resulted in Brown no longer being an open-minded place." There were hisses from the audience.

Students at New York University Law School have also told me that they 16 censor themselves in class. The kind of chilling atmosphere they describe was exemplified last year as a case assigned for a moot court competition became subject to denunciation when a sizable number of law students said it was too "offensive" and would hurt the feelings of gay and lesbian students. The case concerned a divorced father's attempt to gain custody of his children on the grounds that their mother had become a lesbian. It was against PC to represent the father.

17   Although some of the faculty responded by insisting that you learn to be a lawyer by dealing with all kinds of cases, including those you personally find offensive, other faculty members supported the rebellious students, praising them for their sensitivity. There was little public opposition from the other students to the attempt to suppress the case. A leading dissenter was a member of the conservative Federalist Society.

18   What is PC to white students is not necessarily PC to black students. Most of the latter did not get involved in the NYU protest, but throughout the country many black students do support speech codes. A vigorous exception was a black Harvard Law School student who spoke during a debate on whether the law school should start punishing speech. A white student got up and said that the codes are necessary because without them, black students would be driven away from colleges and thereby deprived of the equal opportunity to get an education.

19   The black student rose and said that the white student had a hell of a nerve to assume that he—in the face of racist speech—would pack up his books and go home. He'd been familiar with that kind of speech all his life, and he had never felt the need to run away from it. He'd handled it before and he could again.

20   The black student then looked at his white colleague and said that it was condescending to say that blacks have to be "protected" from racist speech. "It is more racist and insulting," he emphasized, "to say that to me than to call me a nigger."

21   But that would appear to be a minority view among black students. Most are convinced they do need to be protected from wounding language. On the other hand, a good many black student organizations on campus do not feel that Jews have to be protected from wounding language.

22 Though it's not much written about in reports of the language wars on campuses, there is a strong strain of anti-Semitism among some—not all, by any means—black students. They invite such speakers as Louis Farrakhan, the former Stokely Carmichael (now Kwame Touré), and such lesser but still burning bushes as Steve Cokely, the Chicago commentator who has declared that Jewish doctors inject the AIDS virus into black babies. That distinguished leader was invited to speak at the University of Michigan.

23   The black student organization at Columbia University brought to the campus Dr. Khallid Abdul Muhammad. He began his address by saying: "My leader, my teacher, my guide is the honorable Louis Farrakhan. I thought that should be said at Columbia Jewniversity."

24   Many Jewish students have not censored themselves in reacting to this form of political correctness among some blacks. A Columbia student, Rachel Stoll, wrote a letter to the *Columbia Spectator:* "I have an idea. As a white Jew-

ish American, I'll just stand in the middle of a circle comprising . . . Khallid Abdul Muhammad and assorted members of the Black Students Organization and let them all hurl large stones at me. From recent events and statements made on this campus, I gather this will be a good cheap method of making these people feel good."

At UCLA, a black student magazine printed an article indicating there is 25 considerable truth to the *Protocols of the Elders of Zion.* For months, the black faculty, when asked their reactions, preferred not to comment. One of them did say that the black students already considered the black faculty to be insufficiently militant, and the professors didn't want to make the gap any wider. Like white liberal faculty members on other campuses, they want to be liked— or at least not too disliked.

Along with quiet white liberal faculty members, most black professors have 26 not opposed the speech codes. But unlike the white liberals, many honestly do believe that minority students have to be insulated from barbed language. They do not believe—as I have found out in a number of conversations—that an essential part of an education is to learn to demystify language, to strip it of its ability to demonize and stigmatize you. They do not believe that the way to deal with bigoted language is to answer it with more and better language of your own. This seems very elementary to me, but not to the defenders, black and white, of the speech codes.

Consider University of California president David Gardner. He has imposed 27 a speech code on all the campuses in his university system. Students are to be punished—and this is characteristic of the other codes around the country—if they use "fighting words"—derogatory references to "race, sex, sexual orientation, or disability."

The term *fighting words* comes from a 1942 Supreme Court decision, 28 *Chaplinsky* v. *New Hampshire,* which ruled that "fighting words" are not protected by the First Amendment. That decision, however, has been in disuse at the High Court for many years. But it is thriving on college campuses.

In the California code, a word becomes "fighting" if it is directly addressed 29 to "any ordinary person" (presumably, extraordinary people are above all this). These are the kinds of words that are "inherently likely to provoke a violent reaction, *whether or not they actually do."* (Emphasis added.)

Moreover, he or she who fires a fighting word at any ordinary person can 30 be reprimanded or dismissed from the university because the perpetrator should "reasonably know" that what he or she has said will interfere with the "victim's ability to pursue effectively his or her education or otherwise participate fully in university programs and activities."

Asked Gary Murikami, chairman of the Gay and Lesbian Association at the 31 University of California, Berkeley: "What does it mean?"

Among those—faculty, law professors, college administrators—who insist 32 such codes are essential to the university's purpose of making *all* students feel at home and thereby able to concentrate on their work, there has been a celebratory resort to the Fourteenth Amendment.

33   That amendment guarantees "equal protection of the laws" to all, and that means to all students on campus. Accordingly, when the First Amendment rights of those engaging in offensive speech clash with the equality rights of their targets under the Fourteenth Amendment, the First Amendment must give way.

34   This is the thesis, by the way, of John Powell, legal director of the American Civil Liberties Union (ACLU), even though that organization has now formally opposed all college speech codes—after a considerable civil war among and within its affiliates.

35   The battle of the amendments continues, and when harsher codes are called for at some campuses, you can expect the Fourteenth Amendment— which was not intended to censor *speech*—will rise again.

36   A precedent has been set at, of all places, colleges and universities, that the principle of free speech is merely situational. As college administrators change, so will the extent of free speech on campus. And invariably, permissible speech will become more and more narrowly defined. Once speech can be limited in such subjective ways, more and more expression will be included in what is forbidden.

37   One of the exceedingly few college presidents who speaks out on the consequences of the anti-free-speech movement is Yale University's Benno Schmidt:

> Freedom of thought must be Yale's central commitment. It is not easy to embrace. It is, indeed, the effort of a lifetime. . . . Much expression that is free may deserve our contempt. We may well be moved to exercise our own freedom to counter it or to ignore it. But universities cannot censor or suppress speech, no matter how obnoxious in content, without violating their justification for existence. . . .
>
> On some other campuses in this country, values of civility and community have been offered by some as paramount values of the university, even to the extent of superseding freedom of expression.
>
> Such a view is wrong in principle and, if extended, is disastrous to freedom of thought. . . . The chilling effects on speech of the vagueness and open-ended nature of many universities' prohibitions . . . are compounded by the fact that these codes are typically enforced by faculty and students who commonly assert that vague notions of community are more important to the academy than freedom of thought and expression. . . .
>
> This is a flabby and uncertain time for freedom in the United States.

38   On the Public Broadcasting System in June 1991, I was part of a Fred Friendly panel at Stanford University in a debate on speech codes versus freedom of expression. The three black panelists, including a Stanford student, strongly supported the codes. So did the one Asian American on the panel. But then so did Stanford law professor Thomas Grey, who wrote the Stanford code, and Stanford president Donald Kennedy, who first opposed and then embraced the code. We have a new ecumenicism of those who would control speech for the greater good. It is hardly a new idea, but the mix of advocates is rather new.

39   But there are other voices. In the national board debate at the ACLU on college speech codes, the first speaker—and I think she had a lot to do with mak-

ing the final vote against codes unanimous—was Gwen Thomas. A black community college administrator from Colorado, she is a fiercely persistent exposer of racial discrimination.

She started by saying, "I have always felt as a minority person that we have 40 to protect the rights of all because if we infringe on the rights of any persons, we'll be next.

"As for providing a nonintimidating educational environment, our young 41 people have to learn to grow up on college campuses. We have to teach them how to deal with adversarial situations. They have to learn how to survive offensive speech they find wounding and hurtful."

Gwen Thomas is an educator—an endangered species in higher education. 42

QUESTIONS

1. Identify the passages in which Hentoff uses arguments from precept, effect, and similarity.
2. Examine the issue of "fighting words." Considering the genesis of that term, do you feel that this definition applies to the First Amendment issue at hand? Why or why not?
3. What kind of language would you find offensive? Why is it offensive? Do you think racist/sexist/homophobic language actively harms anyone?
4. What kind of future does Hentoff fear if speech codes continue to be enacted in American universities? What aspects of our society would be affected? How would they be affected?
5. The speech codes that Hentoff speaks of are primarily in large, prestigious universities. Do you think the issue pertains to other academic institutions? Posit a cause-and-effect argument concerning speech codes in primary school, high school, or vocational college.
6. Does Hentoff address the concerns that Lawrence voiced in his essay? Compare their versions of cause and effect. What are their similarities? What are their differences? Which do you feel is more compelling?

Is a Hero Really Nothing but a Sandwich?
Ted Tollefson

Ted Tollefson is a Unitarian Universalist minister and is co-founder of the Mythos Institute in Minneapolis. This article is from the *Utne Reader* (May/June 1993).

1   For several years a picture of Warren Spahn of the Milwaukee Braves hung on my closet door, one leg poised in mid-air before he delivered a smoking fastball. Time passed and Spahn's picture gave way to others: Elvis, John F. Kennedy, Carl Jung, Joseph Campbell, Ben Hogan. These heroic images have reflected back to me what I hoped to become: a man with good moves, a sex symbol, an electrifying orator, a plumber of depths, a teller of tales, a graceful golfer. Like serpents, we keep shedding the skins of our heroes as we move toward new phases in our lives.

2   Like many of my generation, I have a weakness for hero worship. At some point, however, we all begin to question our heroes and our need for them. This leads us to ask: What is a hero?

3   Despite immense differences in cultures, heroes around the world generally share a number of traits that instruct and inspire people.

4   *A hero does something worth talking about.* A hero has a story of adventure to tell and a community who will listen. But a hero goes beyond mere fame or celebrity.

5   *Heroes serve powers or principles larger than themselves.* Like high-voltage transformers, heroes take the energy of higher powers and step it down so that it can be used by ordinary mortals.

6   *The hero lives a life worthy of imitation.* Those who imitate a genuine hero experience life with new depth, zest, and meaning. A sure test for would-be heroes is what or whom do they serve? What are they willing to live and die for? If the answer or evidence suggests they serve only their own fame, they may be celebrities but not heroes. Madonna and Michael Jackson are famous, but who would claim that their adoring fans find life more abundant?

7   *Heroes are catalysts for change.* They have a vision from the mountaintop. They have the skill and the charm to move the masses. They create new possibilities. Without Gandhi, India might still be part of the British Empire. Without Rosa Parks and Martin Luther King Jr., we might still have segregated buses, restaurants, and parks. It may be possible for large-scale change to occur without charismatic leaders, but the pace of change would be glacial, the vision uncertain, and the committee meetings endless.

8   Though heroes aspire to universal values, most are bound to the culture from which they came. The heroes of the Homeric Greeks wept loudly for their lost comrades and exhibited their grief publicly. A later generation of Greeks under the tutelage of Plato disdained this display of grief as "unmanly."

Though the heroic tradition of white Americans is barely 300 years old, it 9
already shows some unique and unnerving features. While most traditional
heroes leave home, have an adventure, and return home to tell the story, American heroes are often homeless. They come out of nowhere, right what is
wrong, and then disappear into the wilderness. Throughout most of the world,
it is acknowledged that heroes need a community as much as a community
needs them.

And most Americans seem to prefer their heroes flawless, innocent, forever 10
wearing a white hat or airbrushed features. Character flaws—unbridled lust,
political incorrectness—are held as proof that our heroes aren't really heroes.
Several heroes on my own list have provided easy targets for the purveyors of
heroic perfectionism.

The ancient Greeks and Hebrews were wiser on this count. They chose for 11
their heroes men and women with visible, tragic flaws. Oedipus' fierce curiosity raised him to be king but also lured him to his mother's bed. King David's
unbounded passion made him dance naked before the Ark *and* led him to
betray Uriah so he could take Bathsheba for his wife.

American heroes lack a sense of home that might limit and ground their 12
grandiose ambitions. American heroes avoid acknowledging their own vices,
which makes them more likely to look for somebody else to blame when things
go wrong. Our national heroes seem to be stuck somewhere between Billy
Budd and the Lone Ranger: pious, armed cowboys who are full of energy,
hope, and dangerous naïveté.

Here are some exercises to give you insights into your own ideas about heroes 13
and villains:

1. Draw a time line with markings every five years in your life. For each
   era, name an important hero (male or female). Identify three core qualities each stands for. Look at the overall list for recurring qualities. Who
   or what do your heroes serve?
2. Make a list of enemies, the people who really push your buttons. For
   each specify three qualities that make your blood boil. Now look for
   recurring qualities. What emerges is your "shadow," parts of yourself
   that you fear, loathe, and therefore loan to others. What does your
   shadow know that you don't?
3. Make a collage of your heroes, leaving room for their tragic flaws and
   holy vices. Hang it opposite a large mirror.

QUESTIONS

1. Tollefson provides four qualities he feels define a hero. Do they describe
   someone you especially admire? Are there any other qualities you would
   want to add?
2. Are there any heroic qualities that you feel reflect the society we live in
   today (as opposed to earlier societies or other contemporary cultures)?

3. Do you feel that the American image of the hero as a flawless individual is a positive thing or a negative thing? Why?

4. Look into the personal history of someone you admire. Are there aspects to this person's life that you don't care for? Does knowledge of these aspects affect how you feel about this person?

5. What would an untraditional hero be? (Be creative.)

6. Is it important for people to have heroes? What would Tollefson say? What would your hero say?

Where Have You Gone, Joe DiMaggio?
Matthew Goodman

Matthew Goodman writes about sports for several magazines, including the *Village Voice, Z Magazine,* and the *Guardian.* This essay is
from the *Utne Reader* (May/June 1993).

These days, it seems, the sports pages have come to resemble a police blotter. 1
The fan seeking box scores and game recaps must first wade through news stories about drug abuse among athletes, arrests for drunk driving, betting and
recruiting scandals, and, most disturbingly, reports of rape and other sex-
related crimes. What's going on here? American sports fans ask over their morning toast and coffee. *What's happening to our heroes?*

It's not difficult to understand our desire for athletes to be heroes. On the 2
surface, at least, athletes display many of the classical heroic attributes. They
possess a vital and indomitable spirit; they are gloriously alive inside their bodies. And sports does allow us to witness acts that can legitimately be described
as courageous, thrilling, beautiful, even noble. In an increasingly complicated
and disorderly world, sports is still an arena in which we can regularly witness
a certain kind of greatness.

Yet there's something of a paradox here, for the very qualities a society 3
tends to seek in its heroes—selflessness, social consciousness, and the like—
are precisely the *opposite* of those needed to transform a talented but otherwise unremarkable neighborhood kid into a Michael Jordan or a Joe Montana.
Becoming a star athlete requires a profound and long-term kind of self-absorption,
a single-minded attention to the development of a few rather odd physical
skills, and an overarching competitive outlook. These qualities may well make a
great athlete, but they don't necessarily make a great person. On top of this, our
society reinforces these traits by the system it has created to produce athletes—
a system characterized by limited responsibility and enormous privilege.

The athletes themselves suffer the costs of this system. Trained to measure 4
themselves perpetually against the achievements of those around them, many
young athletes develop a sense of what sociologist Walter Schafer has termed
"conditional self-worth": They learn very quickly that they will be accepted by
the important figures in their lives—parents, coaches, peers—to the extent
they are perceived as "winners." Their egos come to rest, all too precariously,
upon the narrow plank of athletic success.

Young athletes learn that success, rather than hard and honest play, is what 5
brings rewards. And for those successful enough to rise to the level of big-time
college sports, the "reward" is often an artificially controlled social environment,
one that shields them from many of the responsibilities other students face.
Coaches—whose own jobs, of course, depend on maintaining winning programs—hover over their athletes to ensure that nothing threatens their eligibility

to compete. If an athlete gets into trouble with the law, for instance, a coach will very likely intervene—hiring an attorney, perhaps even managing to have the case quietly dismissed. In some schools, athletes don't even choose their own classes or buy their own books; the athletic department does all this for them. It's not unheard of for athletic department staff to wake up athletes in the morning and to take them to class.

6   Given this situation, it's not too surprising that many young American athletes seem to have been left with a stunted ethical sense. Professor Sharon Stoll of the University of Idaho has tested more than 10,000 student athletes from all over the country, ranging from junior high to college age; she reports that in the area of moral reasoning, athletes invariably score lower than non-athletes—and that they grow worse the longer they participate in athletics.

7   Coddled by universities, lionized by local communities, accorded star status by the public, endowed with six- and seven-figure salaries, successful athletes inevitably develop a sense of themselves as privileged beings—as indeed they are. The danger arises when the realistic (and thus probably healthy) understanding of personal privilege mutates into a sense of personal entitlement.

8   Mike Tyson, of course, is the most blatant example of this phenomenon. Having been taught as a young man that he was special—his mentor, Cus D'Amato, reportedly had one set of rules for Tyson and another, more stringent, set for all his other boxing protégés—and having lived his entire adult life surrounded by a cortege of fawning attendants, Tyson eventually came to believe, like a medieval king, that all he saw rightfully belonged to him. Blessed with money and fame enough to last a lifetime, he spent his time outside the ring acquiring and discarding the objects of his desire: houses, automobiles, jewelry, clothes, and women. In the wake of the publicity surrounding his rape trial, countless women have come forward to relate stories of Tyson propositioning them and then, upon being rebuffed, exclaiming in what was apparently genuine surprise, "Don't you know who I am? *I'm the heavyweight champion of the world.*" Needless to say, not all athletes are Mike Tyson; there are plenty of athletes who recognize that they have been granted some extraordinary gifts in this life and want to give something back to the community.

9   Some remarkable individuals will always rise above the deforming athletic system we've created. After retiring from football, defensive tackle Alan Page of the Minnesota Vikings became a successful lawyer and established the Page Education Foundation, which helps minority and disadvantaged kids around the country pay for college. Frustrated by the old-boy network by which Minnesota judges had traditionally been appointed, Page challenged the system in court and finally won election to the state Supreme Court, becoming the first black ever elected to statewide office in Minnesota. Tennis star Martina Navratilova recently joined six other lesbians and gay men as a plaintiff in a lawsuit filed by the cities of Denver, Boulder, and Aspen challenging Colorado's recent anti-gay law as unconstitutional. Thankfully, there will always be some legitimate heroes (or, to use the more contemporary term, role models) to be found among professional athletes.

Still, it's probably misguided for society to look to athletes for its heroes— 10 any more than we look among the ranks of, say, actors or lawyers or pipefitters. The social role played by athletes is indeed important (imagine a society without sports; I wouldn't want to live in it), but it's fundamentally different from that of heroes.

Thanks to the years of hard and uncompromising work that athletes have 11 invested in themselves, sports is often able to provide us a glimpse of that "supreme beauty" that Bertrand Russell wrote of as characteristic of mathematics: "sublimely pure, and capable of a stern perfection such as only the greatest art can show."

Can't we just leave it at that?   12

Questions

1. Based on Goodman's description of the modern athlete, what are the characteristics of the hero?
2. Do these athletes suffer from the tragic flaw that Tollefson describes, or are their problems unrelated to their status as stars? Should their problems influence how we perceive them?
3. Is it important for a fan to understand what the hero's life is really like? Why or why not?
4. Goodman is speaking about athletes, but would the things he says about the successful athlete's frame of mind apply equally to other celebrities? Think about musicians, artists, writers, or actors.
5. What does Goodman mean when he cites Bertrand Russell? What exactly does he feel we should admire about athletic heroes, or any other kind of hero, for that matter?

Have We Outgrown the Age of Heroes?
Walter Truett Anderson

Walter Truett Anderson (b. 1933) is the author of *Evolution Isn't What It Used to Be: The Augmented Animal and the Whole Wired World* (1996) and *Reality Isn't What It Used to Be* (1990). This article appeared in the *Utne Reader* (May/June 1993).

1   It must be very hard for Americans in the 1990s—especially younger Americans—to imagine how it could be possible that, throughout the 12 years Franklin D. Roosevelt occupied the White House, most people didn't know their president was disabled.

2   The history of that elaborate national scam was told a few years ago in a book admiringly entitled *FDR's Splendid Deception.* It's fascinating to read about how it was done, how the photographers and reporters who spent time with FDR (even those from the opposition newspapers who hated him) conspired to avoid publishing any image of the president in a wheelchair. Even more fascinating is *why* it was done—the unquestioned consensus that the public should be shielded from the truth.

3   Times have changed, and are changing. Now, in the era of let-it-all-hang-out-before-somebody-else-hangs-it-out-for-you, we have grown accustomed to such information. We know that President Roosevelt was not a man on a white horse, but a man in a wheelchair. We know, if we care to, about Eleanor Roosevelt's ambiguous sexual orientation. We also know all about John F. Kennedy—his crooked father, his crooked election, the serious case of Addison's disease that was concealed from the public, his ambitious (and apparently near-successful) crusade to become the first president to screw every woman in the United States.

4   We know, and on the whole we don't seem to be too upset about it. Slowly, haltingly, in the messy way such things always happen, we are moving away from the old idea of leadership. Leadership now seems to have less to do with heroism—at least with heroism as we have known it. It is tempting to read the recent death of Superman, that comic-book colossus, as a pop-culture symbol of this transition. If the man of steel is mortal, how can we go on?—unless, of course, we didn't really need immortal men of steel to begin with. Unless we are moving toward a different idea of leaders, beginning to see them as much more complex, vulnerable, dependent, and changeable.

5   I would not exactly call Bill Clinton the perfect embodiment of the new leadership, but certain aspects of his style are instructive. Note, for example, his tendency to base his power on relationships rather than to tower over everybody around him. He chose a vice president who is a peer and an equal—a striking difference from the Batman-and-Robin motif of the previous administration. He lets the world see his wife as a smart, competent woman setting her

own agendas, a marked contrast to the public spectacle of Nancy Reagan gazing in rapt, passive admiration at her man and then playing palace politics in secret.

This shift is not happening only in politics. If you take a look at what is going on these days in such fields as psychology and management theory, you can hardly avoid noticing that a profound shift in social values is under way. New, revolutionary ideas about the human personality are emerging, and so are revolutionary ideas about the dynamics of large organizations. Both of these have something to say about leadership, and about leaders.   6

Various schools of "postmodern" psychology see the individual as more changeable than stable, more multiple than singular. Kenneth Gergen, a psychiatrist at Swarthmore College, believes that in a rapidly changing, culturally pluralistic society the traditional mental-health ideal of firm and fixed identity has become "limiting and in many ways incapacitating." He says that people who demonstrate "elasticity" are healthier and more fulfilled. Other psychologists, therapists, and cognitive scientists are talking about subpersonalities and pluralistic concepts of identity, and widely quoting Walt Whitman's famous line: "I am large; I contain multitudes."   7

This way of thinking about the human personality is politically important in a couple of different ways. First, it enables us to avoid getting too hung up on a one-dimensional image of any leader. We can accept a disabled-but-vigorous Roosevelt, a tainted-but-idealistic Kennedy, an anti-Vietnam War Bill Clinton who is also quite capable of serving as commander in chief in the 1990s. Second, it gives us a different idea of our own internal authority structures. We can, perhaps, begin to be a little less intimidated by a dominant self-image that functions as a sort of psychic dictator telling the rest of our inner voices to shut up.   8

Gergen believes that there is a clear connection between cultural pluralism and the inner psychological pluralism that he and other psychologists have identified. For most of us, there just isn't a single social reality out there that is going to justify an unmovable personal identity.   9

This growing pluralism also offers a clue about where to look for heroes— simple, old-fashioned heroes. We have become too culturally fragmented to unite in admiration of any national hero. Name me one and I'll name you people who hate him or her. But you can find plenty of subnational heroes, demigods and goddesses of this or that subculture. In the absence of national heroes we now have a pantheon of second-string superpeople who are revered by the members of racial, religious, cultural, and ideological groups and more or less ignored by everybody else: Madonna, Jackie Chan, Ice-T, Rush Limbaugh, Shirley MacLaine, Richard Petty, Bill Gates, Wendell Berry, Kim Gordon, Thich Nhat Hahn, Norman Schwarzkopf, Camille Paglia, Billy Graham, Noam Chomsky, Jesse Jackson, David Duke, Adrienne Rich, James Hillman.   10

While the social scientists study the changing shape of culture and personality, the management experts are studying the changing shape of organizations. An amazing transformation has been sweeping over business in recent years. Corporations all over the country are "downsizing," "flattening," moving toward structures based more on flexible networks and teams than on rigid top-   11 down hierarchies. This has been partly forced on them—by economic hard times, by the pressure of foreign competition—but it also reflects a deep, and probably irreversible, change in thinking about what makes a company effective. Some people call it the "organizational revolution."

12   As organizations change, so, of course, do the people in them. Management researchers and theorists are now discovering—and trying to describe—a new type of businessperson. Historically, two character types have prevailed in the business world. One was the rugged individualist, the "self-made man"—Henry Ford, Andrew Carnegie—of the early industrial era. In the post-World War II years, the dominant type appeared to be the other-directed, security-seeking conformist described by William H. Whyte Jr. in his 1956 study, *The Organization Man.* We had not only organization-man business executives but also organization-man presidents—Eisenhower was the classic example—and organization-man heroes: the astronauts, whose "right stuff" was a capacity to function smoothly in huge, technologically complex systems.

13   But the great corporate machines of past decades—General Motors and IBM, say—are not running at all smoothly these days. They have been falling behind their competitors, and so has the organizational philosophy that built them. New models of corporate excellence—such as the "learning organization" proclaimed by Peter Senge in his recent book *The Fifth Discipline*—are coming to the fore. The management gurus are talking about different kinds of employees, "knowledge workers," who cannot be handled according to the old bureaucratic rules. They are also talking about a different kind of executive, the "learning leader" who comes to work prepared to make mistakes and to change course when necessary. Such leaders are valuable because of their capacity to seek out and understand new information. They are not expected to be flawless or to know everything.

14   This is a massive, awkward, complex shift of American values and beliefs, and many things play a part in it. The role of the mass media in shaping public perceptions of leaders can't be underestimated. It was media self-censorship that hid from us the truth about previous leaders; it was manipulation of the media that enabled shrewd operators to rig images of Ronald Reagan, the public-hero model at its most vapid and cynical. Media gabbiness now makes it harder and harder for people to spend much time in public life without having their quirks and their dark sides exposed. This is a rough way for a democracy to grow up, but it's better than continuing to follow an endless sequence of heroes on horseback, would-be supermen with secrets.

15   It would be easy to misunderstand the new image of leadership and heroism, to assume that it dispenses with older values such as vision, strength of character, energy, moral purpose. I don't think it does. As we become more willing to struggle publicly with the vast complexity of human character and to develop a new sense of how organizations run, we are more—rather than less—likely to find leaders with some of those admirable characteristics. We are also likely to send forth a useful message to the many countries that are now beginning to experiment with mass democracy.

QUESTIONS

1. Has our attitude toward heroes changed as a result of changes in our society? Have these changes made the qualities that Tollefson presented outdated? Why or why not?

2. If you accept Anderson's version of the function of heroes in modern American society, how, then, do you perceive the athlete heroes whom Goodman describes?

3. Do you feel that the "pantheon of heroes" that Anderson describes is a better approach to the issue of hero identity, or is it a step in the wrong direction? Why?

4. The heroes of yesterday were part of another culture that didn't seem to be as comfortable with discrepancies of character. Is our attitude today more reasonable?

5. Do you have a "pantheon of heroes"? Who are they? What do you admire in them? What do you dislike?

Chapter 10

REVISING AN ARGUMENTATIVE ESSAY

Good writing is *revised* writing, whether you are writing for academic or professional purposes. Some writers revise as they write, reconceptualizing and editing while they complete a first draft. Others finish a draft, put it aside for awhile, and then revise it. Many do both, revising and editing a first draft, then engaging in additional revisions afterward. Whatever strategy you prefer (waiting until 10 minutes before class to correct a few spelling mistakes does *not* count as a revision strategy), it is important to understand that true revision, as opposed to surface "editing," involves rethinking and sometimes altering the thesis, structure, and support. A common misconception is that revising a paper means simply correcting the punctuation and spelling—that is, cleaning up the surface. Of course, essays written in the genre of argument should ultimately be error free, stylistically effective, and, if possible, eloquent and graceful. But before you concern yourself with error correction and style, you should focus on conceptual and structural issues. This chapter discusses several approaches to revising an argumentative essay.

SUGGESTIONS FOR REVISION

The following suggestions are aimed at helping you revise an essay written for a college class, but many of them pertain to other genres of writing as well, such as a business report or a letter of application—anything you have written that is aimed at having an impact on an audience:

Leave Sufficient Time to Revise

Even if you revise as you compose, it is a good idea to allow at least some time between completing a draft and revising it. If you begin to revise your essay immediately, right after you have completed a first draft, you will probably not be able to view your work objectively and will consequently miss many areas that need improvement. This is the disadvantage of "last-minute jobs"—they don't enable a writer to acquire sufficient distance from the text. However, if you let the essay alone for awhile (even an hour is better than nothing), you will return to it with fresh eyes, viewing it almost as if you were the audience, rather than the writer, and you will be in a better position to notice where revision is needed. To begin the revision process, print a copy of your paper (if you are using a computer) and then leave it for a little while before beginning your revision.

Examine the Thesis by Reading Introductory Paragraphs Aloud

A first draft frequently has thesis problems. It may contain a lot of information discussing the topic but lack a main point; sometimes a thesis in a first draft is too broad to be addressed adequately. To begin revising a first draft, read your first few paragraphs aloud, paying particular attention to your thesis. Then see if you can answer the following questions:

QUESTIONS FOR REVISING YOUR THESIS

Where is your thesis statement?
Does your thesis address a controversy?
Would someone disagree with the position you have taken? In what way?
Does your thesis statement contain the word *because?*
Is the word *because* necessary for this particular thesis?
Have you qualified your position sufficiently?

A useful way to look at your thesis is to consider the impact you wish to have on your audience. Here are some points to consider related to audience:

REVISING YOUR THESIS BY THINKING ABOUT YOUR AUDIENCE

1. What does your audience already know or believe about the topic?
2. Is the aim of your essay to change your audience's thinking or to enlighten your audience in some way?
3. Which aspect of your thesis is your audience least likely to agree with?

To examine your essay in terms of audience, write your thesis statement on a separate piece of paper. Then see if you can answer the following questions:

Before **my audience reads my essay, what beliefs or attitudes toward this topic is it likely to have?**

After **my audience reads my essay, how do I wish its beliefs or attitudes to change or at least be reconsidered?**

What would someone say who disagrees with my essay?

Clarifying the Thesis: An Example of Revision

In his composition class, Paul wrote an essay in response to the following question:

Is there a need for a men's movement?

Here is a first draft of Paul's first two paragraphs. Read these paragraphs aloud, paying particular attention to Paul's thesis:

The Men's Movement

Since the formation of the women's movement, a great many changes have been demanded of men; among other things, they have been asked to be more sensitive to women's needs and more understanding and supportive of women. As a result, a variety of men's movements have developed, designed either to help men change or to defend the often-criticized male. One such movement, of which Robert Bly is considered the leader, supports many of these changes but argues that modern man is not happy and must undergo greater transformations.

In 1990, Robert Bly wrote a book titled <u>Iron John</u>, which has become known as the manifesto of the men's movement that he leads (Bly 307). The story of Iron John involves a boy and his golden ball. While the boy is joyfully playing with the ball, he accidentally allows it to roll into the cage of Iron John, "a large man covered with hair from head to foot" who was found at the bottom of a pond. Throughout his life, the boy makes several attempts to get the ball back but is told by Iron John that he can have it only if he releases Iron John from his cage. In order to set Iron John free, the boy has to steal the key to the cage from underneath his mother's pillow. The scenario of the boy and this bright, beautiful ball represents the youthful innocence, inner harmony, and happiness that Bly believes all men lose early in life. <u>Iron John</u> is symbolic of the "Wild Man" that must be released for us to get back our "golden ball."

Reading Paul's first two paragraphs aloud will enable you to notice the absence of an explicit thesis statement. Because Paul has become so involved with retelling the story of *Iron John,* he has lost track of the purpose of his essay—to answer the question "Is there a need for a men's movement?" This is a problem that occurs frequently in first drafts. Note that Paul's first draft does not refer to the essay question at all, does not indicate that a controversy over this matter exists, and is not presented as an argument.

In his second draft, however, Paul added a thesis statement and refocused his material about *Iron John* so that its relevance to the controversy was more apparent to the reader:

The Men's Movement

Since the formation of the women's movement, a great many changes have been demanded of men; among other things, they have been asked to be more sensitive to women's needs and more understanding and supportive of women. As a result, a variety of men's movements have developed, designed either to help men change or to enable men to reassert their rights. One such movement, of which Robert Bly is considered the leader, argues that because of the women's movement, which has had an emasculating effect on men, modern men are not happy and must seek to reestablish their lost masculinity. However, although Bly is raising points worth considering, a men's movement such as he defines in Iron John cannot be considered necessary in American culture because men still hold a great deal of power. Moreover, a movement such as that advocated by Bly would adversely affect men's attitudes toward women, leading to increased hostility between the sexes.

The "manifesto" of Bly's concept of a men's movement appears in Bly's book, Iron John, published in 1990. The story involves a boy who accidentally allows his favorite plaything, a golden ball, to roll into the cage of Iron John, "a large man covered with hair from head to foot" living at the bottom of a pond. As Bly recounts the story, the boy makes several attempts throughout his life to get the ball back but is told by Iron John that he can reclaim the ball only by releasing Iron John from his cage. Moreover, in order to do so, the boy must steal the key to the cage, which is hidden underneath his mother's pillow. According to Bly, the scenario of the boy and this bright, beautiful ball may be considered a metaphor for the condition of modern man, the golden ball representing the youthful innocence, inner harmony, and happiness that Bly believes all men lose early in life and that, he feels, can be reclaimed only by a men's movement. Iron John is symbolic of the "Wild Man" that must be released for us to get back our "golden ball."

In this second draft, Paul has included a clear thesis statement and placed greater emphasis on establishing the context for his ideas. When he refers to the story of *Iron John,* he does not simply narrate the events, but rather links them to the controversy he is addressing.

Examine Your Essay for Credibility (Appeals to Ethos)

In revising your essay, the following questions will help you assess how credibly you have presented yourself in your essay:

REVISING FOR CREDIBILITY (ETHOS)

1. What sort of impression of yourself are you giving in this essay? Do you present yourself as a thoughtful, believable, and sympathetic person?
2. Have you included sufficient information to suggest that you have "done your homework"?
3. Is this a topic in which personal experience is likely to be relevant? If so, have you included a personal example?
4. Have you included pertinent statements from authorities? Do they strengthen your position, or have you simply quoted from outside material to fill in space?

Examine Your Essay for Appeals to Your Reader (Pathos)

In revising your essay, the following questions will help you assess whether you have adequately appealed to your reader:

REVISING FOR APPEALS TO READERS

1. Have you cited examples that readers are likely to find moving?
2. Have you anticipated objections that readers are likely to have?
3. Are there instances in the essay in which you might directly appeal to your readers' concerns?

Examine Your Essay for Adequate Support (Logos)

In revising your essay, the following questions will help you assess the effectiveness of your support:

REVISING FOR SUPPORT

1. Can you cite at least two reasons or supporting points for the thesis?
2. Are these reasons based on sound assumptions?
3. Have you supported your main points with compelling evidence?
4. Do you need additional evidence or examples?
5. Are statistics relevant to this topic? If so, have you spent sufficient time analyzing them?

Examine Your Essay for Development

In writing a first or even a second draft, writers often leave out important information or give certain points only cursory attention, which means that the essay may require additional explanations, details, or examples. Actually, in revising your paper, you should **expect** that you will need to do at least some additional writing because in a first draft, it is likely that you will have left out at least something. Also, remember that details are what make your writing interesting, so in checking for adequate details, note whether you have included any that evoke sensory images—pictures, sounds, or feelings. Look also for any representative anecdotes that can help your reader understand your ideas and hold your reader's attention as well.

Check Each Paragraph for Function and Connection to the Thesis

As you reread your essay, note the main point of each paragraph in the margin. Then see if you can find words or sentences within that paragraph that refer directly to the thesis. Often an essay will contain a number of good examples, but their relationship to the thesis is not well established. In Paul's essay about the men's movement, for example, Paul discussed Robert Bly's book, *Iron John,* but he did not link that discussion to his main argument. Go through your essay paragraph by paragraph, adding linking words or transitional sentences as needed.

Note Arrangement and Structure

Examine the order of your paragraphs and consider the following questions:

Does each paragraph lead naturally into another?

Have you addressed the opposing viewpoint?

Does the conclusion wrap things up adequately?

Would another arrangement be more effective?

Read Your Essay Aloud, Paragraph by Paragraph, Checking for Sentence-Level Coherence, Fluency, and Correctness

Reading aloud is a useful strategy for all aspects of revision, but it is especially useful for detecting sentence-level problems and areas where the text does not read smoothly. In reading for coherence, fluency, and correctness, think about the following questions:

REVISING FOR COHERENCE, FLUENCY, AND CORRECTNESS

1. Does each sentence lead naturally into another?
2. Are your sentences too short? Can these sentences be combined?
3. Is there a need for additional details?
4. Are your sentences too long? Can these be divided?
5. Have you checked for common mechanical errors such as subject-verb disagreement, faulty pronoun reference, and missing or extraneous commas?
6. Have you used your spell checker?

As you plan your revision, note the changes you would like to make. When I revise, I like to scribble all over my first drafts, jotting down as many thoughts as possible before I lose them. Don't be afraid to write directly on your essay—remember that you can always print another copy. Finally, in thinking about revision, you should leave enough time to utilize whatever human resources you have available to you. If there is a writing lab or center at your school, ask a tutor to give you some feedback on your essay. Or let a friend read it, indicating areas that may not be clear. You don't always have to act on the recommendations of a tutor or a friend, but sometimes that person might notice something that you might have overlooked.

SENTENCE-LEVEL REVISION ILLUSTRATED IN TWO DRAFTS OF AN ESSAY

The following essay was written in response to the following writing assignment:

Topic: heroes in modern society

Using the culture with which you are most familiar, choose a contemporary figure that might be considered heroic. Write an argumentative essay of five to six pages discussing how and why this person ought to be considered a hero. Be sure to formulate a clear definition on which to base your argument.

Read the first draft, noting where you would recommend surface-level revision. Then, in small groups, read the second draft, noting the text in brackets that indicates that a revision was done and explaining why you feel that this section was revised.

FIRST DRAFT

<u>Professor Punk</u>

by David Cota

In our day and age, most heroes are identified as those who seem to stick out in society. Whether it be through extreme wealth, eccentricity, or just straight-out controversy, heroes are those people who can use the media to draw attention to themselves. It seems that the key to being remembered in our fast paced consumer society is just to use the media as a form of attaining notoriety. Basically anyone can be a hero. It's just a matter of marketing yourself so as to gain the interest of the masses. In this society there really aren't very many heroes who actually deserve such a title. In fact, most public figures (even though they may be worshipped by the masses) are not heroes. They are just very business smart media whores who know how to market themselves to make a buck. Most of these people do very little to actually benefit society and make a difference in the world. These people are basically put on a pedestal where they do little more than just look pretty for people to idolize them. Indeed these people are not heroes at all.

So who are the real heroes in our society? I feel that a real hero must make a difference in society and serve some kind of purpose besides just self gain. When I think of this there are several people that come to mind, but one clearly comes out above all the rest. This person is Mr. Greg Graffin, singer and songwriter for the L.A. punk band Bad Religion. Even though most people don't know who Greg Graffin is or just what his band stands for, those of us who do know have been affected by his message of freedom and hope that things can actually be changed for the better. Even though in the past there have been many like him, there is one thing that Greg Graffin has been able to do that other punks have not been able to accomplish. What makes Greg Graffin a hero is that he has been able to bring the world of punk rock and the academic world of scholarship together. With this he has proven that the essence of punk rock is not just mindless teenage rebellion, that one can be educated and still be free from the expected ideas of behavior set out by society (in other words be a punk) and that being educated on a higher level is not selling out to the system, but is actually beneficial in furthering the causes that punk rock promotes and believes in. By no means is this an easy task, yet he has been able to do it without becoming a media whore.

First and foremost, Greg Graffin has dispelled the myth that punk rock is the embodiment of senseless violence or teenage angst. Before he came onto the scene in the 1980s, most punk rockers were seen as misfits that didn't have the means, let alone the intellect, to be taken seriously. Punk was looked at as a phase that some teenagers went through as part of growing up and dealing with the strains of being an adolescent. At this point, punk didn't have a serious role model or leader to give it the credibility that it needed to be respected, not only as an art form, but as a means of communicating valid and interesting points that may otherwise never be voiced by the main stream. When Bad Religion did do their first album, it was basically like all the other punk rock music of the time. Then the band broke up because Greg moved away to go to college to get the knowledge and understanding that would make his band one of the best as far as lyrics when he resurrected it in 1987.

When he did come back, he came back as a grown and well-educated man with a Ph.D. in paleontology and the title of professor Graffin under his belt. No longer could critics of punk rock say that it was just noise of the ravings of disgruntled kids. Greg Graffin became a pioneer of this new kind of punk that was just as strong willed and pungent as its predecessors, but was also so well thought out that it had to be taken seriously. With this, Graffin took up issues like violence, the loss of individuality in our society, and the influence of the mainstream media on our society. He touched on issues that mainstream performers wouldn't touch and that only someone of his intellect could handle. With lyrics like "I ain't no blind supporter/I am a conscious citizen/ and I know we're living too far out of bounds," he spoke out and let the world know that he was informed and that he wasn't scared to take a stand and defend his beliefs. This phenomenon of Bad Religion spread out and soon other bands like it came out and punk was no longer a medium for the frustrated, but was a viable means of conveying ideas about important societal issues.

With this new type of punk that he created, Greg Graffin not only faced the scorn of those who didn't approve of his music but of those who were part of the scene, who saw him as a "sell-out" for having obtained an education. They argued that he had bowed down to the system by becoming a college boy and securing a living, in case his music didn't pan out. To these people he simply responded by telling them straight out that he didn't care what they thought of him because he was himself and was making music on his own terms with his own ideas. Since this is the essence of "punk," it really silenced those critics who didn't like his attitude. As far as the issue of money was concerned, he cited the fact that Bad Religion's music was self-produced and that there was no huge corporation behind them. In fact, he and his bandmates even went through the trouble of starting their own record label (at considerable expense I might add) to insure complete autonomy from any other forces that could possibly affect the artistic integrity of the music or compromise the message of the lyrics. He was no sell-out at all: he had complete control of all the music and all the content of his songs. He was as "punk" as any other punk band member because he not only preached the idea of punk values such as independence from corporations but he also lived them as an example.

Graffin further emphasized that his education had been instrumental in giving him his writing style and the basic knowledge he needed in order to make Bad Religion the powerful and innovative force that it was. He straight out believed that if he had been unable to go to college, Bad Religion may have never existed or may not have had the impact that it did have. He stated in several low key interviews that being a professor allowed him to make these problems known to his listeners and to give them insight that they may not have been exposed to before. He said, "to change things, one must first understand what needs to be changed. This is where awareness and education are involved."

Indeed, Greg Graffin broke all the rules when he became the first professor to front a punk act. He redefined the concept of punk, making it more intellectual, and dismissing those ridiculous ideas that it was just an expression of adolescent anger. He also proved that higher education was not only useful, but instrumental in the process of trying to make things better, whether it be a social issue or just improving as a band. For these reasons, I believe that Greg Graffin deserves to be called a hero.

REVISED DRAFT

(Replaced or deleted words are in brackets. Changed or added words are underlined.)

Professor Punk

by David Cota

In this age of tabloid television [In our day and age], heroes often are identified as those people who are notable in some way. [most heroes are identified as those who seem to stick out in society]. Whether it be their extreme wealth, their eccentricity, or just their involvement in some controversial activity [Whether it be through extreme wealth, eccentricity, or just straight out controversy], heroes are those people who can use the media to draw attention to themselves. It seems that the key to being recognized [remembered] in our fast-paced consumer society is just to use the media as a way to attain notoriety. Basically anyone can be this sort of hero. It's just a matter of marketing yourself in order to gain the interest of the greatest number of people [the masses]. Most public figures (even though they may be worshipped by the masses) do not deserve to be called heroes [In this society there really aren't very many heroes who actually deserve such a title. In fact, most public figures (even though they may be worshipped by the masses) are not heroes.]. They are just business smart and know how to publicize their own peculiarities [They are just very business smart media whores who know how to market themselves to make a buck.]. Most of these people do little or nothing to benefit society or to make a difference in the world. These people are basically put on a pedestal, where they do little more than just look pretty for others to idolize them. Indeed, these people are not heroes at all.

So who are the real heroes in our society? Although some maintain that heroes must be famous, [I feel that] a real hero must make a difference in society and serve some kind of purpose besides just self-gain. One person who clearly demonstrates heroic virtue is Greg Graffin, singer and songwriter for the L.A. punk band Bad Religion [When I think of this there are several people that come to mind, but one clearly comes out above all the rest. This person is Mr. Greg Graffin]. Even though most people don't know who Greg Graffin is or just what his band stands for, those of us who do know have been affected by his message of freedom and of hope that things can actually be changed for the better. Many singers have had similar messages, but Graffin's accomplishment has been to deliver the punk rock message with intelligence [Even though in the past there have been many like him, there is one thing that Greg Graffin has been able to do that other punks have not been able to accomplish. What makes Greg Graffin a hero is that he has been able to bring the world of punk rock and the academic world of scholarship together.]. [With this] He has proven that the essence of punk rock need not be [is not] just mindless teenage rebellion. He has shown that one can be educated and still not conform to [be free from] the standards [the expected ideas] of behavior set out by society (in other words, be a punk). Graffin has demonstrated that being educated [on a higher level] is not selling out to the system, but instead is actually beneficial in furthering the causes that punk rock stands for. Changing the image of punk rock is by no means an easy task, yet Graffin has been able to do it, not by promoting himself, but by promoting ideas [By no means is this an easy task, yet he has been able to do it without becoming a media whore.].

First and foremost, Greg Graffin has dispelled the myth that punk rock is the embodiment of senseless violence or teenage angst. Before he came onto the scene in the 1980s, most punk rockers were seen as misfits who didn't have the means, let alone the intellect, to be taken seriously. Punk was looked at as a phase that some teenagers went through as part of growing up and dealing with the trials of being an adolescent. The music gave voice to a generation that felt oppressed by the idea of a hopeless future. But in its early stages [At this point], punk didn't have a serious role model or leader to give it the credibility that it needed for its ideas to be respected as serious challenges to mainstream culture [not only as an art form, but as a means of communicating valid and interesting points that may otherwise never be voiced by the main stream]. Punk's reaction to powerlessness had been to lash out against the conventional, and the typical punk was a model of self-destruction. When

Bad Religion recorded [did do] their first album, the music was basically like all the other punk rock music of the time—kids screaming angry lyrics to dissonant melodies—and it was reasonably successful. The band broke up because Graffin moved away to go to college, where he got the knowledge and understanding to write some of the best lyrics in the genre when he resurrected the band in 1987 [After the band broke up because Greg moved away to go to college to get the knowledge and understanding that would make his band one of the best as far as lyrics when he resurrected it in 1987.].

When he returned, Graffin had a Ph.D. in paleontology and the title "professor" under his belt [When he did come back, he came back as a grown and well-educated man with a Ph.D. in paleontology and the title of professor Graffin under his belt.]. Instead of abandoning the ideals he had had when he was younger, Graffin made himself a role model for punks and a leader in the movement. [No longer could] Critics of punk rock could no longer say that the music was just the noisy ravings of dis-gruntled kids. Now one of the most prominent punks was a respected scholar whose reputation gave intellectual weight to the ideas in the music. Greg Graffin became a pioneer of a new kind of punk that was just as strong willed and pungent as its predecessors, but that was also so carefully thought out that those outside the movement could take it seriously. Graffin took up issues like violence, the loss of individuality in our society, and the undue influence of the media. He explored questions that mainstream performers wouldn't touch and that only someone of his intellect could handle. With lyrics like "I ain't no blind supporter/I am a conscious citizen/ and I know we're living too far out of bounds," he spoke out and let the world know that he was informed, that he wasn't scared to take a stand, and that he had the intellectual ability to defend his beliefs. The phenomenon of Bad Religion spread. Soon other bands like it emerged, and punk was no longer just a medium for the frustrated and powerless. Graffin had demonstrated that self-destruction is not the only end of the movement, and he helped punk become a viable means of conveying the concerns of a group that feels alienated from society [ideas about important societal issues].

Graffin is heroic because he has remained devoted to the ideals of punk rock, giving a powerful voice to the movement without glorifying himself. Graffin may not be well known outside of punk, but his relative obscurity has contributed to his ability to advance the movement. Punks are punks because they do not have respect for the conventional. In Graffin they have a role model who remains an iconoclast but has done more than simply self-destruct. Many who were part of the scene see him as a "sell-out" for having obtained an education. [With this new type of punk that he created, Greg Graffin not only faced the scorn of those who didn't approve of his music but of those who were part of the scene, who saw him as a "sell-out" for having obtained an education.] They argue that he bowed down to the system by becoming a college boy and securing a conventional living, in case his music didn't pan out. He responds simply by telling them that he doesn't care what they think of him because he is making music on his own terms with his own ideas [To these people he simply responded by telling them straight out that he didn't care what they thought of him because he was himself and was making music on his own terms with his own ideas.]. Because independence and nonconformity are [this is] the essence of "punk," critics within the movement have little more they can say without undermining their own ideals [it really silenced those critics who didn't like his attitude]. [As far as the issue of money was concerned, he cited the fact that Bad Religion's music was self-produced and that there was no huge corporation behind them. In fact,] Graffin and his bandmates even went to the trouble of starting their own record label [(at considerable expense I might add)] to ensure complete autonomy from any other forces that might affect the artistic integrity of the music or compromise the message of the lyrics. Graffin is no sell-out at all: He has complete control of all the music and all the content of his songs. He is as "punk" as any other punk musician on the scene not only because he preaches the idea of punk values such as independence from corporations, but also because he has used his hard-won autonomy to help all of punk live up to the ideals that it espouses [he also lived them as an example].

Graffin [further] emphasizes that his education has been instrumental in giving him his writing style and the basic knowledge he needed in order to make Bad Religion the powerful and innovative force that it <u>has become</u> [that it was]. He [straight out believed] believes that if he had been unable to go to college, Bad Religion may [have never existed or may] not have had the impact that it has had. In several low-key interviews, he has stated that being a professor has <u>given him a broader perspective than he had as just a punk rocker and that this insight has helped him to explore the social questions that are at the heart of punk. His academic training has helped him to articulate these questions in his music and to give his listeners insights that they may not have been exposed to before</u> [that being a professor allowed him to make these problems known to his listeners and to give them insight that they may not have been exposed to before]. He said, "To change things, one must first understand what needs to be changed. This is where awareness and education are involved."

Indeed, Greg Graffin broke all the rules when he became the first professor to front a punk act. He redefined the concept of punk, making it more intellectual and dismissing those ridiculous ideas that it is just an expression of adolescent anger. He also proved that higher education is not only useful, but also instrumental in the process of trying to make things better. <u>Graffin used his education not only to improve his own band, but also to made punk a better force for confronting social problems</u> [whether it be a social issue or just improving as a band]. <u>He could have abandoned his ideals and devoted himself to the world of academics or to the lure of musical stardom, but Graffin remained in the punk scene and has remained loyal to punk ideals. He is a model of a punk who has made good and who has used his own advantage to the advantage of the music.</u> For <u>this selfless dedication to his art</u> [For these reasons], Greg Graffin deserves to be called a hero.

EXERCISE

1. Examine the two drafts of "Professor Punk." What differences can you note between the first draft and the second?

2. Examine the first two paragraphs and the conclusion of both the first and second drafts of "Professor Punk." Make a list of all the differences you can find between the two drafts as they are manifested in the first two paragraphs and the conclusion. How do these changes influence the rest of the essay?

Appendix

Tips for Using the Library Systems of Documentation

Essays written in the genre of argument usually include information obtained from published works, a requirement that makes it important for you to learn to use the library and to cite sources appropriately. The material in this section discusses some tips for using the library and two systems of documentation.

Tips for Using the Library

You may find your first trip to the university library an intimidating experience. There seems to be so much information available, both from books and from electronic sources, that you may not know where to begin to search. Some of my students have told me that when they first go to the library, they spend the first hour just wandering around feeling completely overwhelmed, and sometimes they don't seem to be able to find anything useful. To help you learn to use the library effectively, I would like to pass along a few suggestions that I have found useful in my own research and teaching:

Tip 1: When in Doubt, Ask the Librarian

If you enter a library and have no idea where to begin your search, I suggest that you ask a librarian for help. Do not be afraid that you will ask a foolish question. Librarians have heard all sorts of questions and are very happy to assist you in any way they can. After a librarian understands the nature of your research task, he or she will be able to save you a lot of time by directing you to appropriate materials. There are a number of places you can begin your search: on-line catalogues, periodical databases, dictionaries, encyclopedias, even microfilm. At first, all of these resources will seem confusing to you, but if you ask a librarian, you will soon feel a lot more comfortable. Do not abandon your efforts too soon in frustration. Be persistent and enlist help.

Tip 2: Be Resourceful in Your Search

Most colleges today have computerized their catalogues, which enable students to search for books in a number of ways—by title, author, and subject. If you know the title or author of a particular book, you will be able to find its call number easily through the computerized catalogue. However, if you look under the category of "subject," you will have to use "descriptors" or search terms. Selecting just the right terms may take a bit of work, but once again, the librarian can be of assistance. So if you look for books under a particular subject term and find nothing, do not leave the library, saying that "there was nothing on my topic." Chances are that if you search under another term, you will have more success.

When you conduct a search in an on-line catalogue or database, it is also important to realize that different search words will yield different resource possibilities, even if their definitions are almost identical. Tanya, for example, entered the search term "multiculturalism" and found that this term occurred in 985 records, far too many to browse. She then entered the term "multicultural education" and found that these terms occurred in 461 records—a smaller number, but still far too many to browse. She then entered the terms "multicultural education advantages" and found that there were no records fitting these terms. Finally she entered the terms "multicultural education colleges" and found that these terms occurred in 26 records, a much more manageable number to search.

Another important strategy to use in finding the right descriptors is to pick one source and look at the descriptors that are already listed. Tanya, for example, chose one source from her list:

Author: Bensimon, Estela M.;Tierney, William G.

Title: Shaping the multicultural college campus

Source: *Education Digest,* v59, n3 (November 1993): p67(5)

She then noted the following descriptors:

Multiculturalism—Analysis

Universities and colleges—Social aspects

College students—Race relations

She then could use these descriptors either to narrow or to widen her search.

If you find that your search is yielding too many or too few resources and you can't figure out which descriptors to use, I suggest, once again, that you ask the librarian. He or she may be able to provide search terms that will produce more satisfactory results.

Tip 3: Browse

The research process can lead to a number of unforeseen discoveries, so when you are searching for a particular resource, do not ignore other possibilities.

While you are looking for a particular book on a shelf, glance through some of the other books that are there as well. You may discover a great deal of useful material in a book that you found by accident. The same is true of articles in magazines and journals. After you find an article that you were searching for, browse through some of the other articles in that edition. You may be pleasantly surprised at how much information you find through browsing.

Tip 4: Be Aware of Your Library's Resources

In addition to on-line catalogues, most universities provide students with access to a variety of magazine, journal, and newspaper indexes. At the University of Southern California, for example, the university provides access to periodical and newspaper databases, including full text for *The Chronicle of Higher Education* and other journals, plus access to several news services that provide current information.

For older material, you might wish to consult paper versions of magazine and newspaper indexes. For magazine articles, you might try *The Reader's Guide to Periodical Literature,* which lists articles published in over 100 of the most widely known magazines in the country. The volumes are arranged by year. There are also newspaper indexes for the *New York Times,* the *Wall Street Journal,* and the *Christian Science Monitor.* The *National Newspaper Index* includes indexes for the *Chicago Tribune,* the *Los Angeles Times,* and the *Washington Post.*

To gain an overview of a topic, you might begin with an encyclopedia, such as *Encyclopedia Britannica* or *Encyclopedia Americana.* Other encyclopedias you should be aware of are *Encyclopedia of Education, International Encyclopedia of the Social Sciences, McGraw Hill Encyclopedia of Science and Technology,* and *New Illustrated Encyclopedia of World History.* Other resources you might find useful are collections of abstracts, which can help you understand what an article or book is about before you read it. Some abstract collections you might find useful are the following:

Book Review Digest

Congressional Abstracts

Historical Abstracts

Psychological Abstracts

Sociological Abstracts

Women's Studies Abstracts

Keep these tips in mind whenever you use the library. Above all, don't be intimidated or overwhelmed by the tremendous amount of information available to you. With proper search strategies, you will be able to narrow your search to a manageable number of sources. And remember that the more you use the library and the more willing you are to request assistance from a librarian, the more proficient you will become.

TWO SYSTEMS OF DOCUMENTATION: MLA AND APA

The two types of documentation style that are most commonly used in the genre of argument are the MLA (Modern Language Association) and the APA (American Psychological Association). If you are taking a composition course that is based in an English department, your instructor will probably prefer that you use the MLA. However, it is a good idea to check with your instructor about which system you should use.

Some useful manuals that can be found in your library include:

- *MLA Handbook for Writers of Research Papers.* 4th ed. (New York: MLA, 1995).

  This explains the MLA system, which is preferred in most disciplines in the humanities, including philosophy, religion, and history.

- *Publication Manual of the American Psychological Association.* 4th ed. (Washington, D.C.: APA, 1994).

  This outlines the APA system, which is preferred in most disciplines in the social sciences, including sociology, political science, and economics.

- *The Chicago Manual of Style.* 14th ed. (Chicago: University of Chicago Press, 1993).

  This method uses a system of footnotes inserted into the text. It is often required for research papers in history and for some humanities publications.

THE MLA SYSTEM

Parenthetical Reference and a "Works Cited" Page

When you write a researched essay in the genre of argument, you must include information from secondary sources either in the form of direct quotes, summary, or paraphrase. According to the MLA system, that information must be acknowledged by **parenthetical reference** within the body of your paper and by a "**Works Cited**" page at the end. The parenthetical reference is meant to provide enough information that your reader can locate the full reference in the "Works Cited" page.

A parenthetical reference consists of the author's name (or an abbreviated title if the author's name is missing) and a page number. Here is an example:

Rosenberg says that television "warps our sense of reality because it perpetuates racial stereotypes" (46).

Note that because Rosenberg's name appears in the sentence it does not need to be repeated in the parentheses with the page number. Your readers have enough information here to locate Rosenberg in the "Works Cited" section if they desire to peruse Rosenberg's article themselves. Note also the placement of the quotation marks, the parentheses, and the period. The period goes at the very end, after the parentheses, not inside the quote (this is a common mistake). Follow these conventions correctly or else it will annoy and confuse your reader.

If you do not include the name of your source in the course of your sentence, then it is necessary to include the name and page number in the parentheses:

Many people are not aware that television "warps our sense of reality because it perpetuates racial stereotypes" (Rosenberg 46).

Note that there is no comma between the name of the author and the page number.

Sometimes you may have two sources by the same author. In this case, in order to allow your reader to locate the source within the "Works Cited" section you would have to include the title of the work along with the author's name in the parentheses. For example:

Many people are not aware that television "warps our sense of reality because it perpetuates racial stereotypes" (Rosenberg, "Medium's Influence" 46).

If the work you are referring to is a book, then the title is underlined. If it is an essay or an article, the title is put in quotation marks.

Long Quotations

For quotations that are more than four typed lines (not in the source but in your paper), writers use "block quotations," in which the quotation is indented 10 lines and double spaced. The parenthetical reference occurs one space after the punctuation at the end of the block. Notice also that quotation marks are omitted. Here is an example:

In "Fenimore Cooper's Literary Offenses" Mark Twain criticizes Cooper for his lack of realism:

> Another stage property he pulled out of his box pretty frequently was his broken twig. He prized his broken twig above all the rest of his effects, and worked it the hardest. It is a restful chapter in any book of his when somebody doesn't step on a dry twig and alarm all the reds and whites for two hundred yards around. Every time a Cooper person is in peril, and absolute silence is worth four dollars a minute, he is sure to step on a dry twig. There may be a hundred handier things to step on, but Cooper requires him to turn out and find a dry twig; and if he can't do it, go and borrow one. (Twain 524)

The "Works Cited" Page

References on the "Works Cited" page consist of the author, title, and the publication information (city, publisher, and publication date). The items are arranged in alphabetical order by the last name of the author. If no author is listed, use the first significant word of the title. Each citation begins at the left margin, and additional lines in each citation should be indented one-half inch, or five spaces. Double space between each line and between each citation. The title "Works Cited" should be placed one inch down from the top of the page. Then double space between the title and the first citation.

Here are some examples you can use as models:

A Book with One Author

Rose, Kathleen. <u>Socialization and the Inner City</u>. Los Angeles: Embassy Press, 1991.

Two or More Books by the Same Author

Rose, Kathleen. <u>Socialization and the Inner City</u>. Los Angeles: Embassy Press, 1991.
———.<u>Dropping Out: Alternatives to Academic Careers</u>. New York: Leisure Press, 1992.

A Book by Two Authors

Johnson, William, and Marilyn Reid. <u>Emancipating Your Children</u>. Berkeley: Dome Press, 1987.

A Book with Three Authors

Agassi, Arnold, Jerome Connors, and Malcolm McEnroe. <u>Tennis Etiquette</u>. London: Hillman, 1989.

A Book with Four or More Authors

Dessing, Harmond et al. <u>The Fear of Intimacy</u>. Los Angeles: Coward Press, 1987.

A Book with a Translator or Editor

Ulysses, Stephen. <u>The Agony of the Artist</u>. Trans. Buck Mulligan. Dublin: Whiner Press, 1985.

A Chapter That Is Part of an Anthology or Collection

Stearns, Eliot. "Can Notes Elucidate Meaning?" <u>Understanding Poetry</u>, Ed. Edward Pound, 3rd. ed. London: Cryptic Books, 1982. 3-27.

An Introduction, Preface, Foreword, or Afterword

Simpson, Bart. Introduction. <u>Life is Unfair</u>. By Homer Simpson. Los Angeles: Larson Books, 1991. i-ix.

The "Works Cited" Page: Periodicals

Use the following sequence for listing references to periodicals on the "Works Cited" page.

1. author 2. title of the article 3. name of periodical 4. volume, issue, and page number

Enter the **author's last name at the margin,** followed by a comma, then the author's first name, followed by a period. The **title of the article** should be enclosed in quotation marks, followed by a period placed inside the closing quotation marks. The **name of the periodical** is then underlined with no following punctuation. References to volume, date, issue, and page number depend on the type of periodical you are citing.

Magazines and Journals

In general, magazines begin with page 1 in each issue, whereas journals tend to have continuous pagination for an entire year, and this distinction between separate and continuous pagination determines the sort of information you should include. A volume number, year, and page numbers are sufficient for journal entries because they are paginated continuously. However, for magazines, omit the volume number and provide a month or even a specific day, in the case of weekly publications. Here are some examples:

Magazine (Monthly)

Hoss, Dirk. "How Old Is Too Young?" Maturity May 1990: 21-23.

Magazine (Weekly)

Joseph, James. "Hands-On Experience." Volunteer 6 Sept. 1982: 19-23.

There is no mark of punctuation between the name of the magazine and the date. Also note that if the magazine does not indicate the name of the author, begin with the title of the article, as shown here:

"Economy in Chaos." Time 11 Mar. 1991: 60-61.

Note also that arabic, not roman, numerals are used.

Journal

For journal entries, you should include the volume number, the year within parentheses, followed by a colon and inclusive page numbers. Here is an example:

Tripper, John W. "Dogs that Chew Too Much." The Canine Courier 20 (1989): 262-269.

If the journal begins each issue with number 1, add an issue number following the volume number. Separate the volume number from the issue number with a period. Here is an example:

Phorney, Bill. "Extracting Canine Incisors: Pros and Cons." Journal of American Dentistry 9.6 (1988): 9-12.

Newspaper

For newspaper entries, provide the author's name, the title of the article, the name of the newspaper as it appears on the front page (*New York Times,* not *The New York Times*), and the complete date (day, month, year). Page numbers are listed according to how they actually appear on the page. If the article does not continue on the next page, that is, if it is not printed consecutively, write only the first page number and add a + sign. Thus, if the article begins on page 4 and continues on page 2, you should write 4+.

Here is an example of a newspaper citation:

Reid, Anne. "Dining Out Will Save Your Marriage." San Francisco Chronicle 22 Jan. 1989: 23+.

Other Types of Sources

Some sources are neither books nor periodicals. Here are some other possibilities:

An Interview

If the interview is published, treat it as a work in a collection:

Bly, Robert. Interview. Interviews with Robert Bly. By John Schaffer. Chicago: Westwood Press, 1988. 72-86.

If you are citing a personal interview, identify it by date:

Burton, Theresa. Personal interview. 6 Nov. 1989.

A Broadcast Interview

Clinton, Hillary. Interview. Morning Edition. National Public Radio. KCRW, Los Angeles. 7 Jan. 1993.

Material from a Computer Service

Citations for materials obtained from a computer service are similar to periodical citations. They should also include the publication medium (database or software company), number of pages (or "n. pag." if not paginated), name of the computer network, and date of access.

Link, Flash. "Oh, What a Tangled Web We Weave." Web Weekly 1.1 (1995): 10pp. On-line. Internet. 28 Feb. 1995.

THE APA SYSTEM

Parenthetical Citation

In the APA system, you should refer to outside sources within the body of your text and include enough information that the reader will be able to locate the source in the "**References**" page at the end of your paper. In the APA system the year of publication is included in parentheses immediately after mention of the author's name. If you do not mention the author by name in the sentence in which you are referring to his or her work, then you should include the author's name (or a short title, if the author's name is missing) and the year of publication, separated by a comma enclosed in parentheses at the end of the sentence. If you quote from your source, you must also add the page number in your parentheses, with "p." preceding the page number. For example:

Harding (1993) insists that "proposed budget cuts in our universities threaten the quality of undergraduate education" (p. 6).

As in the MLA system, in the APA system you do not need to include Harding's name in the parentheses because it already appears in the text. Thus, the reader is already aware of the author's name and would be able to find the rest of the information about the source in the "References" section. Note also the placement of the quotation marks, the parentheses, and the period.

In the following example Harding's name is not mentioned in the course of the sentence. Therefore, it is necessary to include her name as well as the page number within the parentheses:

Administrators overlook the fact that "proposed budget cuts in our universities threaten the quality of undergraduate education" (Harding, 1993, p. 6).

A Work with Two or More Authors

If a work has two authors, refer to both within the text. For example:

In a recent study of single mothers (Kelly & Rose, 1991), it was discovered that . . .

  or

Kelly and Rose (1991) discovered that . . .

Note that the "&" sign is used only in parentheses.

If a work has several authors (fewer than six) they should be mentioned in the first reference:

Kelly, Rose, Mangan, Burgess, and Dyer (1991) argue that . . .

However, in subsequent references, you can use "et al." ("and the rest"):

Kelly et al. (1991) argue that . . .

The "References" Page

Similar to the "Works Cited" page in the MLA system, there are also three main components in the APA "References" page—the author, title, and publication information (city, publisher, and publication date). Again, the sources are arranged in alphabetical order by the last name of the author. If no author is listed, use the first significant word of the title. Each citation begins at the left margin, and additional lines in each citation are indented three spaces. Double space between each line, and double space between each citation. Two spaces follow a period, one space follows a comma, semicolon, or colon. The title "References" is placed one and one-half inches down from the top of the page. Double space between the title and the first citation.

Here are some of the major ways in which APA style differs from MLA style:

1. Initials, instead of full first names, are used for authors.
2. Titles of books and articles do not use capital letters, except for the first word.
3. Titles of articles do not use quotation marks.
4. There is a greater emphasis on the year of publication.

Here are some examples you can use as models:

A Book with One Author

Rose, K. (1991). <u>Socialization and the inner city</u>. Los Angeles: Embassy Press.

Notice that the author's first name is indicated by an initial and that only the first word of the title is capitalized.

Two or More Books by the Same Author

Rose, K. (1991). <u>Socialization and the inner city</u>. Los Angeles: Embassy Press.
Rose, K. (1992). <u>Dropping out: Alternative to academic careers</u>. New York: Leisure Press.

Notice that two or more books by the same author are listed in chronological order.

A Book with Two Authors

Reverse all authors' names and separate them with commas. Use an ampersand (&) before the last author.

Johnson, W., & Reid, M. (1987). <u>Emancipating your children</u>. Berkeley: Dome Press.

A Book with a Translator or Editor

Ulysses, S. (1985). <u>The agony of the artist</u>. (Buck Mulligan, Trans.) Dublin: Whiner Press.

A Chapter That Is Part of an Anthology or Collection

Stearns, E. (1982). Can notes elucidate meaning? In Edward Pound (Ed.) <u>Understanding Poetry</u> (pp. 56-71). London: Cryptic Books.

Periodicals

Article in a Journal with Continuous Pagination

Hoss, D. (1990). How old is too young? <u>Maturity, 12</u>, 21-23.

The number following the title of the journal is the volume number. Notice that it is underlined. Also note that commas separate the journal title, volume number, and page numbers.

Article in a Journal Paginated Separately in Each Issue

Joseph, J. (1982). Hands-on experience. <u>Volunteer 6</u> (12), 19-23.

In the preceding case you follow the volume number "6" with the issue number "(12)," which is placed in parentheses.

If the journal does not indicate the name of the author, begin with the title of the article as shown here:

Economy in chaos. (1991, Mar. 11). <u>Time</u>, pp. 60-61.

General Interest Magazines

General interest magazines, which are usually published either monthly or weekly, often cite the date of publication rather than the volume number. For example:

Tripper, J. (1989, April). Dogs that chew too much. <u>The Canine Courier</u>, pp. 262-269.

Newspapers

If you are citing a newspaper article, provide the author's name, the title of the article, the name of the newspaper as it appears on the front page (*San Francisco Chronicle,* not *The San Francisco Chronicle*), and the complete date (day, month, year). Page numbers are listed according to how they actually appear on the page. For example:

Reid, A. (1989, Jan. 22). Dining out will save your marriage. <u>San Francisco Chronicle</u>, p. 23.

Other Types of Sources

Interviews

In the APA system, personal interviews are not included in the reference list but are cited in the body of the paper. Here is an example of how to incorporate a personal interview into your text:

John Gaunt (personal communication, June 21, 1990) indicated that . . .

Published interviews are cited as works in a book or periodical:

Keidis, A. (1987, July). Censorship in the nineties. (Interview). Rolling Stone, pp. 4-7.

Material from a Computer Service

Civil Disobedience. (1988). Grolier's Online Encyclopedia. New York, New York.

If the preceding examples do not provide enough information, consult a style manual. Finally, it is important to remember the following:

1. The genre of argument requires you to acknowledge *all* secondary source material. Do not risk plagiarizing either deliberately or inadvertently.
2. Ask your instructor which style of documentation to use or look at journals in your discipline to see which style is preferred.
3. Do not *guess* the correct form when documenting sources—keep a set of citation conventions handy. Make sure that spacing and punctuation are accurate. Documentation is detailed and can be time consuming. So leave plenty of time to do it correctly.

RESEARCH ON THE WORLD WIDE WEB

(This section was written by Kris Deffenbacher and Mike Reynolds and Jill Nichols at the University of Southern California.)

Introduction

You have probably heard quite a bit about the pleasures and/or the dangers of new computer technology. The positive view of cyberspace, the virtual world of computer links and information, pictures "surfers" cruising around some kind of "highway" that leads them to all sorts of information about a given subject. For example, you might begin using the Web in order to work on a paper arguing about pornography and censorship. Your first stop is the *New York Times* on-line, where a recent article sets the scene; it "links" you to an ACLU "page" on current "web" debates or to a watchdog group's collection of anti-obscenity writings, maybe even to the Bill of Rights on-line, where you can read over the First Amendment and related documents yourself.

But there are also negative views of the Web. You may feel that too much information can be overwhelming. You may be concerned that the Web could be too high-tech to figure out or that the sources on the Web are not reliable—or else that it could provide dangerous information (pornography, for example) to anybody who knows how to find it, without reasonable safeguards.

The following section presents a brief overview of the Internet and the Web and suggests possibilities for further research. This basic introduction to the information superhighway will help get you on-line, provides a starter kit that defines what all this technology is, and illustrates how easy Web research can be. However, although we will accentuate the positive, we also hope to avoid the overly sunny view of endless, simplistic surfing. Web research is a strong supplement and complement to other types of critical analysis, but using a computer will not magically provide answers for you. Surfing and cyberspace require a specific set of skills and critical tools, like any genre or medium of communication. So we will also introduce some of the questions that you, as a Web researcher, can begin to ask as you seek out and find computer resources for your arguments.

The Internet

The term *Internet* was originally used to describe any network that connected two or more computer networks to each other (*inter* = "between," *net* = "networks"). In theory, any network of networks fits the definition (for example, if the five computers in your office are connected to a network of computers at the University of Southern California, that is an internet).

However, when people talk about "the Internet" they are referring to the connection of computer networks across the globe. *The* Internet, or 'Net, has become so large because of a particularly adaptable kind of software (a designed program put into or "on" a computer) that tells computers how to communicate with each other. This software, called TCP/IP, allows any kind of computer to "talk" to any other kind.

The World Wide Web

The World Wide Web is a recent addition to the Internet, and the relationship between the two can be confusing. The Web has been described as being a subset of the Internet, as being a superstructure that sits above the Internet, and as an entirely distinct phenomenon. It would be most accurate, however, to look at the Web as an extension of the Internet—a different way to handle and present the information that "exists" between the networks of computers. For example, information was previously confined pretty much to text; with the Web there are graphics, photos, video, and sound. In short, the *World Wide*

Web is a term that identifies the way computers maintain and view documents using multiple media on the Internet.

The expanded media capabilities have made the Web a really interesting place to do research. In addition, graphically, it is easier for people and organizations to provide and access on-line materials. Consequently, an immense number of schools and colleges, as well as many think tanks, most governmental agencies, and many well-known magazines and journals, have made their print resources available in electronic form—and you should take advantage of this. Although the Web cannot replace library research just yet, it can certainly supplement traditional research, and it offers the advantage of speed and accessibility. You can move from university to university with the click of your mouse, and you can save important articles or quotes directly onto a disk or a hard drive (this is called "downloading"). With the Web there is no need to lug around books, stand in line for the copier, or mark important paragraphs with Post-it notes.

How to Get on the World Wide Web

This section is for beginners—so if you're all hooked up, skip to the next section.

Do you belong to a network already? The first step to getting on-line entails getting specific hardware and software. However, you may already be "in" a network; for example, if you use a computer in an office or in a college computer laboratory, you may already have the proper materials. Many schools offer their students free accounts, or at least free access through the public labs, so check with your school first before worrying about "your" hardware and software.

Hardware: If you plan to get on the 'Net from a personal computer, you need to know a little bit about your hardware (the material parts of your computer)—is it wired and designed to allow 'Net and Web use? Some older computers have too little memory to function well on-line; others may work well with text (more 'Net-based functions) but be unable to handle the high-speed and high-quantity information of many websites. Do you have a modem or phone-line connection? Some computers have built-in modems; others require the purchase of separate modems. Check on this information in your user's manual or call the dealer or manufacturer.

Software: You can get on-line by using TCP/IP software in your computer. This software connects you to the network that will provide full 'Net and Web access. As mentioned, many schools give students free accounts and all the software necessary. Check with them first.

If your school doesn't offer this option, you can always get an account with a local or national provider. Generally you can get all the access you need for under $20 a month. Just look in the Yellow Pages for the names of local Internet access providers. And for information about national providers, just head to your local bookstore and pick up any magazine or book about the 'Net. Most of these list the major companies and/or provide sign-up information and software.

After you are on-line, the 'Net can usually be read through your provider's own software—you won't *need* to find or buy any additional material. For example, your school may use UNIX, which would allow you full textual use of the 'Net—E-mail, bulletin boards, and so forth. However, there are certain types of software that increase your ability to really make use of the Web as a multimedia source. Specifically, you probably want to use a **Web browser.** These browsers create a window in which Web "pages" or files appear, letting you see text and pictures and sounds; formats and possibilities depend on your choice of browser and the readily available plug-ins that improve or expand functions. There are a number of browsers (and plug-ins) available—most of them for free—and you will most likely be provided with one by the school or company that gives you access. If for any reason you are not provided with this software, you can usually download it (get the software onto your computer straight from the Web). The most popular browser currently in use is *Netscape,* and you can find it at this Web address: http://www.netscape.com/.

Using the World Wide Web

After you have access to the Internet and to a browser, you are ready to explore the Web. Enter in the spirit of adventure—all documents are linked to others in a "web" of information that can provide for a far more exciting (though at times more frustrating) reading experience than the more linear one to which we have grown accustomed. When you explore the Web you are entering an ongoing conversation that is always under construction and constantly shifting. For these reasons, it is important that you give yourself some time to become familiar with the Web before you do actual research. Although the Web is fairly user-friendly, you cannot sit down the night before a paper is due and expect to find everything you need. The following steps will help you learn to do research on the Web.

1. *Learn how to navigate.* The different files, or "pages," as they are called, on the Web are connected via hyperlinks. Hyperlinks are words or graphics that, when selected, "jump" you to a new Web page. Although the idea of hypertext is not new (Hypercard and many computer help systems employ it), the hyperlinks that you find on the Web are particularly exciting because they can connect you to any file anywhere on the Internet. A hyperlink on a World Wide Web page can take you to a file that is stored on a computer in Sweden or in Egypt. And it can take you to any type of file; a hyperlink can reference sound files, video clips, graphics, text, and software files. The hyperlinks system is one of the reasons that the Web is such a good research tool: People who design web pages can (and often do) link material from around the world that is available on a single subject.

   At any rate, you should spend some time learning how to identify hyperlinks. (Hyperlinks are usually highlighted or outlined in bright colors, but not always. The safest way to identify a hyperlink is by watching your cursor; it will turn from an arrow to a hand when it passes over a hyperlink.) You should also take some time to become familiar with your browsing software. Most browsers allow you to "bookmark" important Web pages and to move forward and backward among the Web pages you have visited in a session. Familiarity with these functions will save you a lot of time and effort.

2. *Learn how to do research on the Web.* In general, there are three ways that people research topics on the Web. One way is simply to follow links and see where they take you. A lot of information can be found this way, but you don't always know what you are going to find. A second, and less random, way of browsing the Web is to work from lists of sources that other people have compiled. These links are usually listed by category, such as "movies," "Irish culture," or "on-line censorship." A good list should serve only as a base for your search; do not limit yourself to the links that someone else has found useful. Most of these lists are not comprehensive—meaning that they will not link you to all 2,000 Web pages that mention movies. However, there are several Web "libraries" or "catalogues" that are fairly comprehensive, and these can be great starting points when doing research. The less-complete lists are interesting in their own way, though, because they often link to more-eclectic or personal pages than do the large virtual libraries and catalogues. Of all available research tools, a "search engine" such as *Yahoo* or *Lycos* provides the most direct method of finding information about specific topics. A search engine will ask you for key words or phrases and then "search" the Web for documents that include those key words.

3. *Learn to "read" file addresses.* Each Web file has its own unique address, and these addresses can tell you a lot about the file, and thus about the document's value as a source. For example, suppose you are looking for information about the White House, and you find two possible links. One is http://www.whitehouse.gov/, and the other is http://www.earthlink.net/free/billybob_jones/mystuff/politics/whitehouse/. Now the first address is likely to actually belong to the White House and/or president of the United States. We know this by noting the domain name and the location of the subject information. First, the name that comes after the "www" part of the address is a domain name. And all domain names are unique (meaning there can be only one "whitehouse.gov" anywhere in the world). An organization's domain name generally reflects its main purpose. Thus, http://www.ibm.com/ is the website for the IBM computer company, and http://www.airspacemag.earthlink.net/ is the address of the website for *Air and Space Magazine.* The location of the subject information also provides information about the value of a source. The second address we listed is more likely to contain personal thoughts or representations about the White House because of the location of the "whitehouse" refer-

ence in the address. In http://www.earthlink.net/free/billybob_jones/ mystuff/politics/whitehouse/, the word "whitehouse" is a couple of directories below "billybob_jones," and "billybob_jones" is listed under a "free" directory at "earthlink.net." What this address suggests is that Billy Bob has a directory (probably a free one) at a company called Earthlink. And Billy Bob has set up a directory of information he is interested in ("my stuff"), one category of which is "politics." Depending on what kind of information you are looking for, both of these addresses might represent good sources. But the point is that you can often tell what kind of information you are going to find on a Web page just by looking at the address. And the ability to evaluate a source in advance can be an important time-saver when doing on-line research.

Other Suggestions

If you find that you need help using the Web or related software, look for on-line guides. Although most of us are used to turning to books and pamphlets for help, the best guides to the Web are on-line. If you get stuck, use a search engine to search for information about the subject with which you are having trouble. The Web is full of FAQs (frequently asked questions) on all kinds of subjects. And if you really prefer your help to be on paper, just use the "print" command. Anything you see on the Web can be printed out easily.

The MLA handbook, like numerous other writing resources, is now on-line. It will show you how to document on-line sources. Our personal suggestion in terms of documentation is that you save a copy of every document from which you quote. Although many documents stay on-line for years, some are taken down within weeks. If you want proof of your source you may have to provide it yourself.

Genre-Based Analysis on the Web

What kind of an animal is a Web page? How can you figure out the reliability and category of sources on the Web, with their multiple media and the blurring of personal and public presentation? We've presented some basic steps toward evaluation, especially focusing on one singular difference between the Web and other sources: the Web's lack of linearity. Reading the Web doesn't have to follow a linear path from page 1 to page 100; links and the other differences of Web sources explicitly develop "sideways" and "recursive" directions in our critical analyses. Like the writing process, Web research can be circular, self-reflexive, and (rats!) frustrating in ways that seem more obvious than our critical tactics for "normal" print-based reading.

One reason might be a blurring of genres on the Web—not just between media, but between the "types" of arguments one can find. Government sources can be equal parts description, policy, and advertising; "personal" pages are presented publicly, often using "public" and reputable links or sources. This blurring seems disorganized to many analysts; for them, the Web is a source too unreliable to be used academically. To test out some of the genres or rules of discourse on and off the Web, try the following.

ASSIGNMENT: MEDIA/GENRE COMPARISON

Background: This assignment requires you to think about the differences between information obtained through print and information available on-line—newspaper articles and on-line news sources. For example, letters to the editor in your local newspaper may occasionally be heated, but they usually exhibit some degree of decorum. Even the most angry writer will present an explanation of the issue and what she or he is responding to; there are some conventions of writerly behavior followed—or else the letter won't be published. But on the Web's bulletin boards, that decorum is not always observed. Some newsgroups do moderate discussion—if you checked out their FAQ (frequently asked questions about the newsgroup), you'd discover their official rules for interaction. Many such moderated groups officially bar rule-breakers from engaging in the arguments. Other newsgroups, however, are free-for-alls—people "flame" each other (send heated and often abusive replies); argument is much looser, and the rules are harder to figure out, or even completely absent.

Questions

1. What specific rules of argument shape letters to the editor or posts on a use net bulletin board?
2. How do arguments differ when presented on a personal Web page and on the official home page for a politician or government office?
3. Using a specific pair of arguments *on the same topic* but in two different presentations (either Web versus other medium, or two different types of Web presentation), answer the following:

■ What are the rules of discourse for each presentation, and how did you determine those rules?
■ Compare and contrast the rules of discourse. Which is more effective—and in what situations is it more effective? What makes an argument effective? Could the less-effective presentation work better in certain contexts?
■ How do the media (print, graphics) of presentation affect your evaluation of the argument?
■ Analyze the genre of argument being addressed. How does the specific medium of presentation change the genre of the argument, if at all? (For example, what types of evidence become more possible as "citations" on a Web page than in an academic journal? Or on a television show?)

However one defines or evaluates its genres, the Web's ever-changing, hard-to-pin-down shape calls attention to how we create and construct rules of discourse. In part, the Web's lack of concrete form makes it always a work-in-progress, and because of that shifting it becomes a valuable resource for examining how arguments are being shaped and molded to fit certain rules (or not to fit those rules, as is often the case on the Web). One point to remember, though, is that the Web is very, very new. Part of the anxiety about its "lack of form" is due to its relative youth as a medium; rules for understanding the genre of Web discourse might someday develop more clearly and more permanently.

Censorship Assignment on the Web

Overview

One of the most hotly contested debates about the web involves attempts to better and more rigidly define proper rules of behavior on the web. As Peter H. Lewis has written in "No More 'Anything Goes': Cyberspace Gets Censors,"

> Freedom of expression has always been the rule in the fast-growing web of public and private computer networks known as cyberspace. But even as thousand of Americans each week join the several million who use computer networks to share ideas and "chat" with others, the companies that control the networks and sometimes individual users are beginning to play the role as censor.

Readings

Using your Web browser, find the following readings:

Introduction: from "No More 'Anything Goes': Cyberspace Gets Censors," by Peter H. Lewis http://www-scf.usc.edu/~deffenba/lewis.html

Pro-censorship: from "Keep Internet Safe for Families," by Senator J. James Exon http://www-scf.usc.edu/~deffenba/exon.html

Anti-censorship: from "Beware of Chilling Freedom of Expression," by James Herrington http://www-scf.usc.edu/~deffenba/herrington.html

In addition, you must find at least three additional useful sources on the Internet and draw on them in your essay. You will be required to write and present an evaluation of one of these sites. (You can draw from library sources as well, but these must be in addition to the minimum of three Internet sources.) Begin your search by typing keywords into a search engine or with one of the sources linked below. Use this list only as a starting point—surfing around connected sites will help you get a much better feel for this issue than just following someone else's path.

Internet Resources on Media and Computer Law, comprehensive lists on relevant issues. http://www.lib.uiowa.edu/gw/journalism/mediaLaw/media_law.html

Communications Decency Act Ruled Unconstitutional, and the Latest News. http://www.epic.org/CDA/

Netwatchers Cyberzine, a monthly cyberzine covering legal developments in cyberspace. http://www.emitech.com/netwatchers/front.htm

Censorship on the Information Superhighway: a list of "Pro," "Con," and "Neutral" sites. http://www.concentric.net/~abansal/hon399.htm

Writing Prompt

Respond to the following question in a five- to seven-page argumentative essay that includes references to sources obtained on the Net:

Should the U.S. Government regulate the Internet?

This is a *huge* question that you should feel free to narrow in one of a variety of ways. You could focus on the question of online censorship in relation solely to minors, pornography, intellectual property, obscene language, private vs. public transmissions (if there's a difference on the Internet), advertising, and so on.

GLOSSARY

Address: the "location" of the information you're seeking on the Web. The address will provide the server network where the information is stored, as well as the subheadings (individual user's department and name, for example) that that server uses to classify the information. Addresses are usually presented in http form, as in "http://www.usc.edu/."

Browser: a type of software that presents Web material in a user-friendly way, involving multiple media (sounds, pictures, text).

Bulletin boards: groups of users who get together under a subject heading (for example, "alt.fan.xfiles") to discuss that subject. Boards work kind of like E-mail; most of them are accessible through usenet as text-based formats. Some boards work *as* E-mail, in something called a user group—people subscribe to the user group and then receive all postings (mail) to the bulletin board.

Download: to "pull" or save materials off of the Web and store them on your computer or a disk.

E-mail: electronic mail. You will have an Internet account and address given to you upon signing up with a provider; at this address you can receive letters (texts, other stuff if you have the right mail program) from anyone connected to the Internet—"free" of charge (that is, no cost above whatever you may be paying to your provider). A typical E-mail address is "joeshmoe@someschool.edu." These addresses are not the same as Web pages or http addresses.

Emoticons: there are too many of these to name, but they're the little smiley faces that accompany some users' mail or conversations. For example, :) is a smile, but ;) is a smiling wink.

FAQ: stands for "frequently asked questions." FAQs are used, especially in newsgroups, to define the topic and interests of the group as well as its rules, if any, for joining conversation.

Flame: a reaction to something posted on a Web page or on a newsgroup. Flames come in two flavors, as far as we can tell—angry and abusive, a direct reaction to some kind of disagreement; and silly but multiple attempts to *start* some kind of argument based on a warped sense of fun. Some newsgroups prohibit flames; others seem to encourage them. Flames keep discussion lively and a lot more fluid than most conventional forums for debate allow, but they also (be warned) can get amusingly or hatefully obnoxious.

HTML: a programming language used to write Web information onto "pages"—you often see ".html" at the conclusion of addresses, indicating how the page has been programmed. Other languages for programming Web materials, like Java, are also available and becoming more common.

Links: connections to related Web sources. Links are addresses programmed into the page. Sometimes they are presented as the address; sometimes links are shown as icons or pictures. Clicking the mouse on a link will take you to the new source.

'Net or **Internet:** the connection of networked networks of computers— or the links established between any computer or set of computers using TCP/IP language.

Page: Web documents show up on individual screens, as if on a page of a book—ergo the name. A "page" is just a convenient nickname for a specific set of data programmed at a certain address.

SPAM: We can never remember what this acronym stands for, but it means advertising. The Web's currently more-anarchic status has made it ripe for commercial possibilities; many companies have begun establishing themselves on the Web, either as an offshoot of their other functions or solely as a Web-based provider of some product. Any address ending in ".com" uses a commercially based server, and many times you can tell companies by their addresses. Most users hate SPAM.

Surfing: what you do when you get on the 'Net or Web and merely jump around, like the person with the remote control watching television.

Usenet: the 'Net's textual components. Most bulletin boards exist as usenet sources, as do many mail programs.

404 or **Access denied:** a 404 error pops up whenever you try to use a link that does not have a proper address. Because the Web changes so often (people shifting addresses all the time), these errors are fairly common. It's courteous to let the programmer of the link know about the error; sometimes it's just a simple typo in the program.

GOOD STARTING POINTS ON THE WEB

On-Line Web Guides

- Netlinks! Online Cyberspace Guide
  http://www.netlinks.net/
- WWW FAQs (frequently asked questions)
  http://www.boutell.com/faq/

Search Engines

- *Yahoo!*
  http://www.yahoo.com/
- *AltaVista*
  http://altavista.digital.com/
- *Lycos*
  http://lycos.cs.cmu.edu/

Virtual Libraries and Catalogues

- The World Wide Web Virtual Library: Subject Catalogue
  http://www.w3.org/pub/DataSources/bySubject/Overview.html
- The Whole Internet Catalogue
  http://www-elc.gnn.com/gnn/wic/index.html

Evaluating On-Line Sources

- "Teaching Critical Evaluation Skills for World Wide Web Resources," by Jan Alexander and Marsha Tate. Scroll down their list to number 2, "Web Evaluation Checklists."
  http://www.science.widener.edu/~withers/webeval.htm
- "Beyond 'Cool'—Analog Models for Reviewing Digital Resources," by James Rettig. A good overview of the issues involved, with a useful list of "Comparative Criteria for Reviewing Reference Books and Web Sites" near the end.
  http://www.onlineinc.com/onlinemag/SeptOL/rettig9.html

Writing Resources

- *A Guide for Writing Research Papers Based on Modern Language Association Documentation,* by Arthur C. Banks.
  http://155.43.225.30/mla.htm
- *Elements of Style,* by William Strunk, Jr.
  http://www.columbia.edu/acis/bartleby/strunk/

ACKNOWLEDGMENTS

Rushworth M. Kidder, "Should Violence Go Unpunished?" from *Insights on Global Ethics,* December 1994/January 1995. Copyright © The Institute for Global Ethics. Reprinted by permission.

Rushworth M. Kidder, "Hazardous Waste and Gender Equity: Who Decides?" adapted from *How Good People Make Tough Choices,* copyright © 1995. Reprinted by permission of William Morrow & Company.

The New York Times Company, "AIDS Babies Deserve Testing," from *The New York Times.* Copyright © 1994. Reprinted by permission.

Ruth Hubbard, "Test-Tube Babies: Solution or Problem?" from *Healing with Technology.* Reprinted with permission from Technology Review, copyright © 1980.

Harold H. Mosak and Samuel E. Goldman, "An Alternative View of the Purpose of Psychosis" in *Individual Psychology: The Journal of Adlerian Theory, Research and Practice,* Vol. 51:1, March 1995, pp. 46–49; reprinted by permission of the author and the University of Texas Press.

Bruno Bettelheim, introduction to *The Uses of Enchantment.* Copyright © 1975, 1976 by Bruno Bettelheim. Reprinted by permission of Alfred A. Knopf, Inc.

Armin A. Brott, "Not All Men Are Sly Foxes" originally published in *Newsweek,* June 1, 1992. Armin Brott is the author of *The New Father: A Dad's Guide to the First Year* (Abbeulle Press, 1997). Reprinted by permission.

Marina Warner, "The Absent Mother: Women Against Women in Old Wives' Tales" from *History Today,* Vol. 4, April 1991.

Michael Levin, "The Case for Torture" originally published in *Newsweek,* June 7, 1982. Reprinted by permission of the author.

Barbara Huttmann, "A Crime of Compassion" originally published in *Newsweek,* August 8, 1983. Reprinted by permission of the author.

Leah Margulies, "Bottle Babies: Death and Business Get Their Market" from *Business and Society Review,* Spring 1978. Reprinted by permission.

Marcia Eldredge, "Educating Tomorrow's Workers: Are We Ignoring Today's Girls?" from *National Business Woman,* Summer 1992. *National Business Woman* is the quarterly publication of Business and Professional Women/USA (BPW/USA). Reprinted by permission.

Mike Brake, "Needed: A License to Drink" from *Newsweek,* March 14,

That Wound: Critical Race Theory, Assaultive Speech and the First Amendment (Westview 1993). Reprinted by permission of the author.

Nat Hentoff, "'Speech Codes' and Free Speech." This article originally appeared in *Dissent,* Fall 1991. Reprinted by permission of the author.

Ted Tollefson, "Is a Hero Really Nothing but a Sandwich?" originally published in the *Utne Reader,* May/June 1993. Reprinted by permission of the author.

Matthew Goodman "Where Have You Gone, Joe DiMaggio?" originally published in the *Utne Reader,* May/June 1993.

Walter Truett Anderson, "Have We Outgrown the Age of Heroes?" originally published in the *Utne Reader,* May/June 1993. Reprinted by permission of the author.

Author/Title Index

SUBJECT INDEX